John Henry Newman

Tracts - Theological and Ecclesiastical

John Henry Newman

Tracts - Theological and Ecclesiastical

ISBN/EAN: 9783337106294

Printed in Europe, USA, Canada, Australia, Japan

Cover: Foto ©Lupo / pixelio.de

More available books at **www.hansebooks.com**

TRACTS

THEOLOGICAL AND ECCLESIASTICAL

BY

JOHN HENRY CARDINAL NEWMAN

NEW IMPRESSION

LONGMANS, GREEN, AND CO.
39 PATERNOSTER ROW, LONDON
NEW YORK AND BOMBAY
1899

REVERENDO PATRI

ANTONIO BRESCIANI

E SOCIETATE IESV

COLLEGII VRBANI RECTORI

VIRO LECTISSIMO

NOBIS HOSPITIBVS SVIS ET LINGVA PÆNE BARBARIS

ACCEPTISSIMO

HOC·SERENISSIMORVM DIERVM

SVB EIVS TVTELA ACTORVM

QVALECVNQVE MONVMENTVM

COMMENDATVM DICATVMQVE

VELIMVS.

ADVERTISEMENT.

ON collecting into one volume Tracts written at long intervals of time from each other, with the use of various libraries, and of different editions of the Fathers, I have some anxiety lest, in consequence, mistakes should be found in my references, in spite of the great pains I have taken to make them accurate. However, I give here, to the best of my power, a list of the Editions I have followed:—

Africanus, *apud* Routh. Relliqu. Sacr. t. ii.
Ambrosius, *Paris.* 1686, &c. ed. Benedict. seu. Maurin
Anastasius Sinaita, *Ingolstad.* 1606, Gretser.
Athanasius, *Paris.* 1698 (Montfaucon), Maurin.
Athenagoras, *Venet.* 1747, Maurin.
Augustinus, *Paris.* 1689, &c. Maurin.
Basilius Magnus, *Paris.* 1721, &c. Maurin.
Basilius Seleuc. *Paris.* 1622, Dausque.
Bibliotheca Patrum, *Colon.* 1618.
———— *Paris.* Quart. 1624.
———— *Lugdun.* Max. 1677.
———— *Venet.* 1765, &c. Galland
Chrysostomus Joannes, *Paris.* 1718, &c. (Montfaucon), Maurin.
Clemens Alex. *Oxon.* 1715, Potter.

Advertisement.

Collectanea Monumentorum, *Romæ*, 1698, Zacagn.
Collectio Nova Patrum, *Paris.* 1706 (Montfaucon), Maurin.
Conciliorum Collectio Regia, *Paris.* 1715, Harduin.
Concilium Antiochenum, *ap.* Routh. *Rell. S.* t. ii.
Cyprianus, *Venet.* 1758, Maurin.
Cyrillus Alex. *Lutet.* 1638, Aubert.
Cyrillus Hieros. *Paris.* 1720, Maurin.
Damascenus Joannes, *Venet.* 1748, Lequien.
Didymus, *Bonon.* 1769, Mingarelli.
Dionysius Alex. *ap.* Athan. et Rell. S. Routh. t. iii.
Dionysius Rom. *ibid.*
Ephraëm, *ap.* Photium.
Epiphanius, *Colon.* 1682, Petav.
Epistola ad Diognetum, *ap.* Justin. Opp.
Epistolæ Pontif. Roman. *Paris.* 1721 (Coustant.), Maurin.
Eulogius, *ap.* Photium.
Eusebius, Histor. Eccles. ⎫
——— Laud. Constant. ⎬ *Amstelod.* 1695, Vales.
——— Præpar. ⎫
——— Demonstr. ⎬ *Colon.* 1688.
——— c. Marcell. &c. ⎭
Euthymius, *Lips.* 1792, Matthæi.
Facundus, *ap.* Opp. Sirmondi, t. ii.
Gregorius Nazianz. *Paris.* 1778, 1840, Maurin.
Gregorius Neocæsar. (Thaumaturg.) *Paris.* 1622.
Gregorius Nyssen, Opp. *Paris.* 1615, &c.
——— Antirrhet. *ap.* Collectan. Zacagn.
Hieronymus, *Venet.* 1766, Vallars.

Advertisement.

Hilarius Pictav. *Paris.* 1693, Maurin.
Hippolytus, Opp. *Hamburg.* 1716, Fabric.
————— c. Noëtum, *ap.* Opuscula, Routh.
————— Elenchus, *Oxon.* 1851, Miller.
Incerti Dialogi, *ap.* Athan. Opp. t. ii.
Irenæus, *Venet.* 1734, Maurin.
Isidorus Pelus. *Paris.* 1638.
Justinus Mart. *Venet.* 1747, Maurin.
Lactantius, *Lutet.* 1748, Dufresnoi.
Leo Magnus, *Venet.* 1753, &c. Ballerin.
Leontius, *ap.* Bibl. P. *Colon.* et *Venet.* Galland. et Thesaur. Canis. t. i.
Malchion, *ap.* Rell. S. Routh. t. ii.
Maximus, *Paris.* 1675, Combefis.
Melito, *ap.* Rell, S. Routh. t. i.
Mercator, *Paris.* 1673, Garner.
Methodius, *ap.* Bibl. P. *Venet.* Galland. t. iii.
Novatianus, *Londini,* 1728, Jackson.
Opera Varia Sirmondi, *Venet.* 1728, La Baume.
Opuscula Eccles. *Oxon.* 1832, Routh.
Origenes, *Paris.* 1733, &c. Maurin.
Philo, *Francofurt.* 1691.
Phœbadius, *ap.* Bibl. P. *Venet.* Galland. t. v.
Photius, *Rothomag.* 1653, Schott.
Plotinus, *Oxon.* 1835, Creuzer.
Proclus, *Romæ,* 1630, Riccard.
Relliquiæ Sacræ Patrum, *Oxon.* 1814, &c. Routh.
Rusticus, *ap.* Bibl. P. *Colon.* t. vi.
Socrates \} *Amstelod.* 1695, Vales.
Sozomenus

vi *Advertisement.*

Tatianus, *Venet.* 1747, Maurin.
Tertullianus, *Lutet.* 1641, Rigalt.
Theodoretus, Opp. *Halæ*, 1769, &c. Schulze.
——————— Hist. Eccl. *Amstelod.* 1695, Vales.
Theophilus, *Venet.* 1747, Maurin.
Thesaurus Eccles. Canisii, *Antverp.* 1725, Basnage.
Victorinus, *ap.* Bibl. P. *Venet.* Galland. t. viii.
Vigilius Thaps. *ap.* Bibl. P. *Lugdun.* t. viii.
Vincentius Lirin. *ap.* Bibl. P. *Venet.* Galland. t. x.
Zeno, *Veron.* 1739, Ballerin.

I thus complete the references made in the following places to Theodoret's *Hist. Eccles.* :—
Infr. p. 84, ed. Vales, ii. 27, p. 113,
    ed. Schulze, ii. 23, p. 898.
Infr. p. 86, ed. Vales, ii. 8, p. 81,
    ed. Schulze, ii. 6, p. 844.
Infr. p. 88, ed. Vales, i. 4, p. 15,
    ed. Schulze, i. 3, p. 740.
Infr. p. 89, ed. Vales, ii. 22, p. 103,
    ed. Schulze, ii. 17, p. 883.

I take this opportunity of acknowledging the special obligations I am under to the Rev. Fr. Henry Bittleston of this Oratory, as regards this and other of the new editions of my Volumes, for the service he has done me in bringing to my notice, as the proof sheets came down to me, various inaccuracies both of thought and language which required correction.

BIRMINGHAM,
   January 5, 1874.

CONTENTS.

	PAGE
I. Dissertatiunculæ Quatuor Critico-Theologicæ	1
II. On the Text of the Epistles of St. Ignatius	93
III. Causes of the Rise and Successes of Arianism	137
IV. The Heresy of Apollinaris	301
V. St. Cyril's Formula, μία φύσις σεσαρκωμένη	329
VI. The Ordo de Tempore in the Breviary	383
VII. History of the Text of the Douay Version of Scripture	403

CORRIGENDA
Made by the Author for this Edition.

PAGE	LINE	FOR	READ
203	2	too	also
204	25	becoming its First-born	becoming, as He has become, its First-born
205	2	formation	typical order.
209	24	and the External Arianism	and the External, Arianism
229	13	as a categorical	as used for a categorical
234	3	equal	*equal*
243	19	if the second eight	supposing the second eight
„	20	Son of God	*Son of God*
„	25	one	*one*
„	27	what all,	what *all*
„	28	to say with Gregory,	to say *with* Gregory,
244	14	what they do not profess to hold;	what, as I have shown, they even do not profess to hold;
245	11	inquiring into, by the text,	inquiring into, is symbolised by the text,
„	26	The writers of	And again, the writers of
246	1	certainly not by Egyptians,	*certainly not by Egyptians*,
247	22	the eternal if, with Origen,	the Eternal, supposing, with Origen,
248	24	he substitutes	Bull substitutes
250	15	Word	*Word*
258	10	of the Word	of the *Word*
259	19	found to	found substantially to agree

I.

DISSERTATIUNCULÆ QUÆDAM CRITICO-THEOLOGICÆ

AUCTORE JOANNE H. NEWMAN

ANGLO.

MONITUM.

OPUSCULA hæc qualiacunque, ex nupera Oxoniensi Bibliotheca Patrum maxima ex parte desumpta, Latine autem liberius reddita, criticis prudentioribus commendo; id ægre ferens, quod, notulis quibusdam meis domi relictis, minus prodeunt accurata, quam pro ratione studiorum meorum a benevolis sperari potuisset.

ROMÆ,
In Fest. S. Anselm.
1847.

			PAGE
DISSERT.	1.	De quarta Oratione S. Athanasii contra Arianos .	7
	2.	De Ecthesi Ephesina contra Paulum Samosatenum	36
	3.	De formula πρὶν γεννηθῆναι οὐκ ἦν Anathematismi Nicæni	57
	4.	De vocibus ἐξ ἑτέρας ὑποστάσεως ἢ οὐσίας Anathematismi Nicæni	78

DISSERTATIUNCULÆ QUÆDAM CRITICO-THEOLOGICÆ.

DISSERTATIO I.

DE QUARTA ORATIONE S. ATHANASII CONTRA ARIANOS.

QUATUOR illas, quas vulgo vocant, Athanasii Orationes contra Arianos partes esse unius operis, recentioribus criticis persuasissimum est; post ipsum, ut videtur, Photium, qui codice cxl. de πενταβίβλῳ Athanasii mentionem facit. Profecto Montefalconius, ut in re minime dubia, omni probatione præter ipsam librorum structuram supersedendum judicat. "Nihil opus est longiore disputatione, cum clarum sit ex hisce ipsis quatuor Orationibus, nihil eas commune cum ullo alio opere habere; sed ita inter se cohærere, ut unum ipsæ opus simul conficiant, quarum prima sit principium, quarta autem omnium sit finis, quam sane ob causam sola hæc ultima solita terminatur conclusione." Athan. *Opp.* t. i. pp. 403-4. Hæc ille; qui tamen paullo submissius loquitur, cum in *Præfat.* sua

p. xxxv. et in *Vit. Athan.* p. lxxii. concedit eas non esse exaratas certo aliquo consilio prius inito, sed, decursu controversiæ, aliam ex alia, quo res majorem haberet lucem, fuisse productas; id quod præcipue cernitur in secunda et tertia incipientibus, ubi sanctus Doctor, more suo, disputationem jam forte longiorem, propter hæreticorum tamen pervicaciam, continuandam judicat.

Nec minus liquida res est Tillemontio, scribenti; "Les quatre oraisons sont toutes liées ensemble, et en un même corps, comme il paraît principalement, parcequ'il n'y a que la dernière qui finisse par la glorification ordinaire." *Mem. Eccl.* t. 8, p. 701. Et alibi : "Il est certain que ces quatre discours . . . semblent . . . ne faire qu'une seule pièce qu'on aura partagée tantöt en quatre, tantöt en cinq." p. 191.

Tillemontii vestigia sequitur, tanquam pedissequus, Ceillerius, *Ant. Eccl.* t. 5, pp. 217, 218, qui cum Montefalconio consentit posteriores libros, vice quemque sua, anteriorum partes suscipere.

Jam prius Petavio, Incarnationem V. D. tractanti, idem excidit judicium; eo gravius, quod obiter doctissimo theologo elapsum est. Dum enim Epistolam Athanasii *ad Ep. Æg. et Lib.* contendit non esse revera partem Orationum contra Arianos, (ut tum temporis ab Athanasii editoribus habebatur,) quia scilicet illa Epistola non spectet, nisi in parte quadam, ad doctrinam Arianorum, hæc monet: "Non est ejusdem cum sequentibus argumenti, nam *in istis* adversus *Arianam* hæresim disputat etc. . . . prima autem (i. e. *Epist. ad Ep. Æg. et Lib.*) nihil horum facit. *De Incarn.* v. 15, § 9.

Auctoribus tamen tam gravibus atque inter se consentientibus hic contra eundum est; cum plane comprobari possit, ut puto, et sine magno conatu, quartam illam contra Arianos Orationem non esse contra istos hæreticos ab Athanasio scriptam, neque prorsus esse orationem, ne disputationem quidem continuam, sed esse conglutinationem quandam fragmentorum theologicorum, vel annotationum seriem, variæ et longitudinis et materiæ, præcipue de hæresi Marcelli et Photini, aliqua ex parte de Sabellianismo et Samosatenismo, vix aut ne vix quidem contra Arianos. Quam sententiam his argumentis fultam velim.

§ I. De Structura Libri.

1. Jam hoc præmittendum est;—nusquam, ut credo, ab antiquis ad Orationem hanc quartam provocari, tanquam ad partem operis Athanasii "*contra Arianos,*" vel "*de Trinitate;*" cum secunda contra et tertia laudantur a Theodoreto, Justiniano, Cyrillo Alexandrino, Facundo, Concilio Lateranensi sub Martino I. habito, Agathone Pontifice, et aliis, idque illo ipso numerandi ordine qui etiamnum servatur in editione Maurina.[1] Quamvis autem Photii, de toto opere ut quinquepartito loquentis, interpretes esse quodammodo videantur, et Patres Concilii Œcumenici Septimi et Agatho P. Romanus in Sexto, ex eo quod tertiam Maurinam pro quartâ habeant, inde tamen non concludi potest quartam Maurinam, de qua

---

[1] Theod. *Eran.* ii. p. 136. Justin. *ap.* Baron. *Ann.* 538. Cyrill. *Ep.* p. 4. Facund. *Tr. Cap.* iii. 3. Concil. Later. *Sect.* 5, etc.

hic quæstio est, comprehensam fuisse ut quintam partem πενταβίβλου Photii. Nam, quoniam in uno codice hæc Maurinorum quarta vocatur sexta Oratio, alia quædam ibi reperienda est quinta; quæ quidem, Montefalconio judice, est opusculum illud quod vulgo appellatur *De Incarnatione contra Arianos*, quod re ipsa in aliquibus codd. quintæ nomen gerit. Sunt porro codices qui Epistolam *ad Ep. Æg. et Lib.* quæ in codd. solebat esse prima, quartam nominant; alius autem est Montefalconii, ex quo quarta illa Maurinorum plane excidit. Accedit quod in codice quodam Bodleiano (Roe 29, an. 1410) opusculum *De Incarnatione contra Arianos* tres priores subsequitur orationes, quartæ vice. Aliis autem codd. quarta Maurinorum quinta est; aliis Epistola *ad Ep. Æg. et Lib.* est "tertia contra Arianos," Epistola *de Sent. Dion.* in duas partes divisa, pro prima et secunda, ut videtur, habita. Quare, cum adeo varietur in codicibus, nulla præscriptio est ex usu editionum, cur quarta hæc oratio adsciscatur in numerum earum, quæ cum Arianis bellum gerunt.

2. Deinde notandum est, librum hunc ipsa fronte sua prodere se non esse orationem similem illarum quæ ei præierunt. Nam, cum secunda illa et tertia procemium utraque suum habeat, in quo mentio fit gravissimi illius argumenti, quod ab illis est continuandum, nihil contra aut scopo definitum aut ratione ordinatum in quarta incipiente reperitur. In argumentum suum, quicquid sit illud, nullum enim profitetur, præceps ingreditur, propositionem præ se ferens categoricam quandam ex Evangelista desumptam, "Ex Deo Deus est verbum, nam

Deus erat Verbum;" plane omisso verborum illo apparatu et verecunda dicendi pompa, qua in limatioribus suis operibus, res divinas tractaturus, utitur sanctissimus Præsul.

Nec æquabilius aut liquidius fluit postea orationis cursus, sed turbatus semper, incertus, mutabilis. Nam sæpius materies subito profertur nova, ut in sectionibus 6, 9, et 25 editionis Maurinæ; id quod amanuensibus tam plane constitit, ut in quinque codd. temere inseruerint inter sectiones 12 et 13 opusculum *de Sabbatis et Circumcisione*, Athanasio dubie a Maurinis (t. ii. p. 54) ascriptum. Plane diversum est ab hoc genere disserendi animosum illud et bene continuatum sancti oratoris eloquium, qui tam soleat priorem materiem suam producere et tanquam abdere in proxime sequentem, et rem cum re tam callida junctura colligare, ut editori difficillimum sit disputationis cursum ad certa quædam capita revocare.

Accedit quod tres illæ quæ præcedunt Orationes commercium inter se ultro citroque habent, et ad se mutuo respiciunt, et complent definita quædam docendi spatia, quæ terminantur prope exeunte tertia. Integra quædam disputatio, in Scripturis contra Arianos explicandis tota, continuatur a § 37 primæ ad § 59 tertiæ; ante tertiam in locis Propheticis et Apostolicis, per tertiam in Evangelicis versata. Incipit autem, procedit, et terminatur scopo ecclesiastico, seu canone fidei, proponendo, ut divinorum oraculorum justo interprete.[1] At in hac accurata rerum

---

[1] Vid. voces σκόπος, κανών, ἀλήθεια, διάνοια, etc. *Orat.* i. 37, 44, 46; ii. 1, 5, 31, 33, 35, 44, 63, 65, 70; iii. 7, 18, 28, 29, 35, 58, etc.

dispositione nullam plane sedem sibi vindicare potest quartus ille liber seu Oratio Maurinorum.

Quid quod in verborum quoque usu sui similis est quartus liber, aut saltem dissimilis trium Orationum. Nam in quarto, cæteris licet breviore, vocula celeberrima ὁμοούσιον ter reperitur, vid. §§ 10, 12, at eandem in tribus illis prioribus nusquam esse dicendum est, cum solitarius iste locus, *Orat.* i. 9, qui eam continet, symboli quandam fert speciem, ut ex ipso loco intelligitur, neque in propriam Athanasii disputationem cadit. Contra, verbum illud omittitur aliquando in Orationibus tribus, ubi jure posset quæri.[1] Deinde in *Orat.* ii. 78, 79, 80, ut in *Gent.* 40, et 46, *Incarn. V. D.* 20, *ad Serap.* iv. 20, verbum αὐτοσοφία reperitur; at in quarta reprobatur idem, Petavio judice, (*de Trin.* vi. 11,) ut Sabellianum. Tum hoc quoque e minutioribus rebus ad rem nostram acit, quod tres illæ, in Sanctissima Trinitate prædicanda, illustratione uti solent ex luce et ejus irradiatione desumpta; quarta vero, modo ignem non lucem, modo ignem et lucem inducit. Depravato denique textu hæc graviter laborat; illæ non laborant.

3. Profecto, ut antea dictum est, etiam hoc in quæstionem venit, an forte portiones saltem aliquæ hujus libri fragmenta sint tantummodo cujusdam operis, vel plurium operum; vel notulæ rudiores subita manu scriptis man-

---

[1] Vid. ἀλλοτριοούσιος, *Orat.* i. 20; ὁμοίας οὐσίας, ibid. 21, 26, iii. 26; ὁμογενὴς, i. 56; ὁμοφυὴς, ἑτερογενὴς, ἑτεροούσιος, ibid. 58. Cf. *de Syn.* 53, ubi ὁμοιούσιον reprobatur. Cf. item argumentum, non ad consubstantialitatem, sed ad æternitatem Filii a voce εἰκὼν ductum, *Orat.* i. 20, cum illo ab eadem ad consubstantialitatem, *de Decret.* 20, et 23; Greg. Naz. *Orat.* xxx. 20.

Critico-Theologicæ. 13

datæ, prout menti occurrerent ; vel capita controversiarum ; quæ casus rerum temere in unum cumulum congesserit. Peregrinum omnino opusculum, forte non Athanasii, illud *de Sabb. et Circumc.* nonnunquam in medium hunc librum intrusum jam diximus ; præterea, (quod præcipue ad rem nostram facit) idem opusculum in codd. omnibus, excepto uno, quos memorant Maurini, re ipsa consociatur cum fragmento quodam Epistolæ *de Decr.* et Tractatu *In illud omnia,* quasi totum quid, quamquam nihil cum illis habet commune. Alterum exemplum cernitur in Sermone Majore *de Fide,* qui in Montefalconii *Nova Collectione* editus est, qui autem vix aliud est quam series quædam portiuncularum ex variis Athanasii operibus in unum comparatarum. Præterea, quod attinet ad librum nostrum, in codd. quibusdam singuli singulis partibus præponuntur tituli ; ut τοὺς σαβελλίζοντας, κ. τ. λ. in sect. 9 ; in sect. autem 11, πρὸς τοὺς λέγοντας ὅτι, κ. τ. λ. Porro " illi " et " ille " stant nudi aliquando, nullo antecedente nomine. Sed et infractum illud et inordinatum in orationis filo, indicium aliud est multiplicis et disparis materiæ. Quid quod § 25 in duas partes temere secat quod alioqui continuum haberet cursum a 15 ad 36 ; § 11 autem mentionem ultro objicit alicujus rei quam in præcedentibus frustra quæsiveris. Tum §§ 6 et 7, quæ solæ pertinent ad Arianos, jacent inter argumentorum locus Arianis plane alienos, stylum autem sapiunt dilucidum illum et liberum Orationum trium ; qui quidem stylus aliqua ex parte in §§ 14, 17, 27, 28, et 34 reperitur.

Notatu etiam dignum est, a Montefalconio in Monito suo Epistolæ Encyclicæ præfixo esse observatum, phrasim illam οἱ περὶ Εὐσέβιον non adhibitam esse ab Athanasio post Eusebii mortem; "Neque enim sequaces Eusebii jam defuncti usquam apud Athanasium οἱ περὶ Εὐσέβιον vocantur, sed κοινωνοὶ τῶν περὶ Εὐσέβιον vel κληρόνομοι τῆς ἀσεβείας τοῦ Εὐσεβίου." t. i. p. 110. Jam hanc ipsam phrasin (non de rebus præteritis sed tunc præsentibus) legimus in sectione 8 hujus Orationis quartæ; unde sequitur, cum Eusebius discesserit e vivis an. 341, Oratio autem prima scripta fuerit circ. an. 358, illam saltem quartæ Orationis particulam, quæ phrasin οἱ περὶ Εὐσέβιον continet, ante Orationem primam auctoris in manibus fuisse.

Plura adhuc sunt quæ in hac re possint offerri; nam sectiones 1-5, 9, 10, versantur in argumento plane suo, quod in reliquo libro nusquam attingitur. De μοναρχίᾳ tractant; verbo autem ἀρχή utuntur pro *origine*, ut in prioribus Orationibus moris est; cum idem usurpetur pro *initio*, sectionibus hujus libri 8, 25, 26, 27. Porro in disputatione §§ 30-36 singularis usus est epitheti θεῖος ad Christum adhibiti; vox quoque νοεῖν ejusdem loci propria est.

Quod porro singulare est in hoc libro, adeo ut vel stylo signum imprimat, argumentum autem idem non leve quod de serie quadam annotationum polemicarum nunc agimus, non de justo et simplici opere, frequentia illa est vocabulorum hujusmodi, πευστέον 2, e. ἐρωτητέον 3, f. 4, a. λεκτέον 4, init. 6, d. 10, a. ἐλεγκτέον 3, a. 4, e, ἔρεσθαι δίκαιον, καλόν etc., 11, d. 14, a. 23. b. Cujus generis sunt illa quoque, ἀκολουθήσει τὰ ἐν τοῖς ἔμπροσθεν ἄτοπα εἰρημένα, e. g. 2, e. 4, e. 4 fin. 15 init. 25, b. 26 init. quibuscum conferamus elegantiorem periodi cursum, *Orat.* ii. 24, b. καλὸν αὐτοὺς ἔρεσθαι καὶ τοῦτο, ἵν᾽ ἔτι μᾶλλον ὁ ἔλεγχος, κ. τ. λ. ejusmodi sunt etiam τὸ δ᾽ αὐτὸ δὲ καὶ περὶ δυνάμεως, § 3; quæ omnia Aristotelem sapiunt, non Athanasium. Videsis etiam locos Scripturæ sacræ abrupte propositos ut materiem disputandi, ut in §§ 1, 5, 9, et 31.

Aristotelem etiam agit in hoc libro sanctissimus Doctor in effatis suis theologicis proferendis; *e.g.* εἰ ἄγονος καὶ ἀνενέργητος ὁ Θεός, 4 fin. τὸ ἔκ τινος ὑπάρχον υἱός ἐστιν ἐκείνου, 15, c. οὐδὲν ἓν πρὸς τὸν πατέρα, εἰ μὴ τὸ ἐξ αὐτοῦ. 17, d. ὧν οὐκ ἔστιν εἰς τὰς καρδίας ὁ υἱός, τούτων οὐδὲ πατὴρ ὁ Θεός. 22, b. εἰ μὴ υἱός, οὐδὲ λόγος· εἰ μὴ λόγος, οὐδὲ υἱός. 24 fin.

4. Ulterius nunc progrediendum est; liquet enim Athanasium hoc in libro non raro innuere se non doctrinam solum hæreticorum percellere, sed hæreticos ipsos; tamen de nominibus tacet; quod contra fit in Ariana sua controversia, ubi liberrime loquitur de Ario, de Eusebio, de Asterio, et aliis ejusdem sectæ. Hic contra, licet occurrant certe οἱ ἀπὸ τοῦ Σαμοσάτεως, et κατὰ Σαβέλλιον, adversarii plerumque anonymi, unus aut plures, in campum descendunt, vel potius illabuntur; ut colligi potest ex φατὲ 9 init. πίπτουσι 11 init. ὑπέλαβε 13 init. αὐτὸν τοιαῦτα λέγοντα 14, a. οἱ τοῦτο λέγοντες 15 init. κατ᾽ αὐτοὺς 21 init. κατ᾽ ἐκείνους 22, c. Vid. etiam 8, c. 13, c. 20 init. 23, c. 24, a. 25, b. 28 init. Jam si acer ille accusatorius stylus huic libro abest, in hac re saltem, si non in alia, a præcedentibus tribus differt, in quibus illa oratoris vis et fervor animi præcipue cernitur; quid quod hoc fortasse inde colligendum est insuper, neces-

situdinem scilicet aliquam fuisse Athanasio cum quibusdam istarum factionum hominibus, quibus sagax et benevolus præsul, etsi congrediendum, tamen aliquatenus parcendum duxerit.

Deinde observandum est hæresim, de qua per totum pæne librum agitur, etsi Sabellianæ proximam, non fuisse Sabellianam; nam comparatur cum ea, e. g. $\Sigma a\beta \epsilon \lambda \lambda i o v$ τὸ ἐπιτήδευμα, 9, et ὅσα ἄλλα ἐπὶ Σαβελλίου ἄτοπα ἀπαντᾷ, 25. Quinimo, cum hæresis hæresi opponitur in fine § 3, de Arianis aperta mentio est, ut mos est Athanasii, de Sabellianis autem non est mentio, sed de iis qui "Sabellizant," quibuscum scilicet sancto Doctori res erat. Præterea hæresim, quæ agebatur, esse temporis illius, non præteritorum sæculorum, certum est tum ex loquendi modo, quo utitur Athanasius, tum quia cæteræ, quibuscum dimicat in scriptis suis, sunt sui æquales. Namque, etiam cum Pauli Samosateni hæresim aggreditur, non priscam istam sæculi anterioris in arenam immittit, sed immutatam et novam, qualem ipse eam conspexerat in populo Christiano. Nec sane probabile est, in medio illo tot tantorumque errorum certamine, quod Athanasio contigit, prudentissimum virum ad obsoleta quædam, ut Γραϊκὸν καὶ σχολαστικὸν,[1] confugisse.

Quæ omnia suspicionem movent, hæresim, quæ materies est hujus libri, illam esse Marcelli Ancyrani, qui cum Athanasio commilitaverat contra Arianos, et sectatorum ejus; cum omnibus notum sit, simillimo illo Apollinaris exemplo, Athanasium id ipsum facere in disputationibus

---

[1] Plutarch, *Cic.* 5.

suis, hæresiarchæ parcere nomini, hæresim severissime impetere. Quid quod similiter a nominibus abstinet Eusebius in Arianis suis reprobandis (*Eccles. Theol.* i. 9, 10); silet porro Vincentius Lirinensis, si revera in Commonitorio suo Augustinum petit. Idem quoque in Platone fecit Aristoteles; sed in hac re testes supervacanei sunt.

Quod ex ipsa libri structura nihil habet difficultatis, id, collatis inter se dogmatibus, hic Marcellianorum seu Photinianorum, illic eorum quibuscum in hoc libro agitur, plenissimam habebit confirmationem; nempe eo modo, quo Orationes tres hæresim tractant Arianam, disputationem hanc quartam, divulsam licet et incompositam, in Marcelli vel Photini, necnon Sabellii et Samosateni erroribus refutandis versari. Quod cum dicimus, prudentes præterimus sectiones 6 et 7, ad Arianismum procul dubio spectantes, sed in summa operis importunas.

His nostris jam in formam redactis, perjucunda fuit nobis fortuita lectio libelli, inscripti, *In Eusebii contra Marcellum libros Selectæ Observationes*, auctore R. S. C. Lipsiæ, 1787. Laudato Athanasii "quinto libro," ut illum vocat, "contra Arianos," pergit auctor anonymus dicere, "ibi, ut in libro *de Æt. subst. Fil. et Sp. S.* sententiam Marcelli, suppresso tamen nomine, refellit. Quod an aliis sit observatum, ignoro." p. 28.

§ II. De Materie Libri.

Quo melius huic rei satisfiat, triplex hic sumendum est argumentum : primum enim necessitudo illa inter Athanasium et Marcellum in historia istorum temporum, quæ et qualis fuerit, definienda est; deinde enucleanda doctrina Marcelli, Photini, et istiusmodi hæreticorum; tum illa Photiniana hæresis conferenda est cum ea quæ in hoc libro ab Athanasio oppugnatur.

1. Cum Athanasius adhuc junior esset in Episcopatu suo, Marcellus Ancyræ in Galatia Episcopus responsum illud edidit Ariano sophistæ Asterio, ex quo et originem suam et subjectam materiem ceperunt Eusebii *contra Marcellum* et *de Ecclesiastica Theologia* libri, nobis hodie principales testes opinionum Marcelli. Neque Eusebius solum, sed aliquot Concilia Arianorum condemnarunt hominem, qui, Romam petens, ibi Athanasio occurrit circa an. 341; cum uterque præsul a Pontifice, Concilio habito, de Arianorum criminationibus purgatus est.

Purgatus est iterum uterque Concilio Sardicensi an. 347; ab eo tamen ipso tempore, nisi, cum Montefalconio dixerimus, ab an. 336-8 (*Nov. Coll.* p. lii.), postulationes eæ, quæ hactenus ab Arianorum factione urgebantur in Marcellum, inter catholicos etiam circumferuntur. Cyrillus Hierosolymitanus in *Catechesibus* suis an. 347 mentionem facit hæreseos nuperæ Galatarum, quæ Christ sempiternum regnum negaret; ubi Marcellum indicari a sancto oratore, et regio et dogma quæ nominantur liquido demonstrant. Cyrillum excipit Paulinus in Concilio Arelatensi; Paulinum Hilarius; sed Athanasius, cautus homo et clemens, siquis alius, Marcello patrocinatur usque ad circ. an. 360. Idem tamen, confessus tandem Marcellum non longe abesse ab hæresi, a communione, ut traditum est ab Hilario et Sulpicio, hominem semovet. Narrat insuper Hilarius(*Fragm.* ii. 21) inductum esse Athanasium ut hoc faceret, non propter opus Marcelli contra Asterium, sed ob ejus scripta quædam posteriora Concilio Sardicensi. Id autem fecit Athanasius, cum Photinus, Episcopus Sirmiensis, qui hæresim fere illam Marcelli, magistri sui, ante an. 345 ediderat, jam aliquot annos, Catholicis et Arianis consentientibus, a sede sua depositus esset. Marcellus, per totum decennium a sanctissimo præsule repudiatus, quocum tot tantaque ab Arianis pertulisset, tandem ab eodem, morti jam proximo (an. 371) leniore judicio excipitur, ob rem hujusmodi: Basilio Cæsariensi cum Athanasio agenti, ut ne Galatis benignius usus, rei Catholicæ noxam inferret, occurrunt Galatæ, missi ad Alexandriam, qui orarent causam suam, quid autem revera senserint de Christo sine ambagibus expedirent. Eugenius, Diaconus Ecclesiæ Ancyranæ, confessionem catholicam in suorum nomine ibi subscripsit, quam confirmavit manu sua clerus Alexandrinus, necnon, ut videtur, Athanasius ipse, quamquam inter nomina subscripta ille non apparet hodie. Confessio hæc, cui Montefalconius lucem dedit, scripta est in nomine "clericorum et cæterorum qui Ancyræ in Galatia sunt, una cum patre nostro Marcello congregati."

Quo negotio ad finem perducto, et Ancyranus hic, et Alexandrinus ille præsul morti protinus succubuerunt, bellatores ambo in summo Ecclesiæ discrimine, diversa fortuna; plusquam septuagenarius Athanasius, Marcellus autem nonaginta saltem annorum cumulo oppressus, —feliciter grandævus, si reservabatur in hoc, ut errores suos illo extremo halitu vere efflaret. Nihilominus, qui in re historica, non biographia versantur, his, ut mos est in Ecclesia, Marcellus apparet, non ut privatus quispiam, in sua ipsius persona et pœnitentia sua, sed in secta quam genuit, et in maturitate postrema earum opinionum, quæ in ipso semina tantummodo fuerant et elementa pravitatis.

Cæterum, utrum in hominem ipsum an tantummodo in sectatores ejus Athanasius in quarta sua, quam vocant, Oratione invehatur, concludi non potest in alterutram partem, ex illa, seriore utique, confessione ab Eugenio subscripta. Neque Hilarius, Athanasium testatus Marcelli operi contra Asterium pepercisse, nos moveat, ne illo opere utamur in Marcelli placitis eruendis; nam neque in aliis rebus tam fidus in narrando reperitur Hilarius, (ut cum de Liberio loquitur,) ut ex iis quæ plane hæresim sapiunt, Hilarii causa pios sensus extorqueamus. Ea autem sunt hujusmodi.

2. Eusebio teste, placuit Marcello, (1) unam tantummodo in Deitate esse personam; a Sabellio tamen in hoc dissentienti, quod teneret (2) non Patrem continuo esse Filium, Filium Patrem, (id quod υἱοπατορίαν vocant,) sed (3) Patrem et Filium esse nomina mera et nudos titulos; (4) neque exprimere relationes aliquas essentiales in natura divina, sed ex eo originem cepisse (5) quod Verbum Dei sempiternum, seu λόγος ἐνδιάθετος, (quod Divina quædam est Ratio,) sese manifestaverit in carne, in hypostasi scilicet Jesu Christi, Filii Mariæ; (6) hunc itaque unum Deum, seu μονάδα, quodammodo se aperire solere vel dilatare (πλατύνεσθαι) ut nos salvos faciat; (7 et 8) quam dilatationem esse actionem quandam, seu ἐνέργειαν, Verbi, qua

fit προφορικὸς, seu Vox creatrix Dei, cum alioqui sit Ratio interior ; (9) harum autem dilatationum singulare esse specimen Incarnationem Verbi, scilicet dilatationem in carne hominis Jesu, (10) quem susceperit ineunte dispensatione Evangelica, quem exeunte relicturum sit (11). Sequi inde, Verbum non esse Filium, (12) nec Dei Imaginem, Christum, Primogenitum, Regem, sed Jesum esse hæc omnia : quod si ea prædicentur de Verbo in Scripturis V. T. propheticum illud est propter futuram suam in carne manifestationem, (13) neque, dispensatione absoluta, tribui poterunt eadem Verbo, carnem tunc relicturo, regno se abdicaturo, ad Deum redituro, Verbo mero ut antea futuro.

Hæc ille : neque est cur fidem denegemus Eusebio, Ariano homini, vel Arianorum certe fautori, qui, tum contrariarum partium studio tum propter contrariam suam perfidiam, iniquius laturus esset judicium de opinionibus Marcelli. Nam ipsissima verba Marcelli citat scriptor ille ; ab aliorum porro testimonio confirmatur. Præterea si Athanasius in libro hoc quarto hæresim quandam describit simillimam illius quæ Marcello ab Eusebio tribuitur, duplex hoc testimonium Eusebium corroborat, Athanasium interpretatur. Photiniana porro doctrina, a Marcelli auditorio profecta, in iis autem placitis sita quæ ante illam ortam Eusebius assignavit Marcello, argumentum est validum, eruditissimum hunc, licet lubricum, theologum Marcelli animum et consilium recte divinasse.

Nunc singula hæreseos capita, quæ supra percurrimus, testimoniis allatis illustremus.

(1) Unam tantummodo in Deitate esse personam:

Scripturæ adductis verbis, κύριος ὁ Θεὸς in Exod. iii. 5, prosequitur Marcellus: ὁρᾷς ὅπως ἐν ἐπιδεικνὺς ἡμῖν ἐνταῦθα πρόσωπον, τὸ αὐτὸ κύριον καὶ Θεὸν προσαγορεύει; Euseb. p. 132. a. Iterum: τὸ γὰρ ἐγὼ ἑνὸς προσώπου δεικτικόν ἐστιν; p. 133. a. Tum pergit definire πρόσωπον quasi sit idem atque ἡ τῆς θεότητος μονάς. Vid. iterum ἑνὸς προσώπου, ibid. b. Atque iterum: ἀνάγκη γὰρ εἰ δύο διαιρούμενα, ὡς Ἀστέριος ἔφη, πρόσωπα εἴη, ἢ τὸ πνεῦμα, κ. τ. λ. p. 168, c.

(2) Id proprium esse Sabellio, non Marcello, quod υἱοπατόρα doceret; Patrem scilicet esse Filium, Filium autem Patrem. Σαβέλλιος, εἰς αὐτὸν πλημμελῶν τὸν πατέρα, ὃν υἱὸν λέγειν ἐτόλμα. Euseb. p. 76, a. Et Eugenius quoque, in Apologia sua apud Athanasium, anathematizat Sabellium et eos qui cum eo dicerent, αὐτὸν τὸν πατέρα εἶναι υἱὸν, καὶ ὅτε μὲν γίνεται υἱὸς, μὴ εἶναι τότε αὐτὸν πατέρα, ὅτε δὲ γίνεται πατὴρ, μὴ εἶναι τότε υἱόν. Nov. Coll. t. 2, p. 2. Et Basilius: ὁ Σαβέλλιος εἰπὼν, τὸν αὐτὸν Θεὸν, ἕνα τῷ ὑποκειμένῳ ὄντα, πρὸς τὰς ἑκάστοτε παραπιπτούσας χρείας μεταμορφούμενον, νῦν μὲν ὡς πατέρα, νῦν δὲ ὡς υἱὸν, νῦν δὲ ὡς πνεῦμα ἅγιον διαλέγεσθαι. *Ep.* 210, 5 fin.

(3) Patrem et Filium Marcello videri titulos quosdam, in tempore ascriptos sempiterno Deo et Verbo ejus, tunc scilicet, cum ἐνδιάθετος ille λόγος, in Deo inhærens, fieret προφορικὸς in hypostasi Jesu Christi.

Μάρκελλος καινωτέραν ἐξεῦρε τῇ πλάνῃ μηχανὴν, Θεὸν καὶ τὸν ἐν αὐτῷ λόγον ἕνα μὲν εἶναι ὁριζόμενος, δύο δ᾽ αὐτῷ πατρὸς καὶ υἱοῦ χαριζόμενος ἐπηγορίας. Euseb. p. 76, a. vid. etiam. p. 63, c. Itaque, quo melius exprimeret figurata solum locutione Patrem esse Deum, illum appellavit " Patrem Verbi," ἐν τῷ [τὸν Χριστὸν] φάσκειν [τὸν Θεὸν] μηδὲ τοῦ ἑαυτοῦ λόγου κύριον εἶναι, ἀλλὰ καὶ τούτου τὸν πατέρα, ἀφαιρεῖσθαι τὸν πατέρα τὰ ἴδια τοῦ παιδὸς δείκνυσιν. Ibid. p. 38.

Cui suffragata hæreticus ille qui reperitur in *Contr. Sabell. Gregal.* § 5, quem R. S. C., p. 28, putat esse Marcellum. Κἀγώ, φησὶν, ὁμολογῶ γέννησιν· γεννᾶται γὰρ ὁ λόγος, ὅτε καὶ λαλεῖται καὶ γινώσκεται.

Alibi testatur Eusebius a Marcello proponi αὐτὸν [Θεὸν] εἶναι τοῦ ἐν αὐτῷ λόγου πατέρα, ibid. p. 167, c. Quod quidem, etsi vel purum catholicismum sapit, Eusebii ipsius sæpius fortiter arianizantis doctrinæ comparatum, tamen eo nomine in observationem venit, quod Nestorius apud Mercatorem sic distinguit a Sabellio Photinum, " Sabellius υἱοπάτορα dicit ipsum Filium, quem Patrem, et ipsum Patrem quem Filium, Photinus vero λογοπάτορα [Verbumpatrem]." Mercat. t. 2, p. 87.

(4) Verbum esse revera Verbum, ἀληθῶς λόγον, neque nisi improprie Filium : λόγον γὰρ εἶναι δοὺς τὸν ἐν τῷ Θεῷ, ἕν τε καὶ ταὐτὸν ὄντα αὐτῷ ·τοῦτον ὁρισάμενος, πατέρα τούτου χρηματίζειν αὐτὸν ἔφη· τόν τε λόγον υἱὸν εἶναι αὐτῷ, οὐκ ἀληθῶς ὄντα υἱὸν ἐν οὐσίας ὑποστάσει, κυρίως δὲ καὶ ἀληθῶς ὄντα λόγον. ἐπισημαίνεται γοῦν ὅτι μὴ καταχρηστικῶς λόγον, ἀλλὰ κυρίως καὶ ἀληθῶς ὄντα λόγον, καὶ μηδὲν ἕτερον ἢ λόγον. εἰ δὲ μηδὲν ἕτερον, δῆλον ὅτι οὐδὲ υἱὸς ἦν κυρίως καὶ ἀληθῶς, μέχρι δὲ φωνῆς καὶ ὀνόματος καταχρηστικῶς ὠνομασμένος. Euseb. p. 61, a. b.

(5) Verbum esse ab æternitate in Deo, seu ἐνδιάθετος, ut attributum quoddam :

Πλὴν Θεοῦ, disputat Marcellus, οὐδὲν ἕτερον ἦν· εἶχεν οὖν τὴν οἰκείαν δόξαν ὁ λόγος ὢν ἐν τῷ πατρί. Euseb. p. 39, c. Ubi notandum est, phrasin illam ἐν τῷ Θεῷ, teste Montefalconio (*Coll. Nov.* tom. 2, p. lvii.) in suspicionem venisse multis Patribus, utpote suppositam pro illa πρὸς τὸν Θεὸν qua utitur S. Joannes; οὐκ εἰπὼν, observat Eusebius, p. 121, b. ἐν τῷ Θεῷ, ἵνα μὴ καταβάλῃ ἐπὶ τὴν ἀνθρωπίνην ὁμοιότητα, ὡς ἐν ὑποκειμένῳ συμβεβηκός.

Haud aliter Basilius, οὐκ εἶπεν, ἐν τῷ Θεῷ ἦν ὁ λόγος, ἀλλὰ πρὸς τὸν Θεὸν, κ. τ. λ. *Hom.* xvi. 4, p. 137.

(6) Unitatem in Trinitatem esse productam seu dilatatam, rursus autem Trinitatem in Unitatem esse collapsuram.

Dicit Marcellus, εἰ τοίνυν ὁ λόγος φαίνοιτο ἐξ αὐτοῦ τοῦ πατρὸς ἐξελθὼν, ... τὸ δὲ πνεῦμα τὸ ἅγιον παρὰ τοῦ πατρὸς ἐκπορεύεται ... οὐ σαφῶς καὶ φανερῶς ἐνταῦθα ἀπορρήτῳ λόγῳ ἡ μονὰς φαίνεται πλατυνομένη μὲν εἰς τριάδα, διαιρεῖσθαι δὲ μηδαμῶς ὑπομένουσα; Euseb. p. 168, a. b. Etiam pp. 108, b. c. 114, b.

Apud Theodoretum quoque Marcellum tenuisse legimus, ἔκτασίν τινα τῆς τοῦ πατρὸς θεότητος ... μετὰ δὲ τὴν σύμπασαν οἰκονομίαν πάλιν ἀνασπασθῆναι καὶ συσταλῆναι πρὸς τὸν Θεὸν, ἐξ οὗπερ ἐξετάθη· τὸ δὲ πανάγιον πνεῦμα παρέκτασιν τῆς ἐκτάσεως, καὶ ταύτην τοῖς ἀποστόλοις παρασχεθῆναι. *Hær.* ii. 10. Nestorius quoque Photinum citat dicentem: "Vides quia Deum Verbum aliquando Deum, aliquando Verbum appellat, tanquam extensum atque collectum." Mercat. t. 2, p. 87.

(7) Dilatationem hanc sive πλατυσμὸν consistere in actione sive ἐνεργείᾳ τοῦ μονάδος.

Verbum docet Marcellus, ἐνεργείᾳ μόνῃ, διὰ τὴν σάρκα, κεχωρῆσθαι τοῦ πατρός. Euseb. p. 51, a.

Quapropter argumentatur Eusebius, τὴν μονάδα, [ὡς] φησὶ Μάρκελλος, ἐνεργείᾳ πλατύνεσθαι, ἐπὶ μὲν σωμάτων χώραν ἔχει, ἐπὶ δὲ τῆς ἀσωμάτου οὐσίας οὐκ ἔτι· οὐδὲ γὰρ ἐν τῷ ἐνεργεῖν πλατύνεται, οὐδ' ἐν τῷ μὴ ἐνεργεῖν συστέλλεται. p. 108, b. c.

Adeatur quoque ad sextum et septimum anathema Concilii Sirmiensis primi, in quibus Marcellum et Photinum feriri ex quinto Macrostichi facillime concluditur.

(8) Tum primum verbum fuisse in ἐνεργείᾳ, cum mundum crearet:

Οὐδενὸς ὄντος πρότερον, docet Marcellus, ἢ Θεοῦ μόνου, πάντων δὲ διὰ τοῦ λόγου γίγνεσθαι μελλόντων, προῆλθεν ὁ λόγος δραστικῇ ἐνεργείᾳ. Euseb. p. 41, d. Et continuo, πρὸ τοῦ τὸν κόσμον εἶναι ἦν ὁ λόγος ἐν τῷ πατρί· ὅτε δὲ ὁ Θεὸς παντοκράτωρ πάντα τὰ ἐν οὐράνοις καὶ ἐπὶ γῆς προύθετο ποιῆσαι, ἐνεργείας ἡ τοῦ κόσμου γένεσις ἐδεῖτο δραστικῆς, καὶ διὰ τοῦτο ... ὁ λόγος προελθὼν ἐγίνετο τοῦ κόσμου ποιητής. Ibid.

(9) Consistere Incarnationem Verbi in dilatatione [πλατυσμῷ] Monados, vel actione [ἐνεργείᾳ] Verbi in carne, seu homine Jesu Christo:

Εἰ μὲν ἡ τοῦ πνεύματος ἐξέτασις, inquit Marcellus, γίγνοιτο μόνη, ἐν καὶ ταὐτὸν εἰκότως εἶναι τῷ Θεῷ φαίνοιτο· εἰ δὲ ἡ κατὰ σάρκα προσθήκη ἐπὶ τοῦ Σωτῆρος ἐξετάζοιτο, ἐνεργείᾳ ἡ θεότης μόνη πλατύνεσθαι δοκεῖ. Euseb. p. 36, a.

Neque aliter apud Theodoretum: ἔκτασίν τινα τῆς τοῦ πατρὸς θεότητος ἔφησεν εἰς τὸν Χριστὸν ἐληλυθέναι. Hær. ii. 10.

(10) Cum Verbum esset in actione, ἐν ἐνεργείᾳ, seu fieret προφορικὸς, seu procederet, ut opus quoddam navaret, hoc absoluto rediturum esse in illum in quo prius esset statum : Τὸν ἐν τῷ Θεῷ λόγον, narrat Eusebius, ποτὲ μὲν ἔνδον εἶναι ἐν τῷ Θεῷ ἔφασκε, ποτὲ δὲ προϊέναι τοῦ Θεοῦ, καὶ ἄλλοτε πάλιν ἀναδραμεῖσθαι εἰς τὸν Θεὸν, καὶ ἔσεσθαι ἐν αὐτῷ ὡς καὶ πρότερον ἦν. p. 112, c. Vel ut ipsis Marcelli verbis utar, εἷς Θεὸς, καὶ ὁ τούτου λόγος Θεὸς προῆλθε μὲν τοῦ πατρὸς, ἵνα πάντα δι' αὐτοῦ γένηται· μετὰ δὲ τὸν καιρὸν τῆς κρίσεως καὶ τὴν τῶν ἁπάντων διόρθωσιν καὶ τὸν ἀφανισμὸν τῆς ἀντικειμένης ἁπάσης ἐνεργείας, τότε αὐτὸς ὑποταγήσεται τῷ ὑποτάξαντι αὐτῷ τὰ πάντα Θεῷ καὶ πατρὶ, ἵνα οὕτως ᾖ ἐν Θεῷ ὁ λόγος, ὥσπερ καὶ πρότερον ἦν πρὸ τοῦ τὸν κόσμον εἶναι. Euseb. p. 41, c. d.

Quod corroborat Basilius quoque in epistola sua ad Athanasium missa, cum Marcellum testificatur docuisse, λόγον εἰρῆσθαι τὸν μονογενῆ, κατὰ χρείαν καὶ ἐπὶ καιροῦ προελθόντα, πάλιν δὲ εἰς τὸν ὅθεν ἐξῆλθεν ἐπαναστρέψαντα, οὔτε πρὸ τῆς ἐξόδου εἶναι, οὔτε μετὰ τὴν ἐπάνοδον ὑφεστάναι. *Ep.* 69, 2.

(11) Non Verbum sed Jesum esse Dei Filium. Quod quidem, involutum certe in iis quæ jam citata sunt, tamen, cum tam amplum impleat spatium in quarta contra Arianos, Marcello autem et Photino a variis scriptoribus est attributum, hic in pleniore lumine debet collocari.

Ἱερὸς ἀπόστολός τε καὶ μαθητὴς τοῦ Κυρίου Ἰωάννης, dicit Marcellus apud Eusebium, τῆς ἀϊδιότητος αὐτοῦ μνημονεύων, ἀληθὴς ἐγίγνετο τοῦ λόγου μάρτυς, Ἐν ἀρχῇ ἦν ὁ λόγος, λέγων, καὶ . . . . οὐδὲν γεννήσεως ἐνταῦθα μνημονεύων τοῦ λόγου. Euseb. p. 37, b. vid. etiam p. 27 *fin.* Atque iterum, οὐκ υἱὸν Θεοῦ ἑαυτὸν ὀνομάζει, ἀλλ' ἵνα διὰ τῆς τοιαύτης ὁμολογίας [f. ὀνομασίας R. S. C.] θέσει τὸν ἄνθρωπον, διὰ τὴν πρὸς αὐτὸν κοινωνίαν, υἱὸν Θεοῦ γενέσθαι παρασκευάσῃ, [i. e. θέσει υἱὸν Θεοῦ] p. 42, a. Iterum οὗτός ἐστιν ὁ ἀγαπητὸς [i. e. υἱὸς], ὁ τῷ λόγῳ ἑνωθεὶς ἄνθρωπος. p. 49, a.

Apud Epiphanium autem Photinus, ὁ λόγος ἐν τῷ πατρὶ, φησὶν, ἦν, ἀλλ' οὐκ ἦν υἱός. *Hær.* p. 830, b. vid. etiam p. 831.

Eugenius porro, in expurgatione sua, οὐ γάρ ἄλλον τὸν υἱὸν καὶ ἄλλον τὸν λόγον φρονοῦμεν, ὥςτινες ἡμᾶς διέβαλον. Anathematizat autem insaniam Photini et sectatorum ejus, ὅτι μὴ φρονοῦσι τὸν υἱὸν τοῦ Θεοῦ αὐτὸν εἶναι τὸν λόγον, ἀλλὰ διαιροῦσιν ἀλόγως καὶ ἀρχὴν τῷ υἱῷ διδοῦσιν ἀπὸ τῆς ἐκ Μαρίας κατὰ σάρκα γενέσεως. *Coll. Nov.* t. 2, p. 3, d.

Nestorius quoque : "Cogitur Photinus Verbum dicere, non autem Verbum hoc Filium confitetur." Mercat. t. 2, p. 87. Vid. etiam Garner. Mercat. t. 2, p. 314 init.

Accedit quod Marcellus ipse, in apologia sua coram Julio Summo Pontifice habita, præcipue insistit in eo fidei articulo confitendo, qui in his locis periclitatur : e. g. μονογενὴς υἱὸς λόγος, cujus regni, ut testatur Apostolus, non erit finis ;—Verbum de quo Lucas testatur, sicut tradiderunt nobis οἱ ἀπαρχῆς ἀπόπται καὶ ὑπηρέται γενόμενοι τοῦ λόγου· ὁ υἱὸς, τουτέστι ὁ λόγος τοῦ παντοκράτορος Θεοῦ· ἡ δύναμις πατρὸς ὁ υἱός. Epiph. *Hær.* pp. 835, 6.

(12) *Non Verbum, sed Jesum, esse Christum, Primogenitum, Dei Imaginem, Regem.*

Εἴτις τὸν υἱὸν, dicit Eusebius, ᾧ πάντα παρέδωκεν ὁ πατὴρ, λόγον ὁρίζοιτο μόνον, ὅμοιον τῷ ἐν ἀνθρώποις, εἶτα σάρκα φησὶν ἀνειληφέναι, καὶ τότε υἱὸν Θεοῦ γεγονέναι, καὶ Ἰησοῦν Χριστὸν χρηματίσαι, βασιλέα τε ἀναγορεύεσθαι, εἰκόνα τε τοῦ Θεοῦ τοῦ ἀοράτου, καὶ πρωτότοκον πάσης κτίσεως, μὴ ὄντα πρότερον, τότε ἀποδεδεῖχθαι, τίς ἂν λείποιτο τούτῳ δυσσεβείας ὑπερβολή; p. 6, b. d. Locus hic, quem, omissis quibusdam, coarctavimus, omnia illa quæ Marcello assignantur enumerat. Vid. quoque pp. 49, 50; vel, ut ipsis Marcelli verbis utamur de Primogenito, οὐ τοίνυν οὗτος ὁ ἁγιώτατος λόγος πρὸ τῆς ἐνανθρωπήσεως πρωτότοκος ἁπάσης κτίσεως ὠνόμαστο, (πῶς γὰρ δύνατον τὸν ἀεὶ ὄντα πρωτότοκον εἶναί τινος;) ἀλλὰ τὸν πρῶτον καινὸν ἄνθρωπον, εἰς ὃν τὰ πάντα ἀνακεφαλαιώσασθαι ἐβουλήθη ὁ Θεὸς, τοῦτον αἱ θεῖαι γραφαὶ πρωτότοκον ὀνομάζουσι. Euseb. p. 44, b. c. De Imagine autem, πῶς οὖν εἰκόνα τοῦ ἀοράτου Θεοῦ τὸν τοῦ Θεοῦ λόγον Ἀστέριος εἶναι γέγραφε; αἱ γὰρ εἰκόνες τούτων, ὧν εἰσιν εἰκόνες, καὶ ἀπόντων, δεικτικαί εἰσιν· πῶς εἰκὼν τοῦ ἀοράτου Θεοῦ ὁ λόγος, καὶ αὐτὸς ἀόρατος ὤν; ... δῆλον, ὁπηνίκα τὴν κατ' εἰκόνα τοῦ Θεοῦ γενομένην ἀνείληφε σάρκα, εἰκὼν ἀληθῶς τοῦ ἀοράτου Θεοῦ γέγονε. p. 47, a.-d. Vid. etiam p. 142, b.

Et, quod totius argumenti fundamentum est, μηδ' εἶναι αὐτόν τι πρὸ τῆς ἐνσάρκου παρουσίας ἢ λόγον, μηδ' ὠνομᾶσθαι ἕτερον, εἰ μὴ ἄρα προφητικῶς. pp. 82, 83.

(13) Verbum, in fine sæculi, ad Deum rediens, carnem seu humanitatem esse relicturum, regno valedicturum

Quo in articulo, hujus hæreseos summa fere et capite, ut in suo symbolo indicarunt Patres Constantinopolitani multus est Marcellus. Cum "caro non prodest quidquam," quomodo potest habere sempiternam cum Verbo societatem? pp. 42, 3. Præterea Dominus jam dixerat, " Si videritis Filium hominis ascendentem ubi erat prius?" id quod videtur innuere Verbi separationem illam a carne sua, p. 51, c. A Propheta porro diserte dictum est: "Sede a dextris meis *donec* ponam," etc.; et a Paulo: "Oportet illum regnare *donec* ponat," etc. p. 51, d. et a Petro: "Quem oportet coelum suscipere *usque ad* tempora restitutionis omnium," etc. p. 52, a. Porro in id universa œconomia dirigitur, non ut a Verbo, sed ut ab homine, hostis hominis possit subjici, coelum aperiri, p. 49, c. d. οὐδὲ γὰρ αὐτὸς καθ' ἑαυτὸν ὁ λόγος ἀρχὴν βασιλείας εἴληφεν, ἀλλ' ὁ ἀπατηθεὶς ὑπὸ τοῦ διαβόλου ἄνθρωπος, διὰ τῆς τοῦ λόγου δυνάμεως, βασιλεὺς γέγονεν, ἵνα βασιλεὺς γενόμενος τὸν πρότερον ἀπατήσαντα νικήσῃ διάβολον. Euseb. p. 52, a. Præterea, si initium habuerit regnum illud 400 ante annos, non mirum est si habeat finem. p. 50, d. ὥσπερ ἀρχὴν οὕτω καὶ τέλος ἕξειν. p. 52 c. Quod si rogaverit quispiam, Quid tum fiet de carna illa immortali, quondam propria Verbi? respondit Marcellus, δογματίζειν περὶ ὧν μὴ ἀκριβῶς [ἐκ] τῶν θείων μεμαθήκαμεν γραφῶν, οὐκ ἀσφαλές. Euseb. p. 53, a. μή μου πυνθάνου περὶ ὧν σαφῶς παρὰ τῆς θείας γραφῆς μὴ μεμάθηκα. διὰ τοῦτο τοίνυν οὐδὲ περὶ τῆς θείας ἐκείνης, τῆς τῷ θείῳ λόγῳ κοινωνησάσης σαρκός, σαφῶς εἰπεῖν δυνήσομαι. Ibid. b. c.

3. Jam vero, cum hæc fuerit doctrina Marcelli, Photini, et factionis istorum hominum, vix quicquam occurrit in singulis ejus articulis, sic ex ordine collocatis, quod non sit tum expressum tum confutatum in quarta illa, quam vocant, Oratione Athanasii. Cujus rei vis eo major esse debet, quod in historia temporum illorum

Athanasius tam alienus est ab Eusebio, tam familiariter agit eum Eugenio et Basilio. Cum enim dissimilium ingeniorum, diversarum partium viri, ut Athanasius et Eusebius, ejusdem erroris sunt testes, ut reipsa hic aut illic existentis, errorem illum verisimile est et revera existere, et existere in illo loco, cui Eusebius eum assignat, Athanasius saltem non abjudicat. Deinde Basilius, Athanasius, Eugenius, unam rem agunt in historia hujus quæstionis; accusator Basilius, Marcellus et Eugenius rei, Athanasius judex, crimen hæresis cujusdam societas; quare, cum Athanasium eundem de eadem hæresi jam antea scripsisse constet, facilis est conjectura, sanctum Doctorem, cum scriberet, versari in illis ipsis hominibus impetendis, quos postea notat Basilius, horret Eugenius. Verum ad ipsam locorum collationem veniamus, expositis hinc sectæ istius placitis, illinc opinionibus ab Athanasio damnatis.

(1) E sectionibus triginta sex libri quarti, saltem una et viginti id agunt ut refellant eos qui dicerent Verbum non esse Filium: esto septem ex iis respexerint Paulianistas, nihilominus reliquis quatuordecim aliquis inveniendus est scopus, cui plene et unice responsurus est comitatus Marcelli.

(2) Increpat Athanasius commentum dicentium, Verbum Dei, similem verbi humani, non habere substantiam; οὐ διαλελυμένος, ἢ ἁπλῶς φωνὴ σημαντικὴ, ἀλλὰ οὐσιώδης λόγος· εἰ γὰρ μὴ, ἔσται ὁ Θεὸς λαλῶν εἰς ἀέρα. ... ἐπειδὴ δὲ οὐκ ἔστιν ἄνθρωπος, οὐκ ἂν εἴη οὐδὲ ὁ λόγος αὐτοῦ, κατὰ τὴν τῶν ἀνθρώπων ἀσθένειαν. § 1. Vid. quoque *Contr. Sabell. Greg.* § 5, e. Hoc vero idem illud est, conceptis

verbis, cujus Eusebius insimulat Marcellum, e. g. ἐπὶ δὲ τοῦ λόγου, σημαντικὸν αὐτὸν δίδωσι, καὶ ὅμοιον τῷ ἀνθρωπίνῳ. p. 118. Vid. quoque p. 128.

(3) Reprobat Athanasius illud in hæreticis suis, quod dicerent in Natura Divina prius fuisse silentium, tum actionem quandam; τὸν Θεὸν, σιωπῶντα μὲν ἀνενέργητον, λαλοῦντα δὲ ἰσχύειν αὐτὸν βούλονται. § 11, vid. etiam § 12. At Eusebius Marcellum postulat de eodem; ὁ λόγος ἔνδον μένων ἐν ἡσυχάζοντι τῷ πατρὶ, ἐνεργῶν δὲ ἐν τῷ τὴν κτίσιν δημιουργεῖν, ὁμοίως τῷ ἡμετέρῳ, ἐν σιωπῶσι μὲν ἡσυχάζοντι, ἐν δὲ φθεγγομένοις ἐνεργοῦντι. p. 4, d. Alibi objicit Eusebius Marcello posse fieri, ut artifices etiam humani et in silentio sint et in actione simul, interna quadam mentis operatione, p. 167, b.; idem objicit Athanasius, § 11, d.

(4) Non pauca superius dicta sunt de πλατυσμῷ illo μονάδος in carne, idque ἐνεργείᾳ quadam; jam in hac materie tota est una pars libri seu Orationis quartæ, viz. §§ 13, 14, 25. φησὶ γὰρ, dicit Athanasius, ὁ πατὴρ πλατύνεται εἰς υἱὸν καὶ πνεῦμα. § 25. τίς ἡ ἐνέργεια τοῦ τοιούτου πλατυσμοῦ; φανήσεται ὁ πατὴρ καὶ γεγονὼς σάρξ, εἴγε αὐτὸς μονὰς ὢν ἐν τῷ ἀνθρώπῳ ἐπλατύνθη. § 14.

(5) Dogma illud Verbi a Deo procedentis, ad Deum redeuntis, Marcello tribuunt et Eusebius et Basilius; Athanasius autem illi quam impugnat factioni, ipsis adhibitis vocibus προελθὼν et παλινδρομῶν, πρόοδος et ἀναδρομὴ, προεβάλλετο et ἀνακαλεῖται, γέννησις et παῦλα τῆς γεννήσεως. § 12, § 4, e.

(6) Marcellum de Verbo disserentem jam vidimus insistere in phrasi ἐν τῷ Θεῷ: idem fecerunt hæretici illi,

de quibus loquitur Athanasius, vid. § 12 passim, § 2 init. etc. § 4, e.

(7) Eosdem incusat Athanasius, (nisi vellent esse meri Sabelliani,) quod necessario tenerent attributa Dei esse res quasdam per se subsistentes in divina natura, quæ proinde σύνθετος esset: at hoc ipsum deducit Eusebius ex doctrina Marcelli. Athanasius: κατὰ τοῦτο ἡ θεία μονὰς σύνθετος φανήσεται, τεμνομένη εἰς οὐσίαν καὶ συμβεβηκός. § 2. Eusebius: σύνθετον ὥσπερ εἰσῆγεν τὸν Θεὸν, οὐσίαν αὐτὸν ὑποτιθέμενος δίχα λόγου, συμβεβηκὸς δὲ τῇ οὐσίᾳ τὸν λόγον. p. 121, vid. p. 149. d. Iterum Athanasius: εἰ τοῦτο, πάτηρ μὲν ὅτε σοφὸς, υἱὸς δὲ ὅτε σοφία· ἀλλὰ μὴ ὡς ποιότης τις ταῦτα ἐν τῷ Θεῷ. § 2. Iterum Eusebius: εἰ δ᾽ ἓν καὶ ταὐτὸν ἦν ὁ Θεὸς καὶ ἡ ἐν ταῖς παροιμίας σοφία, ἕξις οὖσα σοφὴ ἐν αὐτῷ νοουμένη, καθὸ σοφὸς ὁ Θεὸς, τί ἐκώλυεν, κ. τ. λ. p. 150, b.

(8) Teste Eusebio, Marcellus, dogma suum insinuans, professus est sibi præcipue cordi esse monarchiæ dogma, p. 109, b. quod quidem dogma Athanasius contra, disputationis suæ statim principio, confirmat illæsum prorsus esse et securum in doctrina catholicorum.

(9) Celebre est Marcelli dogma illud de regno Christi ad tempus duraturo, ab initiis quibusdam orto, finem tandem habituro: hæreticorum autem, quos urget Athanasius, haud absimile est illud § 8, quod Filio et existendi et regnandi initium videntur assignasse.

(10) Verbum esse Filium etc. in Veteri Testamento negat Marcellus apud Eusebium p. 131, b. pp. 83-101, pp. 134-140; negant hæretici apud Athanasium, §§ 23-29.

(11) Cum loca illa Veteris Testamenti objicerentur Marcello, profitebatur ea anticipationes esse Novi; εἰ δέ τις, καὶ πρὸ τῆς νέας διαθήκης, τὸ τοῦ Χριστοῦ Ἰησοῦ ὄνομα ἐπὶ τοῦ λόγου μόνου δεικνύναι δύνασθαι ἐπαγγέλλοιτο, εὑρήσει τοῦτο προφητικῶς εἰρημένον. Euseb. p. 43, a. Quare apud Apostolum ad Rom. i. 4, pro ὁρισθεὶς legebat προορισθείς. Euseb. contr. Marc. i. 2.; vid. Anathem. 5um Concil Sirm. Prim.; vid. porro *Select. Observ.* R. S. C. p. 10. Quod idem de Photino quoque narrat Epiphanius, autumasse scilicet eum Vetus Testamentum scriptum esse προκαταγγελτικῶς, προχρηστικῶς. *Hær.* 71, p. 830. At Athanasius quoque de hæreticis suis disputans, ἀλλὰ ναὶ, φασὶ, κεῖται μὲν, προφητικῶς δὲ ἔστω. § 24.

(12) Marcellus, cum testimonio Psalmi 109 urgeretur, voluit "Luciferum" illum esse stellam, quæ Magorum dux fuit. Euseb. p. 48, b. Vid. Epiphan. *Hær.* p. 833, a. Athanasius quoque pro parte sua, per duas sectiones (27, 28) totus est in eodem Scripturæ loco excutiendo.

(13) Accedit denique, quod notatu certe dignum est, idem propemodum sentire Athanasium de natura dogmatis Sabelliani, quod Eusebium, Eugenium, Basilium sensisse supra dictum est. Σαβελλίου τὸ ἐπιτήδευμα, τὸν αὐτὸν υἱὸν καὶ πατέρα λέγοντος, καὶ ἑκάτερον ἀναιροῦντος, ὅτε μὲν υἱὸς, τὸν πατέρα, ὅτε δὲ πατήρ, τὸν υἱόν. § 9.

Profecto plura sunt quæ conferri possint ad Athanasii librum quartum ex Marcelli et Photini hæresi illustrandum; hæc autem qualicumque satis sint quo demonstretur, illud sanctissimi doctoris opus, non adversus Arianos, sed adversus Photinianorum dogma esse exaratum. Neque id multum in hac re valet, quo motus Montefalconius dubitat an opusculum *Contra Sabellii gregales* sit Athanasii, nullam scilicet esse memoriæ proditam Athanasii cum Sabellianorum familiis dimicationem. Nam si reipsa certum est, hunc librum de Sabellianismo quodam disputare, esse autem genuinum, (id quod nemo inficiatur), quid ultra quærendum est? aliorum silentium explicatione eget, sed nihil probat. Opportunum autem est Sirmondi responsum de Hieronymo similiter prætermittente Eusebii tractatus contra Sabellium:—"de infinitis voluminibus quæ ab Eusebio edita testatur, pauca, certe non omnia, Hieronymum commemorasse." Sirmond. *Opp.* tom. i. init.

Jam mihi disputandi tandem finem facturo, in mentem subit Ciceronianum illud, "Utitur in re non dubia testibus non necessariis." At certe nulla moles argumentorum illis nimia est, qui adversarios habeant Montefalconium Benedictinum, Jesuitam Petavium.

Restat ut subjiciatur operi nostro brevis quædam analysis partium seu fragmentorum eorum, ex quibus consistit hic liber.

1. Sectiones septem, 1-5, 9, 10, Monarchiam tractant, et cognatam materiam unitatis, simplicitatis, integritatis divinæ, tum Filii generationis; quarum una § 4, et alterius pars § 3, Arianos alloquitur; reliquæ familias Sabellianas.

2. Duo, 6 et 7, cum Arianis cominus pugnant, nihil autem commune habent neque cum sectionibus quæ præcedunt, neque cum iis quæ subsequuntur.

3. Tres, 8, 11, et 12, comparationem ineunt inter contrarias sectas, præcipue Sabellianam.

4. Tres aliæ, 13, 14, 25, pertinent ad præcipuum quoddam dogma Sabellii et Marcelli.

5. Universæ 21 sectiones, quæ reliquæ sunt, cursum autem pæne continuum habent, 15-24, 26-29, unam rem agunt, Verbum scilicet idem esse ac Filium, contra doctrinam Marcelli et Pauli Samosateni.

DISSERTATIO II.

DE ECTHESI EPHESINA CONTRA PAULUM SAMOSATENUM·

EXTAT in tertia parte Actorum Concilii Œcumenici Ephesini an. 431 habiti, symbolum quoddam sic fere inscriptum: " De Incarnatione Verbi Dei, Filii Patris, Definitio Episcoporum, qui Nicææ in Synodo convenerunt, et expositio ejusdem Synodi adversus Paulum Samosatenum." Ecthesis hæc Patribus Antiochenis, qui Paulum condemnaverunt cir. an. 264-270, vindicatur a Baronio an. 272; J. Forbes, *Instr. Hist. Theolog.* i. 4, § 1; Le Moyne, *Var. Sacr.* t. 2, p. 255; Worm. *Hist. Sabell.* p. 116-119. (vid. Routh, *Rell. Sacr.* t. 2, p. 523); Simon. de Magistris, *Præfat. ad Dionys. Alex.* p. xl.; Feverlin, *Dissert. de P. Samos.* § 9; Fasson, *de voce Homoüsion;* Molkenbuhr, *Dissert. Crit.* 4; Kern. *Disqu. Hist. Crit.* de hac re; Burton, *ap.* Faber, "*Apostolicity of Trinitarianism,*" et aliis. Cum autem *homoüsion* Filii Dei profiteatur, adhibita est a criticis quibusdam, quo probabilius fieret, Athanasium, Basilium, et Hilarium, gravissimos auctores, errasse cum dicerent vocabulum illud Antiochiæ tunc temporis, in Epistola

Synodica Patrum, aut condemnatum esse, aut prudenter omissum. Quæ quidem subdifficilis quæstio non hujus est loci, ubi id tantum agimus, pace eruditissimorum virorum, ut allatis argumentis pro captu nostro commonstremus, ecthesin illam Concilio neque Antiocheno, neque vero Nicæno esse coævam, sed jure referri in tempora et Paulo et Ario posteriora.

Cæterum occurrit hoc Symbolum ap. Harduin, *Concil.* t. 1, p. 1640. Routh, *Relliqu. Sacr.* t. 2, p. 524. Dionys. Alex. *Opp.* Rom. 1696 (1796), p. 289. Card. Mai, *Nov. Coll.* t. 7, 162. Burton, *Testimonies*, p. 397-399. Faber, *Op. cit.* t. 2, p. 287. Ad rem aggrediamur.

1. Ecthesis hæc habet : ὅλον ὁμοούσιον τῷ Θεῷ καὶ μετὰ τοῦ σώματος, ἀλλ οὐχὶ κατὰ τὸ σῶμα ὁμοούσιον τῷ Θεῷ. At multa suadent vocabulum *homoüsion* non habere locum in symbolis sæculi tertii.

(1) Primum, decantata sunt illa Augustini et Vigilii, ex quibus constat tempore Concilii Nicæni *homoüsion* fuisse instrumentum novum, quo munita est fides Ecclesiæ contra Arianos : " Adversus impietatem Arianorum hæreticorum," inquit Augustinus, "novum nomen Patres *homoüsion* condiderunt, sed non rem novam tali nomine signarunt," *in Joan.* 97, n. 4. Alio loco monet: " minus quam oportuit intellectum " esse illud nomen Arimini, " propter novitatem verbi," (*Contra. Maxim.* ii. 14); " quod tamen," subjungit, " fides antiqua pepererat." Vigilius autem, "res antiqua novum nomen accepit *homoüsion*." *Disput. Athan. et Ar. ap. Bibl. Patr. Col.* 1618, t. v. *part.* 3, p. 695. Vid. Le Moyne, *Var. Sacr. l. c.*

(2) Deinde, auctor est Sozomenus, *Hist.* iv. 15, a Semi-arianis Sirmii an. 358 adhibitum esse in confessione sua conscribenda illud ipsum symbolum, quod Antiocheni Patres contra Paulum edidissent; quod quidem certe non adhibuissent amentissimi *homoüsii* insectatores, si in illo ea vox locum habuisset.

(3) Tum ex ipsorum Semi-arianorum testimonio idem conficitur, in iis scilicet quæ ab illis scripta apud Epiphanium reperiuntur. *Hæres.* 73. Profecto ibi provocant ad Concilium Antiochenum contra Paulum habitum, quo melius, *usiam* præseferentes, insinuent suum *homoeüsion;* quod, inquam, contra esset ab illis factum, si Concilium illud in symbolo suo, ut *usiam*, sic *homoüsion* quoque ascivisset.

(4) Neque sane est quod miremur, (hoc enim obiter dici liceat,) si Patres Antiocheni œconomia quadam utendum esse duxerint, in voce *homoüsion* adhibenda. Nam qui primi Pauli causam tractaverunt, Dionysius, Gregorius Neocæsariensis, Athenodorus, fortasse Firmilianus, fuerunt Origenis discipuli, acerrimi impugnatoris eorum qui corpoream aliquam naturam Deo tribuerent; qualem contendit Paulus, testibus Athanasio et Basilio, in vocabulo *homoüsion* innui. De divina substantia tanquam corpore loquitur Tertullianus, *in Prax.* 7, utitur porro, post Valentinianos, voce προβολή, (sicut Justinus cognata phrasi προβληθὲν γέννημα, *Tryph.* 62); at Origenes contra, cum Candido Valentiniano congressus, verbum illud reprobat, Melitonis autem opus, περὶ ἐνσωμάτου Θεοῦ severius notat, (*in Genes. Fragm.* t. 2, p. 25), quasi Deum esse materialem Melito docuerit, vid. etiam *de Orat.* 23. Illa Platonicorum quoque admiratio, quæ in

Origene cernitur, eodem spectat, cum philosophi istius sectæ, quo Deum simplicissimum et perfectissimum esse traderent, soliti sint illum appellare ὑπερούσιον.

Profecto a Plotino Deus appellatur, "origo existentiæ et præstantior *usia*." 5 *Ennead.* v. 11, quia "supereminens omnia est, at non illa, sed causa illorum." *ibid.* c. ult. Quod docuerunt porro materialistæ de necessitate physica, in causa fuit cur Plotinus Dei energiam et voluntatem diceret ejus esse *usiam*, 6 *Enn.* viii. 13. Origenes quoque, "Neque enim *usiæ* particeps est Deus, participes enim facit potius, quam ipse est particeps." *Contr. Cels.* vi. 64. Hinc vox ὑπερούσιον de Deo usurpatur ab Areopagita, *de div. nom.* i. 2, et a Maximo Confessore; qui "οὐσία," scribit, "improprie de Deo dicitur, nam ὑπερούσιος est." *in Areopag. de div. nom.* v. *init.* Vid. etiam Damasc. *Fid. Orth.* i. 4 et 8, pp. 137, 147. Gregorium Naz. quoque, qui Deum augurat esse ὑπὲρ τὴν οὐσίαν. *Orat.* vi. 12. Et Constantinum *ad Sanct. Coet.* 9.

Origenes sane in Joan. t. 20, 16, eo usque progreditur, ut verba reprehendat ἐκ τῆς οὐσίας τοῦ πατρὸς γεγεννῆσθαι τὸν υἱόν; sed ob hanc plane rem, quia arbitratur, perperam quidem, formulam istiusmodi μείωσιν quandam inferre in notionem Dei.

Jam Arianis certe usitatissimum fuit, eo nomine postulare *homoüsion*, quasi, Gnosticorum et Manichæorum more, immaterialitati divinæ injuriam fecerit.

Et Dionysium Alexandriæ Episcopum constat primo horruisse aliquantum hoc vocabulum, tum solum fidenter illud enunciantem et confitentem, cum eum Pontifex Romanus ad id hortatus esset.

Neque illud omittendum est, quod circa idem tempus cum habebantur Concilia Antiochiæ contra Paulum, illam orbis Christianæ partem invaserat Manichæorum hæresis; quæ, utpote verbo *homoüsion* usa in theologia sua, idque materiali sensu, non immerito Patribus metum incuteret, ne vox, in se sanctissima et præclarissima, illo tempore catholico dogmati parum esset profutura.

(5) Quibus perspectis, forsitan expediri poterit ille nodus in historia Patrum Antiochenorum, quod Athanasius, Basilius, Hilarius, una consentientes de verbo *homoüsion* ab illis Patribus improbato, quare improbatum fuerit, inter se non consentiunt. Scilicet, cum *usia*, ut a Petavio dictum est, *de Trin.* iv. 1, in philosophorum scholis, quod unum est et individuum tunc temporis significaret, cognata vox *homoüsion*, de Sanctissima Trinitate usurpata, illis qui a theologia sua mysteria excludebant, alterutrum de duobus erroribus secum ferre videbatur. Nam si verbum illud materiale quid innueret, id jam hæresis erat; si vero immateriale, continuo fieri non poterat, quin illæ duæ Personæ plane essent, non duæ ullatenus, sed omnimodo unum. Quare significaturum esset tandem aut Patris partem (μέρος ὁμοούσιον) esse Filium, sicut volebant Manichæi, aut Patrem esse Filium, sicut Sabelliani. Paulus igitur in Patres Antiochiæ congregatos hoc fere usus est dilemmate: " Nisi vocabulum vestrum Manichæorum est, quod vos negatis, certe Sabellianismum sonat, id quod ego libenter suscipio;" unde et verum erit, quod Athanasius narrat, Paulum dixisse: " Si *homoüsius* est Christus, tres sunt substantiæ in deitate," et verum quod Hilarius, " *Homoüsion* Samosatenus confessus est." Subduxerunt

itaque Patres voculam, ne illam sophista aut de hæresi postularet Manichæorum, aut in Sabellianam vindicaret.

2. Legimus etiam in Ecthesi, μετὰ τῆς θεότητος ὢν κατὰ σάρκα ὁμοούσιος ἡμῖν.

Multa sunt et gravia, cur credamus, formulam illam ὁμοούσιον ἡμῖν temporibus esse tribuendam et Antiocheno Concilio, et fortasse Nicæno, posterioribus.

(1) Si Waterlandio credendum est, ætatem Symboli *Quicunque* eruenti, ὁμοούσιον ἡμῖν pauci tantum ante Eutychen conceptis verbis tradiderunt, post autem plurimi. Exempli causa, provocat vir doctus ad confessionem Turribii Hispani an. 447; Flaviani Constantinopolitani et Leonis Papæ an. 449: Concilii Chalcedonensis an. 451; Felicis III. an. 485; Anastasii II. an. 496; Ecclesiæ Alexandrinæ eodem anno; necnon Hormisdæ, Ecclesiarum Syriæ, Fulgentii, Justiniani, Joannis II. et Pelagii I. in sæculo sexto. "In quibus singulis," inquit, "aut unius naturæ dogma est reprobatum, aut duarum comprobatum, aut τὸ ὁμοούσιον ἡμῖν sancitum; quos quidem articulos frustra quæsiveris in Symbolo *Quicunque*." Opp. t. 4, p. 247. Eodem autem argumento, quo Symbolum *Quicunque*, verba ὁμοούσιον ἡμῖν omittens, collocatur ante Eutychen, Ecthesis hæc Ephesina, iisdem usa, post Eutychen collocabitur.

(2) Illud ipsum, quod ὁμοούσιον ἡμῖν est ab Eutyche repudiatum, indicio est hanc formulam non usurpatam esse ab Ecclesia in confessionibus suis, ante Eutychen; namque id hæreticorum proprium est, Catholicæ traditionis illos articulos respuere, quæ hactenus sunt fidelium tantummodo mentibus, non publicis monumentis, mandata.

"Usque ad hodiernum diem," contendit hæresiarcha in Concilio Constantinopolitano, "non dixi corpus Domini et Dei nostri esse ὁμοούσιον ἡμῖν; confiteor autem Sanctam Virginem esse ὁμοούσιον ἡμῖν, ex qua Deus noster est incarnatus." Hard. *Conc.* t. 2, p. 164, 5. Scilicet in quæstionem venerat, utrum formula quædam reciperetur necne, quæ, cum apprime esset utilis ad nascentem hæresin opprimendam, adhuc tamen privati solummodo fuisset juris et in certis ut plurimum locis usitata. Idem accidisse cernimus in vocabulo φύσις, quod eo plausibilius rejecerunt Eutychiani, quia rarius adhibitum fuisset in scriptis Patrum, tum cum in controversiam vocaretur. De ὑπόστασις, quæ vox alteri erit exemplo hujusce rei, post dicendum erit.

(3) Occurretur forsitan a quibusdam dicentibus, articulum hunc ὁμοούσιον ἡμῖν sancitum esse ab Ecclesia cum Apollinaristis confligente; qui, teste Athanasio *ad Epict.* 2, Christi corpus Divinitati consubstantiale esse jactabant. Concedo utique; sed cum Apollinaristæ dogma ipsi suum brevi deseruerint, (Epiph. *Hær.* 77, 25,) non necesse habuit Eccelsia tesseram aliquam fidei contra perfidiam eorum proferri. Ambæ quippe Apollinaristarum sectæ videntur inter se consensisse in articulo ὁμοούσιον ἡμῖν verbo tenus recipiendo, id solum exagitantes, utrum de carne Domini jam cum Divinitate unita posset ille prædicari, necne; vid. Leont. *de Fraud. Apollin. ap. P. Col. Bibl.* t. 6, *part.* 1. Attamen occurrit certe formula illa in confessione Johannis Antiocheni, circ. an 431. Rustic. *contra Aceph.* ibid. t. 6, p. 2, p. 799, et alibi, ut credo; ea vero non amplius 21 annis antecessit Concilio Chalcedonensi, a quo inter formulas Ecclesiæ illa ὁμοούσιον ἡμῖν recepta est.

(4) Enimvero contra Apollinaristarum ὁμοούσιον θεότητι usitatius est in scriptis Patrum, non ὁμοούσιον ἡμῖν, sed ὁμοούσιον Μαρίᾳ. Scilicet Amphilochius, quasi summam rei explicans, "Apparet certe," scribit, "sanctos Patres dixisse, Filium esse consubstantialem Patri secundum divinitatem, et *consubstantialem Matri* secundum humanitatem." ap. Phot. *Bibl.* p. 789. Proclus, non ὁμοούσιον, sed ὁμόφυλον, scribit, adjecto tamen " Virgine," non "nobis;" τῷ πατρὶ κατὰ τὴν θεότητα ὁμοούσιος, οὕτως ὁ αὐτὸς καὶ τῇ παρθένῳ κατὰ τὴν σάρκα ὁμόφυλος. *ad Arm.* p. 618, *circ. init.* ed. 1630. Vid. quoque p. 613, *fin.* p. 618. Saepius ὁμοούσιον adhibens Proclus in theologia explicanda, hic non adhibet in œconomia. Athanasius quoque : τὸν ἡνώμενον πατρὶ κατὰ πνεῦμα, ἡμῖν δε κατὰ σάρκα. *ap.* Theod. *Eran.* ii. p. 139. Alibi : οὐκ ἐκ Μαρίας, ἀλλ' ἐκ τῆς ἑαυτοῦ οὐσίας σῶμα. *ad Epict.* 2. Vid. quoque verba ὁμογενὴς et ὁμοούσιος inter se opposita, *de Sent. Dion.* 10. Eandem rem exprimit τέλειος ἄνθρωπος, e. g. Procl. *ad Arm.* p. 613, quam quidem phrasin, ab Apollinare rejectam, Eutyches recepit. *Concil.* t. 2, p. 157. Leon. *Epist.* 21.

Contra ab Eustathio an. 325 certe dictum est, Christi animam esse ταῖς ψυχαῖς τῶν ἀνθρώπων ὁμοούσιον, ὥσπερ καὶ ἡ σὰρξ ὁμοούσιος τῇ τῶν ἀνθρώπων σαρκί. *Ap.* Theod. *Eran.* i. p. 56, et ab Ambrosio *ibid.* p. 139. ὁμοούσιον τῷ πατρὶ κατὰ τὴν θεότητα, καὶ ὁμοούσιον ἡμῖν κατὰ τὴν ἀνθρωπότητα; (vid. quoque Leont. *Contr. Nest. et Eutych. Bibl. Col.* p. 977,) quod mirabile sane erit si ab Ambrosio scriptum est, at sancto Doctori paene abjudicatur a Maurinis, *Opp.* tom. 2, p. 729. Quid quod Leontium hunc, in cujus opere occurrit, alium esse atque auctorem illum qui scripserit de Sectis, Coustantii judicium est, *Append. Epist. Pont. Rom.* p. 79, eo autem nomine (quod ad rem nostram facit) quia minus "accuratus" scriptor esset. Attamen videas aliud specimen ejusdem formulæ in Theophilo *ap.* Theod. *Eran.* ii. p. 154.

(5) Neque illud leve est, quod, cum scriptoribus ὁμοούσιον ἡμῖν proferentibus vox οὐσία pro φύσις sive γένος sumatur, ita ut ὁμοούσιον valeat ὁμόφυλον, sensus contra ὁμοουσίου patribus Antiochenis sæculi tertii videtur esse ille quem fert in formula ὁμοούσιος πατρί; nempe ut individuum, non speciem, significet; quod quidem, ut jam vidimus, Paulus pro concesso habet in sophismate suo contra illos Patres torquendo. Quod adeo receptum fuit illis temporibus, ut Hippolytus tantum non diserte neget homines esse inter se unius substantiæ vel οὐσίας; rogat enim, μὴ πάντες ἐν σῶμά ἐσμεν κατὰ τὴν οὐσίαν; *Contr. Noet.* 7. Malchion quoque, in illa ipsa cum Paulo dimicatione, hæresiarcham incusat quod non teneret οὐσιῶσθαι ἐν τῷ ὅλῳ σωτῆρι τὸν υἱὸν τὸν μονογενῆ. Routh. *Relliqu.* t. ii. p. 476. Africanus porro confitetur, οὐσίαν ὅλην οὐσιωθεὶς ἄνθρωπος λέγεται. *Ibid.* p. 125. Quinimo Athanasius ipse videtur uti verbo οὐσία simpliciter de divinitate Verbi, numquam, quantum scio, de humanitate ab eo assumpta. Vid. *Orat.* i. 45, 57 fin. 59 init. 60 init. 62, 64 fin.; ii. 18 init.; iii. 45 init. etc. Inducit autem, quasi inter se contraria, οὐσίαν et ἀνθρώπινον Verbi, *Orat.* i. 41. οὐσίαν et ἀνθρωπότητα, iii. 34 *init.* Sed hac de re plura possent dici, quam hujus disputationis ratio ferret.

(6) Accedit quod Epistola extat quædam a Patribus

Antiochenis, vel quibusdam ex illis, scripta; quæ, de Incarnatione disputans, verbis utitur plane similibus verborum sæculi tertii, plane dissimilibus eorum quæ in Ecthesi Ephesina reperiuntur. Mentionem scilicet facit de Filio "incarnato" et "facto homine," de "corpore ejus ex Virgine sumpto," de "homine ex semine David," de "participatione carnis et sanguinis." Routh, *Rell.* t. 2, p. 473. Atque hæc de formula ὁμοούσιος ἡμῖν, Apollinaris, vel potius Eutychis ævo, primum in fidei confessiones recepta.

3. Hæc quoque notanda sunt in Ecthesi: ἓν πρόσωπον σύνθετον ἐκ θεότητος οὐρανίου καὶ ἀνθρωπείας σαρκός.

Verbum σύνθετον, latine *compositum*, reperitur in fragmento quod extat disputationis Malchionis cum Paulo in Concilio Antiocheno, Routh, *Relliqu.* t. 2, p. 476; at πρόσωπον, sumptum pro antitheto, quod vocant, duarum naturarum, ad seriorem ætatem referendum est.

Concedendum sane est *personæ* vocabulum reperiri in Tertulliano, idque de duabus Christi naturis disputante. *Adv. Prax.* 27. Hoc tamen fere ἅπαξ λεγόμενον est; quamquam Novatianus certe, cui cum Tertulliano magna est necessitudo, loquitur *de Trin.* 21, de "regula circa personam Christi." Sed usurpat ille auctor Christi nomen passim in opere suo, non pro Filio Incarnato, sed simpliciter pro Deo Unigenito: e.c. "Regula veritatis docet nos credere *post Patrem* etiam in Filium Dei Christum Jesum, Dominum Deum nostrum, sed Dei filium etc. c. 9. *init.* Alibi, "Christus habet gloriam ante mundi institutionem," 16. Vid. quoque 13, ubi Christum, non Verbum, carnem sumpsisse docet; alibi autem, inita jam disputatione de "Persona Christi," tamen loquitur de illo ut "secundam personam post Patrem," 26 et 31. Vid. quoque 27.

Quidquid autem hæc valeant, confirmare tamen ausim, (si de re quaquam, quod plane demonstrari non potest, secure potest confirmari), vocabulum πρόσωπον, de Christo incarnato sumptum, non fuisse in usu Catholicorum usque ad tempora fere Apollinaris.

(1) Non occurrit in Athanasii opere contra Apollinarem, scripto circ. an. 370, exceptis locis duobus, de quibus postea; neque in Greg. Naz. *Ep.* 202 *ad Nectarium*, neque *Epp.* 101, 102, *ad Cledonium;* neque in *Dialogis tribus* Theodoreti, nisi in uno loco, quem, Ambrosio a Theodoreto et Leontio tributum, Ambrosii non esse jam diximus; neque in Symbolo Damasi, a quo condemnatus est Apollinaris, vid. *Epp.* Dam. *ap.* Coust. 4 et 5; neque in Symbolo Epiphanii, *Ancor.* 121; vid. quoque 75.

(2) Desideratur idem in iis disputationibus Patrum, ubi, si tum esset in usu, jure erat expectandum; cujus vice aliæ contra suppositæ sunt voculæ et phrases, quæ et iteratione sua formularum pæne gerunt speciem, et varietate sua admirationem movent, cur πρόσωπον quoque in illis locis non reperiatur.

E. c. Irenæus: "Non ergo *alterum* filium hominis novit Evangelium, nisi hunc qui ex Maria etc. et *eundem* hunc passum resurrexisse . . . Etsi lingua quidem confitentur *unum* Jesum Christum, . . . *alterum* quidem passum et natum, etc. et esse *alterum* eorum," etc. *Hær.* iii. 16, n. 5, 6; "*unus* quidem et *idem* existens," n. 7; "per multa dividens Filium Dei," n. 8; "*unum et eundem*," ibid. "Si *alter . . . alter . . .* quoniam *unum* eum novit Apostolus," etc. n. 9. Extenditur disputatio ad c. 24.

Ambrosius: "*Unus* in utraque (divinitate et carne) loquitur Dei Filius; quia in *eodem* utraque natura est; et si *idem* loquitur, non uno semper loquitur modo." *de Fid.* ii. 9. Vid. 58. "Non divisus, sed *unus;* quia utrumque *unus,* et *unus* in utroque . . . *non* enim *alter* ex Patre, *alter* ex Virgine, sed *idem* aliter ex Patre, aliter ex Virgine." *de Incarn.* 35. Vid. 47, 75. "Non enim quod ejusdem substantiæ est, *unus* sed *unum* est," 77, quo in loco verbum *persona* sequitur de Mysterio Trinitatis.

Hilarius: "Non *alius* Filius hominis quam qui Filius Dei est, neque *alius* in forma Dei quam qui in forma servi perfectus homo natus est . . . habens in se et totum verumque quod homo est, et totum verumque quod Deus est." *de Trin.* x. 19. "Cum *ipse ille* Filius hominis *ipse* sit *qui et* Filius Dei, quia totus hominis Filius totus Dei Filius sit, etc. . . . Natus autem est, *non* ut esset *alius atque alius,* sed ut ante hominem Deus, suscipiens hominem, homo et Deus possit intelligi." *ibid.* 22. "Non potest . . . ita *ab se dividuus* esse, ne Christus sit; cum *non alius* Christus, quam qui a forma Dei, etc., *neque alius* quam qui natus est, etc. . . . *neque alius* quam qui est mortuus, etc. . . . in cœlis autem *non alius* sit quam qui," etc. ibid. "ut non *idem* fuerit *qui et,*" etc. *ibid.* 50. "Totum ei Deus Verbum est, totum ei homo Christus est. . . . *nec* Christum *aliud* credere quam Jesum, nec Jesum *aliud* prædicare quam Christum." 52.

Haud aliter Athanasius: ἄλλος, ἄλλος· ἕτερος, ἕτερος· εἷς καὶ αὐτός· ταὐτόν· ἀδιαίρετος. *Orat.* iv. 15 et 29.

ἄλλος, ἄλλος. 30. ἕνα καὶ τὸν αὐτόν. 31. οὐχ ὡς τοῦ λόγου κεχωρισμένου. ibid. τὸν πρὸς αὐτοῦ ληφθέντα, ᾧ καὶ ἡνῶσθαι πιστεύεται, ἄνθρωπον ἀπ᾽ αὐτοῦ χωρίζουσι. ibid. τὴν ἀνέκφραστον ἕνωσιν. 32. τὸ θεῖον ἓν καὶ ἁπλοῦν μυστήριον. ibid. τὴν ἑνότητα. ibid. ὅλον αὐτὸν ἄνθρωπόν τε καὶ Θεὸν ὁμοῦ. 35. Vid. etiam disputationem maxime subtilem in *Orat.* iii. 30-58, ubi tamen vix inveneris verbum unum, quod sit theologicæ scientiæ proprium.

Alia veterum theologorum specimina sunt hujusmodi: "Mediam inter Deum et hominem substantiam gerens." Lactant. *Instit.* iv. 13. Θεὸς καὶ ἄνθρωπος τέλειος ὁ αὐτός. Meliton. *ap.* Routh, *Rell.* t. i. p. 115. "ex eo quod Deus est, et ex illo quod homo ... permixtus et sociatus ... alterum vident, alterum non vident." Novat. *de Trin.* 25. Vid. quoque 11, 14, 21, 24. "Duos Christos ... unum, alium." Pamphil. *Apol. ap.* Routh, *Rell.* tom. 4, p. 320. ὁ αὐτός ἐστιν, ἀεὶ πρὸς ἑαυτὸν ὡσαύτως ἔχων. Greg. Nyss. t. 2. p. 696. ἕνα καὶ τὸν αὐτόν. Greg. Naz. *Ep.* 101, p. 85. ἄλλο μὲν καὶ ἄλλο τὰ ἐξ ὧν ὁ Σωτήρ· οὐκ ἄλλος δὲ καὶ ἄλλος. p. 86.

Vid. quoque Athan. *contr. Apollin.* i. 10; *fin.* 11; *fin.* 13, e. 16, b. ii. 1 *init.* 5, e. 12, e. 18, *circ. fin.* Theoph. *ap.* Theod. *Eran.* ii. p. 154; Hilar. *ibid.* p. 162; Attic. *ibid.* p. 167; Hieron. *contr. Joan. Hieros.* 35.

Haud absimiles loquendi modi, omisso plane vocabulo πρόσωπον, reperiuntur in Epistola illa Patrum Antiochenorum, ad quam jam supra provocatum est: τὸ ἐκ τῆς παρθένου σῶμα χωρῆσαν πᾶν τὸ πλήρωμα τῆς θεότητος σωματικῶς, τῇ θεότητι ἀτρέπτως ἥνωται καὶ τεθεοποίηται. οὗ χάριν ὁ αὐτὸς Θεὸς καὶ ἄνθρωπος. Routh, *Relliq.* t. 2.

p. 473. οὕτω καὶ ὁ Χριστὸς πρὸ τῆς σαρκωσεως ὡς εἰς ὠνόμασται· καθὸ Χριστὸς ἓν καὶ τὸ αὐτὸ ὢν τῇ οὐσίᾳ. ibid. p. 474. εἰ ἄλλο μὲν . . . ἄλλο δὲ . . . δύο υἱούς, *ibid.* p. 485. Malchion quoque, "Unus factus est . . . unitate subsistens, etc." *Ibid.* p. 476.

(3) Constat præterea, vocabulum πρόσωπον a Patribus antiquis de Christo prædicari incerto illo quotidiani sermonis sensu, non theologico ; id quod sæpius vix fieret, si jam recepta esset ea vox in symbola et confessiones Ecclesiæ.

E. c. A Clemente Alexandrino Filius vocatur πρόσωπον, id est, vultus Patris. *Strom.* v. 6, p. 665, et *Pædag.* i. 7, p. 132. Vid. quoque *Strom.* vii. 10, p. 886. Haud aliter ἐν προσώπῳ πατρὸς, Theoph. *ad Autol.* ii. 22. Vid. quoque ὁμοιοπρόσωπον, Cyrill. Hier. *Catech.* xii. 14 fin. Apud Chrysostomum legimus, δύο πρόσωπα, humanum scilicet et divinum, (nisi placuerit cum Tentschero de Patre et Filio illud accipi,) διῃρημένα κατὰ τὴν ὑπόστασιν, *in Hebr. Hom.* iii. 1 fin. ita loquentem, cum paulo ante locutus esset contra Paulum Samosatenum, in quem Ecthesin Ephesinam conscriptam esse creditur. Vid. quoque Amphilochium *ap.* Theod. *Eran.* i. p. 67, qui Christum docet dixisse, Pater major me est, " ex carne et non ἐκ προσώπου θεότητος." His locis πρόσωπον videtur velle aspectum quendam, unum e multis, sub quibus res eadem potest considerari, quod item Athanasio usitatum est ; vid. *de Decr.* 14 ; *Orat.* i. 54, ii. 8 ; *Sent. Dion.* 4. Qua quidem ratione explicandi sunt duo loci, in quibus videtur sanctus Doctor uti vocabulo πρόσωπον, et quidem incommode, in eo sensu quem fert in theologia, viz. *contr. Apoll.* ii. 2 et 10, ἐν διαιρέσει προσὤπων; ubi Lequienius, (in Damasc. *Dialect.* 43) putat se reperisse singulare exemplum vocis πρόσωπον pro *natura* adhibitæ; male quidem, cum ipse Athanasius in altero horum duorum loco se explicans, προσώπων ἢ ὀνομάτων scribit. Quæ cum ita sint, fortasse minus audiendus est Montefalconius, fragmentum quoddam Athanasii non nisi propter ipsam dictionem rejiciens, vid. *Opp.* t. i. p. 1294. Monet enim post Sirmondum in Facund. xi. 2, illum locum continere doctrinam "ab Athanasiana penitus abhorrentem;" idcirco autem, quod versio latina, quam solam habemus, proponit "duas personas, unam circa hominem, alteram circa Verbum." Quod si aliunde ostendi potest non esse Athanasii fragmentum illud, abjudicetur utique. Cæterum in sensu paulum diverso, non tamen in theologico, vocabulo utitur Hippolytus in loco quem Leontius servavit, Hipp. *Opp.* t. 2, p. 45, ed. Fabric., ubi Christus appellatur δύο προσώπων μεσίτης, Dei et hominum.

Præterea apud Hilarium legimus, "utriusque naturæ personam," *de Trin.* ix. 14; "ejus hominis quam assumpsit persona," *Psalm.* 63, n. 3. Vid. eundem *in Psalm.* 138, n. 5. Apud Ambrosium, "in persona hominis," *de Fid.* ii. n. 61, v. n. 108, 124; *Ep.* 48, n. 4. Colligitur autem ex loco quodam Paschasii Diaconi, *de Spir.* ii. 4, p. 194, quem laudat Petavius, *de Trin.* vi. 4, § 3, vocabulum *persona*, pro qualitate seu statu sumptum, etiam in sexto sæculo theologo posse imprudenter excidere. Vid. quoque Cyril. Alex. *Dial.* v. p. 554.

Quapropter ab eodem Cyrillo, in quarto anathematismo suo, adhibita est vox *hypostasis;* εἴ τις προσώποις δυσὶ, ἠγοῦν ὑποστάσεσι, etc. quo quid vellet πρόσωπον clarius efferretur. Vid. quoque diligentiam Vincentii Lerinensis in hac re *Comm.* 14.

(4) Accedit quod mirum quantum distant ea, quæ de antiquorum dictis narrantur a scriptoribus serioris ævi, ab iis ipsis eorum dictis, si quando casu temporum hodie ad nos pervenerint; hic scilicet notiones, justas quidem, sed illas nudas reperimus, illic notiones, easdem certis verborum formulis vestitas; ita ut ipsa locorum collatio demonstret illas formulas non pertinere ad vetustatem. E. g. Ab Ephraëmio Antiocheno accepimus Petrum Alexandrinum, Chrysostomum, Basilium, Nazianzenum, et alios docuisse " duarum naturarum unionem, unam hypostasin, unamque personam." *ap.* Phot. cod. 229, p. 805-7. Optime vero; quis dubitet sanctissimos viros in gravissima materia Catholicas enunciasse sententias? Sed aliud est loqui catholice, prorsus aliud uti iis vocabulis quibus, catholici hoc tempore utuntur, quæ quidem non erant necessaria, non erant in ecclesiastico usu, donec irrepsisset hæreticorum fraus, donec periclitaretur fidelium salus. Jam si Chrysostomum, quem Ephraëmius laudat, adeamus, invenerimus ἕνωσις συνάφεια, ἓν ὁ Θεὸς λόγος καὶ ἡ σάρξ, vix autem ea verba quibus illas notiones Ephraëmius vestit; in Gregorii Epistola ad Cledonium, ad quam idem auctor provocat, ne semel quidem verbum *persona;* in iis autem quæ extant Petri legimus hujusmodi, σὰρξ γενόμενος οὐκ ἀπελείφθη τῆς θεότητος· γέγονεν ἐν μητρᾷ τῆς παρθένου σάρξ. Θεὸς ἦν φύσει καὶ γέγονεν ἄνθρωπος φύσει. Routh, *Rell.* t. 3, p. 344-346.

Maximus quoque Confessor sic interpretatur Gregorium Nazianzenum; " Hoc sane, ut puto, magnus quoque Gregorius Theologus dicere videtur ea magna Oratione Apologetica, dum ait, 'Unum ex ambobus, et ambo per unum:" *quasi diceret*, quemadmodum enim ex ambobus, (*hoc est*, ex duabus *naturis*,) unum (velut totum ex partibus secundum *hypostasis* rationem,) sic et per unum (*hypostasis* ratione ut totum,) ambo (partes *naturæ* ratione, hoc est, duo." *Opp.* t. 2, p. 282.

Profecto quod in hujusmodi locis immutatur a commentatoribus suspecta facit excerpta illa ex operibus Patrum, quæ in aliam linguam reddita ad nos veniunt; ut Ambrosianum illud Leontii; eo magis quia in versionibus latinis, quæ solent Græcorum Patrum textum comitari, verborum formulis reipsa occurrimus aliquando, contra Græcitatis fidem, injuria intrusis, non malo quidem animo, sed quo sensus evidentior fiat.

(5) Hoc quoque, ut arbitror, ostendi potest, scilicet, prout scripta de hac re, quondam antiquorum alicui assignata, eidem decursu temporis a criticis abjudicentur, ita probabile fieri vocabulum πρόσωπον hic aut illic in iis reperiri. Quod in loco Ambrosii cernitur, jam bis citato; at major hic est materies dicendi, quam quæ juste a nobis possit tractari. Alteri tamen exemplo sit, quod exhibet Athanasius. Abesse vocabulum πρόσωπον, theologorum sensu intellectum, a magni Doctoris operibus jam diximus; nunc divertamus ad fragmentum quoddam, in fine tomi prioris Maurini p. 1279 positum. "Olet quidpiam peregrinum," monet Montefalconius; "et videtur maxime sub finem Eutychianorum hæresin impugnare;" ecce autem in eo vocabulum πρόσωπον. Tum, adeatur ad Epistolam, ad Dionysium quendam scriptam, Julio autem Pontifici per-

peram tributam; en tibi vocabulum πρόσωπον, n. 2; vid. Coustant. *Epp. Rom. Pontif.* Append. p. 62. Idem porro reperitur in ἐκθέσει illa τῆς κατὰ μέρος πίστεως, olim Gregorio Neocæsariensi uni ex Patribus Antiochenis, ab Eulogio autem (*ap. Phot.* cod. 230, p. 846) Apollinaristis assignata. Reperitur idem apud Sermonem quendam "in S. Thomam," a Concilio sexto laudatum ut opus Chrysostomi, a Montefalconio autem rejectum, a Tillemontio Edesseno auctori an. 402 tributum, (ed. Maur. *tom.* 8; *part.* 2, p. 14). Hic autem obiter dictum velim, celebrem illam Epistolam Chrysostomi *ad Cæsarium*, de qua tantæ motæ sunt lites in controversia sanctissimæ Eucharistiæ, vocabulum πρόσωπον continere; quod de Hippolyti quoque *Contra Beronem et Helicem* dici potest, si decet de fragmentis illius operis strictim loqui.

(6) Liceat hic apponi locos quosdam antiquiorum Patrum, in quibus vocabulum illud offendimus.

In Epistolis Apollinaristarum inter se dimicantium, an. 381, *ap.* Leont. *Bibl. Col.* t. 6, p. 1033, b. p. 1037, b. p. 1039, b. ubi etiam occurrit ὁμοούσιον ἡμῖν.

In Apollinaris loco quodam *ap.* Theod. *Eran.* ii. p. 173.

In loco auctoris cujusdam adversus Arianos, quem vocat Sirmondus "antiquissimum." Sirm. *Opp.* t. 1, p. 223.

In fragmento Athanasii, nempe ut citatur ab Euthymio apud Petav. *Incarn.* iii. 15, not. 19; et in libro *de Incarn. et c. Arian.* § 2, si Athanasio auctori jure sit ascribendus.

In Gregorii Nyssen. *Antirrhet. contra Apollinarem*, 35.

Vid. quoque *ap.* Damasc. *contr. Jacob.* tom. i. p. 424.

In loco Amphilochii *apud* Damasc. *ibid.* et *ap.* Anast. *Hodeg.* 10, p. 162, et *ap.* Ephraëm, *ap.* Phot. p. 828.

In Ambrosii loco græce reddito *ap.* Phot. p. 805.
In Isidori Pelusiotæ *Ep.* i. 360, p. 94.
In Symbolo Pelagii an. 418, *ap. August. Opp.* t. 12, p. 210.
In Procli *Epist. ad Armenos*, p. 613.

(7) Finem tandem disputandi facientibus forsitan occurretur nobis, Pauli ipsius Samosateni hæresin fuisse Nestorianæ similem; quid autem credibilius, quam Patres Antiochenos, quomodo Hippolytus quadraginta ante annos usus esset vocabulum πρόσωπον in theologia contra Noetum, ita ipsos quoque idem adhibuisse contra Paulum in œconomia tractanda? Ad non constat Paulum revera præiisse Nestorio doctrina sua; quamquam ex Athan. *Orat.* iv. 30 colligi fortasse potest, sectatores ejus tandem a Nestoriana perfidia non longe abfuisse. Nam si ex actis Antiochenis, quatenus hodie extant, judicandum est, doctrinam effudit Paulus fere hujusmodi:—Filium exstitisse, ante adventum suum in carne, solum in præscientia divina, Routh, *Rell.* tom. 2, p. 466; si quis doceret secus, eum duos deos prædicare, p. 467; Filium, ante adventum in carne, fuisse, aut instrumentum quiddam, aut saltem attributum solum, p. 469; humanitatem ejus non ita esse unitam divinitati ut aliter esse non posset, p. 473. Verbum et Christum non unum esse et eundem, p. 474. Sapientiam in Christo esse, sicut in Prophetis, verum abundantius, tamquam in templo; eum autem qui apparuisset, non esse Sapientiam, p. 475; denique, ut summa rei proponitur, p. 484, "non congeneratam fuisse cum humanitate sapientiam substantialiter, sed secundum qualitatem." Vid. quoque pp. 476, 485. Quæ quidem omnia

certo demonstrant, tribuisse Paulum cum Nestorio hypostasin humanæ Christi naturæ; tribuisse autem cum Nestorio naturæ divinæ alteram hypostasin, non demonstrant. Verius dictum erit, antiquiorem hæresiarcham prorsus non admisisse divinam hypostasin in Christo, ut Sabellii commilitonem; quanquam id est verum quoque, Patres Antiochenos, non libenter tantum scelus tribuentes Paulo, ut hypostasin Verbi negaret, ex iis quæ de Christo homine effutiebat, conjecisse eum docere, ut Nestorium postea, duos esse filios, unum æternum, alterum temporaneum, p. 485. Quare Epistola Synodalis, post ejus depositionem a Patribus conscripta, eum docuisse testatur, Christum venisse non de cælo, sed de terra. Euseb. *Hist.* vii. 30. Neque aliter Athanasius Paulum dicit Christum pro mero homine habuisse, ἐκ προκοπῆς ad divinitatem suam evecto.

Cum autem non levis esset similitudo inter Pauli et Nestorii dogmata, (illo capite excepto, quod personalitatem et æternitatem Verbi, Nicææ interea declaratam, teneret Nestorius, rejiceret Paulus,) æquum erat, Nestorio in jus vocato, ad Pauli priorem hæresin, Antiochiæ jam condemnatam, a patribus Ephesi congregatis provocari. Attamen contestatio illa contra Nestorium, quæ, præfixa actis Ephesinis, Hard. *Conc.* t. i. p. 1272, Paulum et Nestorium inter se ordine comparat, ne verbum quidem profert quo concludi possit a Paulo duplicem hypostasin esse excogitatam. Neque, cum narrat Anastasius, *Hodeg.* 7, p. 108, "in sacra Ephesina Synodo demonstratum esse, dogmata Nestorii consonare cum doctrina Pauli Samosateni" Nestorianismum continuo tribuit Paulo, nisi Artemoni quoque tribuit, quem alibi testatur "Christum in duos divisisse." c. 20, p. 323, 4. Ephraëmium autem Antiochenum, cum Paulum dicit "alterum ante sæcula filium, alterum vero postea summa cum dementia asseruisse," *ap*. Phot. p. 814, verisimile est nihil amplius velle, quam uti iis ipsis verbis Patrum Antiochenorum, de quibus paulo ante locuti sumus. Contra, plane colligitur ex Vigilio *in* Eutych. *Bibl. P. Col.* 1618, t. v. p. 731 (omittitur locus in *Ed. Par.* 1624), Eutychianos distinctionem fecisse inter dogmata Nestorii et Pauli, hujus Christum simpliciter pro mero homine habentis, illius eatenus solum usque dum consociaretur Verbo Dei. Marius item Mercator diserte testatur: "Nestorius circa Verbum Dei, *non* ut Paulus sentit, qui non substantivum, sed prolatitium potentiæ Dei efficax Verbum esse definit." p. 50. Idem affirmant, licet non fidelissimi testes, et Ibas, et Theodorus Mopsuestiæ Episcopus, vid. Facund. vi. 3, iii. 2. Leont. *de Sect.* iii. p. 3. Cæterum, si genuinæ essent Dionysii Alexandrini *Epistola adversus Paulum*, et *Responsio ad Pauli Propositiones decem*, tum certo concedendum esset Paulum Nestorio prælusisse; id autem affirmantibus Tillemontio, Fabricio, Natali Alexandro, Bullo, Burtono, et aliis, nos in contrariam sententiam cum Valesio, Harduino, Montefalconio, et Routhio, ire velimus.

Hæc de Ecthesi Ephesina, plurima de re exigua; nisi, ut speramus, iis qui scripta Patrum diligentius tractant, aliqua protulerimus, quæ, in uno loco definita, ad multa transferri possint.

DISSERTATIO III.

DE FORMULA πρὶν γεννηθῆναι οὐκ ἦν ANATHEMATISMI NICÆNI.

SYMBOLO Ecclesiæ, Catholicæ, celeberrima vocula *homoüsion* locupletato, subjunxerunt Patres Nicæni anathematismos quosdam, qui Arianæ perfidiæ præcipua capita ferirent. Ex quibus ille est, de quo pauca quædam hoc loco dicenda censuimus. Non quod formula illa Arianorum sumpta per se difficilior sit intellectu, sed quia placuit doctissimo cuidam viro, de Nicæno autem Symbolo optime merito, nativo verborum sensui subtiliores notiones suas imponi. Quænam illæ sint, quare prolatæ, et qua rationum vi confirmatæ, nunc explicandum est.

Docentibus catholicis Christum esse Deum, Ariani protinus illum esse Deum confitebantur ipsi, at Deum inferiorem quendam, ne scilicet Deos duos introducerent in Ecclesiam. Quibus responsum est, Christum contra revera esse summum Deum, nec tamen duos esse Deos, quia Christus esset Filius Dei; qui autem Dei Filius esset, oportet illum et verum esse Deum nec tamen alterum, sed eundem ac Patrem suum. At in illo ipso vocabulo *Filius*, quod fidelibus jure documento erat veræ divinitatis Verbi Dei, hæreticorum factio collocavit omnem spem suam atque conatum fidei catholicæ convellendæ; argumentabantur enim, cum omnis filius patri junior esset, idcirco Filium Dei non esse æternum, neque habere cætera signa veræ divinitatis. Quare summa quæstionis in significatione *Filii* tandem posita fuit; utrum scilicet Filius Dei, utpote Filius, essentiam totam et universa habuerit attributa Omnipotentis Dei, an contra initium existendi, et alia quæ de rebus creatis prædicantur. Quo autem facilius rem dirimerent, catholici provocabant ad Patres priorum sæculorum, qui scilicet Filio Dei non temporaneum ortum, sed paternæ Divinitatis plenitudinem tribuissent.

At in hoc antiquorum scriptorum testimonio esse quod subtiliore tractatione egeret, jure censuit Bullus, cui lis a nobis intendenda est, quo melius curreret catholicorum argumentum, et eruditioribus persuaderet. Nam scriptores quinque ævi Ante-nicæni, Athenagoram, Tatianum, Theophilum, Hippolytum, Novatianum, quorum duo in catalogo sunt sanctorum, non inficiatus est vir doctus ita de Filio Dei loqui, ut hæreticis ansam præbuerint affirmandi, Patres illos docuisse Verbum Dei factum esse Dei Filium certo quodam tempore, atque ideo quodammodo "extitisse ante generationem suam," eo dissidentes cum Ario quod dicerent Verbum esse æternum, eo consentientes quod Filium æternum esse non dicerent.

Non ideo tamen improbandus est Bullus, quia sollicita mente priscorum famæ, suorum fidei consuluerit. Fateor equidem, non Sanctis, Hippolyto solum et Theophilo, sed

Post-nicænis etiam Sanctis, Hilario et Zenoni Veronensi, in hac materia illud excidisse, quod resecatum vel saltem explicatum prudentiores velint; ut Marano quoque, Balleriniis, et aliis visum est. Scilicet omnes norunt incommodiora hæc gravissimorum scriptorum verba ab hæreticis saltem recentioris ævi in partes suas adduci; nam utrum ab ipsis Arii sectatoribus objecta fuerint catholicis Concilii Nicæni sæculo, alia res est. Profecto notatu dignissimum est Arianos ipsos, cum Ecclesia dimicantes, non provocasse ad Patres priorum temporum usque ad circ. an. 352, pæne triginta post Concilium Nicænum exactis annis, cum, argumentis ex ratione et ex Scripturis, (ut Athanasius loquitur in Epistola sua *de. Sent. Dion.* 1), frustra petitis, "tandem eo audaciæ processerunt, ut etiam Patres calumniarentur." Nimirum primo ad Collucianistas solum suos confugiebant; cum autem multos post annos Patres Ecclesiæ in suos usus convertere cœperunt, etiam tum Origenem solum appellarunt et Dionysium, non Hippolytum, non Theophilum, non alios illos de quibus supra mentio facta est. Quod autem ne versutissimorum quidem hominum illis temporibus in mentem venit, id recentiores ausi, hos ipsos Hippolyti et cæterorum locos in medium protulerunt, ut inde comprobarent dogma suum, Dei Filium non esse ad æternitatem genitum, sed in tempore creatum. Quibus ut occurrat Bullus, eximius alias in hac materie scriptor, Patres reos, in *Defensione sua Fidei Nicænæ*, illato crimine ita liberat, ut non neget tamen illos dixisse, improprie certe, sed aliquo modo, Filium in tempore fuisse genitum. Exceptio autem quam profert hujusmodi est:—plures scilicet eos Patres docuisse Verbi generationes, tropicas illas quidem, sed quæ veræ generationis typi essent et adumbrationes; quales sunt ejus resurrectio a mortuis, item nativitas ex Maria; qualis porro, de qua agendum est, missio ejus a Patre et processio, cum res universæ creandæ essent. Hinc non gravate concedit dictum quoddam fuisse Catholicorum, si non Catholicum dogma, tum ante Concilium Nicææ habitum tum post, "Verbum exstitisse antequam gigneretur;" cujus rei inter alia in testimonium adhibet verba Anathematismi, quorum interpretationem in nos hic suscepimus. Contendit enim Patres Nicænos eo ipso quod condemnarent eos "qui dicerent Verbum non exstitisse ante generationem suam," liquido comprobasse contra istam formulam, "Verbum ante generationem suam exstitisse." Nullus dubitat, ut ipsius verbi utar, "quin hoc pronunciatum Arianorum oppositum fuerit catholicorum istorum sententiæ qui docerent Filium quidem paulo ante conditum mundum inexplicabili quodam modo ex Patre progressum fuisse ad constituendum universa." *Def. N. F.* iii. 9, § 2.

Hæc sane de hac Anathematismi Nicæni clausula argute nimis dicta sunt, et turbant verborum sensum alioqui simplicem et luculentum. Nam procul dubio in illa formula Arianorum, quæ a Patribus percellitur, continetur contra argumentum *ex absurdo*, quod vocant, desumptum; cum ex ipsa vi vocabuli *genitus* confici crederent hæretici, Christum existendi initium habuisse. Confirmabant enim (quasi id inficiari quenquam jam fuerit ipsis verbis sibi discrepare) Filium non exstitisse priusquam gigneretur; alioqui non esset Filius.

Quod interest inter explicationem hanc et illam Bulli, in hoc vertitur;—utrum verba ista Arianorum, "priusquam gigneretur non erat," sint simplex propositio categorica, an argumentum; sint negatio propositionis ei contrariæ, "erat priusquam gigneretur," id quod Bullo placuit; an potius, ut nobis videtur, γνώμη quædam, quam Aristoteles vocat, ἐνθυμηματικὴ, propositio rationem suam secum ferens, in qua, assumpta, non affirmata, contrariæ propositionis vanitate, recta impetitur aliud quiddam, nempe Filium ab æternitate exstitisse. Arbitratur contra Bullus, et Patres Nicænos et Arianos apertis oculis contemplatos esse propositionem hanc, "exstitisse Filium antequam gigneretur;" de hac, certamen inter se instituisse: negasse Arianos, et Catholicos, aut affirmasse, aut saltem permisisse. Profecto ne unum quidem Catholicum virum unquam eam emisisse sententiam non dixerim; affirmasse autem eandem Patres Nicænos prorsus nego.

1. Primum percurrendum erit ad pristinum illud jurgium, quod nascentem hæresin subito Ecclesiæ ostentabat, ut a Socrate narratum est. Testatur enim scriptor ille, Alexandrum, de mysterio Sanctissimæ Trinitatis inter suos disputantem, interpellasse Arium, qui fortiter diceret, (1) si Filium genuerit Pater, ergo genitum habere existendi initium; (2) ergo fuisse quando Filius Dei non esset; (3) ergo eundem subsistentiam suam ex nihilo habere. Socr. i. 5. Quibus e contrario jam collocabimus Anathematismi Nicæni clausulas; "Illos vero qui dicunt, (1) fuit aliquando cum non esset, et (2) antequam gigneretur non erat, et (3) ex nihilo factus est, etc. etc. . . . , anathematizat Catholica Ecclesia." Quarum cum duæ

plenissime respondeant duabus ab Ario in Alexandrum conjectis, cui dubium esse potest, tertiam quoque respondere tertiæ? id est, "antequam gigneretur non erat" idem velle atque illud "si Filium genuerit Pater, habet genitus existendi initium;" id quod nos contra Bullum contendimus. Hæreseos initia non fefellit posterior cursus, namque hic, ut diximus, ipse cardo fuit totius controversiæ, nempe utrum Filius, quia Filius, fuerit necne necessaria lege junior ætate Patre suo. At ubinam contra in historia Concilii Nicæni inveneris mentionem ullam illius propositionis, cui credit Bullus ab Arianis esse reclamatum, "Filium scilicet esse prius quam gigneretur?" Sentit angustias suas vir perspicacissimus, cum ad verba quædam appellat Arianorum in Epistola illorum ad Alexandrum missa, in qua perstringunt hæretici illos qui dicerent "eum qui prius erat, postea genitum esse aut creatum in Filium." Athan. *de Syn.* 16, quos vult Bullus quosdam esse Catholicos. Hos autem credo non esse Catholicos, sed potius sectatores Marcelli et Photini, ut conjicere licet, cum ex Euseb. *Eccles. Theol.* i. 1, ii. 9, p. 114, b. *Contr. Marcell.* ii. 3, tum præsertim ex Anathematismo Eusebianorum in Confessione sua quinta, sive Macrosticho, ubi ita loquuntur; "Execramur eos qui illum simplex ($\psi\iota\lambda\grave{o}\nu$) Dei Verbum non subsistens appellant, Christum autem ipsum et Filium Dei non fuisse ante sæcula contendunt, sed eo tempore ex quo carnem nostram ex Virgine assumpsit; *hujusmodi* sunt sectatores *Marcelli* et *Scotini* (Photini) Ancyrogalatarum." *Athan. de Syn.* 26. Quare fortasse non Catholicos, sed Marcellum et suos respicit Epistola illa Arianorum ad Alexandrum; quod quidem inde confirmatur, quia illo ipso tempore Marcellum Asterius Sophista, Arianorum antesignanus, scriptis suis lacessebat.

2. Notandum præterea est, alias quoque Arianorum formulas, decantatas illas quidem, in quibus summa hæreseos posita est, ut captiosissimos homines decuit, vim quamdam habere enthymematicam. Cujusmodi sunt, "Qui est, eumne, qui nondum esset, fecit ex nihilo, an qui esset?" et "Unumne est non-factum an duo?" Athan. *Orat.* i. 22, et interrogatio illa de "mutabili," quam, cum locum habet in Anathematismo Nicæno, ita exponit Athanasius: "Num libero præditus arbitrio est, an non? an voluntate pro sui arbitrii libertate bonus est, et, si velit, potest mutari, cum mutabilis sit natura; an, ut lapis et lignum, liberam non habet voluntatem in utramque partem se movendi et vergendi?" Athan. *Orat.* i. 35. Scilicet voluerunt hæretici, liberum, quod vocant, arbitrium oportere necessitate quadam ita proprium esse Christi, ut aliter esse non potuerit quin absurdum quid subsequeretur; ex quo conficeretur illum in numero esse creatorum.

3. In *Orat.* i. § 32, scribit Athanasius ἀγένητον illud sive *non-factum* serius esse suppositum ab Arianis in locum priorum suarum captionum: "Cum jam non sit eis integrum his uti vocibus, 'e nihilo est,' 'non fuit antequam gigneretur,' vocabulum *non-facti,* etc. cogitaverunt, ut, cum apud simpliciores Filium factum esse dicunt, eadem rursus illa significent vocabula, nempe, 'ex nihilo est,' 'aliquando non fuit.'" Quo in loco quamvis non disertis verbis dicat "Non-factum unumne an duo?"

pro "Antequam gigneretur non erat" esse substitutum, tamen probabile est certe illum hoc voluisse. Atqui constat formula *non-factum* vel ἀγένητον, ut ea quæ jam diximus aliis verbis proferamus, hoc innui, "Nisi duo sint *non-facta* vel dii, Christus, utpote factus sive genitus, initium habet existendi;" id quod ipsissimum est argumentum illud, quod verbis "Antequam gigneretur non erat," nos assignatum volumus. Cæterum distinctionem illam inter ἀγένητον et ἀγέννητον, de qua loquitur Montefalconius in Admonitione sua in Epistolam *de Decr. Nic.*, a Damasceno notatam, mihi non persuaderi potest esse coævam Athanasio;—sed hoc obiter.

4. Præterea dubium non est quin "Non erat priusquam gigneretur" apud Athanasium idem valeat atque alterum illud "Qui est, eumne, qui nondum esset, fecit ex nihilo, an qui esset?" Scilicet quod Ariani contra Filium effutiebant, id pariter ostendit sanctus Doctor contra ipsum Patrem posse contorqueri. "Num qui est Deus," interrogat, "cum antea non esset, postea factus est, vel estne etiam priusquam gignatur (fiat)?" *Orat.* i. 25. At illud "Qui est eumne qui nondum esset," etc. (ὁ ὢν τὸν μὴ ὄντα, etc.) argumentum prorsus est, non mera propositio, idque ex absurdo ductum; ergo ejusmodi est, "Priusquam gigneretur non erat." Quod plane confirmatur ex Alexandri Epistola Encyclica cum Arii contra Alexandrum prima illa disputatione et Anathematismis Nicænis comparata. Nam, cum ex his triplex conficitur testimonium, quales fuerint formulæ istæ in quibus posita est hæresis Ariana, nulla alia in re sibi discrepat, nisi in hac, quod, omisso "Si Filius, ergo habet initium exist-

endi," ipsius Arii, et "Priusquam gigneretur non erat," Anathematismi, Alexander in Epistola sua supponit ὁ ὢν τον μὴ ὄντα, etc. "Qui est eumne qui non esset," etc. Accedit quod sibi invicem respondent illæ duæ, in locis Gregorii Nazianzeni et Basilii infra laudatis, et in Cyrilli *Thesaur.* 4, p. 29, *fin.*

5. Multa sunt temere jacta in Orationibus Athanasii quæ nobiscum faciunt in hac re. Nam si Arianorum dictum illud, "Non erat antequam gigneretur," argumentum erat, ut nobis videtur, contra Filii æternitatem, tum responsuri essent Catholici, "Vere dictum est Christum non existere antequam gignitur; existere non potest ante, quia gignitur ab æternitate, utpote ab æterno Patre;" id quod re ipsa reperimus dictum ab Athanasio. "Res creatæ fieri cœperunt (γίνεσθαι)," scribit; "at Dei Verbum, cum principium ex quo sit (ἀρχὴν) nullum habeat, merito nec esse nec fieri cœpit, sed semper fuit. Opera igitur principium (ἀρχὴν), cum fiunt, habent; quod quidem principium rebus, quæ fiunt, prius est; Verbum autem, cum non sit ex numero rerum quæ fiunt, ipse potius rerum principium habentium demiurgus fit. Deinde ipsum esse rerum factarum in eo ipso quod fiunt mensuram habet (ἐν τῷ γίνεσθαι), easque Deus ab aliquo principio per Verbum facere incipit, ut perspicuum sit illas non fuisse priusquam gignerentur (πρὶν γενέσθαι); at Verbum non in alio principio habet ut sit, nisi in Patre, qui, ut isti etiam consentiunt, principii est expers; ut ipse quoque Filius sine principio existat in Patre, a quo genitus est, non autem creatus." *Orat.* ii. 57. Neque absimili modo disputant alii Patres. Alterum exemplum

peti potest ex *Orat.* i. 10, ubi pro πρὶν γεννηθῇ supponit Athanasius πρὶν ποιηθῇ; at credo Bullum non esse dicturum, secundum hypothesin suam, Patres ullos antiquos, disputantes de Filio, verba πρὶν ποιηθῇ, ut sua, alicubi adhibuisse. Attamen, "Quis hominum, sive Græcus sive barbarus," scribit Athanasius, "quem Deum confitetur, unam ex rebus creatis ausit dicere, et non fuisse antequam *fieret?*" *Orat.* i. 10. Idem profitetur ipse Arius, suorum certe verborum optimus interpres, cum ad Eusebium Nicomediæ Episcopum scribens, vocabulo γεννηθῇ in κτισθῇ et alia similia mutato, luculentissime ostendit, quod certe non siverit Bullus, se ea esse mente ut argumentum quoddam proferret. "Nos quid sentiamus, et professi jam sumus et nunc profitemur; Filium, antequam gigneretur, *aut* crearetur, *aut* destinaretur, *aut* fundaretur, non fuisse." Theod. *Hist.* i. 4. Nec discrepat ab Ario Eusebius ipse: "*Manifestum omnibus* est, illud quod *factum* est, non fuisse antequam fieret." Athan. *de Syn.* 17.

6. Jam si occurrunt apud Athanasium, quæ Bullo favere videantur, facilem tamen habent solutionem. E. g. "Qui fieri potest," rogat, "ut non sit in numero creatorum, si, ut isti opinantur, non erat antequam gigneretur? siquidem rerum creatarum et factarum proprium est non esse antequam fiant?" *Orat.* ii. 22. Dixerit fortasse Bullus, ex hoc perspicuum esse, Arianos affirmasse Filium "Non esse priusquam gigneretur," Catholicos autem "Esse." Sed non est ita; nam, quemadmodum Patres Nicæni in Anathematismo suo, ut diximus supra, non ipsam Arianæ formulæ propositionem impetunt et feriunt,

sed ejusdem vim argumentativam, ita hic quoque vult Athanasius, non "Quo pacto non est creatus, *nisi erat* antequam gigneretur," sed, "Quo pacto non est creatus, *si illorum argumentum verum est*, non erat antequam gigneretur?" Eodem modo *Orat.* i. 20, cum dicit, "Si non fuerit Filius antequam gigneretur, non semper fuit in Deo veritas," vult, non "*Nisi* fuerit" sed "*Si verum sit illud*, Non fuit Filius," etc. Itaque, non multo post idem dicit de Deo Patre, ut vanissimos sophistas suo sibi gladio jugulet, "Estne Deus etiam priusquam gignitur?" 25. non certe quasi in Patre ullam significet generationem, sed quo argumentum ipsum ut ineptissimum aptius explodat, sive de Patre usurpatum sive de Filio.

7. Et profecto ineptissimam et importunissimam esse hanc interrogationem, non simpliciter veræ cuidam propositioni contrariam, plenissime cum Athanasio consentientes, judicant et Hilarius et Gregorius Nazianzenus. Missam faciunt, quam prorsus ne proferri quidem oporteret. Gregorius scilicet de hac et aliis Arianorum formulis loquens, docet, "Generationem" in Filio, "cum essentia ipsa *concurrere* atque a principio existere;" quod contra fit in hominibus, qui quidem, "ut Levi in lumbis Abrahæ," cum "partim erant, partim procreati sunt, ac proinde partim sunt ex entibus, partim ex non entibus," illud scilicet complent "Fuit antequam gigneretur;" quod Bullus non in hominibus, sed in Filio Dei dici posse arbitratur. Pergit de eadem re magnus theologus: "Quæstionem hanc tuam *absurditatis* multum, *difficultatis* nihil habere aio." Tum captionibus ver-

borum quibusdam aliis prolatis quæ cum Ariana illa possent comparari, "*Ineptius* est" dicit, "id quod a principio erat, *utrum* ante generationem esset (πρὸ τῆς γεννήσεως) *necne*, in quæstionem vocari." *Orat.* xxix. 9.

8. Hilarium fateor Pictavensem in Commentario suo in Matthæum c. 31, n. 3, verba quædam emisisse quæ Bullo favere videantur. Docet enim egregius ille vindex catholicæ veritatis, "Verbum in principio Deum, et hoc a principio apud Deum, et natum esse ex eo qui erat, et hoc in eo esse qui natus est, quod is ipse est penes quem erat antequam nasceretur." Cujus simile est illud quod Bullo favet ex Zenonis Tractatu *de Filii generatione*: "Procedit in nativitatem, qui erat antequam nasceretur." At Zenonem non est cur moremur, diligentem, ut a Balleriniis monstratum est, *Diss.* 1, 2, § 6, Hilarii imitatorem. Quod autem ad Pictavensem ipsum attinet, provocamus ab Hilario imperito ad Hilarium peritissimum Arianorum. Constat enim sanctissimum virum, illa scripsisse antequam in Asiam venisset; "regeneratum autem pridem," ut ipsius verbis utar, "et in Episcopatu aliquantum permanentem, Fidem Nicænam nunquam nisi exsulaturum" conceptis verbis "audivisse," *de Syn.* 91, postea autem, ut Coustantius nos monuit, sese correxisse in celeberrimo suo opere quod *de Trinitate* conscripsit. Illic enim, secus ac voluit Bullus, Arianorum formulam "antequam gigneretur non erat," in sophismatis loco luculentissime ponit. "Adjiciant hæc," de eo scribit. "*arguta* satis atque auditu placentia; Si, inquit, natus est, cœpit; et cum cœpit, non fuit; et cum non fuit,

non patitur ut fuerit. Atque idcirco piæ intelligentiæ sermonem esse contendant, non fuit antequam nasceretur, quia ut esset qui non erat, non qui erat, natus est," xii. 18. Neque aliter illi Arianorum formulæ occurrit; "Unigenitus Deus neque non fuit aliquando non Filius, neque fuit aliquid antequam Filius, neque quidquam aliquid ipse nisi Filius," 15; quod quidem nihil aliud est nisi negatio illius "Fuit antequam genitus est." Pergit, ut Gregorius: "Ubi Pater auctor est, ibi et nativitas est, et vero ubi auctor æternus est, ibi et nativitatis æternitas est." 21. Quid potest esse disertius? Porro pro "fuit ante quam natus est," supponit, "semper natus fuit;" e. g. "Numquid ante tempora æterna esse, id ipsum sit quod est, eum qui erat nasci? quia nasci quod erat, jam non nasci est, sed seipsum demutare nascendo . . . Non est itaque id ipsum, natum ante tempora æterna semper esse, et esse antequam nasci." 30. Concludit, Athanasii sensum vel clarioribus retractans verbis; "Cum itaque natum semper esse, nihil aliud sit confitendum esse quam natum, id sensui, antequam nascitur *vel fuisse vel non fuisse*, non subjacet." 31.

9. Prodeat denique Basilius in dimicatione sua contra Eunomium; cui argumentato, "Aut existentem genuit Deus Filium, aut non existentem," et "Qui est, generatione non indiget," respondit sanctissimus Præsul, "Eunomium, *quoniam* animalia, cum prius non sint, deinde generentur, qui autem hodie genitus sit, heri non esset, hanc notionem in Unigeniti subsistentiam *transferre;* et *quoniam* genitus est, dicere, ante generationem non fuisse." *contra Eun.* ii. 14. Sophisma autem solvit, ut

Patres supra citati, dicendo, Filio esse æternam generationem, ut loquitur Evangelista, cum " æternitati Patris generationem Unigeniti connectit." *Ibid.* 15.

Satis superque de hac re sumus disputati; pro certo jam habeatur, a Concilio Œcumenico, Nicææ congregato, minime sancita esse illa verba quæ Bullo Catholica videntur, "Verbum Dei fuisse antequam gigneretur;" quasi ulla Apostolica traditione aut Ecclesiæ auctoritate nobis commendentur. Quæ cum ita sint, operi nostro hic finis esset imponendus, nisi vir doctissimus, Concilio nequicquam appellato, ad Athanasium ipsum confugisset, Concilii illius magnam partem, quo causam suam apud eruditos feliciore spe posset orare. Opinionem nimirum eam, de generatione quadam Verbi ante mundum conditum in tempore facta, Athanasio ipsi impactam voluit, provocans ad Orationem secundam contra Arianos, *capp.* 61-64.

Illa operis sui parte, copiosissima disputatione inita de verbis Prophetæ, quæ Ariani objiciebant Ecclesiæ, "Dominus creavit me in initio viarum suarum in opera sua," ut in Versione LXX. Interpret. leguntur, provehitur sanctus Doctor ad verba Apostoli, "Primogenitus omnis creaturæ;" quæ proinde ita interpretatur ut doceat Verbum, quod ante sæcula fuit Unigenitum, cum creandus esset mundus, condescensione quadam seu συγκαταβάσει e Patre procedens factum esse Primogenitum. Unde deducit Bullus, illam processionem sive condescensionem auctore Athanasio novam quandam, improprie utique, Verbi in tempore esse generationem.

Jam Verbi condescensionem quandam esse exhibitam in rerum universitate condenda consentiunt omnes; namque ineffabilis procul dubio erat gratiæ et bonitatis, Filium, qui "in principio erat apud Deum," in cogitationem venisse creatorum, et in creatorum fragilitate versari. Sed hoc Bullo non satis est, nisi condescensio illa generatio seu nativitas quædam appelletur. "Catholici quidam doctores, qui post exortam controversiam Arianam vixerunt," ad Athanasium autem provocat, "illam τοῦ λόγου ex Patre progressionem (quam et συγκατάβασιν, hoc est, condescensionem eorum nonnulli appellarunt) ad condendum hæc universa agnovere; et ejus etiam progressionis respectu ipsum τὸν λόγον a Deo Patre quasi natum fuisse et omnis creaturæ primogenitum in Scripturis dici confessi sunt." *Defen. F. N.* iii. 9. § 1. At Athanasium, in hac progressione et condescensione Verbi, voluisse natum denuo esse quodammodo Verbum, et proinde appellatum esse " Primogenitum omnis creaturæ " profecto non puto; contra " Primogenitum " illud, non relationis alicujus, quæ intercederet inter Verbum et Patrem suum, esse significativum, sed plane muneris cujusdam quod, mundum creaturus, pro bono mundi, benignissime in se suscepit Unigenitus. Scilicet ille, qui ab æternitate fuit Unigenitus Patris, in universorum compagine et structura illam Filietatem suam signatam voluit, ita ut typum quendam Unigeniti atque imaginem universa in se exhiberent. Itaque hoc sensu Unigenitus omnis creaturæ se fecit Primogenitum, quod, dum mundum ex nihilo duceret, illo ipso tempore se quoque fecit ideam et normam ejusdem mundi, Demiurgus nimirum et summus Artifex, sese contemplans atque intuens tanquam unicum exemplar suum, ex quo mundum nascentem exprimeret imitando et conformaret. Quare Filius progrediens a Patre non factus est denuo Filius Patris, sed mundo Filius, ut scilicet condescensione sua mundus fieret quodammodo Patris filius, et in cœlestem familiam adoptaretur. Quod si verum est, Primogenitus nihil aliud significare, nisi Filius Archetypus, videbitur. Ad rationes veniamus.

Primum, verbum συγκατάβασις, sive condescensio (quod adeo non generationis in se habet ullum sensum, ut, testibus Vesselio et Suicero, de Æterno Patre, omnium conservatore, a Patribus nonnunquam usurpetur,) quid velit apud Athanasium, legentibus sectiones 78-81 Orationis illius, de qua hic agitur, satis liquebit. Illa disputationis suæ pars incipit et terminatur mentione facta condescensionis Verbi: quare ad eam adeundum est tanquam ad præcipuum quemdam locum, unde vis vocabuli in gravissima hac materia possit erui. Incipit autem his verbis: " Quo res factæ non tantum existerent, sed etiam bene existerent, placuit Deo ut sua Sapientia ad res creatas condescenderet, ut typum aliquem et speciem ipsius Imaginis, cum in omnibus simul, tum in singulis imprimeret; quo nimirum perspicuum fieret et sapientia ornatas esse res factas et digna Deo esse opera. Ut enim nostrum verbum, Verbi, qui Dei est Filius, est imago; ita sapientia in nobis facta ejusdem Verbi, quæ ipsa est Sapientia, imago quoque est," etc. § 78. Quid hic reperimus de Verbo denuo facto Filio? quid non de Filio imaginem sui imprimente in operibus suis? Finem autem facturus Sapientiam introducit sanctus Doctor ita loquentem: " Omnia quidem in me et per me facta sunt: quia autem opus erat ut sapientia in operibus crearetur, ego secundum substantiam quidem cum Patre aderam, sed ad res factas condescendens, meum typum in illis apte imprimebam, ut universus mundus tanquam in uno corpore non secum discordaret sed concordaret." § 81.

Quod ut planius intelligatur, exponendum est Athanasium autumasse, ne ullam quidem rem creationem suam sustinere posse, ut non sanctissimam Creantis manum tanquam refugiat et ad nihilum continuo recidat, nisi eidem simul Demiurgus ipse condescensione quadam suam impertiat gratiam, quo mirabilem illam patienter subeat operationem, per quam in rerum naturam perventura est. "Verbum," scribit, "cum principio Demiurgus esset creatorum, condescendit ad res creatas, ut fieri possent. Neque enim ejus naturam, quæ purus Patris est splendor, ferre potuissent, nisi," græca fortius currunt quam latina, φιλανθρωπίᾳ πατρικῇ συγκαταβὰς ἀντελάβετο, καὶ κρατήσας αὐτὰ εἰς οὐσίαν ἤνεγκε. *Orat.* ii. 64. Quare operibus suis, dum creabantur, ut crearentur, virtutem quandam suam impertiens Artifex Filius, eadem proinde augustissimo filiorum nomine donatus est; συγκαταβάντος τοῦ λόγου, pergit sanctus doctor, υἱοποιεῖται καὶ αὐτὴ ἡ κτίσις δι' αὐτοῦ. Ex quo fit, ut non modo per Filium, verum etiam in Filio, ut Apostolus loquitur, rerum universitas facta esse dicenda sit, cum non exteriore solum mandato, sed intima vi et virtute Spiritus ejus consistant et permaneant omnia. "Nam," ut alibi docet uberrimus ille rerum divinarum interpres, quem sæpius appellasse jucundissimum est, "Deus non solum nos ex nihilo fecit, sed etiam Verbi gratia secundum Deum vivere concessit. At homines ab æternis rebus aversi, sibi ipsis corruptionis mortiferæ auctores facti sunt; qui ex natura quidem mortales fuerunt, sed gratia in Verbi participatione sita naturæ statum effugerunt." *de Incarn. V. D.* 5. Itaque nihil fere est creatum, quod non genitum sit quoque; cum contra non stent in loco suo, sed retro fluant et pereant, nisi vitam quandam a Creatore percipiant intus, superadditam creationi suæ. Proinde Athanasii mos est in scriptis suis, ut res creatas potius appellet genitas quam factas vel opera, γενητὰ seu γεννητὰ, non ποιήματα et ἔργα, quo planius sanctissimam hanc exprimat veritatem: cauto tamen semper, gratiæ illud esse non naturæ, donum Creatoris non creaturæ proprium, quod mundus in se habeat hanc formam pulchritudinis, et cœlestium necessitudinem, et principium stabilitatis. "Res factæ," docet, "cum sint opera, genitæ dici nequeunt, nisi, geniti Filii participes postea effectæ, genitæ et ipsæ dicantur, non sane propriam ob naturam, sed quia Filii factæ sint in Spiritu participes." *Orat.* i. 56.

His perspectis, non difficilis intellectu est mens Athanasii, cum Unigenitum Patris docet esse factum in creatione mundi Primogenitum omnis creaturæ. Nam, cum gratia illa, qua impertita natura rerum in suo loco permanet, variis nominibus respici possit, ut lux, ut pulchritudo, ut sapientia, ut ratio, ut cœlestis adoptio, ut similia, ille supremus Conditor universorum, seipsum mundo impertiens, fit quodammodo mundo et lucis illius principium, et pulchritudinis, et sapientiæ, et rationis, et adoptionis in cœlestium societatem. Itaque, qui ex æterno Sapientia, Lux, Ratio, Filius est Patris, factus est operibus suis principalis quædam Sapientia, et formatrix Ratio, et Lux plenissime irradians et archetypus Filius.

Sapientia autem Patris tandem facta est sapientia mundo, et fecit ut mundus sapiens esset; lux Patris facta est lux mundo, et fecit ut mundus splendesceret; Unigenitus Patris factus est Primogenitus mundo, et fecit ut mundus in familiam Dei adscisceretur.

Profecto fateor hæc omnia in mysterio et fructibus sanctissimæ Incarnationis verissime compleri, cujus gratia ita superat quicquid universæ naturæ a Creatore datum est, ut Athanasius in quodam opere confirmare non dubitaverit, mundi creationem esse per Filium solummodo, dispensationem autem Evangelicam esse in Filio. "Decebat creationis quidem exordium per ipsum fieri, ut res existerent; earum autem instaurationem, in ipso; quæ sane verba inter se differunt. Nam initio quidem omnia per ipsum facta sunt ut essent; postea, ubi omnia defecerunt, Verbum caro factum est, quam scilicet induit, ut in ipso omnia reficerentur. *In illud Omnia.* 2." Quid quod, cum carnem sumeret, imaginem sui mundo exhibuit solidiorem multo et clariorem, et verius se ipsum fecit primogenitum inter creaturas, quam cum, universa conditurus, rerum condendarum ideam se faceret et regulam. Fateor equidem; sed prioris operis præstantiam non imminuunt præstantiora illa quæ subsecuta sunt; id quod Athanasio adeo persuasum est, ut sæpius duo illa una consociet et comparet, extollens quidem meliora, non deprimens quod in se bonum est.

Infinita prope locorum sylva est in sanctis Patribus, ex quibus augustissimum hoc munus Unigeniti, et in rerum natura et in œconomia evangelica, possit illustrari.

"Cum justitia nulla esset in terra, doctorem misit, quasi vivam legem" dicit Lactantius, *Instit.* iv. 25. "Quidquid facturus erat Deus in creatura" docet Augustinus, "jam Verbo inerat, nec esset operibus, nisi esset in Verbo." *In Ps.* 44, 5. Alio loco Filius ab eodem appellatur, "ars quædam omnipotentis atque sapientis Dei, plena omnium rationum viventium incommutabilium." *De Trin.* vi. 11. Cyrillus autem Alexandrinus: "Unigenitus" scribit "secundum naturam; primogenitus propter nos, ut tanquam immortali cuidam radici omnis creatura insita sit, et ex eo qui semper est, germinet." *Thesaur.* 25, p. 238. κατεσφραγίσθημεν, docet idem Cyrillus, εἰς τὸ ἀρχέτυπον τῆς εἰκόνος. *in Joan.* p. 91. Similiter ab Athenagora Filius vocatur ἰδέα καὶ ἐνέργεια omnium rerum materialium; ἡ ἰδέα, ὅπερ λόγον εἰρήκασι, a Clemente Alex. *Strom.* v. 3. ἰδέαν ἰδεῶν καὶ ἀρχὴν λεκτέον τὸν πρωτότοκον πάσης κτίσεως, testatur Origenes, *contr. Cels.* vi. 64 fin. οἷον ἀπό τινος ἀρχῆς, concinit Gregorius Nyssenus, *Catech.* p. 504 fin. Et, ut ad Athanasium redeamus, multus est in eadem doctrina, ut in locis hujusmodi: εἰκὼν καὶ τύπος πρὸς ἀρετήν, *Orat.* i. 21. τύπον τινὰ λαβόντες, et ὑπογραμμὸν, iii. 20. ἐν αὐτῷ ἦμεν προτετυπωμένοι, ii. 76 init. τύπον εἰκόνος ἐνθεῖναι, 78 init. πρωτότοκος εἰς ἀπόδειξιν τῆς τῶν πάντων διὰ τοῦ υἱοῦ δημιουργίας καὶ υἱοποιήσεως, iii. 9 fin. τὴν τοῦ ἀρχετύπου πλάσιν ἀναστήσασθαι ἑαυτῷ. *contr. Apoll.* ii. 5.

Quare jure optimo, ut credo, pro concesso potest assumi, condescensionem illam Primogeniti ad universa constituenda nullam esse adumbrationem æterni mysterii quo Filius a Patre gignitur, sed simpliciter referre ad munus quo fungitur Unigenitus erga opera sua, disponens, stabiliens, vivificans ea quæ condidit. Scilicet idem fere valet πρωτότοκος atque ἀρχὴ τῆς κτίσεως, et μονογενὴς πρωτεύων ἐν τῇ κτίσει, et πρωτότυπον γέννημα, μόνος γεννητὸς ἐν τοῖς γενητοῖς, et cætera ejusdem generis, ut clarissimo etiam Marano credo placuisse in opere suo " De Divinitate Christi ;" neque quicquam facit ad probandum, quod voluit Bullus, Concilium Nicænum iis favisse, (etiamsi non eos omnino reprobaret,) qui dicerent, fuisse Filium antequam gigneretur. Finem igitur ponamus aliquando disputationi nostræ, id solum suggerentes insuper, nempe illa quæ de Athanasii doctrina supra dicta sunt, fortasse inutilia non fore in quibusdam Ante-nicænorum nodis expediendis, quos non Bullus solum, sed eventu feliciore et Maranus et Ballerinii tractaverunt.

DISSERTATIO IV.

DE VOCIBUS ἐξ ἑτέρας ὑποστάσεως ἢ οὐσίας ANATHEMA-
TISMI NICÆNI.

AMBIGITUR inter doctos, utrum, cum Patres
Nicæni eos anathemate feriunt "qui Dei Filium
ex alia *hypostasi* vel *usia* esse sentirent," vocabula *hypostasis* et *usia* rem unam significent an duas. In hac
diversitate judiciorum, jure optimo licet in hanc vel in
illam iri sententiam, cum utramque sustineant ii, quos
neminem in hujusmodi materie secutum esse pœnitebit.
Si *hypostasin* volumus ab *usia* distinctam, Bullum habemus auctorem; si vocabula in unam redacta, Petavium.
Ego profecto Petavium sequor, felix tanto patrocinio,
adductus autem non auctoritate viri, sed ipso factorum
monitu, ut arbitror, et rei veritate.

Bullus, in Defensione sua Fidei Nicænæ, ii. 9, §
11, credit, si eum recte interpretor, singulas notiones,
inter se sejunctas, subesse singulis vocabulis *usiæ* et
hypostasi in hac formula; quasi anathematismus ille, in
quo reperiuntur, duas hæreses uno ictu feriens, et illos
condemnet qui dixerint Filium ex *usia* Patris non esse,
et illos quoque quibus placuerit Filium non esse ex
hypostasi Patris. Et præterea duas revera hæreti-

corum factiones in historia temporum illorum sibi invenisse putat, quæ suum utraque in illo Anathematismo locum habeant.

Petavius contra, *de Trin.* iv. 1, *hypostasin* tunc temporis idem velle atque *usiam* arbitratus, in una propositione Anathematismi mentem docet esse conclusam; eo maxime quia, ante Concilium Alexandrinum an. 362 habitum, sensus *hypostasis* ab *usia* diversus nulla esset publica Ecclesiæ auctoritate munitus. Quocum consentiunt Coustantius (*Ep. Pont. Rom.* pp. 274, 290, 462) Tillemontius, (*Dion Alex.* § 15.) Huetius, (*Origenian.* ii. 2, n. 3.) Thomassinus (*de Incarn.* iii. 1), et Morinus, (*de Sacr. Ordin.* ii. 6.) Maranus autem, (*Præf. ad Basil.* § 1, t. 3, Maur.) Natalis Alexander, (*Sæc.* 1, *Diss.* 22, circ. fin.) Burtonus (*Testimonies to the Trinity*, n. 71,) et Routhius (*Relliqu. Sacr.* vol. iii. p. 189,) si a Petavio dissentiunt, at certe non consentiunt Bullo.

Jam palmarium Bulli hoc est, quod Basilius, cum Sabellianis dimicans, qui, suam rem agentes, dicebant Concilium Nicænum *hypostasi* et *usiæ* unum sensum tribuisse, contra clara voce pronunciat Patres voluisse duas res, cum duabus voculis uterentur, et suam cuique vim tribuisse.

Provocat etiam ad Anastasium testantem, *Hodeg.* 21. (22, p. 342, ed. 1606) Patres Nicænos definivisse tres esse hypostases in sanctissima Trinitate. Quod quidem testimonium, ab Anastasio ipso Andreæ Samosateno ascriptum, Petavius putat esse Gelasii Cyziceni, non gravissimi auctoris; testimonium autem est Amphilochii quoque, idem fere scribentis apud eundem Anastasium *ibid.* c. 10, p. 164. Vid. quoque c. 9, p. 150, c. 24, p. 364, ubi Anastasius ipse loquitur. Accedunt loci ex Dionysio Pontifice Romano, Dionysio Alexandrino, Eusebio Cæsariensi, Origene quoque, a Bullo citati; in quibus singulis cum mentio sit trium *hypostasium*, trium autem similiter *usiarum* nulla in patribus sit mentio, perspicuum est *hypostasin* tunc expressisse notionem aliquam, quam *usia* non exprimeret. Quid quod Athanasius ipse de tribus *hypostasibus* loquitur, In illud Omnia 6. *Expos. Fid.* 2. Vid. quoque *Incarn. c. Arian.* 10. *Orat.* iv. 25, *init.*

Hoc de testibus ipsis: nunc de hæresibus duabus, quæ ex his vocibus tesseram, sibi quæque suam, confecisse dicuntur. Contendit Bullus distinctionem fecisse Semiarianos inter *usiam* et *hypostasin*; ex *hypostasi* Patris esse Filium concessisse, ex *usia* negasse. Quare, quando anathematizat Concilium eos qui ex *usia* Patris negant esse Filium, Semi-arianos ferit; quando eos qui ex *hypostasi*, (credo virum doctum hoc velle, nam non aperte loquitur,) Arianos. Diligentius rem excutiamus.

1. Incipio, non a testibus, sed ab hac interpretatione, quam, quasi ex historia temporum ductam, Anathematismi verbis vir doctissimus imponit. Quinam sunt ii, qui, Bullo judice, negarent ex *hypostasi* Patris esse Filium? Concedatur hic Semi-arianos negasse "ex alia *usia*," at quinam negabant "ex alia *hypostasi*?" Ariani? rejecerunt isti ex *usia* utique, sed de *hypostasi*, tanquam diversa ab *usia*, ne verbum quidem protulerunt. Ego vero nusquam esse tunc temporis illos hæreticos existimo. Hæc autem jacienda erant, caute non conjectura, quasi fundamenta hujus interpretationis; si nulla sunt, corruit ædificium. Nam Bulli

hæc plane principalis et absoluta est propositio, illos qui negarent ex *usia* non esse eos qui negarent ex *hypostasi*. Quærimus duo genera hæreticorum; at non designat ullos homines, qui negarent ex *hypostasi*, ex *usia*, non negarent.

2. Deinde, Semi-arianos tenuisse ex *hypostasi* sensu illo peculiari *personæ*, quem *usia* non habet, hoc unico probat argumento, quod tres illæ Semi-arianorum Confessiones, ann. 341, 344, 351, quæ sigillatim appellantur Marci Arethusii, Macrostichus, et prima Sirmiensis, illos anathemate feriunt qui dicerent Filium esse "ex alia *hypostasi* et non a Deo," prætermissis verbis " ex alia *usia*," quæ inde concludit esse propria Semi-arianorum. Quid velint verba illa prætermissa, mox dicendum erit; interea notatu dignum est, confessionem Philippopolitanam, ex Marci illa Semi-ariana sumptam, Hilarium ita non suspicari, tanquam lacunosam, quia omiserit "ex alia *usia*," ut illam contra defendat eo ipso quod retinuerit, ut putat, tesseram Catholicorum, *de Syn.* 35; quod quidem perinde est, quasi aperte dixerit "ex alia *hypostasi* et non ex Deo," idem velle atque "ex alia *hypostasi* vel *usia*." Accedit quod Athanasius quoque, in narratione sua eorum quæ Nicææ de anathematismo occurrebant, *de Decr.* 20, *fin.* plane omittit *hypostasin;* quasi, dum *usia* staret in loco suo, *hypostasin* sive adjungere sive omittere, idem fuerit.

3. Hoc præterea notandum est, nihil prorsus a Bullo esse prolatum, quo demonstretur Semi-arianos revera reprobasse " ex *usia;* " cum plane constet contra dogma illud recepisse eos, non reprobasse. "Certissimum" esse confirmat, hæreticos eos, qui tres illas confessiones supra laudatas protulerunt, scilicet Semi-arianos, " nunquam

fassos nunquam fassuros fuisse Filium ex *usia* Patris progenitum." Fateor eum hac in re habuisse Petavium consentientem sibi; sed me non perterret tantorum hominum conspiratio, qui Athanasium a me esse noverim. Quod quidem concedit Petavius, Athanasium arbitratus, utpote minus versatum in subtilitatibus Semi-arianorum, credidisse id eos tenere quod non tenerent. "Horum Semi-arianorum," scribit, "quorum antesignanus fuit Basilius Ancyræ Episcopus, prorsus obscura fuit hæresis . . ut ne ipse quidem Athanasius satis illam exploratam habuerit." *De Trin.* i. 10, § 7.

Hæc Petavius; nunc contra audiamus verba Athanasii. "Viros qui alia quidem omnia Nicææ scripta recipiunt, de solo autem *homoüsio* ambigunt, non ut inimicos spectari par est . . . Cum enim *confiteantur ex usia Patris et non ex alia hypostasi esse Filium* . . . non longe absunt ab *homoüsii* voce recipienda. Talis est Basilius Ancyræ, in iis quæ de fide scripsit." *De Synod.* 41. Quo in loco Athanasii illud quoque notabile est, præter ea quæ de Semi-arianorum doctrina testatur, quod *hypostasin* et *usiam* idem plane facit fidelissimus ille hujus historiæ interpres. Neque id omittendum est, quo Semi-arianos pergit urgere, idcirco scilicet eos debere "*homoüsion*" profiteri, quia jam profiterentur "ex *usia*," quod ipsorum tessera "*homæüsion*" non satis posset muniri.

Hilarius item, cum id agit ut ea defendat quæ a Semi-arianis Ancyræ vel Sirmii lata essent, inter alia quæ recte confiterentur, hoc esse testatur, "Non creatura est Filius genitus, sed *a natura Patris* indiscreta substantia est." *de Syn.* 27.

Idem probatur, ni fallor, ex iis ipsis apud Epiphanium scriptis Semi-arianorum, quibus motus credit Petavius, illos hæreticos "ex *usia* Patris" Filio denegasse. Subtilius aliquanto disputat, Semi-arianos tradidisse argutias quasdam de diversis, ut autumabant, actionibus (ἐνεργείας) divinis, quorum una esset actio γεννητικὴ seu generativa, alia κτιστικὴ seu creatrix; unde colligerunt Filium esse, non ex *usia*, sed per actionem illam generativam, ἐξ ὁμοιότητος, ex similitudine Patris. At certe ea quæ plane confitentur Semi-ariani in hac Confessione sua plus valent quam vult Petavius, et "ex *usia*" non obscure significant; υἱὸν ὅμοιον, dicunt, καὶ κατ' οὐσίαν ἐκ τοῦ πατρός, *Hær.* 73, p. 825. b. ὡς ἡ σοφία τοῦ σοφοῦ υἱὸς, οὐσία οὐσίας, p. 853. c. κατ' οὐσίαν υἱὸν τοῦ Θεοῦ καὶ πατρός. p. 854. c. ἐξουσίᾳ ὁμοῦ καὶ οὐσίᾳ πατρὸς μονογενοῦς υἱοῦ. p. 858. d. Vid. quoque vocabulum γνήσιος *ibid*. et Athan. *de Synod.* 41, ut alia, quæ iidem proferunt, prætereamus.

Quod quidem in Collatione illa quoque patet, inter Semi-arianos et Anomœos, Constantinopoli coram Constantio an. 360 habita, cum Semi-ariani, teste Theodoreto, non gravate confessi sunt etiam *homoüsion* illud Catholicorum, idcirco, quia jam confiterentur "ex *usia*." Cum enim Anomœi *homoüsion* condemnatum vellent, Silvanus Tarsus, Semi-arianorum vir primarius, "Si Deus Verbum non est ex nihilo," respondit, "neque creatum, neque alterius *usiæ*, *homoüsius* igitur est Deo qui ipsum genuit, utpote Deus ex Deo, et lumen ex lumine, eandemque cum Genitore naturam habet." *Hist.* ii. 23. Quo in loco, ut in illo Athanasii, notandum est, Theodoretum, cum videtur ipsum Nicænorum Anathematismum citare, tamen omittere verba " ex alia *hypostasi*," tanquam supervacanea, cum " ex alia *usia*," jam memorasset.

Hoc autem Petavio et Bullo concedendum est, Semi-arianos temporis progressu propius accessisse ad Catholicam fidem; ita ut non jure possimus illorum proferre confessionem an. 358, qua probemus quid an. 325 de Filii generatione sensissent. Quippe ex gremio Eusebianorum oriebatur schola quædam et moribus et doctrina gravior, laudata autem ab Athanasio et Hilario; quam postea, Damaso Pontifice, relicta tandem hæreticorum factione, ad fidem Petri magna ex parte constat confugisse. Qui homines quanquam "ex *usia*" confessi sint nondum Catholici, non ideo Eusebii illi duo idem tenuisse censendi sunt, neque Asterius, neque cæteri, qui ipso Patrum Nicænorum tempore, tametsi hæretici, a simplici Arianorum vesania refugerunt. Esto igitur in dubio, ut Bulli causam oremus ultro, utrum Semi-ariani Nicæni "ex *usia*" recepissent an non; tamen certumne est eos contra recepisse " ex *hypostasi* ? " Minime sane; nam ipse Petavius, qui illis " ex *usia* " abjudicat, non voluit iisdem cum Bullo tribuere " ex *hypostasi*." Quæ cum ita sint, historia controversiæ tandem relicta, ut Bullo minus commoda, ad testes veniendum est.

Ex his testibus Gelasius est auctoritate tenui, Anastasius posterioris ævi. Quod autem ex Amphilochio adducitur, satis habiturum esset ponderis, nisi Basilius, eidem conjunctissimus, idem testimonium, idque expressius, dedisset. In Basilium igitur, magnum certe auctorem, tota res recidit; et profecto si unius viri testimonio concedenda est diremptio quæstionis hujus, Basilium protinus sequamur; *hypostasin* et *usiam* inter se differre, dimissis argumentis, plena voce profiteamur. Sed nimirum uni viro, quanquam gravissimo, aliis adversantibus testibus, certe non est confidendum.

Primum illud est, ut supra commonstravimus, Athanasium et Hilarium, non quidem data opera, sed in disputationis cursu, ita *de hypostasi* et *usia* esse locutos, ut significarent vocabula ea unam rem, non duas, voluisse in Anathematismo. Nam commutant illa inter se; *hypostasin* omittunt; omissa autem, tamen Anathematismum tanquam omnibus numeris absolutum æstimant. Præterea Hilarius in *Fragm*. ii. 27, cum velit Anathematismi verba latine vertere, "ex altera substantia *vel essentia*" scribit. Cujus simile fortasse est illud Eusebii in Epistola sua, "ex alia hypostasi *et usia*." c. 7.

Hæc sint præludia quædam, namque Athanasius, in Epistola sua *ad Afros*, ad vocem ipsam pæne definiendam ex proposito aggreditur; "*Hypostasis* est *usia*, neque aliam habet significationem, quam hoc ipsum quod est. Quod Hieremias vocat existentiam, cum dicit," etc. § 4. Quamvis autem alibi loquitur de tribus *hypostasibus*, aliud illud est; nam quia *hypostasis*, numerali diserte addito, vult *persona*, non inde continuo perspicuum est quid tum velit, cum in singulari stat et in alio verborum contextu reperitur. Ego hoc verissimum esse puto, quando trium mentio est *hypostasium, hypostasin* personam velle; sed in Anathematismo Nicæno non legimus "tres *hypostases*," sed "*hypostasin* vel *usiam*;" quemadmodum autem Athanasius, alibi de tribus *hypostasibus* locutus, tamen *hypostasin* in singulari sumptam *usiam* interpretatur (vid. e. g.

Orat. iii. 66, iv. 1, f. 33 *fin.*) ita Patres quoque Nicæni, "hypostasin" proferentes et *usiam* adjicientes, vocabula duo inter se non opposita, sed apposita voluerunt.

Non minus aperte, nec minore auctoritate loquitur Hieronymus: "Tota sæcularium litterarum schola nihil aliud *hypostasim* nisi *usiam* novit." *Ep.* xv. 4. Quid quod de tribus *hypostasibus* disputans in eadem Epistola, liberiora hæc profert, quæ non protulisset utique, si Patribus Nicænis *hypostasis* "persona" sonuisset. "Si jubetis, condatur *nova post* Nicænam fides; et similibus verbis cum Arianis confiteamur orthodoxi." Certe si Basilius validus est testis ex una parte, non minus ex altera gravis est Athanasius, vehemens Hieronymus.

Basilius porro, non Cæsariensis, sed Semi-arianus ex Ancyra, et alii ejus congregales, idem testantur apud Epiphanium: "Hanc *hypostasin* Patres *usiam* vocarunt." *Hær.* 73, 12 fin. Cui suffragatur confessio illa quam Epistolæ Sardicensi assutam invenimus: "unam esse *hypostasin*, quam ipsi hæretici *usiam* appellant." Theod. *Hist.* ii. 6.

Sed occurretur forsitan, Hieronymum, Occidentalem virum, Basilium et Georgium Semi-arianos, non satis fidos in hac re esse auctores, sed prout sua ipsorum aut veritatis traditio, aut hæreticus error ferebat, asseverantius quam consultius de sensu *hypostasi* esse testatos. Esto; at Magnus Basilius contra habuit ille quoque suos amicos, traditionem suam; si enim Occidens unam *hypostasin* prædicaverat, tres *usias* Semi-ariani, ita Orientales contra strenuos fuisse constat in trium *hypostasium*, unius *usiæ* confessione.

Præterea Socrates auctor est, disceptatum fuisse Alexandriæ de *hypostasi* paulo ante Concilium Nicænum de qua tamen "ne verbum quidem fecit Concilium illud." *Hist.* iii. 7, id quod aliter se habet, si inter *hypostasin* et *usiam* a Concilio distinctum est.

Concilium denique Alexandrinum an. 362 habitum, cum decerneret integrum esse *hypostasin* vel pro *usia* vel pro persona adhiberi, non solum eo ipso significavit, vocabulum illud adhuc relictum esse, ut aiunt, in Ecclesia, sed id apertissme declarat in Epistola sua. Si enim *hypostasi* sensum suum jam imposuisset Concilium Nicænum, quid reliquum erat Alexandrinis nisi eum profiteri? Cujus argumenti vim ita intelligit Bullus, ut confugiat ad conjecturam, innovatum fuisse in "veteri vocabuli usu" illo ipso Concilii Sardicensis tempore, reclamantibus et Socrate, qui illum usum ante Concilium Nicænum collocat, *Hist.* iii. 4, 5 et tabula Sardicensi, in qua unius *hypostasis* doctrina ex traditione Catholica repetitur.

Ea quæ adduximus sæculi quarti sunt testimonia; neque aliud sonant, etsi rariora, quæ de eodem vocabulo in sæculis Ante-nicænis traduntur. Socrates hic audiendus est: "Qui Græcam inter Græcos philosophiam tradiderunt, *usiam* quidem pluribus modis definierunt; *hypostasis* vero nullam prorsus mentionem fecerunt. Irenæus quidam Grammaticus, in Lexico per ordinem litterarum digesto, quod Atticistes inscribitur, hanc vocem barbaram esse affirmat. Neque enim apud quenquam veterum scriptorum eam reperiri; ac sicubi fortasse reperiatur, non eo sensu, quo nunc sumitur, usurpari. Etenim apud Sophoclem in Phœnice ea vox insidias significat; apud Menandrum vero condimenta, perinde ac siquis fæcem vini in dolio subsidentem appellet *hypostasin.* Verum licet ab antiquis philosophis hæc vox usurpata non fuerit, sciendum est tamen, recentiores ea frequenter usos fuisse pro *usia."* *Hist.* iii. 7. Ex Ante-nicænis, plurimus est Origenes in vocabulo *hypostasis;* idque, contextu verborum interprete, ut significetur " persona." Loquitur porro de tribus *hypostasibus;* ut Dionysius quoque, ejus discipulus; et Eusebius, ita tamen ut *hypostasin* cum *usia* confundat; item Athanasius, ut supra dictum est, (Orig. *in Joan.* ii. 6, Dionys. *ap.* Basil. *de Sp. S.* n. 72. Euseb. *ap.* Socr. i. 23. Athan. *In illud Omnia,* 6); de duabus Patris et Filii, Origenes, Ammonius, Alexander, (Origen. *in Cels.* viii. 2. Ammon.[1] *ap. Caten. in Joan.* x. 30. Alex. *ap.* Theod. i. 3, p. 740.) Quare videtur illa vox in Ecclesia catholica prius scholæ cujusdam esse propria, nempe Alexandrinæ: post autem exortas hæreses, ne verborum ambiguitas fidelibus fraudi esset, ab Ecclesia ipsa ex scholis in suos usus esse conversa. Profecto, quod alte in mentibus Catholicorum jam inde ab Apostolis insedit, Tria revera esse in Una Divinitate, id, cum a malesana philosophia periclitabatur, placuit Ecclesiæ, Dei monitu, per vocabulum *hypostasis* exprimi. Qua in re cum Bullo et Marano consentio plane; nisi quod Maranus *hypostasin* " summo consensu " receptam esse putat ab Oriente a

---

[1] Hunc autem, cujus multæ in catenis ad N. T. (ad S. Joannem præsertim) occurrunt symbolæ, non esse Ammonium illum sæculi tertii, sed alium quendam sæculi quinti, ecclesiæ Alexandrinæ presbyterum et œconomum, post Combefisium auguratur Fabricius, *Bibl. Græc.* t. v. pp. 714, 722, ed. 1796.

Noeto vel saltem Sabellio exorto, Bullus autem "apud Catholicos Dionysii ætate ratum et fixum illud fuisse, tres esse in divinis hypostases."

Inquirendum est denique, cur, unam rem præ oculis habentes, duobus vocabulis *usia* et *hypostasi* in Anathematismo suo usi sint Nicæni Patres. Respondet Coustantius, *hypostasin* primo scriptam ab illis fuisse, deinde *usiam* provida mente adjectam, ne scilicet *hypostasin* prave verterint Sabelliani, quasi voluerit *persona*. Crediderim præterea *hypostasin* priorem ideo habuisse locum, quia Concilio Œcumenico, sub Latinorum magisterio habito, vocabulum *substantia*, seu *hypostasis*, quasi nativum fuerit et solemne. Quin Damasus, quinquaginta post annos, loquitur de Spiritu Sancto tanquam ejusdem *hypostasis* et *usias* cum Patre et Filio. Theod. *Hist.* ii. 17; longe aliter atque Concilium Œcumenicum secundum, a quo, absentibus quippe Latinis, tres *hypostases* commemorantur. Neque alius fuit nisi Hosius, ex præsulibus scilicet Latinis, (qui ipse Pontificis fuerat legatus Nicææ,) qui controversiam de *substantia* sive *hypostasi*, in Alexandriam induxerit. Sardicæ quoque, quanquam *hypostasis* pro *usia* in Epistolam Synodalem non inducebatur, tamen ex historia Concilii constat, Hosium ibi restitisse iis, quibuscum magna ex parte consentiebat. Hoc porro in controversia fortasse erat sæculo tertio inter Dionysios duos, Pontificem Romanum et Alexandrinum Præsulem, (ut visum est Coustantio, dissentientibus autem Marano et Routhio): cum Alexandrinus tres esse hypostases confirmabat, Pontifex autem tres divulsas ($\mu\epsilon\mu\epsilon\rho\iota\sigma\mu\acute{\epsilon}\nu\alpha\varsigma$) i.e. tres substantias condemnabat, quasi tritheismum sapuerint; Alexandrinus autem regerebat, "Si eo quod tres sunt *hypostases*, divulsas esse dicunt, tres sunt, etiamsi nolint; aliter, Divinam Trinitatem prorsus e medio tollant." *ap.* Basil. *de Sp. S.* 72. Quid quod Occidentalium usus in Athanasio cernitur, semel vel iterum hospite Pontificis Romani; qui, cum Origines, Dionysius, Ammonius, Alexander, populares sui, duo et tres *hypostases* confitentur, ita tamen ipse variat vocabuli sensum, modo unam, modo tres docens *hypostases* in Divinitate, ut videatur prope in se ostendere illam loquendi libertatem, quam in Concilio Alexandrino Catholicis asseruit.

Quæ si recte se habeant, intelligi potest quare, in tribus illis Confessionibus Semi-arianorum, omittatur "ex *usia;*" quia scilicet mittebantur ad Latinos, quos ut conciliarent, utebantur hæretici illo vocabulo, quod in auribus Latinorum clarius soniturum esset; quemadmodum Athanasius contra, ut vidimus, in Epistola sua *de Decr. Concil. Nic.* scribens ad Græcos, omittit *hypostasin*, *usiam* retinet. Neque absimili ratione, quemadmodum Semi-ariani voluerunt prætensa *hypostasi* Occidentalibus blandiri, ita Acaciani contra an. 359, jam ex Constantii favore audaces, illud idem vocabulum, non aliud, Arimini ab Occidentalibus repudiatum voluerunt; ut conspici potest ex illo symbolo, quod, conscriptum Nicæ in Thracia, non solum *usiam*, ut in aliis confessionibus Arianorum, sed *hypostasin* etiam omittit; ea scilicet mente ut Latinis necesse esset, non solum græcum "*homoüsion*," sed latinum "unius substantiæ" rejicere.

Jam vero, si usitatum est philosophorum scholis, illam

magis probabilem judicari hypothesin, quæ ad universa facta vel phænomena, de quibus agit, facillime accommodatur, quid nobis ea quæ jam dicta sunt perpendentibus restat, nisi ut concludamus, vocabulis *hypostasi* et *usia* Anathematismi Nicæni unam rem, non duas significari?

Disputationum harum editioni Romanæ subnotantur hæc:—

NIHIL OBSTAT—Paulus Cullen Censor Theol. Deputatus.
NIHIL OBSTAT—Joannes Perrone S. J. Censor Theol. Deputatus.
IMPRIMATUR—Fr. Dom. Buttaoni Ord. Præd. S. P. A. Magister.
IMPRIMATUR—Joseph Canali Patriarch. Constantinopolit. Vicesgerens.

II.   1870

ON THE TEXT OF THE SEVEN EPISTLES OF ST. IGNATIUS.

(Begun in Notes of the date of 1828, completed in 1870.)

ON THE TEXT OF THE SEVEN EPISTLES OF ST. IGNATIUS.

IN my Essay on the theology of St. Ignatius (Essays, vol. i.), it was assumed that the controversy of the seventeenth century, in which Pearson bore so distinguished a part, had issued in a plain proof of the substantial genuineness of the text of the Medicean and Colbertine MSS. And it was inferred from this as a premiss, that apostolic Christianity was of a distinctly dogmatic character, it being impossible for those who resisted this inference to succeed in explaining away the text of Ignatius, as those MSS. contain it, and only open to them to take refuge in a denial of the premiss, that is, of the genuineness of that text. Then it was added as to such denial, "It is a curious speculation whether, in the progress of controversy, divines, who are determined at all risks not to admit the Church system, will not fall back upon it;—stranger things have happened."

So I wrote in 1838, and what I then anticipated has actually taken place since, though not in the way that I anticipated. I did not fancy that the controversy would have been revived on grounds both new, and certainly at first sight plausible, as has been the case. Those new grounds do not change my own judgment on the matter in dispute; but they have a real claim to be taken into consideration. This I now propose to do.

I.

In the year 1845, then, the late Dr. Cureton gave to the world, from a Nitrian MS. of the seventh century, a Syriac version of three out of the seven Epistles enumerated by Eusebius, viz., those to St. Polycarp, to the Romans, and to the Ephesians; and in this ancient version various characteristic passages, as they are found in the Greek, are absent, and among them some of those on which I have insisted in my Essay. Dr. Cureton claims for this Syriac version (Preface, p. xi.) to be the nearest representative of "what Ignatius himself wrote;" and in this claim he is supported by various critics of great consideration. Nor are the reasons which he and they assign for their judgment of slight account, nor indeed do they admit of a summary refutation in our present partial knowledge of the facts of the case. Before it is possible to close the controversy thus reopened, the Syriac version of the remaining Epistles has to be discovered; or again, it should become clear that there never was any Syriac version of them at all; nor is anything yet known of the history of this new MS., of its derivation, or of the circumstances under which the version it contains was made, such as might explain what may be called the dumb fact of its existence.

One important exception to this remark must be mentioned; a second Nitrian MS. has also been discovered, containing one of the same three Epistles as are contained in the first, viz., the Epistle to Polycarp; and this MS. is of even an earlier date, viz., about A.D. 530—540, and with only so much difference of text from that of A.D. 600—700, as serves to show that the later MS. of the two was not copied from the earlier, and thereby to throw back the date of the version itself at least to the fifth century. The value, however, of this fact, in relation to the question before us, is not great, both because the Epistle to Polycarp anyhow contains little of a dogmatic character, and because, as regards this Epistle, the newly-discovered Syriac differs very little from the hitherto received Greek. Of course the coincidence of those MSS., two Syriac and one Greek, in one text, is a most satisfactory guarantee of the genuineness of that text; but it does not touch the difficulty, which lies in the important differences existing between the Syriac and Greek texts of the other two Epistles, to the Romans and to the Ephesians. In speaking of the agreement of the Syriac and Greek texts of the Epistle to Polycarp, I must not forget to mention that the two last chapters of the Greek are omitted in the Syriac; but these two chapters refer to what may be called personal matters, are of the nature of a postscript, and may have been really such, and thus may have been preserved in some copies, omitted in others, as the case might be, without prejudice to their genuineness. Yet the omission is not without its importance, as it shows that the Syriac copyist had no scruple in curtailing the text he was engaged upon.

Putting aside then the Epistle to St. Polycarp, we come to the real question; that is, what is the force and value of the suspicion cast on the Greek text of the Epistles to the Romans and to the Ephesians, so long received, at least in English schools, by the fact of the omission of important parts of them both in the Syriac MSS.; a suspicion directly attaching to those two, but indirectly of course affecting the other four also, from the probability that, were the Syriac of these four forthcoming (if Syriac there ever was), parallel omissions would occur in them also, as compared with their text as it stands in the received Greek. It must be added, that the very circumstance that only three Epistles have been found in Syriac, is with some critics a reason for thinking that three only were written by Ignatius, or at least only three preserved, though Eusebius speaks in his day of there being seven.

Premising that after all the question, as I have now stated it, is not, in a doctrinal point of view, of extreme importance, inasmuch as the text of the two Epistles, as it is found in the Syriac, retains quite enough of dogmatic teaching, on the Incarnation and the Episcopal *régime*, to answer the purpose for which I have in my Essay used the Greek text, I proceed to state the arguments as they occur to me, in favour of the genuineness of the latter, that is, of the Greek, as contained in those Medicean and Colbertine MSS. which were brought to light by the industry of Isaac Voss and Ruinart.

2.

I have been speaking as if there were only one Greek

text of the Epistles, but, as is well known, there are in fact two, and those two very different from each other. This at first sight would seem to be an additional difficulty, or rather an argument in favour of those who are suspicious of the received Greek, since, if there are three texts extant of one and the same collection of Epistles, differing from each other, there are, on the face of the matter, two chances to one against the correctness of any one of them. However, this *primâ facie* difficulty does not hold in the particular case, as a few words will show.

First, the Greek text, as first published by Valentinus Pacæus in 1557 (in company with sundry spurious Epistles, of which I need not speak here), is very much longer than the Medicean, first published in 1646. Also it bears the marks of a doctrinal terminology, which in the fourth century would be called Arian; the Medicean or shorter edition, on the contrary, is strictly orthodox, as also is the Syriac, that is, so far as it contains passages of a doctrinal character.

Next, the relation of the longer edition to the shorter is this;—not that the two are absolutely divergent from each other, whether in structure or in subject-matter, but that the longer is a sort of paraphrastic enlargement of the shorter or Medicean. It has been usual to call the longer the "Interpolated Edition;" but, thought there are passages in it, which, if the edition does not represent the true Ignatian text, (as I think it does not,) are rightly called interpolations, yet that word is far from conveying a just idea of the relation of the longer on the whole to the shorter and orthodox. The longer Epistles are a continuous paraphrase or amplification of the shorter, unless indeed we please to say that the shorter were intended by their editor to be a compendium or abstract of the longer. Anyhow the two editions thus stand related to each other; they carry on one and the same succession of topics in each Epistle from beginning to end, with a continual, either enlargement or abbreviation of the one by the other, as we may see reason to determine. In both there are the same two prominent subjects—viz., our Lord's two natures, and the authority and sacramental virtue of the Episcopal rule. In the latter of these doctrines both editions speak alike; in the former, as I have already said, the shorter or Medicean edition is orthodox, but the longer edition Arianizes.

3.

The intimate connection of the two editions is obvious at first sight, and need not be proved. What I have to show is, that the longer is a paraphrase of the shorter, not the shorter an abridgment of the longer.

Here, my first remark is this; that there is a grave conciseness in the shorter, which is far more natural in an old man going to martyrdom than the florid rhetoric of the longer, which savours of easy circumstances, plenty of time for words, and a temperament less stern, and a state of feeling less concentrated, than is generated by chronic peril and prospective suffering.

Again, it is never difficult to dilute a vigorous and sententious document, but seldom possible to condense into a series of terse enunciations in logical sequence a composition which is verbose and ornate. Let us compare together several corresponding passages of these editions;—they will decide the point at once. I will put into italics those clauses of the longer, which form the whole text of the shorter.

1. First, from the Epistle to the Trallians, c. 11.

The shorter Edition.

"Flee therefore the evil scions, which bear a deadly fruit; of which, if a man taste, he presently dies. These are not the plants of the Father. For, had they been, they would have shown as branches of the Cross, and their fruit would have been incorruptible; by which (Cross) in His Passion He invites you, who are His members."

The longer Edition.

"*Avoid those evil scions* of his [the evil one], Simon, his first-born son, and Menander, and Basilides, and his whole crew of evil; the man-worshippers, whom also the prophet Jeremias calls cursed. Flee also the unclean Nicolaitans (without any right to Nicolas's name) the pleasure-lovers, the slanderers. Flee also the brood of the wicked one, Theodotus and Cleobulus, *which bear a deadly fruit; of which, if a man taste, he presently dies,* not the temporal death, but the eternal. *These are not plants of the Father,* but a cursed brood; and 'let every plant,' the Lord says, 'which My Father hath not planted, be rooted up.' *For, had they been* branches of the Father, *they would not have been* enemies *of the Cross* of

Christ, but of those who 'slew the Lord of glory.' But now, by denying the Cross, and being ashamed of the passion, they shelter the transgression of the Jews, those God-opposers, those Lord-slayers; for it would not be enough to say, prophet-slayers. *And you Christ invites to His own incorruption, through His passion, and resurrection, who are His members.*"

2. So again, from the Epistle to the Ephesians, c. 9.

The shorter Edition.

" I have known of some, who passed by from thence, as having an evil teaching; whom you have not allowed to cast the seeds of it into you, closing your ears, so as not to admit the sowing, as being stones of the Father's Temple, prepared to be built up by God the Father."

The longer Edition.

"*I have known of some who passed through you, as having an evil teaching of a malevolent and wicked spirit; to whom you have not given an opening to sow the cockle, so as not to admit the error which was preached by them;* being persuaded that that people-misleading spirit speaks, not the things of Christ, but his own, for he utters lies. But the Holy Spirit speaks, not what is His own, but what is Christ's, and not from Himself, but from the Lord, as again the Lord preached to us what was from the Father. For He says, ' The word which you hear is not Mine, but the Father's who sent Me,' and concerning the Holy Ghost He says, ' He shall not speak from Himself, but whatsoever He may hear from Me.' And concerning Himself He says to the Father, 'I have glorified Thee on the earth; the work which Thou gavest Me, I have finished; I have manifested Thy name to men;' and concerning the Holy Ghost, 'He shall glorify Me, for He shall receive of Mine.' But the deceiving spirit heralds himself, speaks his own; for he is a self-pleaser. He glorifies himself, for he is full of arrogance. He is a lying, deceitful, wheedling, flattering, underhand, rambling, trifling, inconsistent, talkative, quibbling, startled thing, from whose force Jesus Christ will deliver you, who has founded you on the rock, *as chosen stones, for the divine building of the Father."*

3. Once more, from the Epistle to the Smyrnæans, c. 6.

The shorter Edition.

"Let no one deceive himself. Heavenly things, and the glory of the Angels, and Rulers, whether visible or invisible, if they do not believe in the blood of Christ, even to them there is judgment. 'He who receives, let him receive.' Let no man's place puff him up. For faith and charity are all in all, of which nothing has precedence in judgment. But consider those who hold other opinions as regards the grace of Jesus Christ, which has come to us, how contrary they are to the mind of God. Charity is not their concern, nor the widow, nor the orphan, nor the afflicted, nor the prisoner or liberated, nor the hungry or thirsty."

The longer Edition.

"*Let no one deceive himself. Unless he believe* that Christ Jesus has lived in the flesh, *and confess Christ's*

Cross, suffering, and *blood* which He poured out for the world's salvation, he *shall not obtain everlasting life*, be he king, or priest, or ruler, or private man, or lord, or slave, or man, or woman. 'He that receives, let him receive.' 'He that hears, let him hear.' *Let not place*, or rank, or wealth, *puff up any one.* Let not dishonour and poverty abase any one. For *faith* towards God, and hope in Christ, the enjoyment of goods in expectancy, *and love* towards God and one's fellow, *are all in all*. For 'thou shalt love the Lord thy God with all thy heart, and thy neighbour as thyself.' And the Lord says, 'This is life eternal to know the only True God, and whom He hath sent, Jesus Christ.' And 'a new commandment I give to you, that ye love one another.' 'On these two commandments hang all the Law and the Prophets.' *Consider then those who hold other opinions*, how they lay it down as a principle that the Father of Christ cannot be known, and how they bear a faithless hatred towards each other. *Charity is not their concern;* they make no account of the promises we are expecting; they reckon on the present as if lasting; they neglect the commandments; they overlook *the widow and orphan*, they spurn *the afflicted*, they mock *the prisoner*."

Such a contrast, though not everywhere to the same extent, runs from first to last between the two editions; showing us, first their intimate connection, next, surely without need of formal proof, that the shorter is the basis of the longer, not the longer of the shorter.

A third hypothesis, indeed, might be made, to the

effect that they both come from some lost original; but to substantiate this, passages ought to be producible from the shorter edition which are not in the longer; whereas the longer may be said to gather up all that is in the shorter, and merely to add to it.

I shall take it for granted then that the writer of the longer Epistles had the shorter before him, when he wrote; and, on this assumption, several important conclusions follow:—1, That the shorter edition is prior in date to the longer. 2, That the writer of the longer considered the shorter to be the genuine work of Ignatius, for otherwise it would not have been worth his while to paraphrase and arrange it. 3, That this recognition of the shorter work at the date of the longer is of a very peculiar kind, having a breadth and force in it rarely found in the case of testimonies to authorship; for it is a testimony, not merely to a title or a heading, to its subject or its drift, or to particular passages in it, and nothing besides, but, being a paraphrase, it is testimony travelling along the entire text, and identifying and guaranteeing every part of it.

The testimony then borne by the paraphrastic edition to the genuineness of the shorter Epistles being so special, it becomes of great importance to ascertain its date.

4.

First, however, I will give two additional reasons in behalf of the chronological priority of the shorter edition.

1. That it is anterior in point of time to the longer is

proved by the scantiness of quotations from the New Testament in the shorter, and the profusion of them which is found in the longer, as the above parallel instances are sufficient to show. It is only in keeping with the date of Ignatius, that he should make few allusions to the Gospels and Epistles. The writers of these were almost or quite his contemporaries, and their friends were his friends. He knew them, or at least remembered them, rather by their conversations than by their writings. He would obviously be guided in his pastoral instructions rather by the lessons which they had once for all engraven on his heart, than by a reference *pro re natâ* to chapter and verse of the documents which they had been inspired to give to the world. And he wrote to those who in like manner would in his person contemplate the first preachers of Christianity, more directly and intimately than in books which, if they had ever seen, they had seen but occasionally and by accident. It would have been unnatural in him, writing to them, to have thought of enforcing his words by New Testament texts. In accordance with this anticipation, we find in the Epistle of St. Clement to the Corinthians, hardly a single reference to any book of the New Testament, though his whole composition is redolent of St. Paul's spirit. The case is the same with the so-called Barnabas and Hermas. It is true that the Epistle of St. Polycarp, on the other hand, written shortly after the death of Ignatius, contains frequent references to both Epistles and Gospels: but then it must be recollected that the writer is not only the specimen of a new generation and a new usage, but wrote at home, among his books, not, as Ignatius, a prisoner, chained to a rude soldier, and carried about from place to place, from Antioch to Philippi, Dyrrhachium, and Rome. It is difficult to suppose that Ignatius could have had at his fingers' ends the multitude of Scripture passages which flow so readily from the pen of the author of the longer Epistles. There are in them as many as ninety texts from the New Testament, and taken from as many as eighteen out of its twenty-seven books. In the shorter edition there are altogether only six of such quotations, and these consisting of but a few words each. If this absence of Scripture texts be a fair test of antiquity, we cannot well assign too early a date to the shorter edition. It will be prior to St. Polycarp.

2. A second reason for the priority of the shorter Epistles may be added, not so strong, yet not without force. I shall presently have occasion to insist upon the Arianisms of the longer; here, I will consider these Arianisms simply as phrases at variance with the phrases in the shorter, and I cannot but think that, at least in some cases, they are not mere fortuitous differences from the shorter text, but deliberate emendations and managements of it. Suppose, for instance, that in an anonymous Anglican sermon, which we fell in with in MS., we read, "His sacred Majesty is king by divine right, for every magistrate, even in a republic, is from God," we might fairly consider that the writer was of a date later than that of Elizabeth or James, because he recognised the then court doctrine of the Right Divine of kings by the very circumstance of going on to explain

it away; whereas no such inference could be drawn about the date of the sermon, supposing we merely read in it, "His sacred Majesty reigns in the hearts of his people," or, "All magistrates are ordained by God, and the king is the greatest of them." In like manner the theological statements in the longer edition of St. Ignatius imply in their language, more or less, a consciousness of an existing text, such as the shorter, which they are intended to correct or to complete.

For instance: in the Epistle to the Romans, in the shorter edition, Ignatius salutes the Roman Church "in the Name of Jesus Christ, the Son of the Father;" in the longer, "in the name of God Almighty and of Jesus Christ His Son."—*Init.*

To the Magnesians: in the shorter we read, "Jesus Christ, who *was with* the Father before the ages, and appeared in the end of time;" in the longer, "who, *being begotten with* the Father before age (or time) *was* the Word God, Only-begotten Son, and at the consummation of the ages continues the same."—C. 6.

And the Epistle to the Symrnæans begins, in the shorter, "I glorify Jesus Christ, our God;" in the longer, "I glorify the God and Father of our Lord Jesus Christ."

And so to the Ephesians: in the shorter, "There is one Physician, fleshly and spiritual, generate and ingenerate, God come in flesh, true life in death, from Mary and from God, first passible and then impassible." But in the longer: "Our Physician is the *One True God*, the *Ingenerate* and unapproachable, the *Lord of all*, and

Father and Generator of the Only-begotten. *Also* we have a Physician, our Lord God Jesus Christ, the Only-begotten Son and Word before all ages, and at last man also of Mary the Virgin, for 'the Word became flesh,' the incorporeal in a body, the immortal in a mortal body, the life in corruption," etc., etc.

Whatever be the force of this second argument, enough has been said without it to show that the longer edition recognises the shorter, and thereby, as I have said, recognises it as the writing of St. Ignatius.

It becomes of great importance then, I repeat, to ascertain the date of the longer Epistles; for at that date, whenever it was, the shorter Epistles were both extant as we have them now, and were considered, at least in certain literary and theological circles, to be genuine. To that inquiry I proceed.

5.

Nor is it a difficult one, if we take the right means for pursuing it. Some critics indeed have recourse to a method highly uncritical, determining the date of the writer by the date of the authors who happen to mention him. If the longer Epistles are first quoted in the sixth or seventh century, that according to them is to be considered about the date at which they were written. On this principle the history of Paterculus must be considered a production of the sixth century, because Priscian, I believe, is the first and only of the ancients who speaks of it. Of course we are sometimes obliged to pursue such unsatisfactory modes of inquiry, because there are no other available; but this is not the case with the longer Epistles ascribed to St. Ignatius: they bear on themselves the evidence of their date, and, though it is always desirable to add external evidence to internal, we have no need to ask of others what we can ascertain for ourselves.

These Epistles, I have said, are characterised by Arian phrases: let us determine then the date at which Arianism ceased to exist in the East of Christendom, its native seat, and we have the latest date which we can fix for these Epistles.

First, what was Arianism? It was the doctrine, that our Lord, though rightly called God, as being the God of the mediatorial system and of the New Covenant, was not the God of the universe; that He was a being separate from God, and therefore, though the sublimest of creatures, super-angelic, only-begotten, still necessarily with a beginning of existence, and with the duties of a minister and subject of His Father, not co-eternal and co-equal with Him. To express and maintain this doctrine, they brought together various terms, separately orthodox, and casually used by one or other of the Fathers before them; in themselves capable of a good sense, but involving a false doctrine in their combination. Now these watchwords of the heresy are found in the longer Epistles, and are sure evidence of the religious opinions of their paraphrast and editor.

1. For instance: Ingenitus ($ἀγέννητος$), "Ingenerate," was the philosophical designation of the First Cause, originally perhaps under the notion that all things

emanated from Him as a parent, and He from no one. It was applied by the Arians exclusively to the Father, by way of insinuating that the Son was not eternal. Hence in the passage quoted above, it was predicated of the Father, in contrast to the Son, that He is "the *only True* God, *Ingenerate*, and Unapproachable." "God of the Universe," or, "Lord *of all things*," is another specific title of the Father, in the Arian Creed, and accordingly the passage in question proceeds, "Unapproachable, Lord *of the Universe*." In the Epistle to the Philadelphians, c. 4, "There is one *Ingenerate*, the God and Father; and one only-begotten Son, the Word God, who is also man." And so in *Trall.*, c. 4, it is made a mark of heresy to hold that "Christ was ingenerate." Vid. also *Magn.*, c. 7; *Smyrn.*, c. 8.

2. Another mark of Arianism was to insist on "the generation of the Son *before all ages*," which is of course a revealed truth, but was used by the Arians as a denial of His co-eternity with the Father, the "ages" being creatures of God, priority to which did not involve eternity *à parte ante*. Again, as *generation* in their mouths implied a beginning of existence, they preferred to say that our Lord "was begotten before all time," to saying "was before all time." Hence it is, that in another passage above quoted, the larger edition gives, "Jesus Christ, who was begotten before time with the Father, the Word God, the only-begotten Son," etc., while the shorter reads, "who was with the Father before the ages."— *Magn.*, c. 7. And so in like manner *Eph.*, c. 18, in the shorter, runs, "Our God, Jesus Christ, was borne in the womb by Mary, according to the economy of God,"

etc.; but in the longer, "The Son of God, who was begotten before the ages, and has constituted all things by the mind of the Father."

3. This last clause brings us to another characteristic of the Arian system. It inculcated that our Lord was made by God in order to be His instrument in creating all things, and that He acted according to His Father's will, mind, or design; whereas the orthodox held that our Lord was Himself the very will, mind, design, Word, and Wisdom of God, and God acted according to His own Mind or Design in acting by Him. Hence, while in the shorter edition Ignatius says to the Ephesians, c. 3, "I exhort you to concur in the mind of God; for Jesus, our inseparable Life, is the Father's Mind," he is made to say in the longer, "for Jesus Christ does all things *according to the* mind of the Father."

4. Another Arianism in the longer Epistles is derived from Philo and the Platonists; viz., that our Lord is a priest, not as incarnate, but as the Word of God before all ages. In *Magn.*, c. 4, He is spoken of as "the true and first Bishop, and the only Priest *by nature;*" whereas Catholics hold that He is Priest by office, as Mediator. So again, *ibid.*, c. 7. "Come together as one man to the Temple of God, as for one Altar, for one Jesus Christ, the *High Priest of the Ingenerate God.*" And in *Smyrn.*, c. 9, "Christ Jesus, the First-begotten, and the Father's only Priest *by nature.*"

5. Another Arianism occurs in *Magn.* 8, where "His Eternal Word" is omitted, and instead of it is inserted "the *generated substance* of a divine energy," words

which, after the Nicene Council, were a denial of the "consubstantial."

6. It was the doctrine of the Arians, Ætius, and Eunomius, A.D. 354, that the Almighty could be perfectly known and comprehended by us. "God knows not His own substance," they said, "more than we do. What He knows of it, that you will find without any distinction in us." Now the writer of the longer Epistles makes Ignatius say, " Consider those who are heterodox, how they are peremptory in saying that the Father of the Christ cannot be known."— *Smyrn.*, c. 6, perhaps with an allusion to Acts xvii. 23.

7. Lastly, in the longer edition there seems to be a denial of our Lord's human soul, another doctrine of Arianism. The writer says, "He assumed a body."— *Trall.*, c. 9. "Truly Mary gave birth to a body, which had God for its inhabitant."—*Ibid.*, c. 10. "He made Himself a body of the seed of the Virgin."—*Ibid.*, vid. also *Smyrn.*, c. 2, and *Phil.*, c. 6, where the writer seems to appropriate to himself the proposition "The God Word dwells in a human body, He the Word being in it, as a soul embodied, because that God, and not a human soul, dwells in it."

I should not have thought it necessary thus formally to draw out the proof of what seems to me so plain on the surface of the longer Epistles, had not great authorities disputed the fact. Such is Cardinal Baronius, who living before the discovery of the shorter Epistles, believed that the longer were written by St. Ignatius. "Ignatii esse germanas, easdemque *sincerissimas*, nemo jure potest dubitare." Still more remarkable is the judgment of Father Morinus, who, writing after the discovery of the shorter edition, not only doubts of its genuineness (which is quite explicable), but actually prefers the larger to it; "Antiqua Ignatiarum Epistolarum editio," he says, "genuinum textum nobis exhibet, nova vero mancum et interpolatum."—*Apud Pearson.* There are cases where conclusions are imperious, and the most authoritative denial of them goes for nothing; such is that of the spuriousness of the longer edition.

But if, as is very clear, the longer edition is the work of Arian hands, we can determine at once its date. Arianism, more than other great heresies, is circumscribed and known in its duration. It had a hold upon the Eastern Church and the Greek language from the beginning to the end of the fourth century. It is not known there, in idea or in phraseology, before the second decade of that century, and it came to an end with the end of it. The longer Epistles then are the production of that century; and probably about the year 354,[1] for then it was, according to Athanasius, that the Arians began to appeal to the Fathers, (note on the author's "Arians," i., 3 fin.). The shorter Epistles therefore were in existence in the middle of the fourth century, and were received, at least in some places, as the genuine work of St. Ignatius, that is, received as such only fourteen years after the death

---

[1] In the title of the longer Epistles, Ignatius is called Bishop of "Antioch *Theopolis.*" As this title was given to Antioch under the reign of Justinian, the existing MS. of the longer Epistles must have been made from a copy not earlier than that date.

of Eusebius. They easily might be, and perhaps were, superseded by the longer, in the course of time, in centuries during which criticism was unknown as a science, and the peculiarities of a dead heresy forgotten.

6.

There are good reasons then for considering that the short Epistles, substantially as we have them, were extant, and received as genuine, at least in the first half of the fourth century. This I have argued from the testimony borne to them by the paraphrastic edition of them which was made in the middle of it; now let us see whether any other testimony is producible in their behalf.

Eusebius, writing in the first years of the fourth century, enumerates Ignatius's seven Epistles, and quotes passages from them. He seems to have known them well; and those which he knew so well, evidently were received by him as genuine, and undoubtedly were genuine, for he was too learned a man to be deceived in this matter. And there was this guarantee of their genuineness, special to them, that upon Ignatius's martyrdom, St. Polycarp collected together those which he could obtain, and sent them to the Church of Philippi, with a letter, still extant, in which he stated what he was doing. Polycarp was martyred in (say) A.D. 166; Eusebius was born about A.D. 264, leaving an interval between the two of about a hundred years for a forgery. Eusebius knew nothing of garbled copies of them. We must reasonably believe then that those Epistles of which he spoke were copies, substantially faithful, of what

Ignatius really wrote and Polycarp edited. Moreover, in that interval references are made to them by Irenæus (A.D. 180), and Origen (A.D. 230), those references being found in the text of the short Epistles. And the question is whether the Epistles which we now have, as they stand in the shorter edition, guaranteed as they are by the longer and interpolated, are those true ones of which Eusebius speaks, and from which Irenæus and Origen quote, or whether in the thirty or forty years between Eusebius and the Arian interpolator, orthodox garblings had been made in the Epistles, and those so skilful as to deceive the interpolator, himself an adept and a judge in forgeries, into the persuasion that the work, which he thought it important to deface with Arianisms, was the genuine work of the primitive martyr. Such a supposition has been actually made and defended; viz., that, as the editor of the longer edition, after (say) 354, encrusted the shorter with Arianisms, so the editor of the shorter had already, before 354, made insertions in favour of orthodoxy, in the original document, such as Eusebius possessed it forty years before, and that the brief Syriac text of the Epistles to the Romans and Ephesians, as lately discovered, is the very and only text, which Eusebius had in his hands, and which Ignatius wrote.

Let this hypothesis be a reserved point, on which I will speak presently; meanwhile, as I am here gathering together the external evidence in favour of the genuineness of the shorter edition, I add, first, that Athanasius, writing in 359, quotes an important passage from the Epistle to the Ephesians, as it stands, not of course in the longer, but neither as in the Syriac (for it is omitted there), but as we now find it in the shorter, without any suspicion of its not being the genuine writing of Ignatius.

Nor is Athanasius the only post-Nicene Father who thus bears witness to the genuineness of the shorter Epistles. Passages are quoted as Ignatius's, by Chrysostom one, by Jerome two, by Theodoret nine; and all are found in the shorter Epistles, none of them agreeing (at least in their doctrinal expressions) with the longer, which those Fathers either did not know of, or simply put aside as one out of various forgeries, of which the Arians had the discredit.

It may be added that Dr. Cureton has published between twenty and thirty extracts from Ignatius's Epistles as in the works of Syrian theologians, all of which are found in the short Epistles, not in the longer, not in the Syriac Epistles.

These Epistles then, substantially such as they are found in their short Medicean and Colbertine form, had possession of the Eastern Church, as if really written by Ignatius, from 359, twenty years after the death of Eusebius; again, the real Epistles of St. Ignatius were extant, and known to ecclesiastical writers from the time of Polycarp to that of Eusebius' history; and the sole question, I repeat, is whether those which were received as genuine from the year 354 or 359, and which we have now, the shorter Epistles, were those genuine ones which Eusebius used in his History A.D. 310, and which Polycarp had edited;—that is, whether there was a substitution or an extensive garbling and depravation of them, in the interest of orthodoxy, in the first half of the fourth century, between 310 and 354 or 359. To this question I now direct my attention.

7.

The question to be answered is this, whether the seven Epistles, as they were found in the shorter edition, and were received as St. Ignatius's by the interpolating Arians in the fourth century, and by Athanasius, Jerome, and Theodoret, are substantially those very Epistles which the holy martyr, going to martyrdom, actually wrote; or, on the other hand, are forged, garbled, and corrupted by the orthodox, and in no true sense his writing. And the obvious mode of answering it, is, as in the case of the longer and Arianised edition, by a reference to the internal characters which the short Epistles present to our notice.

It is not at all easy to succeed in a forgery, or in altering and garbling on a large scale. A man must have much acuteness, much learning, and much wariness to carry through such an enterprise without detection. At least he must be very clever and very ingenious, to be able to maintain the genuineness of a spurious document, against the criticism of a learned and inquisitive age. In such a composition we may be certain there will be blots of some kind or other, doctrinal incongruities, confusion of times or persons, or mis-statement of facts, which extraordinary astuteness cannot altogether guard against, which ordinary sharpness will be sure to detect.

The authors and the champions of supposititious works in ancient times do not seem to have been alive to this;—they were not commonly learned or able men, and in consequence their detection at the present time is easy. Nor, at first sight, is there any reason why the interpolator of these shorter Epistles, if they are interpolated, should be better provided for his task than his fellows. The works, for instance, attributed to the Areopagite, have been rightly rejected as spurious, not to say heretical, in spite of the sanction of ages, as soon as a sufficient knowledge of theology was brought to bear upon them. So again as regards certain works attributed to Dionysius of Alexandria, to Hippolytus, and to Methodius; these have been received as genuine by great divines, but that was only till the history of dogma and of the rites and discipline of the Church was properly studied. Let us see then how much can be brought from the learning of this day against the short Epistles, as they are contained in the Medicean and Colbertine MSS.

It has been imagined, as I have said, that, as interpolations in an Arian sense were made during the Arian controversy, by the Arian party, so prior interpolations were made by the orthodox during the same controversy on the side of orthodoxy, and that the shorter Epistles represent these orthodox corrections and additions. Moreover, this was done, as it would seem, in the interval between Eusebius and the Arian interpolators, so that up to Eusebius (say) A.D. 310 the real Ignatius would have held his ground, and that after (say) A.D. 354 or 359 down to the present time, the world has had nothing better than first the orthodox or Nicene Ignatius, and then the Arian Ignatius following close upon the orthodox, neither of them the real Ignatius. Let us see if this hypothesis will stand.

1. We know the Arian Ignatius, by the definite Arianisms which are found in the longer edition, as I have shown above, such as "before all worlds," "ingenerate," "God of the universe," etc.; now are there any parallel (what may be called) Athanasianisms in the shorter edition, which may be evidence of an orthodoxised Ignatius? I will venture to say there are none at all. The chief mark of Nicene orthodoxy is the word "consubstantial" (homoüsion); does this term occur in the shorter Epistles? It does occur in the spurious Areopagite, in the spurious Dionysius of Alexandria, in the spurious Methodius; it does not occur in these shorter Epistles. Another Nicene symbol is "from the substance;" the Arians introduce "a generated substance" into the longer Epistles, but "from the substance" is not in the shorter. Another mark of the Nicene era is the use of the word hypostasis, or Person; this again is found in the pseudo-Areopagite, but not in the shorter Epistles. That *animus* then of partisanship, which we find in the language of the longer Epistles on the Arian side, is wanting in the shorter Epistles in favour of orthodoxy.

2. What was still more likely than the introduction of the orthodox symbols, was some expressions in reprobation, direct or indirect, of the formal Arian symbols

condemned in the creed of Nicæa; but not a word is to be found levelled against "those poisonous shoots of the evil one," as a forger might have made Ignatius say, who assert that the Son of God was "out of nothing," or "of another substance not divine," or "once He was not," or "was of an alterable nature." Just those heresies are mentioned which were in existence at the end of the first century, and no other. It was playing with edged tools in an impostor thus to manipulate heresies, at a day when little or anything was known of the history of heresies, their authors, tenets, localities, fortunes, and duration; he might escape detection in the fourth century, but he would not escape detection now, if there was anything to detect.

3. One passage indeed there is, anti-Arian in doctrine, though not in its phraseology, which furnishes a good instance of the maxim "exceptio probat regulam." A serious controversy has long been carried on upon the words "not proceeding from Silence (*Sige*)" in the shorter edition in *Magn.*, c. 8, predicated of "the Eternal Word" by the writer, in the sense that He was not like human voices, an utterance breaking in upon a state of stillness, but one that had no beginning. The larger edition simply leaves the passage out, and naturally, for its doctrine is inconsistent with Arianism; but its presence in the shorter has been noted as a sign that, whereas *Sige* was one of the Valentinian Æons, therefore the author wrote after the rise of Valentinus, that is, after the date of Ignatius. This was the only point discoverable in the text of the shorter Epistles which really had to be reconciled with the mainte-

nance of their genuineness. "Illud non negaverim," says Voss, "si locus hic sit sanus, et hæc desumpta sint ex hæresi Valentinianâ, actum videri de Epistolis Ignatianis." Accordingly Pearson devotes as many as forty-six folio columns of his great work to solve the apparent difficulty, at the end of which he says, "Quatuor assertiones attuli, omnes exploratæ veritatis, ita tamen comparatæ, ut si vel una earum vera sit, ea unica omnem argumenti adversariorum vim elidat".—P. 390. And after Pearson, Bull devotes another series of twenty columns to complete the explanation. In our time the difficulty has solved itself; and consistently with the arguments of those Anglican divines. From the newly discovered work on Heresies, commonly attributed to Hippolytus, we find that, before Valentinus, the doctrine of *Sige* was taught by Simon Magus and Menander, in the first century, that is, prior to the date when St. Ignatius wrote his Epistles. Accordingly, M. Bunsen, a fierce adversary, of course, of the genuineness of the shorter Epistles, says candidly, "We must certainly ascribe to pure Simonianism, that is, to the Simonian heresy unmixed with Valentinianism, the system of Gnostic evolutions, of which *Sige*, Silence, is a primitive element. . . . Ignatius, who certainly may have read 'the Great Announcement' [of Menander] as well as he read St. John, might have alluded to it in a letter to the Magnesians, if he ever wrote it."—*Hippol.*, vol. i., p. 356.

4. It may be objected that the strong and abrupt assertions of our Lord's divinity have the appearance of being directed against Arianism; as when the writer speaks of

"the Blood of God" (*Eph.* c. 1, *Rom.* c. 7), and of "Jesus Christ our God, conceived in the womb of Mary" (*ibid.* c. 18, *Smyrn.* c. 1-10, *Rom. init.* c. 3). But it must be recollected that the Arians freely gave our Lord the divine name and authority, and made a boast of doing so, as we see by the longer Epistles (vid. *Eph.* 7, 19, *Trall.* 9, *Rom. init.* 6, *Phil.* c. 6, *Smyrn.* c. 3, *Pol.* c. 3, etc.); it is la Croze's notion that even "theotocos" is of Arian origin; while doing this they reserved the high prerogatives of being "God of the Universe," "Ingenerate," "Self-existing," "Eternal," to the Father. As to the abruptness, or harshness, of the language in which the shorter Epistles ascribe divinity to our Lord, it is only what occurs again and again in Scripture, if Middleton's canons are well founded—vid. Eph. v. 5, 2 Thess. i. 12, Tit. ii. 13, 2 Pet. i. 1, Jud. 4.

5. So much on the theology of the shorter Epistles; as to the emphatic language in which they enforce the episcopal rule, startling as it is at first sight, it admits of an easy explanation. It must be recollected that Ignatius witnessed and took part in the establishment of diocesan Episcopacy, and in consequence it is as natural that his letters should be full of it at the date when they were written, as that Pastorals now should insist on the Immaculate Conception, or protest against mixed education. It was the subject of the day. Hitherto Bishops often lived in community, the Apostles exercising a jurisdiction over the whole Church. As time went on, local jurisdiction came into use. In his last years St. Paul placed local ordinaries in Crete and Ephesus, and

St. John in other cities of Asia Minor, if the seven Angels of the Churches in the Apocalypse are Bishops. He too was now gone, and doubtless the loss of an apostolic presence would at first be grieviously felt in the neighbourhoods which had hitherto been blessed with it. The Greek cities of Asia Minor, in consequence, would be the very places above others where a reactionary disorder was most likely to show itself. Even he, at the end of life, had found the *prestige* of his name insufficient to cope with the self-will of Diotrephes. He left to his successors a double conflict; as against the Ebionite and Gnostic heretics in defence of the Incarnation, so against the opponents of ecclesiastical discipline. And of these two tasks the latter was the more arduous, for it was not so much the enforcement of a tradition, as the carrying out of a development. Hence it is that Ignatius appeals to his own authority, and claims a divine mission in enforcing the claims of the hierarchy. "I cried out, while I was with you," he writes to the Philadelphians, "I spake with a loud voice, 'Give heed to the Bishop, to the Presbytery, and the Deacons.' Now some suspected that I spoke this as knowing beforehand the division of some. But He is my witness, for whom I am in bonds, that I knew it not from flesh of man; but the Spirit proclaimed, saying, 'Apart from the Bishop do nothing,'" etc.—*Phil.*, c. 7.

Here the well-known words of St. Jerome are in point. "Presbyter and Bishop," he says, "are the same; and ere yet, at the instigation of the devil, there were parties in religion, and it was said among the people,

'I am of Paul, and I of Apollos, and I of Cephas,' the Church was governed by the common counsel of Presbyters; but when each began to account his converts as his own people, and not Christ's, then it was decreed through the whole world that one of the Presbyters should be elected and put over the rest, to whom the whole care of the Church should belong, and that thus the elements of schism should be removed."[1]

6. While speaking of the internal character of the shorter Epistles, I will make an additional remark on a point of some obscurity, though on the whole corroborative of their genuineness. Ignatius writes in them to six Churches—five of them are Eastern. He warns each of them against heretics, and exhorts them to unity; sometimes even he mentions by name the Bishop of the Church which he is addressing, and in every case commends him to its obedience. But in the case of the sixth, the Roman Church, he does nothing of the kind. He does not say a word about heresy or schism; he does not refer to its Bishop, or take him (as it were) under his wing. He hardly does more than ask the Romans for their prayers, and he entreats them not to interpose and to prevent his martyrdom. Instead of exhorting them, as he does the other Churches, he says, "I make no commands to *you*, as though *I* were Peter and Paul;" and he salutes them as "the Church, which has in dignity the first seat of the city of the Romans, all-godly, all-gracious, all-blessed," etc., passages which

---

[1] Ad Tit. i. 5.

remind us of St. Irenæus's well-known reference to the "greatest, most ancient, most conspicuous Church founded and constituted at Rome by the two most glorious Apostles Peter and Paul," and to its "potentior" or "potior" "principalitas".

How is all this to be accounted for? We evidently find the writer in a different position of mind, when he addresses the Roman Church, from that in which he addresses others. Would any one so write in the fourth century? At that time there were serious jealousies between Rome and the East, the continuation of those which show themselves in earlier centuries in the history of Polycrates, Firmilian, and Dionysius. A partisan of Rome in the fourth century would not have been so indirect and implicit in his deference to that Church, but would have introduced the doctrine of Roman supremacy with the energy of the contemporary Popes. And an Oriental, however orthodox, would together with St. Basil have been sore at their supercilious indifference, or, with St. Meletius, at their interference in the dioceses of Asia.

8.

So much at first sight; Pearson, however, reviews the internal characters of the shorter Epistles more carefully, and I will translate some of his remarks.

"It is simply incredible," he says, "that an impostor, who lived at the end of the third or beginning of the fourth century, should forge Epistles for Ignatius, without betraying himself by some peculiarity or other of his own age, without allusion to any post-Ignatian rite whatever, or later heresy, or any teaching alien to the mind of the Apostles, or any doctrine borrowed from the schools of Plato, which others were so prompt in professing, or any departure from primitive simplicity—Epistles, on the contrary, which correspond so uniformly to what might be expected of so great a martyr, and which bring out so vividly the tokens of his spiritual gifts. I say emphatically, that there is nothing discoverable in these Epistles, known to Eusebius, which savours of the age suggested by Daillé, or by Blondel, or by Salmasius; nothing of the then existing heresies, nothing of manners or institutions of Christians, then materially changed from what they had been, or of later rites, or ecclesiastical usages, such as led to the detection of the pretended Areopagite. On the contrary, everything in them is strictly conformable to the age immediately following the Apostolic, and very different from an impostor's age. . . . .

"As to Bishops, he calls them simply by the name of their office or order; he gives them no extraordinary title; not that of 'high priests,' 'priests,' or 'rulers,' as they were afterwards called. (The 'Priests' in the Epistle to the Philadelphians are, he says, Jewish priests, p. 414.) Nor does Ignatius make mention of episcopal throne, of ordination, election, or succession, of prerogatives of particular sees, or of appeal to any particular Church to the exclusion of other Churches, or of precepts of obedience, except indeed such as were necessary to avoid schism and to preserve unity. He does not lower

Presbyters, but always associates them with Bishops, declares their dignity and authority, and gives them the most honourable titles. He touches upon no heresies, but those of Ebion and the Docetæ, which, as Theodoret, Jerome, and Epiphanius teach us, were actually prevalent in Asia in Ignatius's day. . . . .

" He teaches nothing about festivals, or stated times of fasting, or of the mode of celebrating Easter, or of the observance of Pentecost or the Sabbath, or of any other rite of which the antiquity is controverted. Such are of frequent occurrence both in the interpolated Epistles, and in the other spurious ones—not in these. Moreover, he speaks of gifts as then ordinarily found in the Church, and of the Holy Ghost speaking sometimes to the writer, which later writers are not accustomed to do. He is very sparing in his quotations from Scripture. He everywhere follows St. Paul's Epistles, which were from the first freely received by all the Churches; but he quotes the Gospels rarely, which were received and discriminated from spurious writings at a later date, while in the second and third century they were in common use among ecclesiastical writers.

" Moreover, the style of these Epistles is one of the most striking evidences of their primitive origin. There is nothing from foreign sources, from Gentile learning; whereas later writers introduced into Christian teaching the sentiments, not to say the dogmas, of the Greeks."— *Vind. Ign.*, pp. 358-360,

9.

Such being the general state of the evidence, external and internal, in behalf of the genuineness of the shorter or Medicean, Greek text of St. Ignatius's Epistles, we are brought at length to the question which has led to the foregoing remarks, and which, after those remarks, is not difficult to determine; viz., how far that text is compromised by the still shorter Syriac text, which has been lately found, of three out of the seven Epistles which were known to Eusebius. I answer as follows:

1. Three out of the seven Epistles have been found among the Nitrian MSS.—viz., in MS. ii. (Cureton) those to Polycarp, to the Romans, and to the Ephesians; again in MS. i. the Epistle to Polycarp. Now we cannot fairly argue, as some have argued, from the fact of there being in MS. ii. only three Epistles, that therefore the remaining four named by Eusebius, (to the Magnesians, to the Trallians, to the Smyrnæans, and to the Philadelphians,) were not written by Ignatius, or have been lost, and that the Medicean Greek of them is spurious; for, if the Medicean MS. is not to be trusted because it contains four Epistles which are not in the Nitrian MS. ii., then the Nitrian MS. ii. is not to be trusted, because it contains two Epistles which are not in the Nitrian MS. i. Ignatius's Epistles then remain seven as far as the Nitrian MSS. are concerned, for the simple reason that those MSS. cannot destroy the authority of the Medicean on that point, without at the same time implicitly destroying their own,

2. Again: there are two copies in the Syriac of the Epistle to Polycarp, and they agree together in their text. This agreement of two MSS. may seem formidable to the solitary Medicean Greek;—so it would be supposing the Greek materially differed from them; but it so happens that its text, except in a few words, is identical with the text of the Syriac. Thus, in the only instance in which the Syriac text seems to have authority as being that of two independent MSS., it does but confirm the trustworthiness of the Medicean Greek.

3. Further: in those cases, on the other hand, in which the Syriac edition differs from the Greek, viz., as regards the Epistles to the Romans and Ephesians, in which it omits passages contained in the Greek, in those cases it differs also from other Syriac editions, not indeed extant, or known to be extant, but which appear once to have existed, because extracts are made from them by writers whose works are contained in Syriac in these same Nitrian MSS. These writers, viz., Severus, Timotheus, and others, quote Ignatius as he stands in the Medicean Greek, not as in the Nitrian Syriac. For instance, the celebrated passage in *Ephes.* c. 7: "There is one Physician," as is quoted above, p. 108, which is garbled in the longer or Arian Epistles, pp. 108, 109, and omitted in the Syriac, is found, just as in the Medicean MS., in the Monophysite work, in MS. vi., and in the work against Julian, MS. viii., and in MS. ix. Again, the striking passage from the same Epistle, contained in the Medicean, "Our God, Jesus the Christ," etc., c. 18, vid. supr. p. 111, which is omitted in the Nitrian text, is

contained in the MS. v. Again: "Suffer me to copy the Passion of my God," contained in the Medicean (*Rom.* c. 6), omitted in the Nitrian, is quoted by Severus in MS. i., by Timotheus in MS. v., and by the anonymous writer in MS. vii. And further: in these and other Syriac MSS., as was implied above, p. 117, passages are quoted from the Epistles to the Magnesians, Trallians, Smyrnæans, and Philadelphians, showing that all seven, and (as far as the quotations go) all of them as in the Medicean text, must have been at one time extant in Syriac, perhaps are extant still, though, as yet, only three have been discovered in that language.

4. Moreover, as was said above, Athanasius, Jerome, and Theodoret, as well as the above Monophysite writers in Syriac, when they quote Ignatius, quote him as we read him in the Medicean Greek; instead of favouring the Nitrian version of him.

5. Nor were the Arians acquainted with the Nitrian Ignatius any better than Athanasius and the other Catholics, or than Severus, Timotheus, and the Monophysites;—else why did not the interpolator use the Nitrian? Why the Medicean? He creates for himself a superfluous difficulty, in selecting the Medicean text for the basis of his edition. It would have been a far easier task to garble the Nitrian text, which has less specially doctrinal in it, than to alter and deform the Medicean, which has much; yet he follows the Medicean.

6. Moreover, Eusebius and Jerome both inform us, that Ignatius wrote his Epistles to warn his brethren "against the heresies, which were springing up and prevailing."—

Eus. Hist. iii. 36. Now there is hardly one allusion to false doctrine in the Syriac; whereas there is much on the subject in the Medicean. The Syriac text then was not the same as that which Eusebius and Jerome knew; on the other hand, the Medicean does answer to it.

7. Such then is at present the position of the Nitrian MSS. of St. Ignatius. They are without history, without vouchers, without location, without correlations; they do not tell their own tale, and there is no one to tell their tale for them.

10.

If, under the circumstances, I am called to do so hypothetically, I should observe as follows:—Nothing, as we all know, is more common in literature, than for an author to introduce into his work large extracts from the works of others. This is the very characteristic of literary history, as we see in Athenæus, Eusebius, and Photius in ancient times, and in Assemanni's Bibliotheca Orientalis, or Bayle's Dictionary in modern. Such works not only embody large fragments of former writers, but often are the very instruments by which those fragments are conveyed and authenticated to later times. Sometimes these are appended to some abstract of the whole to which they belong; sometimes they are such as to hang together as a whole; sometimes they have with them the opening prefaces or salutations and the formal terminations which belong to them. Then, as time goes on, if it is worth while, those passages which are ascribed to one and the same author are brought together from the various works in which they have been preserved, and are edited as his "opera quæ supersunt." Lectionaries and Catenas are similar receptacles of such large portions of ancient works. Such again in modern times are those selections, which are commonly entitled the "spirit," or the "beauties," the "wit and wisdom" of some popular or valuable writer. Sometimes, on the other hand, such collections are fortuitous. Before the use of printing, the industrious transcriber went on copying whatever came to hand, not on any logical principle, but in order anyhow to preserve what otherwise would be lost. Thus No. ii. of these Nitrian MSS. begins with an anonymous fragment of a letter of consolation on the death of a child,—then come the three fragmentary Epistles of St. Ignatius,—and afterwards a letter of St. Gregory Nazianzen, sermons of Mar Jacob, and other writings.

This being borne in mind, it is not unnatural to conjecture that the Epistles to the Romans and Ephesians in the extant MS. were taken as they stood in some lectionary or other collection of ecclesiastical authors Their headings were preserved on principle, in the books from which they were copied; as now in the Catholic Church, though only small portions of Prophets and Apostles are found in the Breviary, never are the titles and opening words omitted, whether in the Ordo de Tempore itself, or in its actual recitation.

In like manner, though Eusebius does not extract the whole of the celebrated Letter of the Gallic Churches concerning their martyrs in A.D. 177, still he gives the formal heading. And so in his quotation from the work of Apollinaris against the Cataphrygians, and from the Letter of the Antiochene Council against Paul of Samosata, *Hist.*, v. i. 16, vii. 30. Thus it is that I would account for the preservation of the initial salutations in the Nitrian text of Ignatius. As to the absence of any decided internal indications of its fragmentary character, this might be admitted to be a difficulty, were not the holy Bishop's style abrupt and sententious in the Medicean also; and it is scarcely possible to say what is completeness and what is not, in compositions which are neither argumentative nor narrative in their character.

Pearson's proof then of the genuineness of the Medicean text of St. Ignatius's Epistles does not seem to me to be affected by the discovery in our day of the Nitrian MSS. In saying this, of course I am contending, as Pearson contended, for its substantial genuineness, not for the fidelity of every word or clause in it.

POSTSCRIPT.

The above remarks upon the genuineness of the Ignatian Epistles have been drawn up from notes which I made as long ago as the year 1828, except, of course, the first and last portions, which are on the subject of the Syriac text of the three which were published in 1845 by Dr. Cureton.

Since finishing them for the press, I have read the observations on Dr. Cureton's discovery by the learned Dr.

Hefele, now Bishop of Rotenburg, in the Prolegomena to his edition of the Apostolical Fathers.

He confirms what I have myself suggested in explanation of the Syriac text, as it stands in the Nitrian MSS., maintaining it to be "non nisi *epitomen* Ignatiarum epistòlarum à monacho quodam Syriaco in proprios usus pios seu asceticos confectam."—lxi. Also, in direct opposition to Dr. Cureton, he insists that the continuity of context is less close in the Syriac than in the Greek, referring in proof to as many as thirteen passages in the three Epistles. The apparent argument from Dr. Cureton's new (third) MS. he meets by considering it of one family with the former two. He refers, moreover, to an Armenian version published by Dr. Petermann in 1849, which on the whole agrees with the Medicean, but was made, as the latter considers, from the true Syriac, not a fragmentary edition, such as Dr. Cureton's, but from a translation of the whole and complete Greek, such as the Medicean represents. The learned writers Denzinger and Uhlhorn, the latter a Lutheran, have written powerfully on the same side.

III.

CAUSES OF THE RISE AND SUCCESSES OF ARIANISM.

(February, 1872.)

CAUSES OF ARIANISM.

SECT.		PAGE
1.	Circumstances of the time	141
2.	Tradition of the Dogma of the Holy Trinity	149
3.	The Tradition how far complete	158
4.	The Tradition how far incomplete	164
5.	First, the Principatus of the Father	167
6.	Its uses in spite of its abuse	180
7.	Secondly, the Syncatabasis of the Son	192
8.	The Temporal Procession	196
9.	The Primogenitus	199
10.	Unadvisable terms or phrases on the subject	208
11.	Thirdly, the Temporal Gennesis	227
12.	The Alexandrian School	237
13.	The Asiatic Writers	242
14.	The Western Writers	265
15.	Conclusion	298

CAUSES OF THE RISE AND SUCCESSES OF ARIANISM.

§ I. CIRCUMSTANCES OF THE TIME FAVOURABLE TO THE SUCCESS OF THE HERESY.

ON reading the history of Arianism the question naturally suggests itself how it came to start into existence so suddenly, and to spread with such rapidity. And a sadder reflection occurs to the Catholic student, as if the Christian body, so long and variously tried by persecution, deserved or promised better, than that its new prosperity should be marred by so deadly a heresy, and that, in every part of the *orbis terrarum*, conterminously with the Church herself. It was not so with other heresies; Sabellianism, Novatianism, and Pelagianism were at least as plausible systems of doctrine, and had as able teachers; but they had no great historical career, as Arianism had. In "The Arians of the Fourth Century" I did not attempt any solution of this difficulty, though I was not ignorant of the works of Mosheim and other learned Germans, who had taken the subject in hand. Here I propose to inquire into it; and, in doing so, I shall at the same time be virtually satisfying an engagement, to which I pledged myself long ago, and which I have never been able to fulfil, viz., to draw up some sort of introduction to the Treatises of Athanasius which I translated for the Oxford Library of the Fathers, and in the course of which the Four Dissertations occur in English, with which I have commenced my present Volume. I shall not be saying much that has not been said before, but I shall be saying it in my own way.

Now first of all, before entering upon the real doctrinal difficulty, let it be observed, that/the long and stubborn struggle in the Empire for and against Arianism, which is so deplorable a phenomenon in the midst of the contemporaneous triumph of Christianity over Paganism, is nothing less than one passage in the history of the perpetual conflict, which ever has been waged, and which ever will be waged, between the Church and the secular power; and was that particular stage of it, which followed in natural course on the termination of the persecutions— the secular power, when foiled in its efforts to subdue the Church from without, next attempting, by entering her pale, to master her from within. It was a new thing in Greece and Rome that religion should be independent of state authority, and the same principle of Government which led the emperors to denounce Christianity, while they were pagans, led them to dictate to its bishops, when they had become Christians. Accordingly, a second conflict was inevitable, whatever might be the shape which it assumed, or the issue upon which it turned. In any case it would be fierce and world-wide.

Next, that it would be a doctrinal controversy, and on one or other of the highest points of theology, nay, and relating to the Object of worship, was probable from the history of the preceding centuries. Christianity was not a mere sentiment or opinion; it was a faith. Its Founder said that He came "to bear witness to the Truth." St. Paul bids us "keep the deposit;" and St. John cautions us against the "spirit of error." The force of these announcements and warnings is illustrated in Christian history from the date of the Apostles to that of Athanasius:—all along there had been doctrinal controversies, especially concerning the Divine Nature, followed up by divisions, impeachments, appeals, trials, and anathemas. Arianism was but the continuation of a series; and, if it was more formidable and eventful than Paulinism or Montanism, this was because it had so large a field to act upon, and so few external hindrances to impede its course. Had the empire become Christian in the time of Noetus, he too might have filled the world with the exploits of his own heresy, as Arius did afterwards.

It was natural then that the first age of the emancipated Church, even more than the ages that followed, should be a time of eager, perilous, and wide-spread controversy; nor need such a phenomenon really perplex us, as if the brave martyrs and confessors of the Dioclesian era had the evil destiny of giving birth to a generation of misbelievers; for the Arianism of the fourth century was not a popular heresy.[1] The laity, as a whole, revolted from it in every part of Christendom. It was an epidemic of the schools and of theologians, and to them it was mainly confined. It did not spread among the parish priests and their flocks, or the great body of the monks; though, as time went on, it gained a certain portion of some of the larger towns, and some monastic communities. The classes which had furnished martyrs in the persecutions were in no sense the seat of the heresy.

Nor indeed were all the theological schools involved in this spiritual malady; it was the more intellectual of them which were recipients of its poison. Western Christendom, at that early date, was far behind the East in acuteness and learning. Of course there were schools in Gaul, Rome, and Carthage, not to mention other places; Tertullian and Hippolytus are the evidence of it; but, whatever was the intellectual proficiency of individuals belonging to these in the fourth century, it was not at hand to save Liberius from the imputation of subscribing a Semi-Arian confession, nor was it any aid to his Legates at the Council of Arles; and the incapacity, which made so many Western bishops at Ariminum unwilling victims of the heresy, would also save them from being, had they been so inclined, its intelligent and active propagators.

It was in the East especially, and, to speak more distinctly, in Asia, that its head-quarters were to be found; and Asia, with Antioch as its metropolis, had a culture

---

[1] Vide Appendix, Note 5, to "The Arians of the Fourth Century," ed. 3.

which the other parts of Christendom had not. Alexandria, which had so firm a tradition and grasp of orthodoxy, was but one city situated at the extremity of the Empire, commanding only the narrow valley of the Nile, and cut off by deserts and by the broad sea from the rest of the Roman world. Antioch, on the contrary, was but the chief of many flourishing seats of learning, and, by means of the public roads, was in easy communication with the whole of Syria, Palestine, and Asia Minor, not to speak of Thrace and Greece. Moreover, its separate Churches, enjoying an autonomy which the Egyptian Churches had not, exercised a freedom of thought, and had a practice in controversy, peculiar to themselves; and, preferring the study of the literal to that of the allegorical sense of scripture, were indisposed to submit either to the authorities or to the proofs on which orthodoxy, such as the Alexandrian, rested the sacred doctrine in dispute. The schools of Asia, then, when once they became advocates of a theological opinion, had far larger resources for its propagation than Gaul or Africa, and far greater influence than Egypt.

Nor was this all; they managed to create for themselves a special controversial advantage, when they undertook the cause of Arius against Egypt, the only zealous champion of orthodoxy. They threw their main force, not against the orthodox doctrine which was the real subject in dispute, but against the symbol of the *homoüsion*, and the conduct of Athanasius. They made the controversy appear a mere question of ecclesiastical expedience, and of ecclesiastical persons and parties. Thus they represented it to the Catholic West. What did the West know about either the one or the other? All they knew was that they had hardly begun to enjoy the peace for which they had so long been praying, when suddenly they were all at war again. When then they seemed to side with the Eusebian party, they were in truth doing little more than making Athanasius a convenient scapegoat for ridding themselves of troubles which they saw no other way out of, not dreaming of tampering with a prime article of the Creed, but expressing their disapprobation of one whom they were taught to believe a restless, violent, party-spirited man, and of his arbitrary formula.

And of this view there might be many honest supporters in the East as well as in the West; for it carried them back to an historical question interesting to themselves personally. The question of the *homoüsion* was not to them new; it was a party question between Antioch and Alexandria. Its adoption at Nicæa was the reversal of an act of the forefathers of the Asiatics in the great Council of Antioch sixty years before. It had in that Council been proposed as a test of orthodoxy, and put aside. It had been put aside, although already used by Alexandrian theologians. But at Nicæa, where the Alexandrian Athanasius conducted the controversy, it had been recalled, it had been definitely adopted. Why was a term to be had in honour in 325, which had been put aside in 264 or 272 as *male sonans* and dangerous? We cannot be surprised then that the *homoüsion*, which perplexed the Western bishops, should have irritated the Orientals; the only wonder is, that East and West had concurred in accepting it at Nicæa. The Acts of the Council there held are not extant, and we are left to determine this point by conjecture. Perhaps the horror which we know seized its Fathers at hearing the blasphemies of Arius, induced them to accept what they found to be the only effectual test against him and his party. Then, after the Council, there would be a reaction in their view of the matter, and the Arians, being a sharp-witted set, would not be slow to take advantage of it. And, with reference to such a reaction, it must be borne in mind, that Ecumenical Councils were at that time a novelty in the Church; and that their sovereign authority and the immutability of their decisions were points not familiar to the apprehension of every bishop. This shows itself in the subsequent events of the fourth century,

Also, it would appear that, out of the Eusebian Councils which followed the Nicene, two only, or rather one, actually absolved Arius. Of course I do not say that those various Councils were clear of heterodoxy: how their members came to consent to such heterodoxy is the question, into which I have in the following pages to inquire; but whatever their shortcomings, Arians they certainly were not. The proper Arian party did not show itself in the Councils till thirty years after the Nicene, under the name of Anomœans, Aëtius and Eunomius being its leaders; the Eusebian Councils in the interval were for the most part composed of Semi-Arians.

This then at first sight as to the successes of Arianism in the East and West upon its start in the fourth century: as to the hold which it got upon the Civil Power, we must bear in mind that the bishops had become at that time an order and a magistracy in the state. They were on terms of intimacy with the Emperors, and if in the Asiatic provinces they were infected, as they certainly were, with the heterodox views of the Antiochene school, they would communicate the heresy in turn to the civil authorities. Athanasius had not the like opportunity of indoctrinating those authorities in the truth. When indeed in his exile he was thrown upon the wide world, then he came across both Constans and the junior Constantine, and at once he availed himself of his good fortune by disposing both of them in favour of the orthodox cause. But he had no access to the presence of emperors when he was at home. The Imperial Court took up its abode from time to time in the great cities of the East; in Thessalonica, Constantinople, Nicomedia, Nicæa, Hierapolis, Ancyra, Cæsarea, Antioch:—I do not think it once went to Alexandria. It must be added that to statesmen, lawyers, and military chiefs, who had lately been Pagans, a religious teaching such as Arianism, which was clear and intelligible, was more acceptable than doctrines which described the Divine Being in language, self-contradictory in its letter, and which exacted a belief in truths which were absolutely above their comprehension. The same consideration will account for the Arianism of the converted Goths, Vandals and Lombards.

Now I proceed to the doctrinal inquiry.

§ 2. THE TRADITION OF THE DOGMA OF THE HOLY TRINITY.

It was the doctrine of Arius that our Lord was a pure creature, made out of nothing, liable to fall, the Son of God by adoption not by nature, and called God in Scripture, not as being really such, but only in name. At the same time he would not have denied that the Son and the Holy Ghost were creatures transcendently near to God, and immeasurably distant from the rest of creation.

Now by contrast, how does the teaching of the Fathers who preceded Arius, stand relatively to such a representation of the Christian Creed? Is it such, or how far is it such, as to bear Arius out in so representing it? This is the first point to inquire about.

First of all, the teaching of the Fathers was necessarily directed by the form of Baptism, as given by our Lord Himself to His disciples after His resurrection. To become one of His disciples was, according to His own words, to be baptised "into the Name of the Father, and of the Son, and of the Holy Ghost;" that is, into the profession, into the service, of a Triad. Such was our Lord's injunction: and ever since, before Arianism and after, down to this day, the initial lesson in religion taught to every Christian, on his being made a Christian, is that he thereby belongs to a certain Three, whatever more, or whether anything more, is revealed to us in Christianity about that Three,

The doctrine then of a Supreme Triad is the elementary truth of Christianity; and accordingly, as might have been expected, its recognition is a sort of key-note, on which centre the thoughts and language of all theologians, from which they start, with which they end.

I propose to show in this Section how the Ante-Nicene Fathers understood this sacred truth, in contrast to the understanding of Arius, availing myself for that purpose of the careful and accurate collection of Testimonies published by Dr. Burton.[1]

1. First, St. Polycarp, Bishop of Smyrna, when at the stake, offered up a prayer to God, which ended thus: "I glorify Thee, through the Eternal High Priest, Jesus Christ, Thy beloved Son ($\pi\alpha\iota\delta\grave{o}\varsigma$), through whom be glory to Thee, with Him in the Holy Ghost, both now and for ever."

Here the Three are mentioned, as in the baptismal form; as many as Three, and no more than Three, with the expression of a still closer association of the Three, one with another, than is signified in that form, viz. as contained in the words, "through," "with," and "in."

2. And this is only one out of several forms of doxology, of the same, or of an earlier date, all connected with the same Triad, and with that Triad only, one of which is attributed to St. Ignatius of Antioch, one to St. Clement of Rome. Also an evening hymn, apparently of the same date, concludes with a doxology to "Father, Son, and Holy Spirit of God," countenancing what I said above, that the

---

[1] Burton's "Theological Works," vol. ii. 1837.

wording of the form of Baptism implied a profession of service to the Sacred Triad in those who were submitted to the rite.

3. And so also the forms of Creed, still extant, of the early centuries. They are all expansions of the baptismal formula, thereby marking that formula to imply, not only worship and service, but faith also, directed towards the Heavenly Three.

4. In like manner St. Justin:—"We worship the Framer of this Universe, and Jesus Christ, our Teacher in these things, having learned that He is the Son of the true God, having Him in the second place, and the Prophetic Spirit in the third rank."

5. Athenagoras. "Who would not be astonished to hear us called atheists, speaking as we do of the Father as God, and the Son as God, and the Holy Ghost; showing both their power ($\delta\acute{u}\nu\alpha\mu\iota\nu$) in unity, and their distinction in order?" In some sense then, he, as believing in one God, must have considered Them One.

Again, expressly:—"The Father and the Son are One: the Son is in the Father, and the Father in the Son, by the unity and power of the Spirit."

Again:—"We speak of God, and of the Son, His Word, and of the Holy Ghost, which are united in power,—the Father, the Son, and the Spirit; for the Son is the Mind, Word, Wisdom of the Father, and the Spirit an off-streaming, as light from fire."

Once more, Athenagoras speaks of "the *knowledge* of God, and of the Word that is from Him, that is, *what* the unity is of the Son ($\pi\alpha\iota\delta\grave{o}\varsigma$) with the Father, *what* the fellowship of the Father with the Son, *what* the Spirit is, *what* the uniting of so many," viz. Three, "and *what* division in their uniting,—the Spirit, the Son ($\pi\alpha\iota\delta\grave{o}\varsigma$), the Father".

In this last passage, Athenagoras justifies our saying that the baptismal form, simple as is its wording, did suggest to the early Christians difficulties and questions, as yet open, and necessitated a theory of doctrine; for it was impossible to go on using words without an insight into their meaning, such as those words in themselves did not supply. Arians would feel this as strongly as Catholics. Next, Athenagoras, in what he says about their meaning, moves in the Catholic direction. He speaks of a *distinction* or *division* in *unity*, as a point to be explained; but, if by unity was meant merely a moral unity, or unity of thought, sentiment, or action, what need was there of any explanation? as if the distinction existing between separate beings could possibly be compromised by such a unity! And, in like manner, a unity, other than moral and seemingly metaphysical, is implied in a former passage, where he speaks of the Son as the Father's " Mind, Word, and Wisdom ".

6. Next, St. Theophilus of Antioch speaks expressly of a " Triad, God, His Word and His Wisdom "; the term " Triad " is also used by Clement of Alexandria, Origen, Hippolytus and Methodius; as "Trinitas" is used by Tertullian and Novatian.

7. St. Irenæus speaks of "the Spirit operating, the Son ministering, and the Father approving," in the salvation of man: of " the Father approving and commanding,

the Son executing and framing, the Spirit supplying nourishment and increase," in man's original formation. He says that "the Father is above all things and the head of Christ; the Word is through all, and the head of the Church; the Spirit is in us all, and is the living water."

8. Clement of Alexandria says, "One is the Father of the Universe, one is the Word of the Universe, and one is the Holy Ghost and the same everywhere." He speaks of "the power of God the Father, the blood of God the Son ($\pi\alpha\iota\delta\grave{o}s$), and the dew of the Holy Ghost."

9. Tertullian says that we should pray not less than three times a day, being "debtors of the Father, Son, and Holy Ghost;" "that all Three are one by unity of substance, and the Unity is developed into a Trinity, Father, Son, and Holy Ghost;" that They are Three, "not in condition, but in degree, not in substance, but in form, not in power, but in aspect; and are of one substance, condition, and power;" that "the Spirit is not from other source (aliunde) than from the Father through the Son;" that "the Spirit is the third from God and the Son, as the fruit from the shrub is third from the root, and the rill from the stream is third from the spring;" that "the words [of Scripture] which are spoken to the Father concerning the Son, or to the Son concerning the Father, or to the Spirit, constitute each Person in His own characteristic [proprietate];" that "we never suffer 'Two Gods' or 'Two Lords' to pass our lips, though the Father is God, the Son is God, and the Holy Ghost is God, and Each is God;" that "Father, Son, and Holy Ghost are undivided

from Each Other;" that "the union of the Father in the Son, and of the Son in the Paraclete, makes Three co-inherents (co-hærentes) the one from the other."

Certainly, if the questions suggested by Athenagoras need an answer, Tertullian has supplied one in bountiful measure. He almost develops the baptismal formula into the Athanasian Creed.

10. St. Hippolytus says, that "even though a man would not, he must necessarily confess God the Father Almighty, and Christ Jesus, God, the Son of God, who became man, to whom the Father has subjected all things except Himself and the Holy Ghost, and that these are thus Three;" that "God's power [or Essence, δύναμις] is one, and as regards that power, God is One, but, as regards the [revealed] Economy the manifestation is triple;" that "we contemplate the Incarnate Word, conceive of the Father through Him, believe in the Son, worship the Holy Ghost."

Again, he says, "I do not say two Gods, but One, and Two Persons, and a Third, the Economy, the grace of the Holy Ghost. The Father is one; there are two Persons, for there is also the Son, and the third is the Holy Ghost." And "We cannot hold one God, unless we really believe in the Father, Son, and Holy Ghost." And "Through the Trinity the Father is glorified; for the Father willed, the Son made, the Holy Ghost manifested." And "The self-existing (ὁ ὤν) Father is above all, the Son through all, and the Holy Ghost in all." And again, "The Jews glorified the Father, but not thankfully, for they did not acknowledge the Son; the disciples knew the Son, but not in the Holy Ghost, and therefore denied Him." Lastly, "To the Son be glory and power with the Father and Holy Ghost, in the Holy Church, both now and for evermore."

11. Origen speaks thus, in the Latin translation, as regards the Son's co-eternity;—what he says will be confirmed, *infr.* p. 165, by a passage preserved to us by Athanasius. "When I speak of the Omnipotence of God, of His invisibility and eternity, my words are lofty; when I speak of the co-eternity of His Only-begotten Son and His other mysteries, my words are lofty; when I discuss the mightiness of the Holy Ghost, my words are lofty:—as to These only is it allowed to us to use lofty words. After these Three, henceforth speak nothing loftily, for all things are mean and low, compared with the loftiness of this Trinity. Let not then your lofty words be many, except concerning Father, Son, and Holy Ghost."

12. St. Cyprian says, "It is written of the Father and the Son and the Holy Ghost, 'And these Three are One.'"

13. St. Gregory Thaumaturgus in his Creed:[1]— "There is One God, Father of the Living Word, ... of an Only-begotten Son: . . Our Lord, Sole from Sole, God from God . . . . and one Holy Ghost, having His being from God, and manifested through the Son to men,

---

[1] For some reason Burton does not quote this testimony, which St. Gregory Nyssen says was preserved in his day in Gregory Thaumaturgus's church, and in his handwriting. Vid. Lumper, t. xiii. p. 287.

the Image of the Son ... in whom is manifested God the Father, who is over all and in all, and God the Son who is through all, a perfect Triad, not separated, nor dissociated, in glory, eternity, and reign."

14. St. Dionysius of Alexandria:—"Neither is the Father estranged from the Son, nor is the Son set apart from the Father; and in Their Hands is the Spirit, who neither of Him who sends nor of Him who conveys can be deprived. How then, while I make use of these Names, can I conceive that they are divided at all or separated from Each Other?" Again: "We expand the Monad into the indivisible Triad, and again we concentrate the completed Triad into the Monad."

15. And Pope St. Dionysius: "We must neither divide the Wonderful and Divine Monad into three divinities, nor destroy the dignity and exceeding greatness of the Lord by thinking Him a creature; but we must have faith in God the Father Almighty, and in Christ Jesus His Son, and in the Holy Ghost." And again he speaks in reprobation of those who "in some sort preach three Gods, dividing the Holy Monad into three hypostases, foreign from each other, and altogether separate; for of necessity with the God of the Universe the Divine Word is one, and in God must the Holy Ghost reside and dwell."

16. And so the Creed ascribed by the Semi-Arians to Lucian their master. Speaking of the baptismal words, he says:—"The Name of the Father is truly Father, and of the Son truly Son, and of the Holy Ghost truly Holy Ghost; the Names not being given without meaning or

effect, but denoting accurately the proper hypostasis, rank, and glory of Each that is named, so that They are Three in hypostasis, but in agreement one."

17. Lastly Eusebius:—" The number Trine was the first to be a type of righteousness by introducing equality: as having a beginning, a middle, and an ending, equal to each other. And these three are an emblem of the hidden, all-holy, sovereign Triad, which, belonging to that Nature which is unoriginate and ingenerate, of all generated substances whatsoever contains the seeds, reasons and causes."—*De Laud. Const.* p. 510.

§ 3. THE EXPLICIT TRADITION OF THE DOGMA ALL BUT COMPLETE.

1. Such being the chain of testimonies in the early centuries concerning the Divine Triad, so far is clear at once, and has to be noted first of all, that it is impossible to view historical Christianity apart from the doctrine of a Trinity. Putting aside the question of the truth or the admissibility of the Arian tenet,—before pronouncing upon Arianism,— so far is undeniable, (as even those have admitted who were the enemies of dogmatic formulas,) that some doctrine or other of a Trinity lies at the very root of the Christian conception of the Supreme Being, and of His worship and service; that, whereas the Object of our faith and devotion is One, still His ineffable Oneness is inseparably associated with the presence of a Triad; that we cannot contemplate the Divine Nature in the light of revelation, without contemplating in connexion with it, Three Powers, Principles, Agents, Manifestations,—or, according to the Catholic dogma, Persons. I have been referring to the principal historical witnesses of the second and third centuries, witnesses summoned from every part of Christendom,— from Rome, Lyons, Carthage, Alexandria, Samaria, Antioch, Smyrna. Faithful to the baptismal form, which indeed by itself is conclusive of the point I am insisting on, they all speak of a Trinity, and, under the same three names used in that form, as their broad view, from first to last, they speak of the special

theistic teaching, which the gospel substituted for the polytheism of the Empire. Three and Three only: nor is there any string of testimonies producible from those early centuries in a contrary sense, though there were individuals, such as Theodotus, Noetus, Sabellius and Paulus, who, differing from each other, differed from the main tradition. The Three Persons are absolutely separated off, as unapproachable, incommunicable, in reference to the created universe, distinct from it in the ideas which They suggest, as the Object of exclusive veneration, a veneration which is equivalent to divine worship. Whether the celebrated passage in St. John's Epistle be genuine or not, it is felicitously descriptive of the Ante-Nicene tradition, when it designates them as the "Three that bear witness in heaven." There is but one passage of an early Father, as far as I know, which is an exception to this rule: I refer to the well-known words of St. Justin, which include under the objects of religious honour, not only the Heavenly Three, but also the good Angels.

2. So much in the first place: next, there is in the foregoing testimonies much more than a recognition of some or other kind of Triad to be associated by us with the idea of the Divine Being. Some of the passages quoted are fuller in their statements than others; but those that say less do not contradict those that say more; their difference from those which are more explicit is only one of defect; they are all consistent with each other, except so far as the Catholic dogma itself of Three in One as now held, may seem self-contradictory, as relating to

truths utterly beyond our comprehension. These passages coalesce and form one whole, and a whole in agreement with the subsequent teaching on the subject of the fourth and fifth centuries; and their doctrine, thus taken as a whole, will be found to contain these four main points:—
(1) Each of the Three Divine Persons is distinct from each; (2) Each is God; (3) One proceeds from Another in succession; (4) Each is in the Other Two. In other words, this primitive ecclesiastical tradition concerning the Divine Being includes the doctrines of the Trinity, of the Unity, of the *Monarchia* or *Principatus*, and of the *Circumincessio* or Co-inherence. To take these four points separately:—

(1) The *Trinitas*, or Divine Triad; viz. that there is a transcendent Three, fulfilling or realising the idea of God. Thus, in the foregoing passages, Theophilus, Origen, and many others use this word "Triad;" Athenagoras speaks of the "division in Their union, and Their distinction in order;" Clement says:—"There is one Father, one Word, one Holy Ghost." Tertullian and Hippolytus speak of "Three Persons;" Gregory of a "Perfect Triad, not separated, nor dissociated, in glory, eternity, and reign;" Dionysius, of our "expanding the Monad into the indivisible Triad."

(2) The *Unitas;* viz., that Each is God, and the One God. Athenagoras says:—"The Father is God, the Son is God, and the Holy Ghost." Clement speaks of "God the Father, God the Son." Tertullian says, "The Father is God, the Son is God, and the Holy Ghost God; Each is God." Gregory that "the Son is All-God (ὅλος) from

All-God;" Dionysius, "We concentrate the completed Triad into the Monad."

(3) The *Monarchia;* that is, that of the Three the Father is emphatically, (and with a singular distinction from the Other Two, as the πηγὴ θεότητος,) spoken of as God. Thus St. Justin and St. Clement speak of Him as the God of the Universe; thus Athenagoras speaks of "God, His Son and Word, and His Spirit;" Irenæus of "God and His Hands;" Theophilus of "God, His Word, and His Wisdom;" and Pope Dionysius of God the Father Almighty, and Christ Jesus His Son, and of the Holy Ghost; as does the Primitive Creed. But, as such enunciations might seem to separate the First from the Second and Third Persons of the Holy Trinity, they are explained by

(4) The *Circumincessio;* or intimate co-inherence of Each Person in the Other Two. Thus Athenagoras:— "The Son is in the Father, and the Father in the Son, by the unity and power of the Spirit;" Tertullian, "Not that we can number Two Gods or Two Lords, although the Father, the Son, and the Holy Ghost, Each is God." And he speaks of their being "Three Co-inherents." The Alexandrian Dionysius says:—"The Father is not divided from the Son, nor the Son apart from the Father, and in their Hands is the Spirit." Pope Dionysius:— "We must not preach Three Gods, dividing the Holy Monad into three hypostases, foreign from each other, and altogether separate: for of necessity with the God of the Universe the Divine Word is One, and in God must the Holy Ghost reside and dwell."

Looking then at the literature of Christianity from the time of St. John to the time of St. Athanasius, as a whole,—as a whole, because proceeding from a whole, that is, from that one great all-encompassing religious association called the Catholic Church, which was found wherever Christianity was found, and represents Christianity historically,—one, however divided by time and place, by reason of the mutual recognition and active intercommunion of its portions, and of their common claims to an apostolical tradition of doctrine, to an absolute agreement together in faith and morals, and to a divine authority to teach and to denounce dissentients,—I say, looking at the Christian literature as a whole, in which what one writer says may be fairly interpreted, explained, and supplemented by what others say, we may reasonably pronounce, that there was during the second and third centuries a profession and teaching concerning the Holy Trinity, not vague and cloudy, but of a certain determinate character:—moreover, that this teaching was to the effect that God was to be worshipped in Three distinct Persons (that is, that there was a divine Triad, of whom severally the personal pronoun could be used), Each of whom was the One Indivisible God, Each dwelt in Each, Each was really distinct from Each, Each was united to Each by definite correlations;—moreover, that such a teaching was contradictory and destructive of the Arian hypothesis, which considered the Son of God, and *à fortiori* the Holy Ghost, to be simply and absolutely creatures of God, who once did not exist, however exalted it might assert them to be in nature and by grace,

So much I take for granted on starting; and then the question follows, which is my proper subject. If the case is as I have stated it, how came it about, that in the face of a tradition of doctrine so strong and so clear, Arianism had such sudden, rapid, and wide-spread successes?

§ 4. THE EXPLICIT TRADITION OF THE DOGMA, LEAVING THREE OPPORTUNITIES TO AN HERETICAL PERVERSION.

I am proposing to answer the question how it was that the heresy of Arius could obtain, as it did, an ascendency in Christendom so sudden, so triumphant, in the face of a universal tradition of doctrine so fatal to the very elements of its teaching; and, in doing so, I must first make an explanation, which will take from the problem a good deal of its difficulty. It was not then Arianism proper, such as I have described it, which had such successes, but that special form of the heresy which was called Semi-Arianism. It was Semi-Arianism which the Eusebian party professed, which their Councils put forth, which the Imperial Court patronised, and into which Liberius and so many bishops of East and West were dragooned or betrayed; a form of error not less un-Christian, but far less revolting than the original heresy. On the other hand, the tradition of East and West, which, as I have shown, was so strong against Arianism, had not the same force, it must be candidly admitted, when directed against the Semi-Arian tenets, being comparatively deficient in its enunciation of those particular points of the Catholic dogma which the Semi-Arians denied. This correction in the description to be given of the antagonist facts, which constitute the phenomenon to be accounted for, is of great importance,—in truth, going far to destroy its paradoxical character.

What Arius professed has been stated above; as to the Semi-Arians, they, with Arius, denied that the Son was the Supreme God, and that He had been from eternity; but they considered Him born of the Divine Substance before all time, and not a creature; and, though not equal to God in nature, as being a Son, and a distinct Being from Him, still ineffably near to Him—the transcendent mirror of His perfections, and the God of the mediatorial kingdom, nay, of the created Universe, as the Vice-gerent of His Father. This is what they maintained;—the more tangible points of their divergence from the Catholic dogma lying in their denial of our Lord's co-equality and co-eternity with the Father. Now it was in these very two points, that the Catholic tradition, as stated above, was weakest, especially as regards the co-eternity.

I do not say that those two points of doctrine, which are necessary to the Catholic dogma of the Holy Trinity, are not also explicity stated by this or that Ante-Nicene Father. For instance, Origen declares distinctly the Son's co-eternity, when he says: "He who dares to say 'Once the Son existed not,' is saying 'Once Wisdom was not;'" and when Tertullian says that "the Father is God, the Son God, and the Holy Ghost God," he implies the co-equality. Doubtless; but still I think I shall be able to show, that not only by simple omissions, but by positive statements, certain Ante-Nicene writers did accidentally give occasion, or at least a shelter, to the Semi-Arianism of the fourth century, and, while showing this, I shall at the same time be able either to exculpate or to excuse those writers, in their involuntary co-operation in a great calamity.

I have to show, then, how this calamity came about; and I shall assign three reasons for it, drawn from the writings of the Fathers of the Ante-Nicene period. The first will be their true doctrine of the *Principatus* of the Father: the second the true doctrine of the *Syncatabasis* or *Condescensio* of the Son; and the third that of the Temporal *Gennesis*.

§ 5. THE FIRST OPPORTUNITY OPENED TO THE HERESY, THE PRINCIPATUS OF THE FATHER.

The *Principatus* of the Father is a great Catholic truth, and was taught in the Church after the Nicene Council as well as before it; but, on the other hand, it might easily be perverted into a shape favourable to Semi-Arianism. This danger is so obvious, that I shall have chiefly to employ myself in this Section in defending the doctrine, not in showing its capability of perversion. Let us consider the place it holds in the Catholic system.

No subject was more constantly and directly before the Christian intellect in the first centuries of the Church than the doctrine of the *Monarchia*.[1] That there was but one First Principle of all things was a fundamental doctrine of all Catholics, orthodox and heterodox alike; and it was the starting-point of heterodox as well as of orthodox speculation. To the orthodox believer, however, it brought with it a perplexity, which it did not occasion to the adherents of those shallow systems which led to heresy. Christianity began its teaching by denouncing polytheism as absurd and wicked; but the retort on the part of the polytheist was obvious :—Christianity taught a Divine Trinity: how was this consistent with its profession of a Monarchy? on the other hand, if there was

---

[1] Vid. references in Suicer *in voc.* and in Forbes's *Instruct. Hist.* i. 18 and 33.

a Divine *Monarchia*, how was not Sabellius right in denying the distinction of Persons in the Divine Essence? or, if not Sabellius, then Arius, who degraded Son and Spirit to the condition of creatures? Polytheists, Sabellians, Arians, it might be objected, had more to say for themselves in this matter than Catholics.

Catholic theologians met this difficulty, both before and after the Nicene Council, by insisting on the unity of origin, which they taught as existing in the Divine Triad, the Son and Spirit having a communicated divinity from the Father, and a personal unity with Him; the Three Persons being internal to the Divine Essence, unlike the polytheism of the Greeks and Romans, the tritheism of Marcion and the Manichees, and the Archical Hypostases of Plotinus. Thus Hippolytus says: "I say, 'Another,' not two Gods, but as light from light, as water from a spring, or a ray from the sun." And Hilary, in the fourth century, confirms him, saying, "The Father does not lose His attribute of being the One God, because the Son also is God, for the Son is God from God, One from One, therefore One God, because God from Himself." *De Trin.* iv. 15. And Athanasius, "We preserve One Origin of Divinity, and not two Origins, whence there is properly a Monarchy." *Orat.* iv. 1.

It was for the same reason that the Father was called God absolutely, while the Second and Third Persons were designated by Their personal names of "the Son," or "the Word," and "the Holy Ghost;" viz. because they are to be regarded, not as separated from, but as inherent in the Father.

In this enunciation of the august Mystery they were supported by the usage of Scripture, and by the nature of the case; since the very notion of a Father carries with it a claim to priority and precedence in the order of our ideas, even when in no other respect he has any superiority over those on whom he has this claim. There is One God then, they would say, "not only because the Three Persons are in one *usia*, or substance (though this reason is good too), but because the Second and Third stand to the First in the relation of derivation, and therefore are included in their Origin as soon as named; so that, in confessing One Father or Origin, we are not omitting, but including, those Persons whom the very name of the One Father or Origin necessarily implies." At the same time it is plain, that this method of viewing the Unity as centred in its Origin, and the *Monarchia* as equivalent to the Monas, might be perverted into a Semi-Arian denial of the proper divinity of Son and Spirit, if ever They were supposed, by reason of Their derivation, to be emanations, and therefore external to the Essence of the Father.

Nor is this all that has to be said upon this point. St. John translates our Lord's words (for the vernacular in which He spoke can only be conjectured), "I and the Father are *one*," by the neuter "Unum;" and he himself, if the passage be his, says: "These Three are one (unum)." In like manner Tertullian says: "They are all one (unum), by unity of substance." Other Fathers say the same. But this use of the neuter had this inconvenience, that it seemed to imply a fourth reality in the Divine Being, over and above the Three Persons, of which the Three Persons partook; as if the Divine Unity were a physical whole; or, if not that, a logical species, which implies Tritheism. This is what the Antiochene Fathers, in the case of Paulus, seem to have feared would follow from the use of the word *homoüsion*, which in consequence they put aside; and we may understand their feeling on the subject, from the harshness with which Eusebius's statement falls upon the ear, when, in the passage quoted above, p. 157, he speaks of the Triad as *attached* or *belonging to* (ἐξηρτημένη) One Divine Nature.

It might seem safer then, as avoiding the chance of misapprehension, to substitute "unus" for "unum," as Augustine has done, and other Fathers, and the Athanasian and other Creeds; "unus" expressing any one or other of the Three Persons, since Each of Them (no matter which of Them is taken) is the One God.[1] But at an earlier date, especially before the Nicene Council, though after it also, the chance of mistake was avoided by contemplating the *usia* or substance of divinity as it resided in the Father, and considering the Person of the Father as symbolical of the unity of substance in the Three, there being no real distinction in fact between the Father's substance and Person;—I say the First Person, and not the Second or Third, both because He had the priority of order as being the Father, and also because the Divine Father was already known to the Jews, not to say to the heathen. Thus, instead of saying "Father, Son, and Spirit, are one

---

[1] Hilary, in the fourth century, refuses to admit "unus;" "ut unum in fide nostra sint uterque, non unus." *De Trin.* i. 17.

substance (unum)," they would say "In one God and Father are the Son and Spirit;" the words "One Father" standing not only for the Person of the Father, but connoting that sole Divine substance which is one with His Person. Thus Pope Dionysius, after insisting on the Divine *Monarchia*, says, "The God of the Universe and the Divine Word are One, and the Holy Ghost must repose and dwell in God; thus in One, as in a summit, I mean the God of the Universe, must the Divine Trinity be gathered up and brought together." Here "the God of the Universe" is not a Fourth, but stands for "the Father," and is equivalent to the One Divine Substance as well as to the First Divine Person, and in Him the Triad of Persons is summed up as One. And thus Eusebius's language of the ἐξηρτημένη τριὰς is by anticipation corrected, not, however, in Augustine's way, by saying that the Three Persons are the "Unus Deus," where "unus" is used indefinitely, but by saying definitely that the Father is the "Unus Deus," with the explanation or understanding that the Son and Spirit are in Him. Thus, Epiphanius, illustrating the more ancient mode of securing the Unity through the *Monarchia*, says, "The Son glorified the Father, that the glory due to the Father might be referred on by the Son to the One Unity." *Hær.* lxix. 53.

I know all this will appear to many men very subtle writing; but they must please to recollect that, when we are treating of matters which we only know in part, our language necessarily seems subtle to those who are determined to know nothing unless they know everything; and that to those who only know Euclid, the reasonings and formulæ of the higher mathematics are so subtle as to be simply unintelligible. The subtlety of inquiry which is demanded by this high theological dogma is the consequence of the fundamental mystery that the Three Persons are Each *really* identical with the One Divine Essence, that is, Each really and entirely God, yet Each *really* distinct from the other.[1] However it is plain that to view the Person of the Father as the same as the Divine Essence, and to refer the Son and the Spirit to Him as the representative of that Divine Essence, was to ascribe a Monarchia or Principatus to the Father in a very emphatic way, and a sort of subordination to the Son and the Spirit, which, scriptural though it was, became a handle to Semi-Arianism, or even a suggestion of it. Therefore, I believe it was that, after the experience of that heresy, instead of Tertullian's "The Three are Unum,' which was inconvenient on the one side, was substituted by St. Augustine, not "The Three are summed up in the First of them," which was inconvenient on the other, but the phrase "The Three are Unus," in which "unus" stands indeterminately for Either of the Three, somewhat in the sense of an *individuum vagum*.

The word "subordination," which I used just now, is a word of Bishop Bull's, and leads me to refer to the chapter of his "Defensio Fidei Nicænæ," in which he treats professedly "De Subordinatione Filii." It is by this aspect of the Sonship that he would account, and

---

[1] "Non omittendum personas tres, etsi invicem *reipsa* distant, *re* tamen idem esse cum essentia, et ab ea *nonnisi ratione* discrepare." Petav. *De. Trin.* iii. 11, 7.

rightly, for various passages in the Ante-Nicene Fathers which have been considered to savour of Semi-Arianism. His explanation of the "subordinatio" is as follows:—

"Naturam perfectionesque divinas Patri Filioque competere et non collateraliter aut co-ordinate, sed subordinate, hoc est, Filium eandem quidem naturam divinam cum Patre communem habere, sed a Patre communicatam, ita scilicet ut Pater solus naturam illam divinam a se habeat, sive a nullo alio, Filius autem a Patre." Hence, "Deum Patrem, etiam secundum divinitatem Filio majorem esse, nempe non natura quidem aut perfectione aliqua essentiali, quæ in Patre sit et non in Filio, sed auctoritate sua sola, hoc est, origine, quoniam a Patre est Filius, non a Filio Pater."

Bull, in spite of his acuteness and learning, seems to have worded this sentence incautiously. He says rightly that the Father is not "natura," but "auctoritate sola," greater than the Son; but if so, why does he say that the Father is "etiam secundum divinitatem Filio major"? whereas the Athanasian Creed says distinctly of the Son, "æqualis Patri secundum divinitatem," and again, "Patris et Filii et Spiritus Sancti una est divinitas," which does not admit of more or less. I consider that what Bull really meant to say in the foregoing passage was that it was a subordination which was interior to the Divine Essence and "secundum filietatem."

In thus speaking then Bull is unjust to his own meaning; when we consider what he really would say, we shall find nothing to criticise in it. I understand his meaning to be, that, without derogating from the absolute co-equality of the Three Persons in the Divine Essence, each of these being in Himself the one, same, and sole God, in the fulness of His being and attributes, nevertheless there is an aspect in which God the Father is personally greater than God the Son, and that the very idea of fatherhood implies a priority to sonship in dignity and order. This also is the doctrine of Petavius, as of all Catholic divines; viz. "Patrem ita dici majorem Filio, qua Filius est, vel qua genitus est, ut non major eodem dicatur qua Deus est, vel secundum naturam et essentiam . . . Filietas ipsa Paternitate quodammodo minor dicitur, vel Filius, qua Filius, Patre, ut Pater est, minor dicitur, quoniam origine est posterior, non autem ut Deus, hoc est, ratione divinitatis, nisi quatenus proprietate hæc afficitur." *De Trin.* ii. 2, 15.

In like manner Thomassin and Maran speak of the Second Person as being the lesser "in quibusdam adjunctis," of a "gradatio Personarum," of a "discrimen ordinis," of (in Tertullian's words) a "decursus Personarum per gradus," of an "ordinis ratio," nay even of a "ministratio," or "subjectio" of the Son.

For myself, returning to Bull, I would rather avoid his word "subordination" in its application to our Lord, since, however grammatically exact, in its effect it is misleading, and I am able to do so by attaching the term discriminative of the Father and the Son in this aspect, not to the latter, but to the former, in keeping with St. Hilary's felicitous paradox, that "The Father is the greater without the Son being the lesser;" *vid.* Hil. *de Trin.* ix. 56, p. 1022. Therefore instead of the "subordinatio Filii," let us speak of the "Principatus Patris."

I have fully allowed that the *Principatus* in the Ante-Nicene times was one of those doctrines which gave a shelter to the Semi-Arian heresy which came afterwards; and I think I have shown, even in the instance of a clear-headed divine like Bull, who desires with his whole heart to believe with Athanasius, that it is easy so to hold it as to be on the verge of heresy. However, I still consider it as an important doctrine, and valuable now not less than when it was more insisted on. It is remarkable that the great Fathers of the fourth century, with their full experience of Arianism, nevertheless continued to enunciate it. What Basil and Gregory did, we, under the guidance and correction of the Church, may safely do also; and if safely, profitably. There cannot be clearer evidence how little the rise of Arianism indisposed them towards the doctrine of the *Principatus*, than their unanimous interpretation of our Lord's words in John xiv., "My Father is greater than I," of our Lord's Divine Nature. These words, from their context, would certainly seem to be spoken of His humanity. He says, "If ye loved Me, ye would rejoice because I said, *I go* to the Father, *for* My Father is greater than I." In His Divine Nature He was not "going" to Him, but as man; therefore the Father's superiority to Him must be spoken of Him as man. But in spite of the direct sense of the words, they are interpreted of our Lord's divinity by almost a *consensus Patrum* in the fourth and fifth centuries; as Petavius enumerates, by Alexander and Athanasius, Basil and Gregory, Chrysostom, Cyril, and John of Damascus among the Greeks; and by Hilary, Augustine and others among the Latins;

though some of them, especially Augustine, interpret them also of our Lord's human nature.

And not only as regards a particular text, but in the staple of their teaching they enforce the *Principatus* of the Father as pointedly as any Ante-Nicene writer.

Thus, if Hippolytus says, "The Father willed, the Son executed," Athanasius responds, "Men were made through the Word when the Father willed;" and, "The works, when He willed, He framed through the Word." *Orat.* i. 29, 63.

Again, if Hippolytus says, "The Father bids (ἐντέλλεται), the Word acknowledges," and "He who commands (κελεύων) is the Father, He who gives ear (ὑπακούει) is the Son;" and if St. Irenæus asks, "Whom else did He *enjoin?*" (præcepit) and speaks of the Father being "well pleased and commanding" (κελεύοντος), and of the Son "doing and framing;"—St. Cyril of Jerusalem replies, "The Father bade(ἐντελλομένου) and the Son constructed all things at His fiat (νεύματι)," *Cat.* xi. 23; and St. Hilary says, that "the Son was *subject* by the compliance of obedience (subditus per obedientiæ sequelam)," *de Syn* 51; and St. Athanasius, "A Word there must be whom God bids (ἐντέλλεται)," *Decr.* 9; and St. Phœbadius, "The Son is subject to the Father, on the ground of their being Father and Son," *contr. Ar.* 15, *ap.* Galland. t. 5.

In like manner St. Justin says, on the one hand, that "The Lord ministered (ὑπηρετοῦντα) to the Father of all;" and Origen, "The Word became minister (ὑπηρέτης);" and Theophilus designates him as ὑπουργός; but, on the other hand, Athanasius says, "Let the Word work the materials, being hidden and working under God" (προστατόμενος καὶ ὑπουργῶν), *Orat.* ii. 22; and Cyril of Jerusalem speaks of Him as "obedient" (εὐπειθής), *Cat.* x. 5; and St. Hilary, after naming His "subjection," *de Syn.* 51, adds (as also more fully, *ibid.* 79), that His "subjectio" is "naturæ pietas," not "creationis infirmitas."

Clement again, ere yet an heretical spirit had wrested words, and the orthodox had become suspicious of them, had said that "the Son's Nature is the *closest* to the sole Almighty;" but Alexander, in the very heat of the Arian controversy, could also speak of there being between the Father and the universe a "mediating, only-begotten Nature, by whom all things were created," *ap.* Theod. *Hist.* i. 4.

I will add three longer passages from Fathers still later than the above, of special authority, and independent one of another.

1. St. Gregory Nazianzen:—"If, when we say that the Father, in being the cause (τῷ αἰτίῳ) of the Son, is greater than the Son, they assume the proposition, 'The being a cause belongs to a being's nature,' and then conclude that that 'greater' belongs to the Father's nature, they seem to be damaging their own reasoning rather than that of their opponents. . . . For we grant that it is the nature of a cause to be greater, but they infer that that is greater in its nature, which is a cause." *Orat.* xxix. 15. And "If the Father were called 'greater,' and not also called 'equal,' perhaps there would be some force in what they allege; but if we find clearly both 'equal' and 'greater,' what will the good men say? . . . Is it not plain that

'greater' refers to cause, and 'equal' to nature?" *Orat.* xxx. 7.

2. St. Ambrose :—"The Son cannot do anything but what He has learned from the Father, because He is the everlastingly abiding Word of God; nor at any time is the Father divided from the Son's working, and what the Son works, He knows that the Father wills, and what the Father wills that the Son knows how to work." *de Sp. S.* ii. 12, *n.* 135.

3. And St. Augustine :—"When there are two men, father and son, if the son is obedient to the father, and when there is reason, asks his father, thanks his father, and is sent some whither by his father, on which he declares that he has not come to do his own will, but the will of him by whom he is sent, now does it follow from hence, that he is not of the same substance with his father? Why, then, when you read such things of the Son of God, do you at once rush into so great a sacrilege of heart and word, as to believe and profess that the Son of God is not one and the same substance with the Father?" *contr. Maxim.* ii. 3, p. 708.

Though Augustine in this extract lays down with much distinctness the doctrine of the *Principatus*, yet the tendency of his theology—certainly that of the times that followed—was to throw that doctrine into the background. The abuse of it by the Arians is a full explanation of this neglect of it. However, what St. Irenæus, St. Athanasius, and St. Basil taught, never can be put aside. It is as true now as when those great Fathers enunciated it; and if true, it cannot be ignored without some detriment to the fulness and the symmetry of the Catholic dogma.

One obvious use of it is to facilitate to the imagination the descent of the Divine Nature to the human, as revealed in the doctrine of the Incarnation; the Eternal Son of God becoming by a second birth the Son of God in time, is a line of thought which preserves to us the continuity of idea in the Divine Revelation; whereas, if we say abruptly that the Supreme Being became the Son of Mary, this, however true when taken by itself, still by reason of the infinite distance between God and man, acts in the direction of the Nestorian error of a Christ with two Persons, as certainly as the doctrine of the *Principatus*, when taken by itself, favours the Arian error of a merely human Christ. The *Principatus* then is the formal safeguard of the Faith against Nestorianism. And (if the thought is not too bold) I may suggest, in coincidence with what I have been saying, that the heresy of Nestorius did, in matter of fact, immediately spring into existence upon this reaction; and St. Augustine, to whom we owe so much for what he has written on the Holy Trinity, lived long enough to be invited on his death-bed to the Ephesian Council summoned by St. Cyril for the condemnation of the Nestorian teaching.

§ 6. USES OF THE PRINCIPATUS IN SPITE OF ITS HERETICAL ABUSE.

I have ventured to say that the view of our Lord as not only God, but definitely and directly as in the Divine Unity the Son of God, is a point of theology of great moment in the doctrine of His incarnation. I will now give distinctly my reasons for saying so, and will begin with a reference to Thomassin's treatment of the subject in his *de Incarnatione Verbi*, l. ii. c. 1, pp. 89, &c. I have done my best to abridge and reduce it without injury to the sense, but, long as it is, still the importance of the subject and the depth and force of his remarks would, I think, be my justification for the following extracts, even had I made them longer.

1. "This," he says, "first of all must be laid down, that it belongs to the Father to be without birth, but to the Son to be born. Now innascibility is a principle of concealment, but birth of exhibition. The former withdraws from sight, the latter comes forth into open day; the one retires into itself, lives to itself, and has no outward start; the other flows forth and extends itself, and is diffused far and wide. It corresponds then to the idea of the Father, as being ingenerate, to be self-collected, remote, unapproachable, invisible, and in consequence to be utterly alien to an incarnation. But to the Son, considered as once for all born, and ever coming to the birth, and starting into view, it especially belongs to display Him-

self, to be prodigal of Himself, to bestow Himself as an object for sight and enjoyment, because in the fact of being born He has burst forth into this corresponding act of self-diffusion.

"Next, however, whereas the nature of Father and Son is one, therefore equally inaccessible and incomprehensible and invisible is in His nature the Son as the Father. Accordingly, we are here considering a personal property, not a natural. For it is especially congenial to the Divine Nature to be good, beneficent, and indulgent; and for these qualities there is no opening at all without a certain manifestation of their hiding-place, and outpouring of His condescending Majesty. Wherefore, since the Majesty and Goodness of God, in the very bosom of His Nature, look different ways, and by the one He retires into Himself, and by the other He pours Himself out, it is by the different properties of the Divine Persons that this contrariety is solved, and the ingenerate Father secures the majesty and invisibility of the Godhead in its secret place; while the Son, who issues thence, manifests Its goodness and sheds abroad Its beneficence. And hence, further, as might be proved from Irenæus and other Fathers, not to speak of the Platonists, the Father is the Son's incomprehensibility and invisibility, and the Son is the Father's comprehensibility and visibility; the Son's Nature is perceived to be invisible and incomprehensible in the Father, and the Father's Nature to be most bountiful and self-communicating in the Son, who, as possessor of a generate and communicated divinity (Deitate genita et donata), rejoices to give what He has received.

"Moreover, since the Incarnation involves some sort of injury (injuriam) to the Godhead, nay even a self-emptying, there is a propriety in the Son's sustaining this rather than the Father, for the Father is the invisible safeguard of Divinity, in that He is its Origin and Fount; and the Son is the principle of Its effusion, nay, the expenditure and emptying out of Itself, saving always that the Father's inviolability is the Son's, and the Son's munificence is the Father's too.

"Again, as the Incarnation, so previous to it the divine adumbrations made to prophets or to patriarchs, would have been strange in the Father, while they were glorious in the Son; for the Godhead in its own Fount is most pure from all humiliation, all the dust of creation, all contagion of foreign natures any whatever; on the other hand, in its Stream, though it is entire, and all and everything that it is in the Fount, it is less strange that it should extravagate and intermingle with the creatures, and (as it were) be, so to say, soiled by its own beneficence.

"And hence again it is that the Scripture speaks of the Father as invisible, and of the Son as the Image of the Invisible God; and says both that God can be seen, and that He cannot. The teaching of the Fathers reconciles the contrariety at once. Invisibility is reserved to the Father, visibility (whether by angelic adumbrations or by an incarnation) is undertaken by the Son.

"Once more. Why was it that the early heretics invented their Eons, and, beyond them all, their First and Inaccessible God, and made the God of Moses, or the Creator, an inferior being? Because they preferred shattering the Divine Nature to viewing it in a plurality of Persons. For the prerogatives which they assigned to their supreme invisible God, these belong to the Father; those which they withheld from Him as unsuitable, are opportune in the Son, viewed as wounding Himself for our needs and our infirmities. Thus Irenæus, Clement, Tertullian, and others, by discriminating the Divine Persons, made provision for the Divine Unity.

2. "And secondly, the Father undertakes no work outside Himself, except through the Son; for the Son is the first and the whole outcoming of the Father, as issuing forth from the depth of His isolation. Therefore, if He creates the earth, through the Son He creates; if He governs it, when created, through the Son He governs it; if He restores it, when ruined, through the Son He restores it. Between the first Fount of Divinity and the far-off creature the Son intervenes; what the Father is within, that is the Son without; what the Father covers, the Son discovers; what the One is potentially, the other is in act; and therefore, of the Father, in the silence of His repose, the Son is the active and effective Image; so that it is congruous that to the Son should be committed the whole administration of the external creation, whether for framing, or ruling, or reforming it.

"Beyond a shadow of doubt does the Scripture declare that the Son is both consubstantial with the Father, yet His Image and Manifestation, and does all things at the mandate of the Father, and by the Father's authority has framed the earth, put on flesh, undergone the Cross. Nor can the Father, in that He is the Still Fountain-head, and the potential principle, and the Silence, do all these things except through the Son, that is, through the motive power, through action and life.

"As, then, the Son cannot of Himself do anything, because He cannot, except from the immobility and potentiality of the Father, start into motion and act, so neither can the Father do anything except with the Son and through the Son, inasmuch as what is in rest and *in potentia* cannot go abroad, except by action and motion. At the same time, what the Father does, though it be through the Son, is His own, since from Him the Son Himself has being.

"All these remarks come to the same point, viz. that the Father works all His works, gives all His gifts to us, through the Son. 'This,' says St. Cyril of Alexandria, 'is a kind of subjection, because the Son seems to lie under the Father's will.'"

Thus Thomassin, in illustration of the help given us towards realising the Incarnation, by what is mercifully revealed to us of the Person who became incarnate; for which knowledge we ought ever to be thankful. And now, under shelter of the teaching of so eminent a theologian, I shall venture to quote some remarks of my own on our Lord as Son or Word, in further illustration of the *Principatus*, as they are contained in two sermons published by me many years ago:—

"It is a point of doctrine necessary to insist upon, that, while our Lord is God, He is also the Son of God, or rather, that He is God because He is the Son of God. We are apt, at first hearing, to say that He is God, though He is the Son of God, marvelling at the mystery. But what to man is a mystery, to God is a cause. He is God, not though, but because He is the Son of God. Though we could not presume to reason of ourselves that He that is begotten of God is God, as if it became us to reason at all about such ineffable things, yet, by the light of Scripture, we may thus reason. This is what makes the doctrine of our Lord's Eternal Sonship of such supreme importance, viz. that He is God because He is begotten of God; and they who gave up the latter truth, are in the way to give up, or will be found already to have given up, the former. The great safeguard to the doctrine of our Lord's Divinity is the doctrine that He is Son or Word of the Father: we realise that He is God, only when we acknowledge Him to be by nature and in eternity Son.

"Nay, our Lord's Sonship is not only the guarantee to us of His Divinity, but also the condition of His incarnation. As our Lord was God, because He was the Son, so on the other hand, because He was the Son, therefore is He man:—it belonged to the Son to have the Father's perfections, it became the Son to assume a servant's form. We must beware of supposing that the Persons of the Ever-blessed Trinity differ from each other only in this, that the Father is not the Son, and the Son is not the Father. They differ in this besides, that the Father is the Father, and the Son is the Son. While They are one in substance, Each has distinct characteristics which the Other has not. Thus we may see a fitness in the Son's taking flesh, now that that sacred truth is revealed, and may thereby understand better what He says of Himself in the Gospels. The Son of God became the Son a second time, though not a second Son, by becoming man. He was a Son both before His incarnation, and, by a second mystery, after it. From eternity He had been the Only-begotten in the bosom of the Father; and, when He came on earth, this essential relation to the Father remained unaltered. Still He was a Son, when in the form of a servant,—still performing the will of the Father, as His Father's Word and Wisdom, manifesting His Father's glory and accomplishing His Father's purposes.

"For instance, take the following passages of Scripture:—'I can do nothing of myself;' 'He that sent Me is with Me;' 'The Father hath not left Me alone;' 'My Father worketh hitherto, and I work;' 'As the Father hath life in Himself, so hath He given to the Son to have life in Himself;' 'Whatsoever I speak, even as the Father said unto Me, so I speak;' 'I am in the Father, and the Father in Me.' Now, it is true, these passages may allowably be understood of our Lord's human nature; but surely, if we confine them to this interpretation, we run the risk of viewing Him as two separate beings, not as one Person; or again, of gradually forgetting and explaining away the doctrine of His Divinity altogether. If we speak as if our Lord had a human personality, then, since He *has* a personality as God, He is not one Person, and if He has *not*, He is not God. Such passages then as the foregoing would seem to speak neither of His human nature simply, nor of His Divine, but of both together; that is, they speak of Him who, being the Son of God, is also man. He who spoke was one really existing Person, and He, that one living and almighty Son, both God and man, was the brightness of God's glory and His Power, and wrought what His Father willed, and was in the Father and the Father in Him, not only in heaven, but on earth. In heaven He was this, and did this, as God; and on earth He was this, and did this, in that manhood which He assumed; but whether in heaven or on earth, still as the Son. It was therefore true of Him altogether, when He spoke, that He was not alone, nor spoke or wrought of Himself, but where He was, there was the Father; and whoso had seen Him, the Son, had seen the Father, whether we think of Him as God or as man.

"Again, we read in Scripture of His being sent by the Father, addressing the Father, interceding with Him for His disciples, and declaring to them that His Father is greater than He. In what sense says and does He all this? Some will be apt to say that He spake *only* in His human nature; words which are perplexing to the mind that tries really to contemplate Him as Scripture describes Him, because they seem to imply as if He were speaking only under a representation, and not in His Person. No; it is truer to say that He, that One All-gracious Son of God, who had been with the Father from the beginning, equal in all Divine perfections, and one in substance with Him, but second after Him as being the Son,—as He had ever been His Word, and Wisdom, and Counsel, and Will, and Power in heaven,—so after His incarnation, and upon the earth, still spoke and acted, after yet with the Father, as before, though in a new nature, which He had put on, and in humiliation.

"This, then, is the point of doctrine which I had to mention, that our Lord was not only God, but the Son of God. We know more than that God took on Him our flesh; though all is mysterious, we have a point of knowledge further and more distinct, viz. that it was neither the Father nor the Holy Ghost, but the Son of the Father, God the Son, God from God, and Light from Light, who came down upon earth, and who thus, though graciously taking on Him a new nature, remained in Person, as He had been from everlasting, the Son of the Father, and spoke and acted towards the Father as a Son." *Serm.* vol. vi. 5.

The second passage runs thus:—

"Obedience belongs to a servant, but accordance, concurrence, co-operation, are the characteristics of a son. In His eternal union with God there was no distinction of will and work between Him and His Father; as the Father's life was the Son's life, and the Father's glory the Son's also, so the Son was very Word and Wisdom of the Father, His Power and Co-equal Minister in all things, the same and not the same as He Himself. But in the days of His flesh, when He had humbled Himself to the form of a servant, taking on Himself a separate will and a separate work, and the toil and sufferings incident to a creature, then what had been mere concurrence became obedience. 'Though He was a Son, yet had He experience of obedience.' He took on Him a lower nature, and wrought in it towards a Will higher and more perfect than it. Further, He learned 'obedience' amid 'suffering,' and therefore amid temptation. Not as if He ceased to be what He had ever been, but, having clothed Himself with a created essence, He made it the instrument of His humiliation; He acted in it, He obeyed and suffered through it. That Eternal Power, which, till then, had thought and acted as God, began to think and act as a man, with all man's faculties, affections, and imperfections, sin excepted. Before He came on earth, He was infinitely above hope and grief, fear and anger, pain and heaviness; but afterwards all these properties of man (and many more) were His as fully as they are ours.

"If any one is tempted to consider such a subject abstract, speculative, and unprofitable, I would observe in answer, that I have taken it on the very ground of its being, as I believe, especially practical. Let it not be thought a strange thing to say, though I say it, that there is much in the religious belief, even of the more serious part of the community at present, to make observant men very anxious where it will end. It would be no very difficult matter, I suspect, to perplex the faith of a great many persons who believe themselves to be orthodox, and indeed are so, according to their light. They have been accustomed to call Christ God, but that is all,—they have not considered what is meant by applying that title to One who was really man, and from the vague way in which they use it, they would be in no small danger, if assailed by a subtle disputant, of being robbed of the sacred truth in its substance, even if they kept it in name. In truth, until we contemplate our Lord and Saviour, God and man, as being as complete and entire in His personality as we show ourselves to be to each other,—as one and the same in all His various and contrary attributes, 'the same yesterday, to-day, and for ever,' we are using words which profit not. Till then, we do not realise that Object of faith, which is not a mere name, on which titles and properties may be affixed without congruity and meaning; but one that has a personal existence and an identity distinct from everything else. In what true sense do we *know* Him, if our idea of Him be not such as to take up and incorporate into itself the manifold attributes and offices which we ascribe to Him? What do we gain from words, however correct and abundant, if they end with themselves, instead of lighting up the image of the Incarnate Son in our hearts?

"We have well-nigh forgotten the sacred truth, graciously disclosed for our support, that Christ is the Son of God in His Divine Nature, as well as in His human. We speak of Him in a vague way as God, which is true, but not the whole truth; and, in consequence, when we proceed to consider His humiliation, we are unable to carry on the notion of His personality from heaven to earth. He who was but now spoken of as God, without mention of the Father from whom He is, is next described as if a creature; but how do these distinct notions of Him hold together in our minds? We are able indeed to continue the idea of a Son into that of a servant, though the descent was infinite, and, to our reason, incomprehensible; but when we merely speak, first of God, then of man, we seem to change the Nature without preserving the Person. In truth, His Divine Sonship is that portion of the sacred doctrine, on which the mind is providentially intended to rest throughout, and so to preserve for itself His identity unbroken.

But, when we abandon this gracious help afforded to our faith, how can we hope to gain the one true and simple vision of Him? how shall we possibly look beyond our own words, or apprehend in any sort what we say? In consequence, we are often led, almost as a matter of necessity, in discoursing of His words and works, to distinguish between the Christ who lived on earth and the Word who is in the bosom of the Father, speaking of His human nature and His Divine nature so separately, as not to feel or understand that God is man and man is God; and thus, beginning by being Sabellians, we go on to be Nestorians, and tend to be at length Ebionites, and to deny Christ's Divinity altogether." *Sermons*, vol. iii. 12.

So much on the doctrine of the *Principatus*, on its use and abuse. It naturally introduces us to the second doctrine which has to be considered, as giving a shelter to Semi-Arianism, viz. the *Syncatabasis* or *Condescensio* of the Son.

§ 7. THE SECOND OPPORTUNITY OPENED TO THE HERESY, THE SYNCATABASIS OF THE SON.

If all that was told us in Revelation about the Holy Trinity was of the same character as the information conveyed in the form of baptism, if we only learned from the inspired word about One Name, the Name of Father, Son, and Holy Ghost, to whom religious service was to be paid, then it would be a reasonable surprise to find writers of the early centuries departing from the theological tone of that sacred formula, and using language derogatory to the supreme dignity of the Son and Spirit. But the case is otherwise; although Scripture tells us not a little concerning those Divine Persons, as They are in Themselves, it tells us much more about Them, as They are to us, in those ministrative offices towards creation, towards the Universe and towards mankind, which from the first They have exercised in contrariety to our higher conceptions of Them. Nor without reason; for it is by means of Their voluntary graciousness that man primarily has any knowledge of Them at all; since, except for that *condescension*, to use St. Athanasius's word, man would not have existed, man would not have been redeemed or illuminated. It is reserved for the close of that series of Dispensations which has innovated upon Eternity, for God to manifest Himself as in Eternity He was and ever has been, as "All in all," and "as He is;" hitherto, "Eye hath not seen, nor ear heard" what He is in Himself; and, in particular as regards the Son and the Spirit, we know them mainly in Their economical aspect, as our Mediator and our Paraclete.

It is natural then, in spite of the baptismal formula, for Christians at all times, without guarding their words, to speak of the Second and Third Divine Persons as subordinate to the Father; for that Economy is the very state of things into which we are all born. St. Michael, indeed, and St. Gabriel, may have had almost from the first a Beatific Vision beyond all economies; but it was natural in St. Polycarp at the stake to address the Father through "the eternal High Priest;" and in St. Justin, when disputing with Trypho, to speak of the "Prophetical Spirit," for such are the pledged relations in which those Divine Persons are revealed towards us in the covenant of Mercy, and no experience had yet taught Saints and Martyrs that such language admitted of perversion.

Moreover, this Syncatabasis, or economy of condescension, on the part of the Son and Spirit, took place, not from the era of redemption merely, but, as I have remarked, from the beginning of all things; and this is a point which, as regards the Eternal Son, must be especially insisted on here. As to the Incarnation, it would have been hard, if the early Fathers might not, without the risk of misconception, have spoken of our Lord, in the acts of His human nature, as inferior to the Father, though even in this respect they have not always escaped censure; but there is in Scripture a record of acts before the Incarnation, which the Church, following

Scripture, has ever ascribed to Him, and which come short of His Supreme Majesty,—acts which belong to Him, not as man of course, nor yet simply as God, not to His Divine Nature, but, as I may say, to His Person, and to the special Office which it was congruous to His Person to undertake, and which He did voluntarily undertake, as being the Son and Word of the Father,—acts, which, if it was in the divine decrees that a universe of matter and spirit should be created, were *ipso facto* made obligatory on the Creator from the very idea of creation, and of necessity must proceed from Him, while they were in themselves of a ministrative character.[1] I refer to that series or that tissue (as it may be called) of acts of creation, preservation, governance, correction, providence, which the Ante-Nicene theologian could not avoid dwelling on, and attributing to the Son, and treating as acts of ministration, (as they really were,) and describing in terms, (whether he would or no,) which heresy would pervert, supposing, in the presence of idolaters and atheists, he was to speak of the Supreme Being at all. Only an Almighty, Ever-present Intelligence is equal to the maintenance of this vast, minutely complex universe; its existence and continuance is His never-ceasing work; but work, as such, is ministration, as being a means to

---

[1] *i.e.* ministration *to the creature;* hence the Epicureans denied a Providence, as implying a God laden with laborious service. But Scripture does not hesitate to speak of God as "*carrying*" His people, as the eagle its young or as beasts of burden the idols, as "*serving* and being *wearied*" with their sins, as "*groaning*" under them, as a wain overladen; Deut. xxxii. 11; Isai. xlvi. 1-3, xliii. 24; Amos ii. 13.

an end; to rule is to serve; to be the Creator is to descend: and the Second Divine Person, in order to create, submitted to a descent, such as was befitting in a Son, and as was compatible, rigorously so, with His co-equality and indivisible unity with the Father.

Nor is this all; whatever anxious care might be taken in guarding the doctrine of His divinity, the contrast between His Eternal Sonship and this Temporal Ministration, reasonable and intelligible as it is in itself, cannot be carried out into the details which Scripture opens upon our view, without affecting our imagination, as if such a ministry were incompatible with Divine Attributes. I mean, if St. Justin, or Clement, or Origen, spoke of our Lord as the Demiurge, or the Moral Governor, or the Judge, such offices indeed, though ministrative, would not seem unworthy of Divine Greatness; but if, with Athanasius and Augustine to corroborate them, they spoke of Him as the God who appeared to the Patriarchs, as the Divine Presence (for instance) or Angel who visited Abraham in his tent, or who spoke to Jacob from the heavenly ladder, or who called to Moses from the Burning Bush, they could not escape the imputation, where critics were unfair, of regarding Him as a secondary or representative deity, as Arius did, though they may be easily defended on the score that they spoke, not of what He was in His own nature, but of the mission which He undertook in the economy of grace. And therefore it may be quite true, without their being to blame, that they have in matter of fact accidentally opened the way or furnished an excuse for heresy

§ 8. THE TEMPORAL PROCESSION.[1]

I have something more to say still. In regard to truths so far above us, it is impossible for us to draw the line precisely between such of our Lord's acts as belong immediately to His Sonship, and those which belong to His office; since, even as regards our human relations, we often have a difficulty in determining their limits. According to our opportunities or circumstances we take upon ourselves duties which are not simply obligatory upon us, but are brought upon us by our position, or called for by their appropriateness; and we are often unable, if we attempt it, to trace up each act to its right principle. Jacob toiled and endured sun and frost for many years in his duties of a shepherd in Padan-aram; how many of his acts were absolutely due to Laban, on the ground of his being a hired servant, and how far did he give a free service either for love of Rachael, or as Laban's son-in-law and representative? Where did obligation end, and generosity begin? David, again, in defence of his father's flock, smote the lion and the bear; how far did duty compel him to that fight, and how far was it spontaneous zeal? It may be difficult to decide; but still the two ideas are quite distinct, service and devotion;

---

[1] The phrase "*temporalis processio*" is used by St. Thomas. Qu. 43, art. 2, of the Son's Incarnation. It is here used analogously for His coming to create, &c., as by Billuart *de Trin. Diss.* 1 art. 2, § 4.

and we do not deny that Jacob was the son-in-law and nephew of Laban, and David the son of Jesse, because we fall into the error of thinking that there was a strict obligation upon them personally, to show the solicitude which they exercised in fact for the flocks committed to their charge.

And so as regards the acts of our Lord as recorded in Scripture, and the colour given to them by the early Fathers. They may have attributed acts to His Nature, which belonged to His Person or to His office, without thereby intending to deny that He had an intrinsic divinity, and had undertaken a temporal economy. He was the Son of God, equal to the Father; He took works upon Him beneath that Divine Majesty; they were such as were not obligations of His Nature, nor of His Person, but they were congruous to His Person, and they might look very like what essentially belonged to Him; but after all, they were works such as God alone could undertake. He was Creator, Preserver, Archetype of all things, but not simply as God, but as God the Son, and further, as God the Son in an office of ministration; perhaps His creative acts might be called services, as afterwards He took upon Himself "the form of a servant;" or at least they might so be called by this or that early Father. Such writers might be mistaken in so terming them; and there were many questions in detail which they might doubt about or answer variously:—why He was called an Angel; how He was High Priest, by nature or by office; in what sense He was First-born of creation; in what aspect of His Person "He cannot do anything of Himself;" nay, even such a question as, Did the Word become the Son? which will come before us in the sequel. Errors in these details, if they made them, would not prove that the writers did not hold distinctly the fundamental truth that the Co-eternal Word became in the beginning the ministrative Word, who created and upholds all things; and, if they actually did profess that He was the Creator, how does it invalidate or obscure such a profession, that they held also that He created at the Father's will? No creature could create, but a Son might serve. Thus the Fathers of the first four centuries may have enlarged on the acts natural or congruous to His Divine Person, and the medieval theologians may have rather dwelt upon the thought of Him in His absolute Divine Perfections as co-equal with the Father; but it is as unjust to say that Origen, Hippolytus, Dionysius or Methodius introduced Arianism, as to say that Alexander, Athanasius and Basil favoured it, merely because they, one and all, in their writings contrast the Son with the God and Father of all, as being the First-born in creation, or, to use the Platonic term, the Prophoric Word, giving existence, life, light, order, and permanence to the whole world.

At the same time I do not deny, on the contrary I am proposing to show, that this doctrine of the *Syncatabasis* of the Son, true as it is, did, as well as the *Principatus* of the Father, accidentally shelter and apparently countenance that form of Arianism, which gained such sudden and wide extension in Christendom on the conversion of the Empire to Christianity.

§ 9. THE DOCTRINE OF THE PRIMOGENITUS.

Because our Lord is a Son, therefore it is that He could make Himself less than a Son; and, unless He had become less than a Son, we should not have learned that He was a Son, for His economical descent to the creature is the channel of our knowledge. This is what I have been insisting on; also, that, since His original Personality thus led on to His Temporal Procession, therefore it is not easy to determine when He acts as the Son, and when merely as the Minister of the Father, and the Mediating Power of the Universe. For instance, in treating of the doctrine of the Incarnation, we find it a question in controversy to determine, whether our Lord's ignorance of the Day of Judgment, Mark xiii. 32, is to be predicated of His Divine Person, or of His human nature, or of the Mediator, as such. Again, since He came "in the form of a servant," was He really made a servant? Again, since He took upon Himself a created nature, can we call Him a creature? He is a Priest, but how? as God or as man? has He, as Emmanuel, one will or two? If, then, these are questions to determine, even when we start from a fact so tangible as His humanity, can we wonder that there should be difficulties, and a danger of mistake, when even the most saintly and most acute minds exercise themselves in treating of what is beyond the phenomena of human experience, viz., His *Syncatabasis*, or original "Descent to the creature" in order to its existence, life, rule, and conservation? For instance, I should have styled this *Condescensio* by the name of a "Mission," from the analogy of the Incarnation, except that I thought it not clear that "Mission" is an allowable term, theologically, to apply to it, and whether it should not rather be called a προέλευσις or "going forth". Others have thought (I consider erroneously) that this προέλευσις can be called, and has in early times been called, a *gennesis*, or divine generation. It requires experience in the history of theological terms to decide such questions; and we may freely grant that the early writers, who could not have the experience of times to them future, may have varied and erred in their language about our Lord, and that, in the interest of grievous heresies, without imputing to them any departure from orthodoxy themselves.

To show this in detail, I cannot do better than draw out the great Athanasius's account of our Lord's *Syncatabasis*, as involved in the creation and preservation of the universe, and then against his statements, so high in their authority, set some of the mistakes in relation to it which are to be found in the language or the thought of certain Ante-Nicene writers, in spite of their general concurrence in his teaching. This I now proceed to do.

That it should have been the will of God to surround Himself with creatures destined to live for ever, after an eternity in which He was the sole Being in existence, is a mystery as great as any in religion, natural or revealed. If it were possible for change to attach to the Unchangeable, creation was the act in which change was involved;

and, in fact, in order to be intelligible, we are obliged to speak as if He then did pass from a state of repose to an age of unintermitted, everlasting action. The steps of the process in which this change (so to call it) consisted, as Athanasius and other Fathers describe them, are as follows:—

1. First, "He spoke the word;" to whom did God speak? to His Word and Son. "And it was done." Who did it? At the Father's bidding, the Son at once brought the work into effect.

2. But word and deed are consecutive acts, whereas with God they are one act. And to say that the Father addressed the Son is to draw a line, however fine, between the Two, whereas they are transcendently one and the same Being. When, then, it is said, "He spoke the Word," what is meant, is "He uttered the Logos," as elsewhere, "By the Word of the Lord were the heavens made." His Logos is His command, His effectual, self-operating command. Accordingly, it is more consistent with, more conservative of, the co-equality and indivisibility of the Father and His Word, to consider the Word not addressed, but as Himself the Divine *Fiat*, the Hypostatic Will and Operation, the Counsel, Idea, Design, Purpose, and Effective Force, the Wisdom and Power, which called up the universe out of nothing.

3. This going forth of the Hypostatic Wisdom and Power of God, manifesting Himself externally in creative act, was the commencement of His Temporal Economy, and the immediate introduction of His *Syncatabasis*.

4. For that first act of creation could not stand alone;

other acts necessarily followed. Creation and conservation must go together. The finite could not stand of itself; nay, the finite could not have borne the direct action of the Infinite upon it, as it started into existence under the Divine Hand, unless by the Infinite Itself it had been fortified to bear Its touch; otherwise it would have fallen back into its original nothing, annihilated by the very process of creation. In order, then, to give effect to His work, He who was at the first instant external to it, must, without a moment's delay, enter into it and give it a supernatural strength by His, as it were, connatural Presence (*vid. supr.* p. 73).

"The Word," says Athanasius, "when in the beginning He framed the creatures, condescended (συγκαταβέβηκε) to them, that it might be possible for them to come into being. For they could not have endured His absolute, untempered nature, and His splendour from the Father, unless, condescending with the Father's love for man, He had supported them, and taken hold of them, and brought them into substance." *Orat.* ii. 64.

This was the first act of His *Syncatabasis*.

5. It was also the first act of grace, of a gift made to the creation, over and above its own nature, and accompanying that nature from the first:—a divine quality, by which the universe, in the hour of its coming into being, was raised into something higher than a divine work, and was in some sort adopted into a divine family and sonship, so that it was no longer a γενητὸν but a γεννητὸν, and that by the entrance, presence, manifestation in it of the Eternal Son.

"By this condescension of the Word," says Athanasius, "the creation also is made a son through Him (υἱοποιεῖται ἡ κτίσις)." *Ibid.; vid.* also *Orat.* i. 56, and *contr. Gent.* 42.

6. Thus He who was the Son of God became in a certain sense Son towards the creation for the sake of it and in it. He was born into the universe, as afterwards He was born in Mary, though not by any hypostatic union with it. This birth was not a figure of His eternal generation, but of His incarnation, a sort of prelude and augury of it.

Thus Athanasius speaks of it:—"If," he says, "the Word of God is in the world, which is a body, and has taken possession of the whole and all its parts, what is wonderful or absurd in our affirming that of man too" (that is, in the Incarnation) "He has taken possession? . . for if it becomes Him to enter into the world and to be manifested in the whole of it, also it would become Him to appear in a human body, and to make it the subject of His illumination and action." *De Incarn. V.D.* 41.

7. Thus the Only-begotten of the Father imputes His Divine Sonship to the universe, or rather makes the universe partaker of His Divine Fulness, by entering, or being (as it may be called) born into it; not, of course, as if He became a mere Anima Mundi, or put Himself under the laws of creation, but still by a wonderful and adorable descent, so as to be, in spite of His supreme rule, the First-born of His creation and of all that is in it, as He afterwards became the First-born of the pre-

destinate, and as St. Paul says, "is formed in their hearts."[1]

"The Son is called First-born," says Athanasius, "not because He ranks with the creation, but in order to signify the framing and adoption of all things through Him (τῆς τῶν πάντων δημιουργίας καὶ υἱοποιήσεως)." *Orat.* iii. 9.

8. And, as the supernatural adoption of human nature under the gospel involves a real inward sanctification, so the elevation of the universe in the Divine Son includes an impress of His own likeness upon it. He made Himself its Archetype, and stamped upon it the image of His own Wisdom. He gave it order and beauty, life and permanence, and made it reflect His own perfections. As

---

[1] Πρωτότοκος is not an exact translation of *Primogenitus*, though Homer, as Petavius says, may use τίκτω for *gigno*. It is never used in Scripture for "Only-begotten." We never read there of the First-born of God, or of the Father; but First-born of the creation, whether the original creation or the new. The Presence of the Son interpenetrates and permeates the world, though in no sense as its soul. Pantheism in natural theology is the error parallel to Monophysitism in revealed. As far as I know, St. Athanasius does not use the comparison, which is found in the creed attributed to him, between the compound nature of man and the mystery of the Incarnation. If our Lord is not fettered by His human nature, when "made flesh," much less is He subjected to His own universe by becoming, as He has become, its First-born, its Archetype and Life. Athanasius protests against both errors in *Incarn. V.D.* 17. οὐ γὰρ συνεδέδετο τῷ σώματι, ἀλλὰ μᾶλλον αὐτὸς ἐκράτει τοῦτο, κ.τ.λ. *vid.* the whole passage. At the time of writing these grand orations, *contr. Gent.* and *de Incarn.*, Athanasius was not more than twenty-five, perhaps only twenty-one; though they have the luxuriance of youth, yet they are standard works in theology.

He was the beginning of the creation of God, in respect of time, so was He its first principle or idea in respect to typical order.

"In my substance," says Athanasius, speaking in the name of Wisdom, "I was with the Father; but, by a condescension (συγκαταβάσει) to things made, I was applying to the works My own impress, so that the whole world, as being in one body, might be, not at variance, but in concord with itself." *Orat.* ii. 81.

9. It follows that, while the creation was exalted into sonship, the Son, in exalting it, was lowered. His condescension seemed to make Him one of His own works, though of course the first of them; for the greatest and highest glory of creation was not what it had by nature, but what it had by grace, and this was the reflection and image of Him who created it. Thus, as viewed in that reflection, He was a created wisdom, His real self being confused, so to speak, with the reflection of Him; as now we might speak of a crucifix as "golden," "silver," or "ivory," and as being made, when we are not really speaking of Him who was fixed to the Cross, but of His image.

"The Only-begotten and Auto-Wisdom of God," says Athanasius, "is Creator and Framer of all things; but, in order that what came into being might not only exist, but be good, it pleased God that His own Wisdom should condescend to the creatures, so as to introduce an impress and semblance (τύπον καὶ φαντασίαν) of the image of Wisdom on all in common and on each, that the things which were made might be manifestly wise works, and worthy of God; . . . and, whereas He is not Himself a creature, but the Creator, nevertheless, because of the image of Him created in the works, He says Himself of Himself, ' The Lord created Me a beginning of His ways for His works.'" *Orat.* ii. 78.

Thus much Athanasius:—I will corroborate his doctrine by various passages of Augustine, as they occur for the most part in the eighth volume of the Benedictine edition of His works.

He tells us that God created all things by His Word and Only-begotten Son: that in the Word " are all things that are created, even before they are created," and that " whatever is in Him is life, and a creative life ; " that " whatever God was purposed to do, was already in the Word, nor would be in the things themselves, were they not in the Word ; " that " all nature is corruptible, and thereby tends to nothing, because it is made out of nothing ; " but that " as a speaker utters sounds, which have a meaning from the first, so, while God created the world from unformed matter, He withal created its form together with it ; " that "while all nature tends to nothing, as coming out of nothing, it is really good as it comes from Him ; " that " its good is threefold, consisting in proportion, beauty, and order ; " that " those things which have any beauty are divine gifts ; " that " the Word, who is equal to God, is the Art of the Omnipotent Artificer, by whom all things are made, an unchangeable and incorruptible Wisdom, abiding in Itself, changing all things:" that "He is a transcendent, living Art, possessed by the Omnipotent and Wise God, full of all ideas that live and are unchangeable ; " that we must distinguish between "the two titles 'Only-begotten' and 'First-born,' interpreting the former by the words 'In the beginning was the Word,' and the latter by the Apostle's saying that He is 'First-born among many brothers;'" that, since "they were not such by nature, by believing they received power; that His Son might be Only-begotten with the Father, and First-born towards us;" pp. 81-2, 177, 501-3, 553-5, 850-1, &c.

And this is precisely the doctrine of St. Thomas as regards the "First-born:"—"In quantum solus est verus et naturalis Dei Filius, dicitur unigenitus; in quantum per assimilationem ad ipsum alii dicuntur filii adoptivi, quasi metaphorice dicitur esse primogenitus." Qu. 41, art. 3 (p. 195, t. 20, ed. 1787). And what is true of the new holds of the original creation.

This doctrine, expounded by St. Athanasius, confirmed by St. Augustine and St. Thomas, is in tone and drift very unlike Arianism, which had no sympathy with the mysticism and poetry of Plato; but it had a direct resemblance to the Semi-Arian edition of the heresy, and, if put forward without its necessary safeguards and corrections, as we find them in those great doctors, was likely to open the way to it. To such instances of true doctrine incautiously worded, and imperfectly explained, I shall now proceed.

§ 10. UNADVISABLE TERMS AND PHRASES IN EARLY WRITERS.

I am now to give instances of incorrect and unadvisable terms and statements in some of the early Fathers, founded upon the doctrine of the *Syncatabasis*, as I have drawn it out, which may be taken for Semi-Arianism, and gave some countenance to it, when it was openly professed. And I shall arrange them under three heads, according as they belong to our Lord's three titles,—the Word, Wisdom, and the Son.

The Divine Word.

Our Lord, as the Word of God, is considered first, as in the bosom of the Father, next, as proceeding from Him to create, form, and govern the universe. This contrast is sometimes expressed by the terms ἐνδιάθετος and προφορικὸς, the internal and the external Word. These terms are taken from heathen philosophy; nor are they often used by the Fathers, but the idea they convey has a Christian meaning, and requires terms equivalent to these to express it, if these, on account of their associations, are inexpedient. Heathen terms are not in themselves inexpedient, since St. John uses the word "Logos," which the Platonists, as well as Philo, had used before him; and, as these philosophers also use the two words, Endiathetic and Prophoric, in order to denote a change of condition in the Eternal Word, which Christianity also acknowledges, it was but natural in Christian writers to follow the precedent of the Apostle, and, as he designated the Second Person of the Trinity the Logos, in like manner to call him Endiathetic, viewed in His relation to God, and Prophoric, viewed in His relation to creation.

The history of the words is this:—Logos, as we know, stands, in Greek, both for reason and for speech; and, since the inward thought is immediately connected with and passes on into language, as its corresponding development, it was natural to consider the mental and vocal act as virtually one, as the common term expressing them suggested, as if a thought were only an inchoate word, and a word only a perfected thought. Hence came the Logos Endiathetic and Prophoric of the Stoics, who thus both distinguished and identified thinking and speaking. Still more appropriately were these terms applied by the Platonists to their Divine Logos, to express his state of repose and then of action. From the Platonists the terms passed over to Christian writers.

It was natural that the latter should thus adopt them; still they did not commonly use them; some of them did, but others looked on them with suspicion, convenient and expressive as they were, for the reason that heretical authors, as well as Platonists, had used them for their own purposes. The one term without the other would obviously be the symbol of a heresy; the Inward Word betokened Sabellianism, and the External, Arianism. Both together might represent the Catholic Truth, and accordingly they are used for the Divine Word as in the bosom of the Father, and as manifested in creation, by St. Theophilus, prior to the Nicene Council, and St. Cyril[1]

---

[1] So I understand Petav. *de Trin.* vi. 1, § 8.

of Alexandria after it; but, on the whole, they were avoided by the Fathers on account of their associations.

"Nothing essentially belonging to God could be external to God; if, then, Catholics held their Logos to be Prophoric, that was enough to prove that He was not God." This is what the Arians said, whether that External Word was a Divine action or a Divine messenger. Hence it was that Catholic writers disowned the Logos Prophoricus. Thus, long before the rise of Arianism, Ignatius had said of our Lord, that He was "God's Eternal Word, not proceeding from silence," as a sound or voice does; and Athanasius, with various other Fathers, says that "He is not Prophoric, a sound of words." Arius, on the other hand, assuming what Athanasius denies, says, "Many words does God speak; which of them is the Son?" To obviate this inference, the Fathers spoke of the Word as a substance, hypostasis, or nature. 'Ως ἐκ λογικοῦ λόγος, says Athanasius, οὕτως ἐξ ὑποστάσεως ὑπόστατος, καὶ ἐξ οὐσίας οὐσιώδης καὶ ἐνούσιος, καὶ ἐξ ὄντος ὤν. *Orat.* iv. 1.

Logos was not the only term, which, from its properly denoting an attribute or act, was denied by the Arians, except in a figurative sense, to the Divine Son. Some Latin writers translated it by "Sermo;" which carries with it an idea of imperfection and complexity, since conversation or talking is made up of parts, and has no determinate limits. Tertullian feeling this, though he uses "Sermo" himself, observes, "Ergo das aliquam substantiam esse sermonem? Plane." *adv. Prax.* 7. Hence, in contrast, Augustine says of the more usual title, "Verbum," and in opposition to Arius, as above quoted, "Unus est Deus, Unum Verbum habet; in Uno Verbo omnia continet." *In Joan. Tract.* 22.

There are other epithets in Ante-Nicene writers, intended specially to exclude the notion of separation between the Father and the Son, and on that account, as I noticed above, imaging the Son as the utterance or *fiat* of the Father, and not as directly addressed by Him, which, in like manner, might be perverted to obliterate His Divine personality; such as His being the Father's "commanding," or " planning," or " operating." But titles such as these were given to Him by the Catholic Fathers after Arianism as well as before; and, if it is no offence in the Post-Nicene to have taken this licence, much less is it in the Ante-Nicene. If Augustine, for instance, might speak of Him as the " Jussio" of God, then might Justin be allowed to call Him the ἐργασία or "Operatio," and Origen to call Him the " Mandatio ; " and if Augustine might designate Him as the "Ars Patris,"[1] Theophilus is not to blame for applying to Him the title of διάταξις. Yet such titles, as well as that of the Prophoric Word, denoting, in the first instance, divine indeed, but unhypostatic acts, could not really belong (as the Arians might say) to the Son, except figuratively, since Catholics, as well as they, held Him to be an hypostasis. Hence, Athanasius seems to deny that He can be called *jussio*, which Augustine sanctioned; οὐ προφορικὸς, οὐδὲ τὸ προστάξαι θεὸν, τοῦτό ἐστιν ὁ υἱός. *Orat.* ii. 35.

But, even though the Prophoric Word were allowed to

---

[1] *contr. Serm. Ar.* 3, t. 8, p. 627; *de Trin.* vi, 10.

be an hypostasis, as Athanasius urged, that would not rescue the phrase from the Arian use of it; for, anyhow, that term implied that the Word was sent forth from the Father; therefore, He was external to Him; and what was external to the Divine Essence could not really belong to it. Indeed, this was the primary tenet of the whole heretical party, that the Son was a second Being, as distinct in His substance from the Father as from any one of us, though the Semi-Arians said He was a sort of emanation from God, but the Arians proper that He was His creature. This, too, as it would appear, is just what Philo meant by the Prophoric Word; and, when Catholics used Philo's term, they might be plausibly represented as using it in Philo's sense.

And this Arian view of the Logos received additional support from the received Catholic interpretation of certain passages in the Old Testament, and the designation of "Angel" so unhesitatingly given to the Word by the early Fathers. The title, as properly meaning "messenger," is cognate to the idea of a mission; and this is the true explanation of their use of it. It is one of our Lord's titles springing out of His voluntary Syncatabasis; at the same time, unless read with this necessary explanation, it seems to imply a created nature. St. Justin, for instance, speaks of the Word's appearing as an Angel to Abraham, wrestling with Jacob, appearing in the Burning Bush, and announcing to Joshua the fall of Jericho. Still, this is only what the Post-Nicene Fathers, after the experience of Arianism, said also. "He is called an Angel," says Athanasius, "because He alone reveals the Father." *Orat.* iii. 13. And Hilary:—" In order that the distinction of Persons might be absolute, He is called God's Angel; for He who is God from God, is also the Angel of God." *de Trin.* iv. 23. And as to particular apparitions, Athanasius says that it was our Lord who wrestled with Jacob; Hilary, that it was He who spoke words of comfort to Hagar; Cyril of Jerusalem, that it was He who conversed with Moses on the Mount; Basil, that it was He who appeared to Jacob in a dream; Chrysostom, that He appeared to Abraham; and Cyril of Alexandria, that He appeared to Moses in the Bush. If Athanasius is to be spokesman for these great Fathers, the so-called Angel was not our Lord in the prerogatives proper to His Divine Person, but in one of those manifestations which belonged to His "condescension," and to the office which was the form of it. He was the First-born, as of the material universe, so also of the Angelic Choirs; not, indeed, as partaking the nature of Angels, any more than the nature of the material world, but as present and living in His creatures by an economy of ministration. But, if Athanasius may speak of Him, not in His proper nature, but in His *Syncatabasis*, why may not Justin?

There are passages, however, of St. Methodius,[1] harsher than any that occur in Justin, and it would be unfair to pass them over without expressing an opinion upon them. I cannot deny they sound like Semi-Arianism; yet I do not see why they should not be interpreted on the principle of the *Syncatabasis*, as well as those which I have already mentioned. He says that our Lord is "the most ancient

---

[1] Photius considers his works have been practised upon by heretics.

of the Æons and the First of the Archangels." *Conviv.* iii. 4. May not this be taken to mean that He was the Prototocos or First-born of Angels, that He entered into them all, that is, into the spiritual world as into the material, and was the Archetype, on which they were both created and super-naturalised?

The context, in which these words occur, will confirm such an interpretation of them, and at the same time be defended by it, for the context is at first sight more difficult than the language itself already quoted. Methodius says:—

"Observe how orthodox Paul is in referring Adam to Christ, accounting Adam to be not only a type and an image of Christ, but even this, viz. that he even became Christ, because of the Pro-æonian (πρὸ αἰώνων) Word having fallen upon him (ἐγκατασκῆψαι). For it was fitting that the First-born (πρωτόγονον) of God and the First-Offspring and Only-begotten, even Wisdom, should, as being intermingled with man (κερασθεῖσαν), have become man (ἐνηνθρωπηκέναι), in the Protoplast and First and First-born of men. (And this" [also] "Christ was" [viz. when He came on earth] "a man filled with the pure (ἀκράτῳ) and perfect divinity, and God contained in man.) For it was most becoming that the most ancient of the Æons and the First of the Archangels, who was intending (μέλλοντα) to come among men (συνομιλεῖν), should inhabit Adam, the most ancient and first of men."

That is, it was fitting that He who condescended to appear as the First-born of the angelic creation should also become the First-born of the human race, as He afterwards in the true Incarnation became the first of the predestinate.

As to the notion of an indwelling, not hypostatic, of the Son in a creature, it is in this sense that we speak of our Lord's appearing to Abraham or to Jacob; He appeared to them *in* a created Angel. Again, St. Paul says of himself, "Christ liveth *in* me;" and the Psalm runs, "Nolite tangere christos meos," in accordance with our Lord's words "Why persecutest thou *Me?*" And Catholics hold as *de fide*, that certainly at communion our incarnate Lord is really present *in* the communicant.

There is another passage of Methodius which creates some difficulty, in which Origen too, nay, at first sight even Irenæus, may be said to be implicated, and which carries us back to Philo, whose language I must first report.

Philo, then, in one place speaks of the Supreme God as "He that is" (Jehovah), and as accompanied by His Two Powers, God and Lord (*de Abrah.* p. 367, ed. 1691), titles which Mosheim (in Cudworth "Syst. Intell." iv. 36) considers to stand for the Hebrew Elohim and Adonai. Philo's words are, "The Father of all is in the centre, who in the Holy Scriptures is called by His proper name, 'He that is.' Those on each side of Him are His most ancient and nearest Powers; that is, the one called the Operative, the other the Kingly. The Operative is God, for by It He established and ordered the Universe, and the Kingly is the Lord." He proceeds, "Attended (δορυφορούμενος) by each of these Powers, He who is in the centre presents to the perceptive intellect an appearance (φαντασίαν) at one time of One, at another of Three." It must be added that some such notion is in the Cabbalistic writings. God who is between the Cherubim is the Supreme Being, supported by His two primeval creations, which, according to Epiphanius, the Ebionites considered to be the Son and the Holy Spirit. (Heber, *Bampt. Lect.* ed. 2, p. 175, *vid.* also Philo, *Quis hæres*, p. 504.)

Philo, as far as I know, ascribed no "condescension" to his Logos, for he considered him a creature, or, at least, an emanation, as well as his companion Angel. He speaks of him as a second God (*vid.* Euseb. *Præp. Ev.* vii. 13, p. 323, ed. 1688); as an Archangel between God and man, neither increate nor a creature, an intercessor with God, a messenger from Him (*Quis hæres*, p. 509), as the first-born Son, His Viceroy (*de Agricult.* p. 195), the created idea or plan, the κόσμος νοητὸς on which the visible world was made (*de Opif. mund.* p. 5, *Quis hæres*, p. 512). There is nothing then in him which needs explanation when he speaks of the Almighty and His two ministering attendants; but if a writer such as Irenæus uses language of a like character, he must be interpreted, not by Philo, but by other statements of his own and by the doctrine of his brother theologians. Indeed, when closely inspected, the doubtful language of this great Father explains itself.

He says:—" Not that the Father needeth Angels in order to create, &c. . . . for His Offspring and Image minister to Him for all purposes, that is, the Son and Holy Spirit, the Word and Wisdom, of whom all the Angels are servants and subjects." (*contr. Hær.* iv. 7, 4.) Again: "God needed not Angels for the making of those things which He had predestined with Himself should be made; as if He had not Himself His own Hands, for there are ever-present with Him His Word and Wisdom, the Son and Spirit, through whom and in whom He made all things at His free-will, and to whom He says 'Let us make man after our Image and Likeness.'" (iv. 20, 1.) The phrase "Hand of God" is used as a title of the Son by Athanasius, Cyril and Augustine, and implies the Homoüsion, that is, that the Son and Spirit are included within, not external to the Divine Essence. Elsewhere, Irenæus says in confirmation of this, "All these things the Father made, not by Angels, nor by any powers divided from His own Intelligence, for God needs not any of these, but by His Word and Spirit." (i. 22, 1.)

Allowing then that the Second and Third Divine Persons have, in and since the creation, condescended to ministrative offices, no offence can be taken with statements, such as those of Irenæus, which, assuming this, clearly maintain, on the other hand, Their co-existence in the Divine Unity. Though this condition is not denied in the following passage from Methodius, still he unpleasantly uses the language of Philo. He is commenting upon the two olive-trees in Zach. iv.:—

"The Angel answered, 'These are the two sons of fatness, who stand by the Lord of the whole earth,' meaning the Two primeval ($ἀρχεγόνους$) Powers, which attend on God," ($δορυφορούσας$, Philo's word also,) *Conv.* x. 5. He had in the context been speaking of the Son and Spirit under the images of the Vine and the Fig.

As to Origen, he seems to have followed the theologians of the Cabbala (according to St. Jerome *Ep. ad Pam. et Oc.* t. i. p. 524, ed. Val.), when he considers the Seraphim in Isaiah vi. to be the Second and Third Divine Persons. Here again, as in the instance of Methodius, the question arises, did he so think of Them in Their own nature, or in the ministrative office They had graciously assumed in the economy of creation and redemption, and as inhabiting the Seraphim?

One other incorrectness, and one which does not admit of a satisfactory explanation, must be pointed out in Methodius, in which others also are implicated, but not Origen, who is as distinctly Catholic in regard to it as Methodius, his severe critic, is not. Catholics, as we have seen in the extracts from Athanasius, were very explicit in teaching that the Divine Word was the Living Idea, the All-sufficient Archetype, the Divine διάταξις, the transcendent Ars, on which the universe was framed. The Son interprets and fulfils the designs of the Eternal Mind, not as copying them, when He forms the world, but as being Himself their very Original and Delineation within the Father. Such was the doctrine of the great Alexandrian School, before Athanasius as well as after. Origen calls Him the αὐτοσοφία, and the ἰδέα τῶν ἰδεῶν; and Clement the φωτὸς ἀρχέτυπον φῶς, and the ἀρχὴ καὶ ἀπαρχὴ of all things; and Athenagoras the ἰδέα and ἐνέργεια of creation. Hence it was that He was fitted, and He alone, to become the First-born of all things, and to exercise a *Syncatabasis* which would be available for the conservation of the world. The African Tertullian before Arianism, as well as Augustine after it, says in like manner that in Him were "the thoughts and dispositions of all things, which were as if they were already, as existing in the Divine Intelligence." *adv. Prax.* 6 *fin.*

Different from this is the language of Philo, who either held that the Word wrought *after* the Divine "Archetypal exemplars," or again, as I have said above, was the Divine *created* plan of the world; anyhow, not the Divine Idea; and Eusebius follows him in this denial. "As a skilful painter," he says, "taking the archetypal ideas from the Father's thoughts, He [the Word] transferred them to the substance of His works." *Eccl. Theol.* p. 165. This mistake was not guarded against by Methodius; he speaks of our Lord adorning the world by imitation, κατὰ μίμησιν, of the Father. *Ap.* Phot. *Bibl.* p 938. Novatian falls into the same error (p. 175, ed. Jackson), calling the Son expressly "imitator." *Vid.* also Tatian *contr. Græc.* 7, who says κατὰ τὴν μίμησιν.

2. *The Divine Wisdom.*

Wisdom is another chief title given to our Lord, which was wrested from its true meaning, as contained in the Ante-Nicene writers, by the Arians who succeeded them. It signifies the Word, especially considered as having become a gift to the universe, that is, as the First-born viewed in His Supreme Excellence and Perfection. Hence, whereas there are two chief acts of the Demiurge, first to create, then to fashion and furnish; in the latter of these acts, that is, in stamping His Image upon the world in its order, harmony, and beauty, He is Wisdom, as in creating and sustaining it He is the Word. Again, since in the Gospel Dispensation it is the Third Divine Person who is the Giver of life, grace, strength, and glory to the spiritual creation, and since Divine Wisdom, as seen in the material creation, manifests itself in analogous gifts, it is not strange that in the writings of the early Fathers, Wisdom is sometimes found to be the symbol of the Holy Ghost, not of our Lord, as in passages of Theophilus and Irenæus, as above quoted.

This leads to a remark very pertinent to the matter in hand. We know that in Scripture the same word "Spirit" is used indiscriminately, and (if I may so speak) used confusedly, both for the Holy Ghost and for His gifts. Even He Himself is called a gift in the Hymn, viz. "Altissimi Donum Dei," as if He had really no personality; and much more is it common with St. Paul to speak of His gifts and graces as if identical with Himself, as if what is merely His work were really He. Thus we read of Christians "walking in the spirit," of the "spirit of adoption," of "the law of the spirit of life," of "giving" and "receiving the spirit." Nor are we without some instances of a parallel usage in Scripture, as regards our Lord's titles. Thus "Christ" is said to be "born in our hearts," and "the engrafted Word" is said to "save our souls." And so again, our members are said to be "members of Christ," and our Lord is said to be persecuted in His disciples, as I remarked above.

In this way it is that the early Fathers speak of Him,

and most appropriately, under the name of Wisdom, as a work or creation. Thus Tertullian speaks of the "Sophia condita, initium viarum in opera ipsius" (*adv. Herm.* 45), and Clement of the πρωτόκτιστος σοφία. (*Strom.* v. 14, ed. Potter.) This is the plain doctrine of Athanasius, as stated in the following passage, which is a continuation of what I have above quoted :—

"If, as the Son of Sirach says, 'He poured her out upon all his works,' . . and such an outpouring signifies, not the substance of the Auto-Wisdom and Only-begotten, but of that wisdom which is copied off from Him in the world, how is it incredible that the All-framing and True Wisdom, whose impress is the wisdom and knowledge poured out in the world, should say . . as if of itself, 'The Lord created Me for His works'? For the wisdom of the world is not creative, but is that which is created in the works, according to which 'The heavens rehearse the glory of God, and the firmament announces the work of His Hands.' This if men have within them, they will acknowledge the true Wisdom of God, and will know that they are made really after God's Image. And, as some king's son, when his father wished to build a city, might cause his name to be printed upon each of the works that were rising, both to give security of the works remaining by reason of the show of his name on everything, and also to make them remember him and his father from the name, and, having finished the city, might be asked concerning it, how it was made, and then would answer, 'It is made securely, for, according to the will of my father, I am imaged in every work, for there is a creation of my name in the works;' yet in saying this does not signify that his own substance is created, but the impress of himself by means of his name; in the same manner, to apply the illustration to those who admire the wisdom seen in the creatures, the True Wisdom makes answer, 'The Lord hath created Me for the works,' for the impress which is in them is Mine, and I have thus condescended in My framing them." *Orat.* ii. 79.

St. Cyril of Alexandria expresses this created Wisdom in another way, after Scripture, calling the Divine Word, relatively to us, a seed; whereas if He were literally a seed within us, then the plant of grace, as showing itself in our thoughts, words, and deeds, would be Himself, which is pantheistic. "The Word of God," he says, "'enlighteneth every man that cometh into the world;' not in the way of a Teacher, as Angels do, or men, but rather as God, in the way of a Framer, doth He sow in each whom He calls into being the seed of Wisdom." *In Joan.* p. 75. This figure of speech occurs several times in Justin, and surely without any blame to him. He speaks of the heathen writers " seeing truth, though dimly, through the innate seed of the Word." *Apol.* ii. 13. "Of the spermatic Divine Word," *ibid.*, and of those " in whom dwells the seed from God, the Word." *Apol.* i. 32. It is scarcely necessary to refer to St. Peter's words concerning Christians being born again, " not of corruptible seed, but of incorruptible, through the Word of God who liveth and remaineth for ever."

If St. Athanasius may, without offence, call the Eternal Word and Wisdom a creature, that is, figuratively, and

St. Cyril speaks of him as if a seed, it does not appear why there should not be a sufficient explanation producible for St. Justin and others calling him a Work, though this has seemed to many writers, Catholic as well as Unitarian, to give matter for a controversy. For instance, Justin calls him ἔργον τῆς βουλῆς τοῦ προβάλλοντος αὐτὸν πατρὸς, *Tryph.* 76, that is, *after* He was προβληθὲν, He became an ἔργον; Tatian calls Him ἔργον πρωτότοκον, *contr. Græc.* 5, and St. Dionysius of Alexandria a ποίημα. If the name of Athanasius is not great enough to shelter such expressions from criticism, I refer objectors to the following passage from the Angelic Doctor:—

"Filius," he says, "in Scripturis dicitur creatura, *Eccli.* xxiv. 5, &c. Cum dicitur, 'Sapientia est creata,' potest intelligi de sapientia quam Deus indidit creaturis; *Eccli.* i. 9. Neque est inconveniens, quod in uno contextu locutionis loquatur Scriptura de Sapientia genita et creata, quia sapientia creata est participatio quædam Sapientiæ increatæ." *Qu.* 41, 3, t. 20, pp. 194-5.

3. *The Divine Son.*

As the terms Word and Wisdom have each two senses both in Scripture and in the Fathers, the one relative to God, the other to the creature, so has the term "Son". It means the Only-begotten and the First-born, as I have shown above; and, as misconceptions concerning the two former titles were a sort of shelter to the prevalent heresy of the fourth century, so were misconceptions concerning the Divine Son.

1. Very little remains to be said about the term "First-

born". The figure is used of our Lord six times in Scripture, and in each case it is distinct in meaning from "Only-begotten". (1) First, St. Paul speaks of His becoming in His incarnation the "first-born among many brethren," *Rom.* viii. 29; and he connects this economy with their being conformed to His Image, and gifted with grace and glory. (2) In the same sense we read of Him in the Apocalypse as "the Beginning of the creation of God" (that is, the new creation), *Apoc.* iii. 14. (3) He is "the First-born of the dead," *Apoc.* i. 5.; that is, the cause and first-fruits of our Resurrection. (4) Also, *Col.* i. 18. (5) The "First-born of *all* creation," *Col.* i. 15; as being the efficient and formal cause whereby the creation was born into a Divine adoption. And (6) St. Paul speaks of God's "bringing the First-born into the world" (*Hebr.* i. 6), whereby "the world" may be meant either the material universe, or the world of men.

In none of these passages does the phrase "First-born of *God*" occur; the word refers, not to His generation, but to His birth (that is, His figurative birth) into the Universe, or into the family of Adam, or from the grave. St. Athanasius notices this contrast between "Only-begotten" and "First-born". "If He be called First-born of the creation," he says, "it is because of His condescension to the creatures, according to which he has become a Brother unto many. . . . It is nowhere written of Him in the Scriptures, 'the First-born of God,' nor 'the creature of God,' but it is the words 'the Only-begotten,' and 'Son,' and 'Word,' and 'Wisdom,' that signify His relating and belonging to the Father. But 'First-born' implies descent to the creation. . . . The same cannot be both Only-begotten and First-born, except in different relations; that is, Only-begotten, because of His generation from the Father, and First-born, because of His condescension to the creation, and to the brotherhood which He has extended to many." *Orat.* ii. 62.

The treatises of Petavius, *de Trinitate* and *de Incarnatione*, are works of such vast extent and such prodigious learning, that it is not safe to say what is not contained in them. I will only observe, then, that I do not recollect meeting with passages in them which recognise the above doctrine of St. Athanasius concerning the "First-born." Petavius seems to take the title Πρωτότοκος in its Latin sense of Primogenitus, and thence, contrasting it with Unigenitus, to inquire which Fathers use it of our Lord's divine nature, and which Fathers of His human; whereas there is a class of ideas and epithets which belong neither to the one nature nor to the other separately, but to both, that is, to His mediatorial office, and embrace both natures, as Petavius would be the first to acknowledge. Such especially is our Lord's Priesthood; and analogous to this incarnate mediatorship is His office of Demiurge. It is quite true that, as Petavius shows, there are writers, both before and after the Nicene Council, who understand "First-born" as simply belonging either to the one or the other of His natures; but that is no reason why he should not do justice to the doctrine of Athanasius, a doctrine taken up by his successor, Cyril, who, speaking of the title "First-born" and the creatures, says, οὐχ ὡς πρῶτος ἐκείνων ὑπάρξας, ἀλλ' ὡς πρῶτος τῆς υἱοῦ προσηγορίας γενόμενος αὐτοῖς αἴτιος. *Thesaur.* p. 241, c. *Vid.* also *ibid.* p. 238, ἵνα ὥσπερ ἀθανάτῳ τινὶ ῥίζῃ, &c.

2. So much, then, on the "First-born"—the other title of the Son, viz. the "Only-begotten," introduces us to the third and most important of the three sanctions, which the Arians claimed, in favour of the heresy, from the Ante-Nicene writings. It will be the subject of my concluding Sections.

§ 11. THE THIRD OPPORTUNITY OPENED TO THE HERESY THE TEMPORAL GENNESIS.

Hitherto I have found scarcely anything in the thought or language of the Ante-Nicene Fathers, which, even though suggestive accidentally of the subsequent Semi-Arianism, does not admit of an orthodox sense, and has not the sanction of the Post-Nicene Fathers. The *Principatus* is the doctrine of St. Gregory Nazianzen and of St. Augustine; the *Syncatabasis* is the special teaching of St. Athanasius. Such doctrines are in no respect inconsistent with the consubstantiality, co-eternity, and co-equality of the Son with the Father. So far is clear; but I have something more to say concerning certain early writers, which I wish I could explain as satisfactorily. I do not know how to deny, that, both in the East and in the West, there are writers, otherwise Catholic and orthodox in their theology, who use language concerning the Divine Sonship, which can hardly be distinguished from what in St. Augustine's day would have been considered heretical, or close upon heresy.

The doctrine, which they favour, is the Temporal *Gennesis;* viz., that the Eternal Word was not the Son from everlasting, but became the Son before the creation in order to be its Creator; and this doctrine, afterwards repudiated by the Church, is. it is plain, in real connexion historically, and in apparent connexion theologically, with Arianism. I say "in real historical connexion," because where it had first appeared, there Semi-Arianism was most successful, and where, as in Egypt, it had not been tolerated, Arianism in no shape gained a footing. And I say, "in only apparent theological connexion" with the heresy, because, while the Arians, of all shades of misbelief, repudiated the Nicene Homoüsion, these writers, whose language is so equivocal on the point in question, all taught the cardinal truth, of which the Homoüsion is the symbol, viz., the true divinity, in union with the Father, of the Word and Son. All could have subscribed to the Nicene Creed and to its Anathematisms.

That these writers held both the eternity, and the hypostatic existence of the Word, I think beyond a doubt. I am not for an instant supposing that, with Marcellus of Ancyra in the fourth century, and with the heretics whom Justin speaks of (*Tryph.* 128) in the second, they considered the Son to be a mere energy or action, or a temporary expansion, of the Divine Essence, and not the Divine Essence Itself; still that they believed in His eternity, viewed as the Son, I cannot persuade myself, if their language is the index of their belief; and this is the point on which I shall insist. Nor will it satisfy me even if some of them assert the existence of the Son, "before all ages;" this indeed would be enough, if it were all they said; in that case I could account the phrase to stand for "eternity". For what do we know of eternity except that it is the state of things before time? It is a negative idea; it has no epochs; as soon as we let time go, we are forthwith merged in eternity. The phrase then "before all ages," any how may mean, and often does strictly mean, eternity; and it would have been conclusive that those who used it of the Son were believers in the eternal *gennesis* but for this,—that, whereas it need not mean eternity, those who use it in fact show us that it need not, by bringing up again the notion of time after they have seemed to drop it, viz. by such propositions as that the *gennesis* took place " *when* the Father willed to create the worlds," that our Lord "was *before* He was begotten," and the like. By such expressions they imply that the *gennesis* after all had a relation to time; and then it is that it occurs to the inquirer that "*before* all worlds" is also of the nature of a date, and, being a phrase not absolute but relative, is inadmissible as used for a categorical enunciation of the Son's eternity. Besides, the text in the Septuagint Version, Proverbs viii. 12, which was the stronghold of the Arians, because it spoke of Divine Wisdom being *created*, also speaks of him as πρὸ τοῦ αἰῶνος, showing that the pro-æonian state, contemplated at least by the translator, was not eternity, as containing in it an act of creation, that is, an act which belongs to time. And further still; it was possible to hold the eternal *conception* of the Son in the Divine Essence, as a distinct Person, without holding His *birth* to have been from eternity, and to understand *gennesis* not to mean *generation* but *birth*.

Some light will be thrown upon these points as I proceed; meanwhile, fully conscious as I am how comprehensive a view it requires, and how minute and familiar a knowledge, of the literature of the first centuries of Christianity, if one is to have a right to pronounce definitely what is in it and what is not, still, writing under the correction of that consciousness, I will venture to say as much as this;—first, that authors of the East and West, who are distinct in calling the Word "eternal," as well as " before all ages," are not distinct in calling the Son "eternal;" and next, that, while they speak of His *gennesis* taking place in order to creation, and as dated by creation, they add not a word to show that in such statements they meant (as Bull has thought) merely a certain figurative *gennesis*, and that there had already been another and a true *gennesis* from all eternity.

Now to open the question :—

Christians in that early period had difficulties about the Divine Nature, which do not trouble us now. The most cultivated minds came to the Church from heathenism, and brought their ideas of the One God from Plato, if the philosophical contemplation of the Divine Being and His Attributes was not altogether new and strange to them. Was He All-powerful, All-knowing, All-merciful? Was He so from all eternity, so that He never could be without the attributes which those titles signify? If so, the subject of them, the created universe, must be eternal also. How could He have attributes, which during the antecedent eternity had no exercise ? how could they have exercise without an existing creation ? If creation had a beginning, He had a birth (so to speak) of attributes since that beginning, which He had not had before it.

Nor was this all. The dilemma, which arose out of the contemplation of the Divine Attributes, was involved also in that of the Divine *gennesis*. That *gennesis*, or internal act of God, had its purpose and scope in His external act, the creation of the universe. It was the means towards creation; as then the attribute of Power implied a created world, so did the doctrine of the *gennesis*, and, if the creation was not from eternity, neither was the *gennesis*.

This necessary connexion between the two divine acts, the one internal, the other external, the gennesis and the creation, which was so widely assumed, as a principle, in the Ante-Nicene Church, is not altogether foreign to later theology. That is to say, if I understand Petavius rightly, the mission of the Son to be in due time incarnate, is included in His *gennesis;* and, if so, the *syncatabasis* or mission (as it may be called) to create, is included in the *gennesis* also. "Missio," he says, "nihil aliud est, quam æterna productio communicatioque naturæ, in qua illud est, ut in tempore opus aliquod externum appareat. Sicut, 'Patrem docere Filium,' est doctum et scientem genuisse, ut auctor Breviarii scribit, et 'judicium dare Filio' est judicem ipsum gignere, ut ait Chrysostomus, sic 'mitti a Patre Filium' est gigni naturam hominis assumpturum et suo tempore assumentem . . . . Non enim cogitandum est, duas ac separatas esse processiones Personæ Filii, quarum una est æterna, altera temporalis." *De Trin.* viii., i. § 10.

And the same doctrine, I suppose, is implied in the words which St. Thomas quotes from St. Augustine, *Quæst.* 34. *art.* 3: "In nomine Verbi significatur, non solum respectus ad Patrem, sed etiam ad illa quæ per Verbum facta sunt operativa potentia;" on which St.

Thomas says: "Importatur in Verbo ratio factiva eorum quæ Deus fecit."[1]

This connexion between the Divine act of the *gennesis* and the Divine act of the creation, real as it was, was pushed to that extreme by early theologians, as to lead to their holding that, if the *gennesis* was from eternity, so was the creation, and, if the creation was not from eternity, neither was the *gennesis*. From this common ground two schools took their start, but in opposite directions; the one holding that each of the two Divine acts, the other that neither of them, was from eternity. And of these schools two great writers may be considered the representatives respectively; of whom Origen affirmed that the creation was from eternity, as well as the *gennesis*, and Tertullian affirmed that the *gennesis* had a beginning as well as the creation.

1. Origen, for instance, says: "As there cannot be a Father without there being a Son, nor an owner without there being a possession . . . . so neither can God be called Omnipotent, unless He has those on whom to exercise power; and therefore, that He may be shown to be Omnipotent, *all things must necessarily subsist.*" *de Princ.* i. 2, 10.

Tertullian, on the other hand:—"Because God is a Father, and God is a Judge, it does not therefore follow that He was Father and Judge always, because He was

---

[1] And so Augustine again, "Si, ut Deus, præceptum accepit, nascendo id accepit non indigendo. In Verbo enim Unico Dei omnia præcepta sunt Dei, quæ ille gignens dedit nascenti," *contr. Maxim.* ii. 14, 9.

God always. For He could not be Father before there was a Son, nor a Judge before there was sin. *There was a time when neither sin nor Son was,*—sin to make the Lord a Judge, Son to make Him a Father." *contra Hermog.* iii.

2. But here I remark as to Origen's doctrine, that he held the eternity of the *gennesis*, not as a mere deduction from his general doctrine of the eternity of creation, as if the Son were one of the creatures, and *gennesis* a kind of creation; for, in passages preserved by Athanasius, he expressly says that the Son is from eternity because He is from and in God, and is co-eternal in His eternity. "When was not in being that Image of the Father's ineffable and nameless and unutterable subsistence, that Impress and Word, who knows the Father? for let him understand well, who dares to say, 'Once the Son was not,' that he is saying 'Once Wisdom was not,' and 'Word was not,' 'Life was not.'" Again: "It is not lawful, nor without peril, if, because of the difficulty of understanding it, we deprive God, as far as in us lies, of the Only-begotten Word, ever co-existing with him." *de Decr.* 27. Thus Origen includes the Son, not in the world's eternity, but in God's eternity.

And, on the other hand, as regards Tertullian's denial of our Lord's eternity as the Son, we must not thence at once conclude, that he denied the eternity of His *hypostasis* as the Word. Indeed, his strong expressions in enunciating the Catholic dogma of the Trinity, some of which I have quoted above, necessarily include substantial orthodoxy in respect to its separate portions. What do his reiterated notices mean of the Divine Triad, of the Three Persons, Each of Them God and one and the same God, and his placing Them on one line, *equal* except in order of naming Them, (for instance, " Duos definimus Patrem et Filium, etiam Tres cum Spiritu Sancto,") if They were not in some true sense Three from all eternity ? He whom he called the Son was no other than the Eternal Word, even though the name "Son" belonged to Him only upon his becoming the Creator of all things.

3. Again, as to Origen's notion of the eternity of the Universe, it must be recollected that, though in matter of fact creation is not from eternity, yet it might have been, had God so willed. At least so says Suarez: " Duobus modis posse rem aliquam vel productionem esse æternam, uno modo ex intrinseca necessitate sua, quomodo Divini Verbi generatio æterna est; alio modo absque necessitate simpliciter ex libertate causæ volentis ex æternitate eam efficere. Repugnat creationi quod sit ab intrinseco æterna. Non est de ratione creationis novitas essendi actualis, &c. Negatur æternitatem repugnare rationi creaturæ. Ad Patres dici potest, loqui ex suppositione fidei, quæ docet nullam creaturam esse ab æterno creatam." *Metaph.* p. 1., pp. 409, 410, 412, ed. 1751. It must be recollected, too, that St. Thomas lays it down, " Quod mundum incepisse, sola fide tenetur, et demonstrative probari non potest." And he says: " Voluntas Dei ratione investigari non potest, nisi circa ea quæ absolute necesse est Deum velle." *Quæst.* 46. art. 2. That in Origen's time the " Novitas rerum creaturum " could be called an article of faith, is very doubtful.

And then, on the other hand, as to Tertullian; it is true that to suppose the *gennesis* to be a divine act, not from eternity, but in time, is an offence, not only against the perfection of the Triad, but primarily against the simplicity and unchangeableness of the Divine Monad; but much may be said in his excuse. His religious knowledge was not ours: truths are taken for granted now on all hands, which had to be learned one by one then. The "de Deo" was not yet a formal theological treatise, familiar to the Schools, and found but a poor substitute in the writings or the floating *dicta* of heathen philosophy, recommended though they might be to Christian writers by reason of the Being or Attributes of God being natural truths, and only indirectly belonging to Revelation. Now it was in regard to the simplicity of the Divine Nature, that Plato and his numerous followers, with their doctrine of Divine Ideas, were most in fault. Moreover, if creation, as Tertullian rightly held, was a temporal act, while it was a received maxim, as Victorinus lays it down, "Facere motus est,"[1] he would not feel the force of that objection to a temporal divine birth, afterwards urged by the Arians (*e.g.* by Candidus, Galland, *Bibl.* t. viii. p. 140), viz., "Omnis generatio mutatio quædam est." And again, he might argue, that such a temporal act need not be inconsistent with the Divine Immutability, though human reason could not see how it was consistent with it, supposing there was no violation on the other hand of the Divine Unity, hard

---

[1] *ap.* Galland, *Bibl.* t. viii. p. 149. *Vid.* also Origen, *ap.* Method. μεταβάλλειν τὸν ἄτρεπτον συμβήσεται, εἰ ὕστερον πεποίηκε τὸ πᾶν.

as it was to understand this, in the dogma of a Tri-une God. And in corroboration we must consider, that even now among orthodox believers external to the Church, there is much confusion in their conception of the Son and the Spirit, as if these Divine Persons were *in* the Divine Nature rather than directly God, a confusion of thought inconsistent with a clear apprehension of His absolute simplicity and unity.

With this introduction, let us now collect the suffrages, so to speak, of Eastern, Western, and Alexandrian authors for and against the Temporal *Gennesis;* that is, the tenet that the Hypostatic Word was the Son, not from everlasting, but by a Divine act coincident with or equivalent to His manifestation as Prophoric, when in the beginning of all things He proceeded from the Father by a *syncatabasis*, to create, inform, and govern the universe, material and spiritual.

I shall take the Alexandrians first, then the Orientals or Asiatics, and lastly the Western or Latin writers.

§ 12. THE ALEXANDRIAN SCHOOL.

That the Logos existed with God from eternity, and, I will add, in an *hypostasis*, ἐνυπόστατος, is confessed or implied by the Ante-Nicene writers generally; that the Logos was also the Son, and, as the Son, was begotten of the Father before all things, is also their general doctrine. But the question before us relates to His eternal pre-existence, considered *as Son*, or the eternity of the *gennesis;* and, whatever we shall have to say about certain other theologians, this fundamental truth was held and taught without a dissentient voice by the Fathers of the Alexandrian School, so far as their writings have come down to us, taught by them with a prominence, clearness and consistency, which is decisive of Catholic Tradition on the subject.

By writers of the Alexandrian School, I mean such as the following:—Athenagoras, Clement, Origen, Dionysius, Gregory Thaumaturgus, Theognostus, Pamphilus, Alexander, and Athanasius.

1. ATHENAGORAS, the earliest of them, is the least explicit; for, while he says that the Divine Being is ἀϊδίως λογικὸς, he does not directly speak of an ἀΐδιος υἱός. However, if he does not affirm the eternal *gennesis*, at least he speaks as if he did not hold the temporal. He speaks of the Son, *after* the act of creation, as being "*in* the Father;" this is to dissociate the *gennesis* from the act of creation, and to disclaim the "Logos Prophoricus". He

says: "The Son of God is the Father's Word, in conception and action, ἰδέᾳ καὶ ἐνεργείᾳ, for by Him and through Him all things came to be, the Father and the Son being one, the Son being *in* the Father, and the Father *in* the Son, in the unity and power of the Spirit." *Leg.* 10. This passage teaches also the *homoüsion*, for it teaches the *circumincessio*. Elsewhere he speaks of the Word's going forth; but retaining the word ἰδέα as well as ἐνέργεια, he guards against the error, afterwards Semi-Arian, which I have noticed above in Novatian and Methodius, of supposing the Son to create after a pattern in the Father, whereas He is Himself the Archetype of the Universe. That office of Archetype involved a *Syncatabasis*, and Athenagoras uses language of it quite in accordance with that of Athanasius. In that office He is not simply the Son of God, but, as Athenagoras says, His παῖς, as if His minister and is the πρῶτον γέννημα, not of, but for the purposes of the Father; and, as he hastens to explain, for the ministry of creation, as being its Idea and Motive Power, bringing order into chaos, ἰδέα καὶ ἐνέργεια προελθών, and Himself in the creation the first-fruits of His own work. Such a doctrine, such phraseology is identical with the thought and language of Athanasius about the "First-born".

2. CLEMENT:—"Everything which excels the Gnostic (or Christian philosopher) accounts precious according to its worth, and estimable. Among things sensible, rulers and parents and every elder. In matters of learning, the oldest philosophy and the most primitive prophecy. In things intellectual, that which is most ancient in origin (γενέσει); viz. Him who is apart from time and beginning

(ἄχρονον καὶ ἄναρχον), the Beginning and Firstfruits of all things, the Son." *Strom.* vii. *init.* Here the Son, not simply the Word, is both ἄναρχος ἀρχή and ἀπαρχή; both the first origin and the first-born, the Unigenitus and the Primogenitus, and, not only beyond time, but actually without beginning.

3. ORIGEN:—I have lately quoted a passage of Origen's, in which he speaks of "the Only-begotten Word as ever co-existing with God," *supra*, p. 233, *vid.* also p. 155, and considers it a misbelief to say that "Once the Son was not;" thus by anticipation denouncing the Arian formula, as Pope Dionysius did, with more authority, shortly after him. Again he says *In Jerem. Hom.* ix. 4. ὁ σωτὴρ ἀεὶ γεννᾶται (Routh, t. iv. p. 304), as St. Augustine "semper nascitur Filius," *Ep.* 238, 24. And in the same sense Origen interprets "This *day* have I begotten Thee," as meaning the ever-present Now of Eternity. *In Joan.* t. i. 32.

4. ST. DIONYSIUS was accused before the Pope just named, of saying that "God was not always a Father and the Son was not always a Son;" that "the Son was not before His *gennesis*," and that "once He was not, for He was not everlasting," which were afterwards the Arian formulæ. He answers:—"Never was it that God was not a Father . . . . Whereas the Father is eternal, the Son is eternal, being Light from Light. Since there is a parent, there is also a child. They both are and are ever . . . . . The Son only was ever co-existing with the Father, and is full of Him who exists, and is Himself from the Father." Vid. Athan. *De S. Dion.* 13—15.

5. ST. GREGORY THAUMATURGUS, in his Creed, speaks of "One God, Father of a living Word, of Substantive Wisdom and Power, and Eternal Likeness; a Father, Perfect of Perfect, of an Only-begotten Son." And of "One Lord .... True Son of True Father, Invisible of Invisible .... Eternal of Eternal." *ap.* Galland. t. iii. p. 385.

6. THEOGNOSTUS, in the sole fragment of his Hypotyposes extant, does not indeed use the word "eternal" as a predicate of the Son, but he applies to Him those images, which the other Fathers adduce in proof of His eternity, and of the eternity of the Word, viz. that He is like a ray from the sun, the vapour from water, and the like. He says:—"The substance of the Son sprang from the Father's substance, as the radiance of light, as the vapour of water. . . . . Nor does the Father's substance suffer change, though it has the Son as an Image of Itself." *ap.* Athan. *de Decr.* 25.

7. PAMPHILUS, in the fact of his defending the theology of Origen, subscribes to it himself. Now one of the points of faith which he brings forward from Origen's comment on Genesis, is the eternity of the Son. "On the point that the Father is not before the Son, but that the Son is co-eternal with the Father, Origen speaks thus in his first book on Genesis:—'God had no beginning of being a Father, impeded, as men who become fathers, by incapacity of becoming such till a certain time. For, if God is always perfect, and can be a Father, and it is an excellence to be the Father of such a Son, why does He delay and withhold Himself from

what is in itself an excellence, and being, so to say, as soon as He can, Father of a Son?" *ap.* Routh, *Reliqu.* t. iv. p. 302.

8. ALEXANDER, at the first rise of Arianism:—"They say that once the Son of God did not exist; and that He who did not first exist came into being afterwards . . . and by the hypothesis of 'He was from nothing,' they also overthrow the Scripture record that He existed ever . . . Since that hypothesis is evidently most impious, it is of necessity that the Father was always Father; for He is Father of the ever-present Son, on account of whom He has the name of Father, &c. . . . To the Son we must pay the due honour, ascribing to Him the *gennesis* without beginning (τὴν ἄναρχον γέννησιν), from the Father, and using of Him only the words 'was' and 'always,' and 'before all time'." *ap.* Theod. *Hist.* i.

9. Lastly, ATHANASIUS:—"If He be called the eternal Offspring of the Father, He is rightly so called. For never was the substance of the Father imperfect, that what is proper to It should be added afterwards; nor as man from man, has the Son been begotten, so as to be later than the Father's existence; but He is God's Offspring, and, as being proper Son of God, who is ever, He exists eternally." *Orat.* i. 14.

§ 13. THE ASIATIC WRITERS.

We have seen how emphatically the Alexandrians, from first to last, are witnesses of the co-eternity of the Son, as Son, with the Father. This being their unanimous profession or understanding, it is, at first sight, natural to expect that writers in the other parts of Christendom will be found to profess the same doctrine, and to profess it as unequivocally. It is a reasonable expectation; because, as we have seen above, the writers in question are in such full agreement with the Alexandrians in the substance and in the details of their teaching on the subject of the Holy Trinity. Their silence on a twentieth point, it may be urged in their favour, after agreement with the School of Alexandria upon nineteen, may equitably, or even must reasonably, be supplied from the view which the Alexandrians actually take of the sacred dogma. Again, their own teaching on those nineteen points obliges us, it may be said, to think that in mere logical consistency with themselves, they really did hold that twentieth point, on which they happen to be silent. If they hold that our Lord is consubstantial with the Father, in accordance with the subsequent Nicene formula, if they hold our Lord to be an *hypostasis*, or to have a personality, whether they consider Him Word or Son, if they believe that distinct *hypostasis* to have existed from eternity in the unity of the Father, what room is there for difference between them and the

Alexandrians? What is the subtlety, which modern criticism can hit upon, to throw doubt upon what is so clear?

Such anticipations, I grant, are reasonable;—however, there is a silence which speaks; and there are subtleties which belong, not to the critic, but to the subject-matter of his criticism. Whether the silence, and whether the language, of the writers in question be such as to bear out what I have said of them, we have now to inquire.

I have adduced eight or nine Alexandrians stating in one way or another, that the Divine *gennesis* is from eternity. No other Alexandrian can be found to speak otherwise. I am going to adduce as many writers from other parts of Christendom, and in like manner shall suppress none. Is it unreasonable to expect that all of them, or that some of them, will in one way or other say what the Alexandrians say? Will it not be a strange accident if a first eight all speak in behalf of a certain truth, and a second eight are all silent, or at least not distinct upon it, if the second eight held it as well as the first eight? That truth is, that the Word was the Son of God from eternity; does not the unanimity in speech and in silence on one side and on the other, go for something in proof, not only that those who all speak, held it, but also that those who are all silent, did not hold it?

What I want is that any one of those Asiatics and Westerns to whom I am now betaking myself, should say, in behalf of the eternal *gennesis*, what all, or almost all, the Alexandrians say. I want them to say with Gregory, " True Son of True Father, Eternal of Eternal;" or with Origen, in St. Augustine's language, " Semper gignit

Pater, semper gignitur Filius;" or with Dionysius, "The Son is ἀειγεννής;" or with Clement, "He is ἄναρχος ἀρχή;" or with Alexander, "Ever Father, ever Son;" nay, even with Athenagoras, that the Son at and after the era of creation was in the Father as well as from Him, and was its ἰδέα as well as its ἐνέργεια. Nay, it would be something if I found them concordant in professing that the *gennesis* was πρὸ αἰώνων as well as πρὸ κτισμάτων. How is it that, even before the Arian controversy, the Alexandrians abound in such statements, and the writers, to whom I am proceeding, during the same period, are so wanting in them?

This surely is a strong negative argument against their really holding what, as I have shown, they even do not profess to hold; but there is a positive argument against them also. They have a doctrine of their own; I do not mean that every one of them brings it out in fulness, but that it is one to which all of them contribute, and to which they one and all converge; for, as I thought it reasonable, when collecting testimonies on the doctrine of the Holy Trinity, to interpret one writer by another, when they evidently all belonged to one family of thought, so here too I consider I shall be able to show such an intrinsic and substantial agreement between these writers on the point in question, as to allow me fairly to take the incomplete and indirect statements upon it, one by one, to which they commit themselves, as complements and elucidations of each other.

Their doctrine then, which was consistent with their holding firmly the consubstantial and co-eternal unity of the Persons of the Blessed Trinity, was this:—that the

Word was with God from eternity; One with Him, yet distinct from Him, and not merely an attribute or power;—that he was in "corde" or "in utero Patris," till the universe was to be created, and then He was born in order to be its Creator; the external act by which God surrounded Himself with beings animate and inanimate, spiritual and material, being accompanied by a corresponding internal act in the Divine Essence. Thus the Alexandrian teaching was symbolised by the text, "Ego hodie genui te," "hodie" meaning eternity; and the opinion, which I am now inquiring into, is symbolised by the text, "Ex utero ante luciferum genui te;" the doctrine of the *Syncatabasis* and the *Primogenitus*, as I have described it, being held by all alike, whether at Alexandria or elsewhere.

It will be convenient, then, to reduce the doctrine of these Asiatics and Latins to these three heads: first, the Logos in the bosom of the Father, or (to use the philosophical word) Endiathetic, which I shall denote by the letter A; next, the Logos born to be a Son, or Prophoric, B; and, lastly, the Logos Prototocos, C.

Under the name of East I include the countries from Thrace to the borders of Egypt; the countries especially illuminated, in the middle of the fourth century, by Basil and Gregory Nazianzen of the school of Origen, who took up the work which Athanasius had so long carried on before them. And again, the writers of those countries, prior to the time of these Fathers, are such as these :— Ignatius, Polycarp, the writer to Diognetus, Justin, Irenæus, Tatian, Theophilus, Methodius, and Eusebius. To these may be added, as a witness to the doctrine taught him, (whether by Asiatics or Latin ecclesiastics, *certainly not by Egyptians*, for he seems never to have known them) the Emperor Constantine.

Of these I put aside St. Ignatius, St. Polycarp and St. Irenæus from my inquiry. Neither Ignatius nor Polycarp indeed asserts the eternity of the Son; Irenæus does, and his assertion of it, considering his relation to Polycarp, may fairly be taken to speak both for Polycarp and for Ignatius. It would be strange, indeed, if they could be supposed to hold any contrary doctrine, since they are rightly included in what may be called the Apostolic family; and that is why I contrast them with those who came after them whether of the East or the West. They are historically connected with each other; they have not the like historical connexion with others. That these two primitive saints and martyrs should not give expression to the doctrine of the eternity of the *gennesis* is not wonderful, considering how little we have of their writing, and that neither of them wrote about the Holy Trinity. Of Irenæus it might be expected, because he writes at great length, and on a variety of heresies relating to the Object of our worship; and Irenæus, as I have said, does make profession of it.

In *contr. Hær.* iii. 20, he says, " Non tunc cœpit Filius Dei, existens semper apud Patrem ;" and, *ibid.* ii. 55, *fin.* he speaks of the "semper co-existens Filius Patri."

Leaving those, then, who necessarily had the immediate tradition of the Apostles, and whose testimony, as far as given, concurs with that of the unanimous Alexandrian

School, with the authoritative decisions (as we shall see) of the Ante-Nicene Church, and with the doctors of the Fourth and Fifth centuries, let us inquire into the Asiatic writers who were between these two eras of St. Ignatius and of St. Augustine, and contemporaneous with the Alexandrians aforesaid.

But here, again, I must pass over Hermas too, be he a Greek or Latin author, for the same reason that also leads me to pass over St. Cyprian, because he nowhere treats theologically of our Lord, either as Word or as Son of God.

1. I begin, then, with the EPISTOLA AD DIOGNETUM; though neither can this beautiful fragment of a very ancient author be expected to give us clear information on the definite point which I am enquiring about. He says, speaking of the Logos:—

Οὗτος ὁ ἀπ᾽ ἀρχῆς, ὁ καινὸς φανεὶς, καὶ παλαιὸς εὑρεθεὶς, καὶ πάντοτε νέος ἐν ἁγίων καρδίαις γεννώμενος· οὗτος ὁ ἀεὶ, σήμερον υἱὸς λογισθεὶς, c. 11. Certainly there is nothing here implying the Temporal *Gennesis;* on the contrary, the unknown writer will be maintaining the Eternal, supposing, with Origen, he understood by σήμερον the day of eternity. But I doubt if the context will admit of this interpretation of the word. *Vid.* Methodius, *infra*, p. 258. He seems to me to contrast οὗτος ὁ ἀεὶ with σήμερον υἱὸς, and again the υἱὸς is evidently to be explained by the words ἐν καρδίαις γεννώμενος, as if he said, "He, the Word, was from everlasting, (A) and is now, as the first-born in the hearts of His holy people, the Archetypal Son (C)."

I fear I must say that Bishop Bull is not as exact as I should wish him to be in his treatment of this passage. He paraphrases it thus:—" Habet *Filius* Dei novas aliquas et quasi recentes nativitates ... nunquam tamen revera novus et recens *ipse* fuit, sed Filius *Dei Patris semper* et *ab æterno* extitit." Where does the author, whom Bull is paraphrasing, say one word of any "nativitas" except the "nova," which is mystical? where does he contrast a true generation with that mystical? where does he say that the Son of God is from eternity? He speaks of the Word, not of the Son, as eternal, unless indeed σήμερον means "eternal." This Bull does not pretend to show, yet he says, " Filius Dei .. ὁ ἀεὶ .. aperte dicitur, nempe in Epistola ad Diognetum," &c., p. 168, ed. 1721.

2. JUSTIN suffers from a like misinterpretation. How can Bull not know that the point he has to prove as regards certain of his authors, is their witness to the eternal *gennesis?* He actually discusses the difficulty arising from the fact that a certain number of them seem to deny it. He has to prove the eternity of the Son, not the eternity of the Logos; yet, as in the case of the author last quoted, so as regards St. Justin Martyr, when Justin speaks of the eternal Logos, Bull substitutes the word " Son." He says, " Testimonia quædam ex eodem [Justino] adducemus, quæ co-æternam τοῦ λόγου, *sive* Filii Dei cum Patre suo existentiam apertissime confirment." *F. N.* iii. 2, *init.* ed. 1721. Then he proceeds to quote two passages which speak only of the eternity of the Logos, not of the Son. As to the latter of these, the word "Son," or its equivalent,

does not occur in it at all; as to the former, Grabe, whose annotations have for their object to defend and to support Bull's hypothesis, candidly confesses that both text and stopping must be corrected in a direction adverse to the necessities of Bull's argument.

Now let us consider St. Justin's theology; for myself, indeed, though I have done my best to master what he has written, I distrust too much whether my eyesight or my power of sustained attention, to speak with the fullest confidence; but, speaking under correction of these defects, I will say, that, though I have found passages in the Alexandrians, I cannot find a single passage in St. Justin, in which the Son, or the only-begotten, or the *gennesis*, is declared to be from everlasting, except in such phrases as "before all creatures," which are short of the directness of the Alexandrian School.

(1.) The following is the passage, on which Bull principally relies in proof of St. Justin's taking the orthodox view of the point in question. I quote it with Grabe's correction and stopping, introducing the three letters, which I have assigned as notes for the Endiathetic Word, the Prophoric, and the Primogenitus respectively.

Ὁ υἱὸς ἐκείνου, ὁ μόνος λεγόμενος κυρίως υἱὸς, ὁ λόγος πρὸ τῶν ποιημάτων, καὶ συνὼν, (A)—καὶ γεννώμενος, ὅτε (B) τὴν ἀρχὴν δι' αὐτοῦ πάντα ἔκτισε καὶ ἐκόσμησε (C). *Apol.* ii. 6. Grabe's Latin runs: "Verbum ante omnes creaturas et coexistens (Patri); et nascens, quando [non quoniam . . .] primitus cuncta per eum condidit et ornavit." p. 170. It is observable Justin does not even use the phrase πρὸ αἰώνων, but πρὸ τῶν ποιημάτων.

There is no mention in this passage of the eternity of the *gennesis;* rather it is said to have taken place when the world was to be created. Nor does Bull's second passage or collation of passages, to the effect that our Lord was the " I am " of the burning bush, avail better for his purpose ; vid. *ad Græc.* 21, *Apol.* i. 63, and *Tryph.* 60. Doubtless our Lord is from eternity, and Justin believed Him to be the one true God ; but I am looking for a categorical passage declaring that the Son always existed as the Son ; such as Origen's " the Only-begotten Word, ever-coexisting with Him," or " Who dares say, ' Once the Son was not ' ? " I will set down some other passages of Justin; none of them, I think, rise above the level of the foregoing. I have no doubt of his holding the co-eternity and consubstantiality of the *Word;* but does he anywhere profess the everlasting *gennesis?*

(2.) Ἰησοῦς Χριστὸς, μόνος ἰδίως υἱὸς τῷ θεῷ γεγέννηται. λόγος αὐτοῦ ὑπάρχων, καὶ πρωτότοκος καὶ δύναμις. *Apol.* i. 23.

(3.) Υἱὸς . . . ὃς, καὶ λόγος πρωτότοκος (C) ὢν τοῦ θεοῦ, καὶ θεὸς ὑπάρχει. *Ibid.* 63.

(4.) Ἀρχὴν, πρὸ πάντων τῶν κτισμάτων, ὁ θεὸς γεγέννηκε δύναμίν τινα ἐξ ἑαυτοῦ λογικὴν, (B) ἥτις καὶ δόξα κυρίου ὑπὸ τοῦ πνεύματος τοῦ ἁγίου καλεῖται, ποτὲ δὲ υἱός, ποτὲ δὲ σοφία, ποτὲ δὲ ἄγγελος, ποτὲ δὲ θεός, ποτὲ δὲ κύριος καὶ λόγος. . . . ἔχειν γὰρ πάντα προσονομάζεσθαι, ἔκ τε τοῦ ὑπηρετεῖν τῷ πατρικῷ βουλήματι (C) καὶ ἐκ τοῦ ἀπὸ τοῦ πατρὸς θελήσει γεγεννῆσθαι (B). [Ἀλλ' οὔ?] τοιοῦτον ὁποῖον καὶ ἐφ' ἡμῶν γενόμενον ὁρῶμεν· λόγον γάρ τινα προβάλλοντες, λόγον γεννῶμεν, οὐ κατ' ἀποτομὴν, ὡς ἐλαττωθῆναι τὸν ἐν ἡμῖν λόγον προβαλλόμενοι, καὶ ὁποῖον ἐπὶ πυρὸς ὁρῶμεν ἄλλο γινόμενον, &c. &c. *Tryph.* 61.

The Benedictine Editor who follows Bull in his explanations, fully admits that St. Justin is not here speaking of an eternal *gennesis*, but of one before and in order to creation; at the same time, with Bull, he will not allow that Justin speaks of a real, but of a figurative and improper *gennesis*. Where does Justin speak of any other gennesis but this temporal one? and what grounds are there for saying this is not real and natural?

(5.) Τοῦτο τὸ τῷ ὄντι ἀπὸ τοῦ πατρὸς προβληθὲν γέννημα, (B) πρὸ πάντων τῶν ποιημάτων συνῆν τῷ πατρὶ καὶ τούτῳ ὁ πατὴρ προσομιλεῖ (A) ... ἀρχὴ (C) πρὸ πάντων τῶν ποιημάτων τοῦτ᾽ αὐτὸ καὶ γέννημα ὑπὸ τοῦ θεοῦ ἐγεγέννητο. 62.

(6.) Προϋπάρχειν θεὸν ὄντα πρὸ αἰώνων (A), τοῦτον τὸν Χριστὸν, εἶτα καὶ γεννηθῆναι ἄνθρωπον γενόμενον ὑπομεῖναι. *Ibid.* 48.

(7.) Υἱὸν αὐτὸν λέγοντες, νενοήκαμεν, καὶ πρὸ πάντων ποιημάτων, ἀπὸ τοῦ πατρὸς δυνάμει αὐτοῦ καὶ βουλῇ προελθόντα (B). *Ibid.* 100.

(8.) Μονογενὴς γὰρ, ὅτι ἦν τῷ πατρὶ τῶν ὅλων οὗτος, (A, ἰδίως ἐξ αὐτοῦ λόγος καὶ δύναμις γεγενημένος, (B) καὶ ὕστερον ἄνθρωπος διὰ τῆς παρθένου γενόμενος. *Ibid.* 105. This is a near approach to the statement which I am looking for. To say that "the Word was born" is like saying that the birth was from everlasting, for the Word is eternal; still, St. Justin may have meant "that the Word was born into Sonship or to become a Son;" that is, became the Logos Prophoricus. In like manner, above, (n. 3, p. 250,) he speaks of λόγος πρωτότοκος; where Bishop Kaye would interpose καὶ unnecessarily. *Vid.* also above, p. 251, λόγον γεννῶμεν. And Tatian, ὁ λόγος γεννηθείς, and Theophilus, τὸν λόγον ἐγέννησε προφορικόν, *infra,* p. 253 4, &c.

(9.) Ἐπάλαισεν Ἰακὼβ μετὰ τοῦ φαινομένου μὲν, ἐκ τοῦ τῇ τοῦ πατρὸς βουλῇ ὑπηρετεῖν, θεοῦ δὲ, ἐκ τοῦ εἶναι τέκνον πρωτότοκον τῶν ὅλων κτισμάτων (C). *Ibid.* 125.

(10.) Τὴν δύναμιν ταύτην γεγεννῆσθαι ἀπὸ τοῦ πατρός, δυνάμει καὶ βουλῇ αὐτοῦ, ἀλλ' οὐ κατ' ἀποτομὴν, ὡς ἀπομεριζομένης τῆς τοῦ πατρὸς οὐσίας, &c. *Ibid.* 128.

I have referred to this passage, because it contains an avowal of the Homoüsion, as *supr.* n. 4.

In none of the above passages is the *gennesis* said to be ἀεὶ, from eternity; nay, it is not even said to be "before all time," πρὸ αἰώνων; the idea commonly in Justin's mind is creation, and the birth of the Son "before creation," πρὸ τῶν κτισμάτων. In the one passage, in which he speaks of "before ages" *supra* (6), he is not speaking of our Lord's *gennesis,* but of His Divinity. There is nothing to show that he confines πρωτότοκος, as Athanasius, to denote a word of office. His usual word to express the Son's ministration is rather ὑπηρέτης, ὑπηρετεῖν.

3. TATIAN, the disciple of Justin, is far more explicit in his statement of that doctrine which is not altogether foreign to the theology of his master. I am obliged to make a long quotation from him :—

Θεὸς ὁ καθ' ἡμᾶς οὐκ ἔχει σύστασιν ἐν χρόνῳ, μόνος ἄναρχος ὢν, καὶ αὐτὸς ὑπάρχων τῶν ὅλων ἀρχή· πνεῦμα ὁ θεὸς ...
... Θεὸς ἦν ἐν ἀρχῇ, τὴν δὲ ἀρχὴν λόγου δύναμιν παρειλήφαμεν. ὁ γὰρ δεσπότης τῶν ὅλων, αὐτὸς ὑπάρχων τοῦ

παντὸς ἡ ὑπόστασις, κατὰ μὲν τὴν μηδέπω γεγενημένην ποίησιν μόνος ἦν· καθὸ δὲ πᾶσα δύναμις, ὁρατῶν τε καὶ ἀοράτων αὐτὸς ὑπόστασις ἦν· σὺν αὐτῷ τὰ πάντα (σὺν αὐτῷ γὰρ) διὰ λογικῆς δυνάμεως αὐτὸς καὶ ὁ λόγος, ὃς ἦν ἐν αὐτῷ (A), ὑπέστησε. Θελήματι δὲ τῆς ἁπλότητος αὐτοῦ [at His absolute will] προπηδᾷ λόγος [vid. ἥλατο, Sap. xviii. 15.] (B). ὁ δὲ λόγος, οὐ κατὰ κενοῦ χωρήσας [*i.e.* creating as He went forward] ἔργον πρωτότοκον τοῦ πατρὸς γίνεται (C). τοῦτον ἴσμεν τοῦ κόσμου τὴν ἀρχήν. γέγονε δὲ κατὰ μερισμὸν, οὐ κατ᾽ ἀποκοπήν· [with a participation of God, not a separation;] τὸ γὰρ ἀποτμηθὲν τοῦ πρώτου κεχώρισται, τὸ δὲ μερισθὲν, οἰκονομίας τὴν αἵρεσιν προσλαβὸν, [as taking upon itself the office of an economy] οὐκ ἐνδεᾷ τὸν ὅθεν εἴληπται πεποίηκεν. ὥσπερ γὰρ ἀπὸ μιᾶς δᾳδὸς, &c. &c., οὕτω καὶ ὁ λόγος, προελθὼν ἐκ τῆς τοῦ πατρὸς δυνάμεως, οὐκ ἄλογον πεποίηκε τὸν γεγεννηκότα. καὶ γὰρ αὐτὸς ἐγὼ λαλῶ, (B) καὶ .... διακοσμεῖν τὸν ἐν ὑμῖν ἀκόσμητον ὕλην προῄρημαι. (C) καὶ, καθάπερ ὁ λόγος ἐν ἀρχῇ γεννηθεὶς, (B) ἀντεγέννησε τὴν καθ᾽ ἡμᾶς ποίησιν (C), αὐτὸς ἑαυτῷ τὴν ὕλην δημιουργήσας, (C) οὕτω κἀγὼ, &c. .... Λόγος γὰρ ὁ ἐπουράνιος, πνεῦμα γεγονὼς ἀπὸ τοῦ πατρὸς, καὶ λόγος ἐκ τῆς λογικῆς δυνάμεως, (A) κατὰ τὴν τοῦ γεννήσαντος (B) αὐτὸν πατρὸς μίμησιν, εἰκόνα τῆς ἀθανασίας τὸν ἄνθρωπον ἐποίησεν, (C) &c. *contr. Græc.* 4—7.

In this passage, which displays a force and clearness superior to Justin's, Tatian follows his master in professing the Homoüsion, by his use of Justin's illustration of the "fire from fire". This illustration, too, shows that, in what he says of the procession of the Logos, he is speaking of a real and proper *gennesis*, not an allegorical, while at the same time, as Maran the Benedictine editor admits, he is evidently speaking of a temporal *gennesis*. It is observable that he does not use the word "Son" once.

The words in the last sentence, λόγος ὁ ἐπουράνιος, πνεῦμα γεγονὼς ἀπὸ πατρὸς, call for a remark. They may be thought to imply that the (everlasting) Word was begotten, which would be an eternal *gennesis*, or at least they identify the two ideas of Word and Son, so that either the Word is but temporal, or the Son is eternal. However, I should understand the words λόγος πνεῦμα γεγονὼς (and the λόγος γεννηθείς), as I have translated Justin's λόγος γεγενημένος (n. 8, p. 251, 2, and *infra*, p. 283) of "the Prophoric Word". It must be allowed, indeed, since, according to the remark of Dionysius of Alexandria, our words are in some sense our children, that the everlasting Word is, as such, in some sense a Son of God, and so far the *gennesis* in Justin's sense is eternal. This admission, however, does not exclude its being temporal more exactly, if, as I think, these Fathers considered our Lord's *gennesis* as a process. From eternity He was conceived, as if "in utero," and before time and creation He was born. He was not born from eternity.

With Athanasius Tatian connects the title "First-born" with the Word's work of creating and informing all things; in calling the First-born Himself a work, he has the sanction of St. Athanasius and St. Thomas, whom I have quoted above. The phrase προσλαβὼν τὴν αἵρεσιν suggests the voluntariness of His *Syncatabasis*, an idea which I do not find in Justin, who seems rather to make the οἰκονομία or ὑπηρεσία to belong to our Lord's Nature;

but I have softened the harshness of this notion, *supr.* "*On the temporal procession.*"

His κατὰ τὴν μίμησιν is wrong theology, as I have noted above, when referring to St. Methodius and Novatian, *supr.* p. 219. It connects his view of doctrine with that of writers, who, historically, have no relations with him; as his emphatic start, "God was alone," will be presently seen to connect him with Novatian, St. Hippolytus and Tertullian.

Tatian at length fell into heresy; but it was not a heresy affecting his belief in the Holy Trinity; and it was after his writing the treatise from which the above extracts are made.

4. ST. THEOPHILUS writes with more authority than Justin or Tatian. He was a bishop, and of the great see of Antioch, being the sixth in descent from St. Peter. His testimony is in point of distinctness an advance upon Tatian's, as Tatian's is upon St. Justin's.

Ἐξ οὐκ ὄντων τὰ πάντα ἐποίησεν. οὐ γάρ τι τῷ θεῷ συνήκμασεν· ἀλλ' αὐτὸς ἑαυτοῦ τόπος ὤν, καὶ ἀνενδεὴς ὤν, καὶ ὑπερέχων πρὸ τῶν αἰώνων, ἠθέλησεν ἄνθρωπον ποιῆσαι ᾧ γνωσθῇ· τούτῳ οὖν προητοίμασε τὸν κόσμον· ὁ γὰρ γενητὸς καὶ προσδεής ἐστιν, ὁ δὲ ἀγένητος οὐδενὸς προσδεῖται. ἔχων οὖν ὁ θεὸς τὸν ἑαυτοῦ λόγον ἐνδιάθετον ἐν τοῖς ἰδίοις σπλάγχνοις (A), ἐγέννησεν αὐτὸν μετὰ τῆς ἑαυτοῦ σοφίας ἐξερευξάμενος πρὸ τῶν ὅλων (B). Τοῦτον τὸν λόγον ἔσχεν ὑπουργὸν τῶν ὑπ' αὐτοῦ γεγενημένων, καὶ δι' αὐτοῦ τὰ πάντα πεποίηκεν. οὗτος λέγεται ἀρχή, ὅτι ἄρχει καὶ κυριεύει πάντων τῶν δι' αὐτοῦ δεδημιουργημένων (C). Οὗτος οὖν ὢν πνεῦμα θεοῦ, καὶ ἀρχή, καὶ σοφία, καὶ δύναμις ὑψίστου, κατήρχετο εἰς τοὺς προφήτας, κ.τ.λ. . . . οὐ γὰρ ἦσαν οἱ προφῆται ὅτε ὁ κόσμος ἐγίνετο· ἀλλ' ἡ σοφία ἡ ἐν αὐτῷ οὖσα ἡ τοῦ θεοῦ (C) καὶ ὁ λόγος ὁ ἅγιος αὐτοῦ ὁ ἀεὶ συμπαρὼν αὐτῷ (A). *ad Autol.* ii. 10.

Again: ὁ λόγος ὁ τοῦ θεοῦ, ὅς ἐστι καὶ υἱὸς αὐτοῦ . . . . ὡς ἀλήθεια διηγεῖται, τὸν λόγον, τὸν ὄντα διαπαντὸς ἐνδιάθετον ἐν καρδίᾳ θεοῦ (A). πρὸ γὰρ τι γίνεσθαι, τοῦτον εἶχε σύμβουλον, ἑαυτοῦ νοῦν καὶ φρόνησιν ὄντα, ὁπότε δὲ ἠθέλησεν ὁ θεὸς ποιῆσαι ὅσα ἐβουλεύσατο, τοῦτον τὸν λόγον ἐγέννησε προφορικὸν (B), πρωτότοκον πάσης κτίσεως (C), οὐ κενωθεὶς αὐτὸς τοῦ λόγου, ἀλλὰ λόγον γεννήσας, καὶ τῷ λόγῳ αὐτοῦ διαπαντὸς ὁμιλῶν . . . θεὸς οὖν ὢν ὁ λόγος, καὶ ἐκ θεοῦ πεφυκώς, κ.τ.λ. *Ibid.* 22.

Here, as in the foregoing authors, there is a clear expression of a belief in the *Homoüsion;* our Lord is in the Father's ἰδίοις σπλάγχνοις, ἐν καρδίᾳ θεοῦ, ἐνδιάθετον, ἐκ θεοῦ πεφυκώς, &c. &c. And, moreover, in such expressions, as in the passage of Tatian, we have the plain proof that the *gennesis* thus spoken of is a real proper *gennesis*, and not a metaphorical; for if metaphorical, there was nothing in it to call for these phrases which insist on His proceeding from the very οὐσία of God. Moreover, in Theophilus the philosophical words, Endiathetic and Prophoric, at length come to the surface, which are implied as ideas in Justin and Tatian, as also in Hippolytus and others, as we shall see *infra*. Further, Theophilus knows of no other *gennesis* but the temporal, for he confines the idea of *gennesis* to the Word's becoming *prophoric*; ὁπότε ἠθέλησεν ποιῆσαι, ἐγέννησε προφορικόν. And the phrases ἐν σπλάγχνοις, ἐν καρδίᾳ are to be remarked, in connexion with the "ex utero" of

Psalm 109, on which I have already insisted; and still more so with the singular word συνήκμασεν. God is always from eternity in His perfection or maturity; "but," says Theophilus, "nothing was in its maturity *with* God;" in other words, the Logos was ἐν καρδίᾳ θεοῦ, but had not yet attained that perfection which took place when He became prophoric, or was born into Sonship. This idea will be further illustrated when we come to consider the doctrine of St. Hippolytus. I understand Theophilus's word ὑπουργός of the *Syncatabasis*, though it is a less honourable title than Justin's ὑπηρέτης, and perhaps than the παῖς of Athenagoras and Hippolytus, and far below the dignity of πρωτότοκος. However, it is corrected, if it needs correction (for Athanasius seems to use it, *Orat.* ii. 22), by the words ἄρχει and κυριεύει which follow, and by σύμβουλος, which also strongly expresses the Word's personality; *vid.* also βοηθός, ad *Autol.* ii. 18. Also, it must be observed that he uses the phrase πρὸ τῶν αἰώνων for the *divine* eternity, as Justin, *supr.* p. 252.

5. ST. MELITO was Bishop of Sardis in the latter part of the second century. There is nothing in what remains of him specially bearing upon the subject before us; it may be noted, however, that twice he uses the phrase "before the ages;" viz. πρὸ τῶν αἰώνων (Routh. *Reliqu.* t. i. p. 112) and προαιώνιος (*ibid.* p. 116), and in both places in the sense of eternity (as being applied to the Word's divinity), with Justin and Theophilus.

6. ST. METHODIUS, bishop, first of Patara in Asia

Minor, then of Tyre, is best known as having written against Origen, though he agrees with him, as we have seen, in those representations of the ministrative office of the Son and Spirit, which I have had to explain. There is a passage in his *Convivium Virginum* which is asserted on all hands as decisive of his adhesion to the doctrine of the eternal *gennesis;* it is as follows :—

"Those who are receiving the illumination [of baptism] φωτιζόμενοι, receive the lineaments, features, and manly aspect of Christ, the resemblance of the *Word* being stamped upon them . . . . [Hence] the oracular voice from above from the Father Himself to Christ, on His coming for the purification of water in the Jordan. 'Thou art My Son, this day have I begotten Thee.' He declared that He was His Son without the mention of limit or time, ἀορίστως καὶ ἀχρόνως. ' Εἶ' γὰρ αὐτῷ ἔφη, καὶ οὐ ' γέγονας'· ἐμφαίνων μήτε πρόσφατον αὐτὸν τετυχέναι τῆς υἱοθεσίας, μήτε αὖ προϋπάρξαντα μετὰ ταῦτα τέλος ἐσχηκέναι, ἀλλὰ προγεννηθέντα καὶ ἔσεσθαι καὶ εἶναι τὸν αὐτόν. τὸ δὲ, 'Εγὼ σήμερον γεγέννηκά σε, ὅτι προόντα ἤδη πρὸ τῶν αἰώνων ἐν τοῖς οὐρανοῖς, ἐβουλήθην καὶ τῷ κόσμῳ γεννῆσαι, ὃ δή ἐστι, πρόσθεν ἀγνοούμενον γνωρίσαι." *Conviv.* viii. 9, *ap*. Galland, t. 3, p. 719.

In this passage it is certainly said that the Son "is," not "was made;" that He is the Son without limit of time; that He has not merely obtained a Sonship recently, which will one time come to an end, but that, whereas He was before the ages in heaven, and was afore-begotten, so He will ever be in existence, and so is He one and the same. But granting all this, I am not sure in these statements of any implication of the eternal *gennesis*. Methodius seems to me to say that "'to-day' is the day of the Church, during which incessant regenerations take place, of which the Son (who is prior to the Church, nay, prior to all creation, as having no beginning in time, and who will outlive the Church) is the great Archetype, ever coming to the birth, ever coming into the world, for the world's illumination." This, indeed, is nothing else than the doctrine of "the First-born," applied, as in *Rom.* viii. 29, *Hebr.* i. 6, *Apoc.* i. 5, to the new creation. The concluding words "to beget Him to the world, that is, to manifest Him who was before unknown," are parallel to passages in Justin, *Tryph.* 88, *fin.*, and *Epist. ad Diogn. supr.*, and Hippolytus, *infr.* p. 270, *fin.*

7. THE EMPEROR CONSTANTINE has not even the authority of a layman in the Church; but what he so confidently states on the subject of the Divine Sonship, he certainly did not invent himself, but learned from some high persons in the East or West. It will be found substantially to agree with the doctrine of Tertullian as stated above, p. 232, in affirming that God is not a Father from all eternity, except *in posse*, not actually. "Our most religious Emperor," says Eusebius, "did in a speech prove, that the Son of God was in being even according to His divine *gennesis*, which is before all ages (A); since, even before His actual *gennesis* ($\pi\rho\grave{\iota}\nu$ $\gamma\epsilon\nu\nu\eta\theta\hat{\eta}\nu\alpha\iota$ $\dot{\epsilon}\nu$ $\dot{\epsilon}\nu\epsilon\rho\gamma\epsilon\dot{\iota}\alpha$) (B), He was in virtue ($\dot{\epsilon}\nu$ $\delta\upsilon\nu\acute{\alpha}\mu\epsilon\iota$) with the Father without *gennesis* ($\dot{\alpha}\gamma\epsilon\nu\nu\acute{\eta}\tau\omega\varsigma$), the Father being always Father, as always King and always Saviour." *ap.* Athan. *Decr. fin.*

8. And now, by way of contrast, let me refer to the doctrine of that Eusebius who reports to us the theology of Constantine. While I cannot deny that such a theological view, in which the Emperor was sheltered by passages of such orthodox writers as I have named, might easily be misunderstood in an Arian or Semi-Arian sense, —both the heretical party and the authors I have cited speaking of the Son as being formally born, upon and in order to, the creation of the universe, and as if not generated from eternity,—after all there is this vast difference between the heretics and these Catholic Ante-Nicenes, that the Catholics were firm believers in the Homoüsion, and the others, on the contrary, rejected it. The latter considered that the Son had an individual existence as each of us has, and was in all respects separate from the Father as we are, whether, as Arians, they thought Him a mere creature, or, as Semi-Arians, a second and secondary God. The Catholics, on the other hand, some of whom I have cited and some I have still to cite, testify in set terms to the consubstantiality or simple individuality of Father and Son. I have already given the statements of these Asiatic Ante-Nicenes; now I will show this contrast as exhibited in the language of Eusebius, a Semi-Arian, using for the purpose some of the passages brought together by Petavius, *de Trin.* i. 11.

He lays it down, for instance, as revealed truth. that " after the unoriginate and ingenerate essence (οὐσίαν) of the God of the Universe, which is incommunicable and above all comprehension, there is a *second* essence and divine Power, the origin of all created things, and first subsisting, and begotten (γεγενημένην) from the First Cause (αἰτίου), the Word, Wisdom, and Power of God." *Præp.* vii. 12, p. 320, ed. 1688;

That "The Only-begotten of God Himself, and First-born of the universe, the origin of all things, exhorts us to account His Father alone as true God, and to worship Him alone." *ibid.* vii. 15, p. 327;

That "though the Radiance co-exists with the Light (συνυπάρχει) and is its complement (for without its Radiance Light could not subsist), and co-exists together with it and in itself (καθ' αὐτὸ), the Father exists *before* the Son (προϋπάρχει) and subsists before the Son's making (τῆς γενέσεως αὐτοῦ προϋφέστηκεν), in that He alone is ingenerate (ἀγένητος); and, whereas the Radiance does not shine forth by any choice on the part of the Light, but by a certain *inseparable accident* of its essence, the Son subsists the Image of the Father by His purpose and choice." *Demonstr.* iv. 3, p. 147, 8;

That "he who holds two *hypostases* is not obliged to admit two Gods; for we do not determine them to be equals in honour;" that "the Son Himself teaches us that His Father is His God;" whereas "the Son, when He Himself is compared to the Father, will not be God of His Father, but . . . . the Image of the Unseen God, &c., and He venerates, worships, and glorifies His own Father as being God." *contr. Marcell.* ii. 7, p. 109.

I have brought together other passages of Eusebius, in annotating on Athanasius, vol. ii. art. *Eusebius*.

If the Semi-Arian Eusebius thus vitally differed

from Justin and Theophilus, much more did the Arians.[1]

9. Nor is this all. It must be considered that the authors whom I have cited, whatever be the authority of some of them, cannot be said to speak *ex cathedra*, even if they had the right to do so; and do not speak as a Council may speak. When a certain number of men meet together, one of them corrects another, and what is personal and peculiar in each, what is local or belongs to schools, is eliminated. Now we have the voice of a great assembly of Asiatic Bishops in the third century speaking on the very doctrine of our Lord's Divinity; I mean the Council or Councils of Antioch, between A.D. 264 and 272. One of these Councils was attended by as many as seventy Bishops. They were convened at Antioch against the heresiarch Metropolitan, Paul of Samosata, and they published an exposition of the Catholic dogma, which supplies us with that very article of it which I desiderate in Tatian and others. I cannot deny, and indeed I cannot but be pleased, that the Alexandrians had a share in this good work. Dionysius, their then Bishop, was the first to move against Paulus; he wrote against him, and, when he could not attend the Council, as being in his last illness, he sent

---

[1] I am not forgetful of the strong passages brought together by Cave in behalf of Eusebius's orthodoxy. I would gladly believe that he became more orthodox after the Nicene Council, at least upon a main point on which the Arian controversy turned. The passages most in his favour appear to be in his *Laud. Constant.*, written ten years after the Council; but this is too large a subject for a note.

a formal letter to its Fathers, from his death-bed, on the grave subject of their meeting. Moreover, the most eminent members of the Council were closely connected with Origen as a teacher; Athenodorus and Gregory were his converts, and for many years his pupils; and Firmilian, if not his pupil, as Gregory Nyssen affirms, at least was his warm friend and patron, and studied the Scriptures with him in a long sojourn in Palestine. I do not say this, however, to weaken the authoritative force of the Council as an Asiatic body, though doubtless this Alexandrian element was of the greatest service in its deliberations.

Into their dogmatic Letter they introduce one of those plain cardinal words incompatible with the doctrine of the temporal *gennesis*, which I have looked for in vain as yet out of Alexandria. They speak of the Son, not merely as before all creatures, or ages, but absolutely as eternal. They say, "This *Son* .... knowing both in the Old and the New Covenant, we confess and preach as being begotten, the Only-begotten Son, Image of the Invisible God, First-born of all creatures, Wisdom and Word and Power of God, in existence before ages, not in foreknowledge, but in substance and hypostasis Son of God .... Him (the *Son*) we believe, *being ever* with the Father (σὺν τῷ πατρὶ ἀεὶ ὄντα), to have accomplished the Father's purpose for the creation of the Universe." Moreover, as if protesting against the mischief done by the doctrine of the "prophoric Word," the "Word begotten into Sonship," they assert that He is "One and the same in substance." Routh. *Reliqu.* vol. ii. pp. 466, 468, 474.

At the last of these Councils, one of which drew up the Letter in which these words occur, the word *homoüsion* which the Alexandrians had maintained, I confess, was withdrawn; but it was withdrawn on an objection of Paul's, for which it was thought necessary to consult, not for any reason arising out of the meaning and drift with which it was afterwards used at Nicæa. However, that withdrawal, whatever may be said of it, does not impair the force of what the Council did positively enunciate. What that enunciation brings home to us is this,—that we may follow the facts of ecclesiastical history, whithersoever they lead us (as in this question of the incomplete utterances of early Saints), without any misgiving that, in doing so, we shall be doing damage to the tradition of the early Church, as a witness in behalf of the faith of St. Athanasius and St. Augustine.

§ 14. THE WESTERN WRITERS.

The theological literature of the East in the first centuries can hardly be said to have suggested Arianism; but it was a sort of shelter for it, when it made its appearance. I shall have to speak in very much the same way of certain writers of the West during the same period, who were more copious and more able than the Orientals. St. Justin or St. Theophilus cannot pretend, in force of intellect or originality, to vie with Tertullian, or with Hippolytus in fertility or in authority.

The theological writers in the West during the period which I have taken in Asia and Egypt (viz., down to the middle of the fourth century, to Eusebius and Athanasius inclusive), are St. Hippolytus of Rome, the Roman author of the lately discovered *Elenchus Hæresium*, Tertullian of Rome and Carthage, Novatian also of Rome; St. Zeno of Verona, St. Hilary and St. Phœbadius of France, and Lactantius and Victorinus of Africa. Of Cyprian I spoke above.

Of the four Roman writers in this list, three were in direct variance with the Holy See on matters of discipline, which they maintained ought to be stricter than the Popes judged to be prudent. The earliest of these three seems to be the author of the *Elenchus Hæresium*, discovered some twenty or thirty years ago, who is so scandalous in his treatment of two contemporary Popes, Zephyrinus and Callistus; a learned and able writer, but fierce and reckless in his enmities, and incontrollable in his temper. Another, the African Tertullian, is the most powerful writer of the early centuries. He is said to have lived in Rome, for many years apparently, and was there ordained Priest; then, when at length driven to his own country by the hostility of the Roman clergy, he set himself to inveigh against the laxity of morals which he considered to be tolerated by the Popes, and died in the profession of Montanism. The third is Novatian, a Roman priest, so highly placed and so specially respected, that, during the vacancy of the Holy See, he was chosen by the Roman clergy to be their spokesman in their correspondence with St. Cyprian of Carthage; a man of unblemished, or rather austere character, and dying for the Christian faith in the Valerian persecution. He too, scandalised by the relaxation of discipline in his day, became the author of the unhappy schism which goes by his name. His sectaries stood by the Catholics, and suffered with them for the cause of orthodoxy, during the Arian tyranny. He is said to be the first Anti-Pope, and to have contrived his own consecration by means quite unworthy of his high character; but, bearing in mind how Pope Callistus suffers from his unscrupulous adversary, I am slow to admit what may really be a party representation of him. He, as Callistus, has no opportunity of speaking for himself.

Greater still in reputation, without any slur upon his character or conduct (though some have attributed to him a temporary Novatianism some twenty or thirty years before Novatian) is Hippolytus. He stands, or rather stood, while his writings were extant, in point of authority, range of subject, and ability, in the very first rank of theologians in the Ante-Nicene times, and perhaps has no rival at all, as a theologian, during that period, except his master, St. Irenæus. At present we have little more than fragments of his writings, and it is a mystery how Origen's works have come down to us, who has ever been in the shade, and not those of Hippolytus who has ever been in the brightest light of ecclesiastical approbation. A senator of Rome, as some consider, before he became a servant of the Church, he is said to have been a disciple of the holy Bishop of Lyons, and he followed him in being in succession Bishop, Doctor, and Martyr. Within a century of his death a church had been erected near the Basilica of St. Laurence in honour of a martyr of his name, and it became a popular shrine and resort of pilgrims; and there is reason for concluding that he was the Hippolytus to whom it was dedicated.[1] I say so, because there it was that in the 16th century a marble statue of him was found, which is still to be seen in the Vatican, an historical portrait, as some consider, with a list of his works engraven upon the episcopal chair on which he is seated. He is the first commentator *in extenso* upon Scripture among Christian writers, and his annotations are said to have been used by St. Ambrose in his own *Hexameron*. He is on the Catalogue of theolo-

---

[1] There is no difficulty in believing that other martyrs of the same name were afterwards associated with him in the church which was dedicated to him, as occurs in the instance of other saints.

gians given us by Eusebius, St. Jerome, Theodoret, and Leontius, and, together with St. Irenæus, is quoted largely by Theodoret in that writer's controversies with the heretics of his day. Moreover, Pope Gelasius, A.D. 500, uses him as one of his authorities in his work against the Eutychians, and Pope Martin in the Lateran Council of A.D. 649 appeals to him in his own condemnation of the Monothelites.

That a name so singularly honoured, a name which a breath of ecclesiastical censure has never even dimmed, should belong, as so many men think just now, to the author of that malignant libel on his contemporary Popes, which is appended to the lately discovered *Elenchus*, is to my mind simply incredible,—incredible, not simply considering the gravity of tone in what remains to us of his writings, and mainly indeed in the *Elenchus* itself, but especially because his name and his person were, as I have been pointing out, so warmly cherished at Rome by Popes of the fourth, fifth, and seventh centuries. Rome has a long memory of injuries offered to her majesty; and that special honours should have been paid there to a pamphleteer, as we now speak, who did not scruple in set words to call Pope Zephyrinus a weak and venal dunce, and Pope Callistus a sacrilegious swindler, an infamous convict, and an heresiarch *ex cathedra*, is an hypothesis which requires more direct evidence for its acceptance than has hitherto been produced. I grant that that portion of the work which relates to the Holy Trinity as closely resembles the works of Hippolytus in style and in teaching, as the libellous matter which has got a place in it is incompatible with his reputation;—in the present discussion, however, it matters not what becomes of a difficulty which is mainly historical or biographical. Here I shall place him first among the Western writers, on account of the weight of his authority in early times, the clearness and terseness of his style, and the completeness of his doctrinal view. After him I shall proceed to his companions, Tertullian and Novatian.

1. HIPPOLYTUS, *contr. Noetum*, 10.

"God, existing (ὑπάρχων) alone, and having nothing contemporaneous (σύγχρονον) with Himself, purposed to create the world."

Existing alone; so Tatian, μόνος ἄναρχος, ὑπάρχων ἀρχή, *supr.* p. 253; and *infr.* p. 276, Tertullian, "Ante omnia Deus erat solus;" (vid. also Marcellus, πλὴν θεοῦ, οὐδὲν ἕτερον ἦν. Euseb. *supr.* p. 24.)

"He conceived in thought (ἐννοηθείς) the world (A); He willed, spoke, and made it. To Him forthwith presented itself the thing that came into being (γενόμενον) as He would."

Clement says, ἡ ἰδέα, ἐννόημα τοῦ θεοῦ· ὅπερ οἱ βάρβαροι λόγον εἰρήκασι τοῦ θεοῦ. *Strom.* v. 3, ed. Potter. In Hippolytus, then, ἐννοηθεὶς may perhaps refer to the Word as endiathetic.

"It is enough for us to know only this, that contemporaneous with God there was nothing besides Himself; and that He being sole (μόνος) was many (πολύς); for not Word-less (intellect-less), or Wisdom-less, or Power-less, or Thought-less (ἀβούλευτος) was He, (A) but all things were in Him, and He was the whole (τὸ πᾶν)."

"When He would, as He would, He manifested His Word (B), at seasons determined with Him [i.e. Himself], by whom He made all things (C). When He wills, He does; and when He has in mind, He performs; and when He speaks, He manifests; and when He moulds, He exercises wisdom (σοφίζεται). For all things that have come into being (γενόμενα) He contrives, by means of Word (Reason) and Wisdom, by Word creating and by Wisdom embellishing. He did then as He would, for He was God."

"Embellishing" or "furnishing" is a reference to Gen. ii. 1, "So the heavens and the earth were finished, and πᾶς ὁ κόσμος αὐτῶν," "et omnis ornatus eorum." So Justin and Tatian, *supr.* pp. 250, 253. And so Methodius *de Creatis*, vii. *ap.* Galland, t. 3, p. 802.

"And of the things which were coming into being He begat (ἐγέννα) the Word to be His Leader, and Counsellor, and Operator (ἀρχηγὸν, σύμβουλον, ἐργάτην)."

And so Theophilus, ἐγέννησεν τὸν λόγον, ὑπουργὸν, ἀρχὴν, σύμβουλον, &c., *supr.* p. 256.

"Which Word having in Himself invisible (A) He makes visible (B) to the world, during its process of creation (κτιζομένῳ). Speaking a first voice, and begetting Light from Light (B), He sent Him forth (προῆκεν), a Lord to the creation (κύριον)."

Tatian, προπηδᾷ λόγος, *supr.* p. 253; and Theophilus, ἄρχει ὁ λόγος καὶ κυριεύει πάντων, *supr.* p. 256.

"His own Mind (νοῦν), to Himself alone hitherto existing as visible (A), but to the world, that was coming into being, invisible, Him He makes visible, that, by becoming manifest, the world might see Him and might thereby be sustained ($\sigma\omega\theta\hat{\eta}\nu\alpha\iota\ \delta\upsilon\nu\eta\theta\hat{\eta}$) (C)."

This salvation or preservation through the presence and manifestation of the Word, is that indwelling virtue of the Primogenitus, on which Athanasius dwells in such various ways. The sight of Him is life or salvation to the Universe, as His incarnate birth is said by Methodius, *supr.* p. 258, to be a manifestation of the unknown.

"And thus there stood by Him Another (B). In saying Another, I do not say two Gods, but as Light from Light, or as water from a fountain, or as a ray from the Sun."

Here is the doctrine of the Monarchia, against which Eusebius offends and the holders of the Three $\dot{\alpha}\rho\chi\iota\kappa\alpha\grave{\iota}$ $\dot{\upsilon}\pi o\sigma\tau\dot{\alpha}\sigma\epsilon\iota\varsigma$. Also the doctrine of the Homoüsion; whereas Eusebius, *supr.* p. 261, says, that the Father and Son are not like light and radiance, so far as this, that the Father can have been without the Son, and that the Son is not the necessary complement of the Father.

"There is one Power, that from the All-in-all ($\dot{\epsilon}\kappa\ \tau o\hat{\upsilon}$ $\pi\alpha\nu\tau\acute{o}\varsigma$); and the All is the Father, from whom there is a Power, the Word (A). And He is Mind ($\nu o\hat{\upsilon}\varsigma$), which, progressing ($\pi\rho o\beta\grave{\alpha}\varsigma$) in the world (B), was manifested as the Minister ($\pi\alpha\hat{\iota}\varsigma$) of God (C). All things are through Him, and He alone from ($\dot{\epsilon}\kappa$) the Father." *contr. Noet.* 11.

$\Pi\alpha\hat{\iota}\varsigma$ is elsewhere too used in this sense by Hippolytus, as in *de Antichrist.* 3 and 61. It was by His *Syncatabasis* in the creation of all things that, though a $\upsilon\dot{\iota}\grave{o}\varsigma$, the Word became the Primogenitus, or $\pi\alpha\hat{\iota}\varsigma\ \theta\epsilon o\hat{\upsilon}$. The term also belongs to Him as incarnate, *vid. Act.* iv. 27-30.

Hippolytus presently adds:—'$A\lambda\lambda$' $\dot{\epsilon}\rho\epsilon\hat{\iota}\ \mu o\acute{\iota}\ \tau\iota\varsigma\cdot\ \xi\acute{\epsilon}\nu o\nu$

μοι φέρεις, λόγον λέγων υἱόν... Ὁ μακάριος Παῦλος λέγει
... ὁ θεὸς τὸν ἑαυτοῦ υἱὸν πέμψας ἐν ὁμοιώματι σαρκὸς
ἁμαρτίας,... ποῖον οὖν υἱὸν ἑαυτοῦ ὁ θεὸς διὰ τῆς σαρκὸς
κατέπεμψεν ἀλλ' ἢ τὸν λόγον, ὃν υἱὸν προσηγόρευε διὰ τὸ
μέλλειν αὐτὸν γενέσθαι ;... οὔτε γὰρ ἄσαρκος καὶ καθ'
ἑαυτὸν ὁ λόγος τέλειος ἦν υἱός, καίτοι τέλειος λόγος ὢν
μονογενής· οὔθ' ἡ σὰρξ καθ' ἑαυτὴν δίχα τοῦ λόγου ὑπο-
στᾶναι ἠδύνατο, διὰ τὸ ἐν λόγῳ τὴν σύστασιν ἔχειν. οὕτως οὖν εἷς υἱὸς τέλειος θεοῦ ἐφανερώθη. *Ibid.* 15.

This passage is too important not to be set down in the Greek. Bull and others attempt to soften what is extreme in its statement, but they hardly can be said to do so with complete success. St. Theophilus, as *supr.* p. 255, says, that at the epoch of creation "nought" had attained the fulness of maturity but God, who was ever all-perfect, as if the Son, while "in utero Patris," had not arrived at His perfection. St. Hippolytus seems to carry this idea further, viz. that, as the Son was necessary as the hypostasis of His human nature, so again His human nature co-operated towards the perfection of His Sonship. Marcellus parallels Hippolytus's διὰ τὸ μέλλειν αὐτὸν γενέσθαι with his own προφητικῶς, &c. *supr.* pp. 28-33.

I find one passage in Hippolytus in which he makes a statement which I had not found elsewhere except among the Alexandrians, and which ought to be recorded. In his *Didascalia*, ed. Fabric. part i. p. 246, we read ὁ πρὸ αἰώνων μονογενής. There is a stronger passage in the Vienna *Catena*, ed. Fabr. ii. p. 29: ἀεὶ ἦν τῷ ἰδίῳ συνυπάρχων γεννήτορι, &c. Neither of them is inconsistent with the doctrine of the "in utero." Also, it is difficult to trust the superscription of names in such collections; *e.g.* in some of them Hippolytus is called "Bishop of Rome," *vid.* also *supr.* p. 88, note. I should add, I cannot accept as genuine the fragments *contra Beronem et Helicem*, as Bull and Fabricius do.

2. The Author of the *Elenchus*, who comes next to be considered, writes upon the subject in discussion as if he had Hippolytus's treatise before him or by heart. He says:—

"God who is one, the first and only, and Creator and Lord of all things, had nothing contemporaneous with Himself" (x. 32, p. 334).

"Only," μόνος; as Hippolytus, Tatian, Tertullian, and Novatian. σύγχρονον ἔσχεν οὐδέν is almost *verbatim* from Hippolytus.

"He then being the Only God and Universal, first having conceived in thought a Logos (A), begets,"—

ἐννοηθείς, as Hippolytus: ἀπογεννᾷ brings out the idea of ἐννοηθείς, which I have suggested above is intended by Hippolytus to refer to the Endiathetic Word. The author proceeds to speak still more plainly,—

"Begets Him (B), not a *logos* as a mere utterance (φωνήν), but as being an Endiathetic λογισμός," (that is, a δύναμις, not an act,) "of the All-in-all (τοῦ παντός)." 33.

He who was begotten or born, or became a Son, was the aboriginal Logos or λογισμός, that connatural indwelling Power called Logos, not a mere accidental, external sound, or voice from God. It was the Endiathetic Word, born into Prophoric action. He uses the τὸ πᾶν, as Hippolytus, *supr.* p. 269.

"Him alone of all beings He begat: for Being the

Father Himself was, the *gennesis* from whom (ἐξ οὗ τὸ γεννηθῆναι) was the cause (of existence, αἴτιον) to those things which were coming into being (C). The Word was in Him, undertaking (φέρων) the will of Him who begat Him (C), not being unskilled in the Father's conception (οὐκ ἄπειρος τῆς ἐννοίας)."

Here seems to be the same shade of error which leads Methodius and others to speak of our Lord as a Son acting κατὰ μίμησιν τοῦ πατρός. The idea is continued in the words which next follow, in which too, as in St. Justin, the Son is spoken of as the "First-born of God," not "First-born of the Universe," as St. Athanasius would speak.

"For together with His going forth (προελθεῖν) from Him who begat Him (B), having become His First-born (C), He has, as an utterance (φωνήν) in Himself, the ideas conceived in the Father's mind (ἐννοηθείσας ἐν τῷ πατρικῷ); whence, at the bidding of the Father (κελεύοντος πατρός) that the world should come into being, did the Word accomplish every separate portion of it, thus pleasing God (C). . . Whatsoever things God willed, did God make. These things He fashioned (ἐδημιούργει) by His Word, nor could they become otherwise than they became . . . And besides them He framed out of all composite substances the ruler of them all, [Adam?] fashioning him (δημιουργόν, qu. δημιουργῶν), not wishing to make him a god and failing, nor an angel (be not deceived),[1] but a man. For had He wished to make thee a god, He could have done it; thou hast the Word

---

[1] A parallel μὴ πλανῶ is found in Hippol. *de Antichr.* 2.

as the Archetype" [by which to frame such a hypothetical creature] (ἔχεις τοῦ λόγου τὸ παράδειγμα); "but He wished to make a man, and a man He has made thee..."

I thus interpret παράδειγμα as characteristic of the πρωτότοκος; for if we translate it, "you see what He can do by the instance of what He did in the case of the Word," as if our Lord were not true God from the Father's substance, but a made god, we contradict the words that follow: "His Word is alone from (ἐκ) Him ... therefore He is God, existing as the substance of God (οὐσία ὑπάρχων θεοῦ)." This is the doctrine of the Homoüsion.

Lastly, he says:—Τὰ πάντα διοικεῖ ὁ λόγος ὁ θεοῦ, ὁ πρωτόγονος πατρὸς παῖς (C), ἡ πρὸ ἑωσφόρου φωσφόρος φωνή (B).

He is παῖς, servant or minister, as in Hippolytus, *supr.* p. 271, by reason of His *Syncatabasis*. Πρὸ ἑωσφόρου; this seems to be his substitute for πρὸ κτισμάτων, a phrase which I do not find in this author, nor in Hippolytus: nor the phrase πρὸ τῶν αἰώνων, except *supr.* p. 272; but I have not confidence enough in my own accuracy to assert a negative.

3. TERTULLIAN must have this credit given to him, that, as I showed above, he, among all the Ante-Nicene writers, is most accurate and explicit in his general statements of the doctrine of the Holy Trinity. Especially is he clear upon the Homoüsion. This is a merit which remains to him, into whatever extravagances he fell in other points; and it must be kept in view, much as we may lament his error on the particular question before us.

I have already quoted from his Treatise against Hermogenes one passage, *supr.* p. 232, in which he lays down distinctly the proposition which, except on the hypothesis that the Eternal Logos was "generatus in Filium," is simply Arian; viz. "Fuit tempus cum Filius non fuit." In his treatise against Praxeas, he gives fuller expression to that tenet, and in singular accordance with the doctrine of Hippolytus and Theophilus: he says, c. 5-7 :—

"Before all things God was alone; He Himself was world, place, and all things for Himself. He was alone, for there was nothing external to Him."

Here is that initial statement, which we have found, on starting, in Tatian and others, as to the aboriginal solitariness of God. And of His Self-sufficiency;—as the αὐτὸς ἑαυτοῦ τόπος, ἀνενδεὴς ὤε, of Theophilus, and the τὸ ὂν ἦν of the *Elenchus*. Tertullian continues:—

"However, not even then was He alone; for He had with Him that which He had in His own Self, that is to say, His Reason (Ratio) (A). For God has Reason (rationalis Deus), and Reason was in Him before [all things]; and thus it was that all things were from Him. Which Reason is His Intelligence (Sensus)."

Bull (*Def. F. N.* iii. 10, p. 209) says that the Greek of *sensus* is ἔννοια. If so, Tertullian is pursuing the line of exposition taken by Hippolytus and the *Elenchus*, *supr.* pp. 269, 273.

"This Reason the Greeks called *Logos*, which also stands for our word *Sermo* (Word); and therefore it has become a custom with our people, translating roughly, to say that the Word was in the first beginning (primordio) with God; whereas it is more exact to consider Reason more ancient. For God had not the Word (non Sermonalis Deus) from the beginning (B), but Reason (Rationalis Deus) (A), and that even before the beginning (principium); and because the Word Itself, as being informed (consistens) by Reason, evidences Reason to be prior, as being the Word's substance (substantiam suam)."

"Substantia sua," that is, the hypostasis, or substantial stay of the Word; as if the Word was by itself a manifestation, and Reason the reality in God. We may argue hence, Bull says, that Reason, being a substance, is a Person. This, indeed, Tertullian says distinctly presently, and says that the Word, as identical with Reason, is that Person, using the term *Persona;* but I do not see with Bull that the term substance or hypostasis means *Person* here, but *stay,* stay of the Word; in the same sense, as God is the *hypostasis* of creation.

". . . With His Reason thinking and disposing (disponens), He made that to become His Word, (viz. Reason,) which by the Word He was exercising (B) . . . When you silently converse with yourself, this inward action you will observe is carried on by reason, which suggests to you a word for every movement of your thought and every stirring of your intelligence (sensus). Every act of thought is a word; every act of intelligence is reason . . . Therefore the word is in some sense your double (secundus), by means of which you speak when you are thinking, and think when you are speaking. How much more fully then does this take place in God, whose image and likeness you are even accounted (*vid.* Dionysius in Athan. *de S. D.* 23). . . Accordingly, I may without rashness lay down, first of all, that, even then, before the framing of the Universe, God was not alone, as having in Himself Reason, and the Word in Reason, so as to make that Word His Second (secundum a se) by exercising it within Himself (agitando intra se) (B)."

All this answers to the doctrine of the Logos Endiathetic and Prophoric; and this intrinsic agitation of which he speaks, is, as will appear lower down, the *gennesis* of the Word, the transition of the *Ratio* into the *Sermo;* and the very word "agitando," which is used literally, (not morally,) evidences, as I have said, that the radical error of these early theologians lies in their imperfect apprehension of the Nature of God, Its simplicity and Immutability, as if His Essence allowed of internal alteration.

"This force and disposition of the Divine Intelligence (vis et dispositio sensûs) is in Scripture signified also by the name of Wisdom; for what is wiser than the Reason or the Word of God? Hear then Wisdom, which had been laid deep (conditam) as a Second Person (A). First of all, 'The Lord created Me a beginning of His ways for His works; before He made the earth, before the mountains were placed, and before all the hills He begat Me.' That is to say, in His own Intelligence laying deep and begetting. Next, recognise in the passage Wisdom's presence with Him (assistentem) in this fact of Its being separated off from Him. 'When He was preparing the heaven,' he says, 'I was with Him . . . for

I was delighted every day with His Person.' . . . Then it is that the Word Himself takes His form (speciem) and His clothing (ornatum), His sound and voice, when God says, 'Let there be Light.' This is the perfect birth of the Word (B).''

"Sophia assistens" is parallel to the καὶ οὕτως παρίστατο αὐτῷ ἕτερος of Hippolytus; and this expression, "stood by Him," or "was present to Him," answering to the ὁ λόγος ἦν πρὸς τὸν θεόν of St. John, separates off the doctrine of these Fathers from the Sabellianizers, such as those spoken of by St. Justin, or the party of Marcellus, or such as Praxeas, against whom Tertullian is writing, who, if Marcellus may be taken to represent them, were disposed to substitute ἐν τῷ θεῷ for πρὸς τὸν θεόν, in order to obscure the personality of the Word, *vid. supr.* p. 24. Tertullian has spoken of the *Ratio* of God being "in semetipso." *supr.* p. 276.

For the right meaning of "the Lord hath created Me," I refer, *supr.* p. 205, to Athanasius.

"Hæc est perfecta nativitas Sermonis:"—therefore that nativity was once imperfect. This reminds us of the συνήκμασεν οὐδὲν αὐτῷ of Theophilus; also of the τέλειος υἱός of Hippolytus, though he associates the Incarnation with the τελειότης. The Second Person, according to them, had from the first, from eternity, the nature of a Son, even when Endiathetic or *in utero*, as Tertullian speaks presently, but that Sonship came to its perfection in His becoming, or as He became, prophoric.

Let me add that Phœbadius (*ap.* Galland, t. 5, p. 253) seems to be referring to Tertullian, and setting him right, when he says " Hæc est nativitas perfecta Sermonis, hoc est, principium sine principio." That is, the ἄναρχος ἀρχή of Clement. Tertullian continues:—

"This is the perfect birth of the Word, while He proceeds from God, being laid deep (conditus) by Him first in order to the thought [of creation] under the name of Wisdom (A), then generated (B) to give effect [to that thought] (C)."

"Conditus" might almost be translated "conceived" in contrast with actual birth.

"Then generated to give effect to that thought, viz. 'when He prepared the heaven, I was present with Him,' [and] thereupon making God a Father to Himself [parem *leg.* patrem], by proceeding from whom He became a Son,—being First-born as generated before all, and Only-begotten as alone begotten from God, in a proper sense, from the womb of His heart, as the Father testifies, ' My heart has burst forth with a Word most good' (B)."

Here Tertullian, like Justin, understands the title of "First-born" to refer to the Divine Sonship, not like Athanasius to the Word's *Syncatabasis.* "Ex vulva cordis ipsius" answers to the ἐν τοῖς σπλάγχνοις and ἐν καρδίᾳ of Theophilus, and the "cordis ejus nobilis inquilinus" of Zeno, and the "in gremio" and "in μήτρᾳ" of Victorinus, as we shall find *infra.*

. . . "Nor need I longer insist on this point, as if the Word were not from God both under the name of Wisdom and Reason and of the whole Divine Mind and Spirit; who was made the Son of that God, from whom by going forth He was generated (B). You ask me, do I lay down that the word is some Substance formed (constructam) by the [Divine] Spirit and the carrying on [traditione] of Wisdom? Just so . . . I say that nothing could have proceeded from God empty and void, inasmuch as not being put forth [prolatum] from what is empty and void, and that That cannot be without a substance which proceeded from so great a Substance, and has produced so great substances . . . Whatever, then, was the Word's substance, That I call a Person, and for That I claim the name of Son; and, in acknowledging Him for a Son, I am maintaining that He is the Father's Second."

"The Father's Second," that is, a Reiteration of the Father, not a name, or quality, or act, but a substantial Person, as he has said all along.

Such is Tertullian's teaching, as clear and decided in character,—as grand, viewed as an exposition of Catholic Truth on the general doctrine of the Trinity,—as it is distinctly faulty as to one point, the Son's co-eternity, considered as the Son—the consequence of an error which has its root, I repeat, in his defective apprehension of the Divine Attributes.

4. NOVATIAN is commonly considered to be the author of the Treatise *de Trinitate*, as if on the authority of St. Jerome, but nothing depends on the Treatise being Novatian's, as in any case it is a work of the Ante-Nicene period.

"What shall we say then? Does Scripture set forth two Gods? How then does it say, that God is One? or is Christ not God?" &c. c. 30, p. 231, ed. Jackson.

Here is the same objection proposed, on the score of the

Monarchia, which we find in Hippolytus, *supr.* p. 271, and in Tertullian, adv. *Prax.* c. 4.

"God the Father is Founder and Creator of all things; alone without origin, the invisible, illimitable, immortal, eternal, and one God." c. 31, p. 236.

This is like the start of Tatian, Theophilus, Hippolytus, and Tertullian, *supra*.

"Out of whom, when He willed, The Word, His Son, was born," or "The Word was born to be a Son (B)," (Sermo Filius natus est.) In the former of these renderings he will agree in the use of terms with Tertullian; in the latter, Him, whom Tertullian calls *Ratio* before and *Sermo* after His birth, Novatian calls *Sermo* before it. In either rendering Novatian considers the *gennesis* temporal, for he says "*quando* voluit." So ὁπότε ἠθέλησεν, Theophilus, *supr.* p. 256, and Hippolytus, p. 269.

"Whom we understand to be not a mere voice, &c. . . . but the substance of a virtue sent forth from God (prolatæ a Deo)."

"He then, whereas He is begotten from the Father, still is ever in the Father, [i.e. a parte ante]: I say 'ever in,' not as maintaining that He was not born, but that He was born. But we must pronounce Him to be ever in the Father, who is before all time, for no time can be assigned to Him, who is before time."

Here Novatian understands "before time" to mean "from eternity," with Justin and Melito, *supr.* pp. 251, 257, and Zeno, *infra*.

"For He is ever in the Father, or else the Father is not ever Father." Here Novatian implies that the Father has been ever a Father, in opposition to Tertullian; but, since he has said above that the birth of the Son was "*quando* voluit Pater," which is inconsistent with eternity, I think it natural to take the words in one of those other senses which they admit, in which they are in harmony with the "quando."

For instance, Tertullian himself, though he denied that God was a Father from eternity, would probably or certainly allow that He was Father *in posse*, together with the Arian Theognis and the Emperor Constantine. And such an explanation or evasion receives some shelter from St. Thomas's solution of the parallel question about creation. "Actio (not merely the posse) Dei est æterna, sed effectus non est æternus." *Vid.* Sylv. *in Quæst.* 45, p. 344.

Also, if Novatian, as the other authors I have quoted, considered that the Word's inherence *in* God before the *gennesis* was an existence "in *vulva* cordis ipsius," as Tertullian speaks, this would be assigning not only a potential, but actually an incipient Paternity to the Father from everlasting.

And further, it is plain that the very idea of "the Word" implies a *filietas*, and if the Word is eternal, so is the *filietas*. I have already referred to Dionysius, who says, "Words are our children," *vid.* Athan. *de Sent. Dion.* 23. *Vid.* the λογοπάτωρ of Marcellus and Photinus, *supr.* p. 23.

Novatian, then, might hold that the Father was Father from eternity, because there lay hid within Him He, who had the nature of a Son (both as being the Word, and as being the Son in the event), yet might hold also that the actual *gennesis* or *nativitas* was temporal. He proceeds:—

"He then, when the Father willed, proceeded from the Father; and, whereas He was in the Father, He proceeded out of the Father; and, whereas He was in the Father, because He was out of the Father, henceforth (postmodum) He was with the Father, because He proceeded from the Father, namely, that Divine Substance, whose name is the Word (B)."

The "cum Patre" answers to St. John's πρὸς τὸν θεόν, *John* i. 1, and to Hippolytus's παρίστατο and to Tertullian's "assistens;" and they all interpret St. John as speaking of the state of the Word, not before, but after the *gennesis*.

"Worthily is He before all things; but He is after the Father, since by Him all things were made, who proceeded from Him, at whose will all things were made (C). He was God, proceeding out of God, constituting the Second Person, after the Father, as being the Son, but not robbing the Father of His prerogative of being the One God," &c.

A passage presently follows so remarkable for beauty and completeness of statement, and for concurrence in the later theology, that I will quote it in the original:—

"Unus Deus ostenditur verus et æternus Pater; a quo solo hæc vis Divinitatis emissa, etiam in Filium tradita et directa, rursum per substantiæ communionem ad Patrem revolvitur. Deus quidem ostenditur Filius, cui Divinitas tradita et porrecta conspicitur; et tamen nihilominus unus Deus Pater probatur, dum gradatim reciproco meatu illa Majestas atque Divinitas ad Patrem, qui dederat eam, rursum ab illo ipso Filio revertitur et retorquetur."

Here are the doctrines of the Consubstantiality and Coinherence.

5. LACTANTIUS is of no authority in himself any more than Constantine; nor should I cite him, if he stood alone. The force of his testimony lies in his being one of a number, who may be said to appeal and respond to each other. And in particular his doctrine is in its main points remarkably coincident with that of his fellow-Africans, Tertullian, Zeno, and Victorinus. He would seem then, not indeed in the details, but still in the substance of his statements, to be reporting what he learned from his ecclesiastical teachers. One idea he has, indeed, which must be original with him; I do not find it in the writers I have been enumerating, and it has just the appearance of a clever antithesis of his own or some other private person, by way of systematising divine truths. He contrasts our Lord with the Archangel who fell, as if they had anything in common. "God," he says, "before He commenced this fabric of the world, produced (produxit) a spirit like to Himself (B), who was possessed (præditus) of the virtues of God the Father .. Then, He made" [he does not say "produced"] "another, in whom the nature (*indoles*) of his Divine origin (*stirpis*) did not remain. Accordingly, he was poisoned with his own envy, and passed over from good to evil." *Instit*. ii. 9, ed. 1748.

But here at least is the temporal *gennesis* in agreement with Tertullian and the rest.

"He was twice born; first in spirit, afterwards in flesh. Whence it is said in Jeremias, 'Before I formed Thee in the womb, I knew Thee.'" *Inst.* iv. 8.

Here again is the expression "*in utero*," though it directly applies to His human birth; and, as the other three Africans concur in using this image of the Divine Sonship, and among the Greeks Theophilus, we may suppose that Lactantius too, at least includes under it a reference to our Lord's heavenly as well as to His earthly nature. To the same effect he continues:—

"Also in the same prophet: 'Blessed He who was before He was born,' which has happened to no one else but Christ, who, being the Son of God from the beginning, is regenerated anew according to the flesh."

It would be obvious to take the birth spoken of in these words, "He was before He was born," of our Lord's human nature, were it not that it was a known formula in reference to His Divine Nature, the denial of which was anathematised at Nicæa. It is found also, with reference to our Lord's Divine Nature, long after the Nicene Council, in St. Hilary and St. Zeno, as we shall see *infra*. I do not say that Lactantius understands it in that sense in this passage. I quote the passage merely to give another instance of the common knowledge and use of the formula among Catholics. In respect to its admitting both an orthodox and a heterodox sense, it is somewhat parallel to the μία φύσις σεσαρκωμένη.

"Holy Writ teaches . . . that that Son of God is God's Word (Sermo), or again, His reason (Ratio) . . . Rightly is He called the *Sermo* and *Verbum* of God . . .

whom God conceived, not in the womb, but in the mind (non utero, sed mente)."

That is "in utero mentis," a figurative "uterus." It is to be observed, he uses the word "conceived," thus carrying out the idea of a birth, but there is nothing to show that he did not believe at least the conception to be from everlasting.

. . . "If any one wonders that it should be possible for God from God, by the putting forth (prolatione) of His voice and breath, to be generated, he will cease to wonder, when he has acquainted himself with the sacred voice of the Prophets." *Ibid.*

Here he speaks of the Sonship as commencing with that "prolatio vocis et spiritûs" which was introductory to creation, that is, of a temporal *gennesis*.

That, with the foregoing writers, he holds the Consubstantiality and the Coinherence, is plain from the following passage :—

"How is it, that, whereas we profess to worship one God, nevertheless we assert that there are two, God the Father and God the Son? . . . Neither can the Father be without the Son nor the Son be separated from the Father. . . . Since then it is the Father who constitutes the Son, and the Son who constitutes the Father, there is One Mind to both of Them, one Spirit, one Substance; but the Father is, as it were, the exuberant Fount, the Son as if the stream that flows from it; the One is like the Sun, the other as the Ray . . . When by the prophets one and the same is called the Hand of God, and the Power, and the Word, certainly there is no division between Them . . . The One is as if

Two, and the Two as if One ... Rightly Each is called the One God; for, whatever is in the Father flows on to the Son, and what is in the Son comes to Him from the Father." *Ibid.* iv. 29.

6. ST. HILARY did not teach the same doctrine after his banishment into Phrygia, as he taught before it. When he returned, he taught, as in his work *de Trinitate*, that our Lord was Son from everlasting; but at first, as in his comment on the Psalms, he used the celebrated formula, which, in agreement with Tertullian, Novatian, and others, seems to imply that the *gennesis* was temporal. He always held the "Consubstantial," though he did not hear of the Nicene Council or Creed till thirty-one years after the Council was held. "Though I had been regenerated," he says, "and had continued some time in the Episcopate, I never heard the Nicene Faith till I was on the point of exile; but to me the meaning of Homoüsion and Homœüsion was suggested by the Gospels and Apostles." *de Synod.* 91. In him then we have a specimen of pure Western belief, uninfluenced by the controversies of the day. That this is the right view to take of him is confirmed to us by the parallel avowal of the Gallic Council of Arles, A.D. 360, in its letter to the Orientals:— "Verbum *usiam*," its Fathers say, "a vobis quondam contra Ariomanitarum hæresim inventum, a nobis semper sancte fideliterque susceptum est." Hil. *Opp.* p. 1353; where the remarkable words "quondam a vobis" show how little the Gallic Church of that day realised to themselves the true character of the Nicene act. Its Bishops believed, not on the word of a Council "sometime

held in the East," but upon the authority of their immemorial tradition.

Such being the significancy of St. Hilary's testimony, what does he tell us in his work on St. Matthew about the Divine *gennesis*? He tells us that He who was the Word from eternity, became the Son in order to creation. "The Word," he says, "was in the beginning God, and with God from the beginning. He was born from Him who was, and He that was born had this prerogative, viz. that He it is who ' erat antequam nasceretur; ' that is, there is the same eternity of Him who begat, and of Him who is begotten." *Matt.* xxxi. 3.

Here we seem to see the reason why this formula, "Erat antequam nasceretur," which to us has an heretical sound as implying the temporal *gennesis*, was used by great theologians as Hilary, and was recognised as existing, yet not reprobated, nay, indirectly sanctioned by the Nicene Fathers when they anathematised those who denied it. It was an obvious escape from the Arian argument, "A son has, as such, a beginning of existence." This formula virtually answered, "Yes, as a son He had a beginning, but He was the eternal Word before He was the Son. As in the fulness of the times the Eternal Word became the Son of man, so in the beginning of days He had become the Son of God."

However, St. Hilary unlearned this doctrine after his visit to Asia Minor and Alexandria. In Asia Minor he would have proof of the dangerous use which the Semi-Arians made of the formula, and at Alexandria he became the personal friend of Athanasius, who inherited the

Alexandrian antagonistic and true teaching. Perhaps he would read in Athanasius's fourth Oration his condemnation of those who said, πρὸ τοῦ γεννηθῆναι, ἐν τῷ θεῷ ἦν ὁ λόγος, and, ὁ λόγος ἐν τῷ θεῷ ἀτελὴς, γεννηθεὶς, τέλειος γέγονεν. *Orat.* iv. 11, 12. Accordingly, in his *de Trinitate*, Hilary, without distinctly condemning the ancient and widely spread opinion which he had himself held, lays down that both the formula in which it was embodied, and its contradictory, are alike unmeaning; for, if the *gennesis* is from everlasting, our Lord neither was, nor was not, before He was born. "Cum natum semper esse," he says, "nihil aliud sit confitendum esse quam natum, id sensui, antequam nascitur 'vel fuisse,' vel 'non fuisse,' non subjacet." *de Trin.* xii. 31.

7. However, the opinion did not die with Hilary; it has the sanction of St. Zeno of Verona some years after Hilary gave it up. Zeno was consecrated in 362, and died close upon the second Ecumenical Council in 381, leaving to posterity a certain number of discourses, doctrinal and hortatory, written with great force and elegance. In these his conformity in all respects with the Nicene doctrine is, as might be expected, entire; he is distinct upon the consubstantiality, co-eternity, co-inherence, and co-equality of the Father and Son; but when he comes to the question, Is the *gennesis* eternal? he speaks after the usage of his African fellow-countrymen.

"The beginning," he says, in ii. 3, "without controversy, is our Lord Christ, whom the Father before all ages did embrace (amplectebatur) in the profound impenetrable secret of His own Mind (A), and with a knowledge which was all His own, not without the affection felt towards a Son, but without the manifestation of Him. Therefore that ineffable and incomprehensible Wisdom propagates Wisdom, and Omnipotence Omnipotence (B). From God is born God, " De Ingenito Unigenitus, de Solo Solus, de Toto Totus, de Vero Verus, de Perfecto Perfectus, Totum Patris habens, nihil derogans Patri."

Here observe the tenses, " amplectebatur" and "nascitur." That this "nativitas" is not the eternal Ballerini simply grants; but with Bull, he maintains that the word denotes the Father's decree or the Son's procession to create the world, an hypothesis for which I cannot see that he advances any argument, for the connexion of two events is no argument for their identity.[1] Also observe the expression," Filii *non sine* affectu ;" he does not say, " with the affection," in order to signify that it marked the beginning of that relation which was perfected in the " perfecta nativitas," as Tertullian speaks, prior to creation. Of course the love of the First Divine Person to the Second was infinitely full from all eternity; but Zeno is here speaking of the Paternal love towards a Son. He goes on :—

" He proceeds unto a nativity, 'qui erat antequam nasceretur,' equal to the Father in all things, for the Father in ipsum alium se genuit ex se, ex innascibili scilicet sua illa substantia," &c.

Here Zeno uses the very formula, which was sheltered at Nicæa, which we have found in Hilary and Lactantius, and which is the recognised symbol of the temporal

---

[1] On this subject vid. " Arians," Note ii. ed. 4th.

gennesis, as held by Tatian, Theophilus, Hippolytus, and the rest, as the homoüsion is of our Lord's proper divinity.

Again, in ii. 4, Zeno says: "Erat ante omnia manens, unus et idem alter, ex semet ipso in semet ipsum Deus, secreti sui solus conscius (A), cujus ex ore, ut rerum natura, quæ non erat, fingeretur, prodivit Unigenitus Filius (B), cordis ejus nobilis inquilinus, exinde visibilis necessario effectus, quia orbem terræ erat ipse facturus (C), humanumque visitaturus genus," &c.

Here by "visibilis effectus," as by "revelamine" in the former passage, he connects his doctrine with the ἀόρατον ὄντα ὁρατὸν ποιεῖ of Hippolytus. Observe also the contrast between "cordis inquilinus," and "ex ore," after the manner of Tertullian.

Again, in ii. 5, which is in part a repetition of ii. 3, he says, "Excogitatarum ut ordinem instrueret rerum (C), ineffabilis illa Virtus incomprehensibilisque sapientia e regione cordis eructat Verbum, Omnipotentia se propagat," &c. Here "excogitatarum" seems to answer to the ἐννοηθείς of Hippolytus.

It is remarkable that he says a few lines later:—"Temperat se propter rerum naturam Filius, ne exsertæ majestatis Dominum non possit mundi istius mediocritas sustinere." This reminds us of the doctrine of Athanasius, *supr.* pp. 73, 202. And this explains, as Ballerini suggests, the words of Tertullian, which have been charged with a denial of the co-equality of the Son, whereas he is speaking of the *Syncatabasis*. "Invisibilem Patrem intelligemus pro plenitudine majestatis, visibilem vero Filium agnoscemus pro modulo derivationis." *adv. Prax.* 14.

If it needs explanation, that a Saint and Martyr, many years after the Nicene Council, should, as far as his language goes, countenance a tenet which by Augustine's time had been forbidden; I should point on the other hand, to the fact, equally remarkable, that that Council makes mention of the formula which embodied it without condemning it, nay, with an express condemnation of those who denied it, and next, to the assurance which was given by the Alexandrian Council to the whole world in 362, the year of Zeno's consecration, that it was enough to accept the words of the Nicene Creed, with I suppose, its anathemas, in order to be an orthodox believer.[1]

8. VICTORINUS, who wrote almost contemporaneously with Zeno, has as little authority, taken by himself, as Lactantius, but is valuable as one of a company of consentient writers, both as supporting and completing their statements. He was an African, and, while a heathen, taught rhetoric at Rome. Augustine relates the circumstances of his conversion, and how, when the hour came for his making profession of his faith, and he had the option given him of making it privately, he declined the

---

[1] Without withdrawing what I have maintained above in *Dissert.* 3, pp. 57, &c., that the "non erat antequam nasceretur" of the Arians was an enthymeme of their own directed against Catholics, I do not see my way to deny that Tertullian before Arius, and Zeno after him, and various other writers between their dates, used on their part the "Erat antequam nasceretur" deliberately and independently as a positive formula.

considerate suggestion. "When he stood up," says St. Augustine, "the spectators whispered his name one to another, with a voice of congratulation, and there ran a low murmur through the joyful multitude, 'Victorinus, Victorinus!'" The Saint continues: "And, when that man of Thine, Simplician, related this to me, I was on fire to imitate him." Victorinus was converted in 360 or 361; and, as he was advanced in years, the works which he drew up against the Arians cannot have been written much later than that date.

St. Jerome calls them very obscure, and Gennadius considers them deficient in knowledge of Scripture. I am not considering them here in either of these respects; but in respect of their doctrinal enunciations, whether the catechetical instruction, which accompanied his conversion, was given him in Rome or in Carthage. It is enough for my purpose, if he has a clear view of doctrine, and that in coincidence with the writers whom I have quoted, and in illustration of them. Now, while he is clear upon the Consubstantiality, &c., he distinctly teaches that the *gennesis* was a process; that our Lord from eternity was God and from God, but still only in God, "in corde," "vulva," or "utero;" as such He was the Logos, the "alter et idem" of Zeno, (Victorinus uses the term *fœtus*,) which was at length to become a Son; that, when the world was to be created, He was born and manifested, became the Son, and acted as the principle of order and beauty, the life, the sustaining power, of the universe. I shall quote him under A, B, and C, symbols which I have all along used as designating respectively the Word Endiathetic, the Word

Prophoric, and the Primogenitus. It will be observed that he holds the Homoüsion and the Coinherence.

A. "Erat circa Deum Logos, et in principio. Ergo semper fuit." *de Gener.* 16; *ap.* Galland, t. 8.

"'In principio' esse, non generatum esse significat. Non genitus est Logos, quum Deus ipse Logos sit, sed quiescens et silens Logos." *Ibid.* 17.

"Unigenitus qui est in gremio Patris . . . in gremio, et in μήτρᾳ substantiæ ὁμοούσιον; uterque, et substantia et divinitate consistens; uterque in utroque; et cognoscit uterque utrumque." *adv. Arium,* i. 15.

"Gravida occultum habet quod paritura est. Non enim fœtus non est ante partum, sed in occulto est." *de Gen.* 14.

B. "Et generatione pervenit in manifestationem ὄν operatione, quod fuit ὄν potentia. Absconditi manifestatio generatio est." *de Gen.* 14.

C. "Universalis Logos Filius Dei est, cujus potentia proveniunt et procedunt in generationem omnia et consistunt. Ipsius ergo potentia, procedens et simul existens cum Patre, facit omnia et generat." *adv. Arium,* i. 22.

"Quod Filius Logos est in actionem festinans substantia; vita enim Logos, et intelligentia Logos, processit in substantiam eorum quæ sunt intellectibilium et hylicorum; et idcirco actio ipsius Logi propter imbecillitatem percipientium ipsum et patitur et passibilis est, vel potius passibilis dicitur." *Ibid.* i. 24.

These last words excellently express Athanasius's idea of the *Syncatabasis.* With Justin and the rest,

Victorinus recognises the ministrative, servile, and passible condition of the Primogenitus, (not in His divine nature of course, but) in His voluntary office, terminating as it did in His incarnation and passion, a condition which arose out of the necessary imperfection of that created universe with which, for its exaltation, He condescended to be implicated.

I have already, in speaking of the Asiatic Writers, drawn attention to the striking dogmatic utterance of the great Council of Antioch in the third century, declaratory of the eternity of the Divine *Gennesis;* a still more authoritative Voice issued about the same time from the West, from the Apostolic See, and to the same effect. It is a great misfortune that the series of dogmatic Tomes of the Ante-Nicene Popes have not been preserved to us; a fragment of one of them remains, and it accidentally contains an assertion, indirect but clear, of the very doctrine we desiderate in certain other writers, the eternal existence of the Son. It is in Pope Dionysius's notice of some supposed heresy at Alexandria, which over-zealous ecclesiastics had brought before the Holy See. The portion which remains to us of his letter is written in a tone of authority and decision befitting an Infallible Voice. After censuring some quasi-tritheistic error, he proceeds:

" Equally must one censure those who hold the Son to be a work, and consider the Lord has come into being, as one of things that really came to be; whereas the divine oracles witness to a generation suitable to Him and becoming, but not to any fashioning or making. A blasphemy then is it, not ordinary, but even the highest, to say that the Lord is in any sort a handiwork; for if He *became* Son, once He was not; *but He was always.*"

He goes on to explain the words in Proverbs, "The Lord created Me," &c., and it is remarkable how throughout his remarks he ignores the hypothesis of a temporal *gennesis,* knowing only the temporal birth from Mary and the Divine Sonship from everlasting.

§ 15. CONCLUSION.

And here I conclude my inquiry into the historical origin of Arianism, perhaps rather abruptly, and certainly without exhausting it. I cannot hope to have read all that ought to be read upon it, or to have covered the whole ground which it occupies, or to have done full justice to the views of other commentators and critics, or to have guarded my own from all objections. So far is certain, that, whatever have been my pains, I cannot have escaped errors in matters of detail, though I have no misgiving about the substantial correctness of what I have written.

POSTSCRIPT.

May 2, 1883.—My attention having been accidentally called to certain passages in this Tract iii., I have been led to ask myself whether I have always succeeded in bringing out my real meaning with that distinctness which was imperative on so important a subject, and the more so because of the reverence due to the times and persons of whom I had to treat.

Then I reflected that a fresh edition of the Volume, in which I might avail myself of the opportunity of revision, could hardly be expected in my lifetime.

The result has been that I have made at once such alterations in the foregoing pages as I felt to be necessary, without waiting for a future which might never come to me.

J. H. N.

IV.

THE HERESY OF APOLLINARIS.

(From Notes, dated August 22, 1835.)

THE HERESY OF APOLLINARIS.

§ 1.

THE Apollinarian heresy is at first sight antithetical to Arianism; Arians denying our Lord's true divinity, and Apollinaris His true humanity

[For a good and interesting account of Apollinaris, *vid.* Wake against Bossuet, *Appendix* in vol. 28 of "Popish Controversy;" *vid.* also Petavius *de Incarn.* i. 6, v. 11-13, and Tillemont, *Mémoires*, t. 7, p. 602, edit. 1706. Basnage and Bayle are unfair, selecting from the report of early writers about his opinions just what they choose.]

2. But only at first sight; for the very tenet, which constitutes the Apollinarian heresy, viz. the denial of the existence of any mind or intellect, νοῦς, in our Lord's human nature, was already professed, and in a still bolder form, by the Arians.

[The Arians denied, not only the νοῦς in our Lord's soul, but they refused to ascribe to Him a soul of any kind; whereas the Apollinarians did not deny Him a soul, so that intellect was away, that is, an animal soul. This was not among the original Arian errors. Perhaps they were cut short in their full profession of heresy by the prompt indignation which their denial of our Lord's divinity excited. Denial of His human soul is not found as one of their tenets in the letters of Alexander, Arius, &c., at the beginning of the controversy, nor in the historical accounts of it, A.D. 319-341. It is apparently mentioned by Athanasius, *Adelph.* 1, (with the words, νῦν δὲ κατ' ὀλίγον ὑποκαταβαίνοντες,) and *Apoll.* i. 15, A.D. 371-2. And later still by Gregory Naz. 1 *Ep. ad Cledon.* t. 2, p. 87, by Theod. *hær.* iv. 1, and August. *hær.* 55. King (*Creed*, p. 230) considers it as only partially received among the Arians. It was received, as we find from Theod. *supr.* and *Eranist.* ii. pp. 73, 80, by the Eunomians, the extreme party among them, A.D. 357. The Benedictine Editor of St. Hilary, *Præf.* n. 119, also says, "Neque hic error erat omnium qui Ario favebant communis, sed insignium quorundam Arianorum proprius." He mentions Potamius (vid. Phœbad. *contr. Arian.* p. 251); also, Ursacius and Valens (Theod. *Hist.* ii. 8); and, referring, but not assenting, to Baronius (*Ann.* 324, n. 100), Eusebius. Theodoret (*supr.*), and Leontius (*de Sectis*, iii. 4, p. 365), say, that the Arians adopted the tenet to baffle the Catholics, who are accustomed to explain texts indicative of infirmity in our Lord, by referring such to His human nature. However, it was but the natural or necessary result of their original heresy, and of their dislike of mystery in religion. If the Word was not God, why should He not act as, and instead of, the soul of a man?

The Arians were not the only forerunners of Apollinaris. Origen (*de Princ.* ii. 5) seems to refer to other such, and Hippolytus (*contr. Noët.* 17) when, after speaking of our Lord's soul, he adds, λογικὴν δὲ λέγω.

3. Again, it must be recollected, that the heresies concerning the Holy Trinity and the Incarnation, even though on paper they look contrary to each other, do in fact, when analysed, run together into one. For they are all opposed to the one Truth, and are thereby a negation of those ultimate principles of thought, on which that Truth rests; and thus really, one and all are ranged on one line over against the Truth alone, which seems at first sight to lie between them.

[Thus Arianism and Sabellianism, though diametrically opposed to each other in a drawn-out scheme of doctrine, substantially agree together, and are contrary to the Catholic Faith, inasmuch as the True Faith asserts or admits the existence of mysteries in any human view of the Divine Nature, and both heresies virtually deny it. Again, the Platonic doctrine of the Logos ἐνδιάθετος and προφορικός, the Word conceived in the mind and the Word spoken, a Divine attribute and a Divine energy, leads either to Sabellianism or to Arianism;—to Sabellianism, since the Divine Word, Endiathetic, is not a Person; to Arianism, since the Personal Word, Prophoric, is not strictly Divine. And again, Arians, Sabellians, Nestorians, and Monophysites, agree together in the assumption on starting, that nature and person are always coincident in intellectual beings; vid. Damasc. *contr. Jacob.* ii. t. 1, p. 398; Leont. *in Nestor.* i. p. 660; Vigil. Thaps. *contr. Eutych.* ii. 10, p. 727; Anast. *Hodeg.* fin. ii. p. 70, vi. pp. 96, 98, ix. p. 140, xvii. p. 308.

4. And thus, over and above any direct and avowed identity of doctrine between Apollinarianism and Arianism, there are, as it were, underground communications between the one and the other. For instance, as we shall see presently, inasmuch as Apollinarianism tends to the doctrine of the consubstantiality of the Divine Son with His assumed flesh, so does it necessarily favour the Arian denial of His consubstantiality with the Father.

[Thus St. Ambrose: "Emergunt alii [Apollinaristæ], qui carnem Domini et divinitatem dicant unius esse naturæ.... Jam tolerabiliores sunt Ariani, quorum per istos perfidiæ robur adolescit; ut majore contentione adserant [Ariani] Patrem, Filium, et Spiritum Sanctum unius non esse substantiæ, quia isti [Apollinaristæ] divinitatem Domini et carnem substantiæ unius dicere tentaverunt." *Incarn.* 49.]

5. However, Apollinaris does not seem to have been aware that there was really but one falsehood in theological

teaching, as there was but one truth. Perhaps he was deceived by the ethical differences of his teaching from that of the Arians; and, as he disliked them, and had zealously opposed them to his own temporal disadvantage, he might easily be induced to think in consequence, that no views which he was putting forward would advance the interests either of Arianism or heresies cognate to it.

[The literary remains of Apollinaris, as of the Eutychians, display an unction, very unlike Arianism, which made its way by means of a pretentious logic. These teachers write devotionally rather than controversially. Eutyches in particular refused to argue, out of reverence, as he said, towards our Lord. Whenever his inconsistencies were urged upon him, he said the subject was beyond him. He considered our Lord ἀτρέπτως τραπῆναι, and that in His own secret way, quomodo voluit et scit. *ap.* Leon. *Ep.* 21. He professed to dislike φυσιολογεῖν. *Concil.* t. 2, pp. 157, A.D. 164, &c., &c. Leontius remarks on this evasion, *contr. Nest.* i. p. 665. The same character of mind manifests itself in the *Eranistes* of Theodoret's dialogues. Vid. *Dial.* i. p. 18, fin. μή μοι λογισμούς, &c., also i. p. 11, ii. p. 105. Leo, speaking of Eutyches, says that his heresy was "de imperitia magis quam de versutia natus." *Ep.* 31, p. 854; *vid.* also *Epp.* 30, p. 849; *Epp.* 28, p. 801; 33, p. 865; 34, p. 870; 35, p. 877; 88, p. 1058. After Eutyches there was a change; vid. Leont. *de Sect.* vii. 3, 4. Severus and his party were skilful controversialists; Damasc. *contr. Jacob.* ii. and x. Maxim. t. 2, p. 280. Anast. Hodeg. pp. 20, 308, &c. As to Apollinaris, he was a man of education, and wrote with force as well as with warmth, and his followers had soon the evil repute, not only of clever disputation, but also of literary forgeries, as indeed had the Monophysites also. The Pseudo-Areopagite is by Lequien attributed to Monophysites (*Dissert. Damasc.* ii. 14, &c.), while Leontius has a work *de fraudibus Apollinistarum.*]

6. Moreover, he might easily persuade himself that he was but following out and completing, clearing and defining

and protecting the teaching of the Fathers. The great truth which they had ever propounded, was that the Eternal Son had come into the world in our nature—language which implied that His Personality was divine, and His manhood only an adjunct to it, instrument, or manifestation. The Word was clothed in flesh, he would say; He dwelt, acted, revealed Himself in the flesh, but this was as far from being a real addition to His own self, as a garment or an instrument is from being a part of a man. A garment is made to fit the wearer; so must our Lord's human nature be shaped and adjusted for a union with His divine. It had not a substantive character; it was not an hypostasis; else it would have a personality of its own; accordingly, it could not in all respects be similar to the ordinary make of human kind.

[There are two meanings to the word "substantive," as to the word "hypostasis;" τὸ ἁπλῶς ὄν, καὶ τὸ καθ' ἑαυτὸ ὄν; Leont. *de Sect.* vii. 2; bare existence, and self-existence, as in grammar, a noun adjective in contrast with a noun substantive. We may allowably say that our Lord used His manhood after the manner of an attribute, but still that manhood did really exist. St. Cyril, who has been accused of Apollinarianism, was so impressed with the danger of giving it an opening in his own teaching, that, in spite of "hypostasis" being by his day so generally used in the sense of "Person," he does not scruple to maintain in his Anathematisms that our Lord's manhood was an hypostasis. "Palam est," says Petavius, *Incarn.* vi. 2, n. 3, p. 274, "ibi," that is, in his Anathematisms and his defence of them "hypostasin pro persona non accipi, sed pro solida, vera, et non imaginaria re, sive rei extantia."]

7. In like manner, he would say, as a man was not a garment, so our Lord was not a man; that is, strictly speaking, He had not a manhood; He was God clothed in our nature.

[Apollinaris did not refuse to call our Lord "man;" Leont. *de fr. Ap.* p. 705, c. And Eutyches says, "In veritate, non in phantasmate homo factus," *ap.* Leon. *Ep.* 21, p. 741; nay, τέλειος ἄνθρωπος, *Conc.* Hard. t. 2, p. 157, yet he said our Lord's body was ἀνθρώπινον, not ἀνθρώπου, Leon. *Ep.* 26, 30; *Concil.* t. ii. p. 165. And the *Eranistes, Dial.* ii. p. 82. But the last-named pleads hard to be excused doing so: τὸ μὲν εἰδέναι τὴν ληφθεῖσαν φύσιν προὔργου τίθεμαι· τὸ δέ γε ἄνθρωπον ἀποκαλεῖν τῆς οἰκουμένης τὸν σωτῆρα, σμικρύνειν ἐστί. *Dial.* ii. p. 83. And, τί τὸ ἀναγκάζον ὑμᾶς ἄνθρωπον ὀνομάζειν τὸν σωτῆρα; *ibid.* p. 78. Also he says, it is περιττόν to call Him man, p. 85; again, that before His passion He was called man, but not after, p. 93. And the Apollinarian in Incert. *Dial.* v. 2-14, gives eight reasons in proof that our Lord is not man. These teachers preferred to speak of His ἔνσαρκος παρουσία, *Concil.* Hard. t. 2, pp. 163, 197, 235, after the precedent given by Athanasius, *Adelph.* 1, and by Cyril, *Catech.* iii. 11; xii. 15; xiv. 27, 30, and by Epiphanius, *Hær.* 77, 17.]

8. But, if our Lord could not be, strictly speaking, considered to be a man, and had not a human personality, it was plain in what His nature differed from ours. The mind or νοῦς was the seat of personality; therefore He had no mind. This absence then of *mind* from His manhood was the characteristic tenet of Apollinaris. He said that our Lord had no *mind*, because He had no human personality; just as Catholics said, that since He had in all respects a human nature, He had a human mind.

[εἰ ἄνθρωπος, καὶ διανοητικός· εἰ δὲ οὐ διανοητικός, οὐδ' ἄνθρωπος. Greg. Nyssen. *Antirrh.* 22, *fin.* οὐκ ἄρα ἀνθρωπίνη σάρξ, ἡ μὴ κοινωνήσασα ψυχῇ λογικῇ. Incert. *Dial.* iv. 9. *ibid.* v. 16. οὐ γὰρ ἄνουν ζῷον, ὁ ἄνθρωπος. Greg. Naz. 1. *Cledon.* t. ii. p. 35. Moreover, our Lord's mind is the very medium, by which a union was possible between the Divine and the human, according to Origen, *Princ.* ii. 6, n. 3. Naz. *Orat.* ii. 23, p. 24. Incert. *Dial.* iv. 2. Damasc. *Fid. O.* iii. 6, p. 213.]

9. Thus, instead of securing especial honour to the Person of Christ, they landed themselves at once in a tenet especially dishonourable to Him. If our Lord's human nature had no intellectual principle included in it, His Divine Self would be constrained to take its place, and act for it, as a sort of soul of the body; but what an indignity, what a subjection and imprisonment, what a state incompatible with the very idea of divinity, for the Eternal Word to be made to share with the flesh a human individuality! This, which is the *reductio ad absurdum* of Apollinarianism, will of course come before us more directly presently.

10. This is what comes of Reasoning in the province of theology, unless in the first place we inquire our way by Scripture and Tradition, and then proceed to reason under the information thence afforded us.

[St. Basil, *Ep.* 263, p. 406, speaks of Apollinaris as working out his theological views by logical processes; and Leontius says of him, διϊσχυρίζετο τὸ δόγμα αὐτοῦ, οὐκ ὑπὸ ῥητοῦ τινος, ἀλλ' ἀπὸ περινοίας. *de Sect.* iv. 2, p. 636, vid. Anast. *Hodeg.* p. 98.]

§ 2.

1. Apollinaris denied that our Lord was perfect man, that He had a *rational* soul in addition to His Divine Nature; and he did so, on the ground that the doctrine of a humanity complete at all points, with a human mind, rendered an Incarnation impossible, as introducing a second being or person into the constitution, as he might call it, of Emmanuel. He argued, as if from the nature of the case, that nothing could be taken up by the Divine Word into His Personality, which was already in itself individual and one; for, otherwise, it would be impossible to maintain the ἄκρα ἕνωσις, the *summa unio*, between the Divine Word and His assumed nature, and that this maintenance was our primary duty.

[The *summa unio* was the first principle of the Apollinarians; vid. Theod. *Eran.* p. 189, *fin.* and Leont. *de fr. Ap.* p. 705, where Apollinaris almost uses the phrase as a symbol, and is vehement in his maintenance of it against Diodorus; *e.g.* "Ludis summam unionem," &c., vid. also Jobius, *ibid.* p. 702. However, in Pseudo-Justin, *ap.* Leont. *contr. Nest.* p. 668, and Grab. *Spicil.* t. 2, p. 198, it is (according to the Benedictine editor of Justin, *Append.* p. 488, and Lequien in Damasc. t. 1, p. 420) a Nestorian phrase. Again, it is Catholic in Proclus *ad Armen.* p. 613, in Eulogius *ap.* Photii *Bibl.* p. 768, 10, p. 812, 20, Anast. *Hodeg.* c. 13, pp. 228, 240, and in Maximus, *Epp.* t. 2, p. 273. Of course all parties claimed to preserve in their own teaching what really was a first principle in the doctrine of the Incarnation.]

2. Then the Apollinarians proceeded thus:—
Δύο τέλεια could not in any real sense coalesce and

unite; for this would be like saying that one and one do not make two. As well might two human minds run together into one, as God and man be united, without some accommodation or adjustment in the human nature to the Divine. Does not the Church herself admit this? for what is her denial of personality to our Lord's human nature, but a confessed incompleteness in that nature? Moreover, what is the seat of personality but the νοῦς or mind? and how can we consistently deny personality to our Lord's manhood, yet ascribe νοῦς to it?

[Unum perfectum, non duo perfecta. Leont. *de fr. Apoll.* p. 707. Naz. *Ep.* 1. *Cledon.* p. 88, πῶς οὐ δύο ἡγεμονικά; Incert. *Dial.* iv. 3, 5. μὴ εἶναι θεὸν τέλειον μετὰ ἀνθρώπου τελείου. Nyssen. *Antirrh.* 22. Athan. *Apoll.* i. 2, 16. Epiph. *Hær.* 77, 23. *Ancor.* 77. The Catholics in answer denied that personality was involved in the idea of νοῦς, so that a man might be perfect in the nature and attributes of man, yet have no personality.]

3. To say that our Lord, Emmanuel, was perfect man was to consider Him as ἄνθρωπος θεοφόρος, a man full of God or deified, whereas really He was θεὸς σαρκοφόρος, God incarnate.

[Vid. Valentinus in Leont. *de fr. Ap.* p. 702, col. 2, *fin.* They wrote this confession of the " God incarnate " on their doors and garments. Naz. 2. *Cledon.* p. 96.]

4. They accused Catholics of holding two sons, the Son of God and the son of Mary, instead of the One Person of Emmanuel; comparing them to the Paulianists.

[That is, of what was afterwards the heresy of Nestorius. Athan. *Apoll.* i. 21. Nyssen. t. 2, p. 694. Theod. *Eran.* iii. p. 193. Leont. *de fr. Ap.* p. 701 C. and τοῦτο ἕπεται τῇ Παυλιανικῇ διαιρέσει. Vid. Constant. *Epp. Pont. App.* p. 63.]

5. Also, they said that Catholics added a fourth Person to the Blessed Trinity, and placed a man before the Holy Ghost.

[Athan. *Epict.* 2, 9. *Apoll.* i. 9, 12. Epiph. *Hær.* 77, 4-10. *Ancor.* n. 77. Ambros. *Incarn.* 77. Leont. p. 707 A. Procl. *Armen.* p. 614.]

6. Moreover, they argued that, if our Lord is man as He is God, we are called upon both to worship Him and not to worship; which cannot be done: therefore the Catholic doctrine is not true.

[Naz. Ep. 1. *Cledon.* p. 89. Incert. *Dial.* v. 28. Leont. p. 707. Catholics did not say that He was man *as* He was God. They even admitted the illustration of a garment as applied to His humanity; vid. Petav. *Incarn.* vii. 13, and *infra*, and they maintained that it had no personality; only they maintained also that nevertheless it was complete in its nature, and therefore that it included an intellectual soul or νοῦς.

7. Further, they said that a human intellect was unnecessary to the Incarnate Word, whose infinite intelligence would supply every need which a human mind could answer; and, if unnecessary, to teach it was to introduce a gratuitous difficulty into theology.

[περιττὸς γὰρ ἦν, φησὶν, ὁ νοῦς, τοῦ θεοῦ λόγου παρόντος. Theod. *Hær.* v. 11, p. 420.]

8. Nay, it was mischievous as well as gratuitous; for it interfered with the simple idea and object of the Incarnation, which was the manifestation of the Invisible God.

[To support this view they referred to Baruch iii. 35-38: "After this He was *seen* on earth and *conversed* with men;" vid. Theod. *Eran.* i. p.

17. Naz. *Ep.* 2. *Cledon.* p. 95. Athan. *Apoll.* ii. 4. Nyssen. t. 2, p. 694. Incert. *Dial.* iv. 1, *fin.* and ii. *init.* If a manifestation were all that was necessary, a phantom would answer the purpose as well as a real body. We shall find this consequence carried out by the extreme Apollinarians.]

9. Whatever tended to represent the union of God and man as more than a simple manifestation of the Invisible, they considered to obscure the truth. An outward form was enough, for it exactly answered the purpose of being an organ, an instrument of manifesting Him.

[The Apollinarian Valentinus says, "Amictum et vestem ac tegumen mysterii occultati assumpsit, et pro hominibus apparuit; nec enim aliter spectatores Dei fieri poteramus, nisi per corpus." Leont. p. 703. And Jobius: "Carnem unisse sibi, et esse unam personam indivisibilem mediam inter Deum et hominem, et conjungentem creaturas divisas cum creatore." *ibid.* p. 702. And Apollinaris himself: "Organum, et quod movet instrumentum, unam naturaliter perficiunt operationem." *ibid.* p. 706. "Venerabile, magnum, supramundanum σκεύασμα. *ibid.* The body of Christ is a σχῆμα ὀργανικόν. Athan. *Apoll.* i. 2, 14. Incert. *Dial.* iv. 5, *fin.* "Let us glorify Him," says Apollinaris in Theod. *Eran.* ii. pp. 173, 174, ὡς τινὰ βασιλέα ἐν εὐτελεῖ φανέντα στολῇ· ὁρῶντες καὶ αὐτὸ τὸ ἔνδυμα δοξασθέν. *vid.* also Ambros. *Incarn.* 51.

However, the orthodox disputant, in Theod. *Eran.* i. pp. 22, 3, speaks of the flesh of Christ as a παραπέτασμα and προκάλυμμα, referring to Hebr. x. 20; and the *Eranistes* is shy of adopting these words, perhaps under the notion that those words mean a veil rather than a medium of vision. In *Hær.* v. 11, p. 422, Theodoret calls the word προκάλυμμα heretical, as applied to the flesh of Christ, contrasting it with the idea of it as the ἀπαρχή of the whole race. *Vid.* Note on Athan. *Orat.* ii. 8, Oxf. trans., or *ibid.* ed. 2, art. in voc. παραπέτασμα.]

10. They proceeded to argue that the human mind was necessarily sinful, and that in consequence it was an

impiety to suppose that it was a portion of that manhood which our Lord assumed.

[It would seem from this as if the Apollinarians thought sin was of the nature of the soul, after the manner of modern Calvinists. Leontius seems to make this their main argument; ἔλεγε γὰρ ὅτι ὁ νοῦς ἁμαρτητικόν τι ἐστίν. de Sect. iv. 2, p. 636 He goes on to say himself, "The more need of our Lord's soul to sanctify ours." vid. also de fr. Ap. pp 702, 706. Athan. Apoll. i. 2, 14, 15. Naz. Ep. 1. Cledon. p. 89. Epiph. Hær 77, 26. Eran. i. p. 13. Incert. Dial. v. 2, 9.

Another form of this objection was, κόσμου μέρος κόσμον σῶσαι οὐ δύναται. Athan. Apoll. ii. 7. Incert. Dial. v. 2.]

11. Such were the argumentative grounds of the heresy. Its advocates disposed of the difficulty arising out of the Scripture passages which speak of our Lord's soul, by asserting that the animal or physical soul was meant in them, or if the rational constituent or νοῦς, then that the Divine Word, which supplied the place of a soul, was called soul there. And thus He was "perfect man ;" the divinity supplying that in His manhood which was necessary for its perfection. But without the Word, He was not "perfect man," any more than one of us has a perfect manhood, when, by the departure of the soul, he lies a corpse.

[The Word then was the νοῦς of the σύνθετον, of the Christ or Emmanuel. The Apollinarians considered our Lord οὐκ ἄψυχον, οὐδ' ἄλογον, οὐδ' ἄνουν, οὐδ' ἀτελῆ, the θεότης supplying the deficiency ; Naz. Ep. 2. Cledon. p. 94. This divinity was Christ's "inner man ;" ἀντὶ τοῦ ἔσωθεν ἐν ἡμῖν ἀνθρώπου, νοῦς ἐπουράνιος ἐν Χριστῷ. Athan. Apoll. i. 2. And on the other hand, τὸ σῶμα καὶ ἡ ψυχὴ ὁ ἔξωθέν ἐστιν ἄνθρωπος ibid. 13, vid. also 19.

[This explanation will serve to enlighten us as to an evasion, to which they had recourse in some of their creeds, which seem orthodox. Thus in the Creed included in the Ephesine Acts, (*vid. supr.* p. 37,) our Lord is said to be ὅλον θεὸν καὶ μετὰ τοῦ σώματος . . . καὶ ὅλον ἄνθρωπον μετὰ τῆς θεότητος; where the καὶ before the first μετὰ seems to direct us to the evasion. They meant to say that He was perfect God, His body *exclusive*, and perfect man, His Divinity *inclusive*. And so again, τέλειος ἄνθρωπος ἐν πνεύματι in Constant. *Epp. Pont. App.* p. 75; where πνεῦμα stands for the Divine Nature, an archaism, which they seem to have affected, because it brought their triple view of human nature into connexion with St. Paul, 1 Thess. v. 23, the human πνεῦμα there spoken of, or intellectual spirit of an ordinary man, being changed for the Divine Spirit or Word in the manhood of Emmanuel.

They were called διμοιρῖται, as allowing Him only two out of the three constituents of human nature. Basnage strangely mistakes here. *Via. Naz. Ep.* 202, τριτημόριον.]

§ 3.

1. Such were the statements and arguments, by the aid of which the Apollinarian tenet was recommended to the acceptance of Catholics; but, whatever might be their value, their outcome was nothing short of a negation of our Lord's Divinity, as absolute, if not so immediate, as Arianism.

Apollinaris taught, as a special means of securing that all-important dogma, and of securing the *summa unio*, the hypostatic simplicity, of the two natures in the Word incarnate, that He, the Infinitely great God, had become the soul of a human being.

["Hoc est, Verbum carnem factum esse, unitum esse carni, ut humanus spiritus." Leont. p. 702 D.]

2. That is, that He had united Himself to what, viewed apart from His presence in it, was a brute animal; this position being no mere inference of opponents, but what the Apollinarians taught directly and purposely, in order, as they said, to deprive His humanity of that (viz. the intellectual principle) which emphatically constitutes man.

[*Vid.* passages quoted above, pp. 308-314.]

3. Moreover, that the whole, the σύνθετος οὐσία, which the Word formed with that brute creature, has a completeness and entireness, surpassing that of the Word Himself.

[He taught, says Gregory Naz., θεότητα τοῦ μονογενοῦς μέρος γενέσθαι τοῦ ἀνθρωπείου συγκράματος *Ep.* 202, p. 168. ᾧ καινὴ κτίσις, says Apollinaris himself, καὶ μίξις θεσπεσία, θεὸς καὶ σὰρξ μίαν ἀπετέλεσαν φύσιν. Eulog. *ap.* Phot. p. 850.]

4. Let it be observed, he did not merely say that the Incarnation was analogous to the union of soul and body, as the Athanasian Creed rightly teaches, and as the Eutychians afterwards perversely maintained, but that it was an actual instance of that union. The Word was the very soul of a human body. The Word and the flesh went together to make a compound nature, a *σύνθετος οὐσία*, which was neither the one nor the other, as in the case of men generally, being both present, but both changed in that resulting whole. What, separately taken, is ghost and corpse in man, becomes in their union soul and body, each new in itself, as well as in the unit which they together constitute. A change in the Divine Nature of the Word! This then was Apollinaris's expedient for protecting this sacred truth against the blasphemies of Arius.

[Leont. *de Sect.* viii. 8, p. 649. σαρκινὸν τὸν λόγον. Nyssen. t. 2, p. 694. ἀλλοίωσις τοῦ λόγου. Athan. *Apoll.* i. 2. ὁ λόγος εἰς σάρκα καὶ ὀστέα καὶ τρίχας καὶ ὅλον σῶμα μεταβέβληται. *Epict.* 2. ὁ πρῶτος, says Theodoret of Apollinaris, τῶν φύσεων τὴν κρᾶσιν εἰσάγων. *Eran.* p. 174. σύνθετον οὐσίαν οὐδεὶς εἰπεῖν ἐτόλμησε, πλὴν Ἀπολλινάριος. Ephraëm. *ap.* Phot. p. 804. *vid.* also p. 850. Damasc. *contr. Jac.* p. 402. *vid.* Tertull. *in Prax.* 27.]

5. There was no escape open to Apollinaris from these consequences, except the fresh error, into which he seems to have been forced, viz., that of denying that our Lord's body remained human, and of maintaining that it had a celestial nature.

[He argues, Leont. p. 706 B, that, if it can be said, "The Word became flesh," it may also be said, "The flesh became the Word." "Verbum caro factum est, ut caro fieret Verbum." Pseudo-Athan. *ap.* Anastas. *Hodeg.* xiii. p. 230. He argued that our Lord's body was consubstantial with the Divinity, and not with our bodies, otherwise, it could not have life in itself, and become a principle of life to others, but must need quickening and nourishment, as others need. Leont. p. 705 E. Diodorus affirmed that His nature was the same as that of other men, though His conception and birth were different; on which Apollinaris asked what was the use of a divine generation and birth, if a corresponding nature did not follow. *ibid.* D.]

6. Or further still, except the heresy of maintaining that our Lord's body became nothing more than a phantom, such as Angels might wear in order to their intercourse with men.

[ἀνάγκη λέγειν, ἢ τὴν εἰς σάρκα τροπὴν αὐτὸν ὑπομεμενηκέναι, ἢ δοκήσει τοιοῦτον ὀφθῆναι. *Eran* p 10.]

7. So much on the heretical tenet, viewed in itself; next, as to its bearing on our Lord's mission.

If the Incarnation is mainly or solely intended as a manifestation of the Divine Nature, how is it a satisfaction for human sin?

[οὐκ οἷόν τε ἦν ἕτερον ἀνθ' ἑτέρου ἀντιδοῦναι λύτρον· ἀλλὰ σῶμα ἀντὶ σώματος, καὶ ψυχὴν ἀντὶ ψυχῆς δέδωκε ... τουτέστιν τὸ ἀντάλλαγμα. Athan. *Apoll.* i. 17.

παρέδωκεν [ἡ ἐκκλησία] τὸν θεὸν καὶ λόγον ἐπιδημήσαντα ... ἵνα καὶ παθῇ ὑπὲρ ἡμῶν ὡς ἄνθρωπος, καὶ λυτρώσηται ἡμᾶς ἐκ πάθους καὶ θανάτου ὡς θεός. *ibid.* i. 20.

εἰ μὴ καὶ τὸν ἔσωθεν καὶ τὸν ἔξωθεν συνεστήσατο ἑαυτῷ ὁ λόγος, ... πῶς τὸ ὑπὲρ τοῦ παντὸς ἀντέδωκεν ἀντίλυτρον; *ibid.* i. 19. Vid. Leon. *Serm.* 63, p. 249.]

8. What becomes of our boast, that our enemy has been foiled by the very nature over which he had triumphed, and that that nature has been shown capable, and been made the subject, of the most intimate union with Infinite sanctity and wisdom?

[ὅπου κεκράτητο ἡ ψυχὴ ἡ ἀνθρωπίνη ἐν θανάτῳ, ἐκεῖ ἐπεδείκνυται ὁ Χριστὸς τὴν ἀνθρωπίνην ψυχὴν ἰδίαν οὖσαν, . . ἵνα, ὅπου ἐσπάρη ἡ φθορά, ἐκεῖ ἀνατείλῃ ἡ ἀφθαρσία, &c. Athan. *Apoll.* i 17. *vid.* also 7. ii. 6, 17. Epiph. *Ancor.* 78 a. Ambros *Incarn* 56. Naz. *Ep.* 1. *Cledon.* p. 85.]

9 How is it a union of Himself with our nature, such, as to be the germ of its new life, and the first-fruits of its renovation in holiness?

[ὅλου τοῦ ἀνθρώπου, ψυχῆς καὶ σώματος, ἀληθῶς ἡ σωτηρία γέγονεν ἐν αὐτῷ τῷ λόγῳ. Athan. *Epict.* 7. τὸ ἀπρόσληπτον, ἀθεράπευτον. Naz. *Ep.* 1. *Cledon.* p. 87. ἐκεῖνον ἔσωσεν, ᾧ καὶ συνήφθη. Leont. *de Sect.* iv. 2, p. 626. οὐ προκάλυμμα τῇ θεότητι μηχανώμενος, ἀλλὰ διὰ τῆς ἀπαρχῆς παντὶ τῷ γένει τὴν νίκην πραγματευόμενος, τελείαν τὴν ἀνθρωπείαν φύσιν ἀνέλαβε. Theod. *Hær.* v. 11, p. 422. *vid.* also *Eran.* iii. p. 297. Leon. *Serm.* 72, p. 286. Vigil. T. *adv. Eut.* i. p. 724 Athan. *Orat.* iii. 33. Nyssen. t 2, p. 696. Damasc. *F. O.* iv. 4, p. 255.]

10. Much as it is to have a perfect pattern set before us, how is this pattern practically available, unless an inward grace is communicated from His Person to realise this pattern in us?

[λέγετε, τῇ ὁμοιώσει καὶ τῇ μιμήσει σώζεσθαι τοὺς πιστεύοντας, καὶ οὐ τῇ ἀνακαινίσει καὶ τῇ ἀπαρχῇ, καὶ πῶς . . . οὐ γὰρ ἦλθεν ἡ θεότης ἑαυτὴν δικαιῶσαι, οὐδὲ γὰρ ἥμαρτεν, ἀλλ᾽ ἐπτώχευσε δι᾽ ἡμᾶς, &c. &c. Athan. *Apoll.* ii. 11. τὸ ἐκτὸς ἡμῶν καθαρίζουσι μόνον διὰ τοῦ καινοῦ προσωπείου. Naz. *Ep.* 2. *Cledon.* p. 95.]

11. I do not mean of course that he would not deny the consequences which I have been urging against his doctrine; but I am concerned here, not with him personally, but with that doctrine itself. We may be sure that he felt its difficulties; and this consciousness is the natural explanation of his inconsistencies, which are not few.

He was an eloquent writer, and an able disputant, and boldly affirmed what, according to the undeniable logic of his opponents, he ought to have denied. In one fragment, for instance, he says our Lord's body was glorified, ὡς ἥρμοττε σώματι θεοῦ καὶ σωτῆρι κόσμου, καὶ σπέρματι ζωῆς αἰωνίου, καὶ ὀργάνῳ θείων ἐνεργειῶν, καὶ λυτικῷ κακίας ἁπάσης, καὶ θανάτου καθαιρετικῷ, καὶ ἀναστάσεως ἀρχηγῷ. *ap. Eran.* ii. pp. 173, 4. *vid.* also p. 256. These are fine words, but were they reconcilable with his heretical tenet?

§ 4.

1. These inconsistencies, which form the decisive testimony of Apollinaris himself against his own teaching, will partly be seen in his own statements as they remain to us, as contrasted with his profession of the whole Catholic creed, and partly in the extravagances of his followers.

First, as to his own statements :—

[His opinions to be found in his fragments preserved, 1. by Theodoret, and 2. by Leontius, and 3. in the report of Gregory Nazianzen (Leont. p. 707 C), Gregory Nyssen, and Basil.]

He said that, 1. Our Lord was born of the Blessed Virgin (Leont. p. 701 C, p. 702 D, Incert. *Dial.* iv. 9 *fin.*). 2. He had no rational principle but the Eternal Word (p. 706 C, D). 3. His body or flesh was an organ or outward form of the Divine Power (p. 706 D). 4. The Only-begotten was a constituent of a compound nature (p. 704 C). 5. What was virtually a new nature in Him was made out of the divinity and the flesh (p. 704 A). 6. Though they remained in their own nature (*ibid.*). 7. His flesh was of a created nature (p. 702 D). 8. It remained after the union (p. 701 E, A, C. *Eran.* pp. 171, 2). 9. It was consubstantial with ours (p. 702, C, D. p. 704 A. *Eran.* p. 170). 10. It was not consubstantial with God (p. 701 E,

p. 702 D). 11. It was consubstantial with God, by communication of name, not by change of nature (p. 704 E). 12. It was not from heaven, considered as flesh (p. 701 B, p. 705 A). 13. As being the flesh of Christ, it is God (p. 702 D, p. 704 B). 14. Our Lord was the "cœlestis homo," "propter spiritum cœlestem" (p 702 D). 15. His flesh, though not from heaven, (p. 701 B) 16. Still possessed the names and the properties of the Word, so as even to be increate (p. 705 E, p. 176 A). 17. It was not changed from created to increate, but was increate, as far as it was God (p. 706 B). 18. It was increate, considered as God (p. 705 B). 19. The man was consubstantial with God (p. 705 C) 20. His flesh was of one substance with the Word (p. 706 D). 21. It was connatural with the Divine Nature (p. 705 B). 22. It was consubstantiated with the Divinity (p. 705 D). 23. It was from the beginning in the Son (Naz. *Ep.* 202). 24 The Word remained God, not changed into a bodily substance (p. 705 D. *Eran.* p. 70).

2. Next, as to his followers, some were unwilling to lose the shadow of an orthodox profession, however nominal; while others were prepared to go all lengths, orthodox or not. Some desired to retain a positive doctrine; others recklessly split up their party into fragments as numerous as their doctrinal varieties, bringing it to an end by virtue of the very principles on which it had started.

[ὑμῖν πάντα ἐπινενόηται, ἵνα μίαν τῆς ἀρνήσεως κατασκευάσητε γνώμην, &c. Athan. *Apoll.* i. 21.]

3. Both parties claimed Apollinaris as their master.

[Valentinus, the moderate, says, "Magister noster Apollinarius blasphemos et insanos scripto vocavit eos, qui," &c. Leont. p. 703 D. Timotheus, the extreme, "cum Magister noster Apollinarius dicat," &c. p. 704 C.]

4. Both parties taught that our Lord's body was originally consubstantial with ours, and that it was made divine. But it was debated between them, whether by being made divine, it was changed merely in properties, or was changed into the divine substance.

[Valentinus says, "Nobis consubstantialis est secundum carnem; unio honoravit naturam, non fecit corpus consubstantiale Deo," p. 703 C. Timotheus says. "Natura quidem consubstantialem nobis esse carnem, unione vero esse divinam." p. 704 B.]

5. Valentinus, of the moderate party, maintained that its properties alone were affected by the presence of the Divine Word, not its substance.

[He writes his *Apologia* "contra eos qui dicunt dicere nos esse corpus consubstantiale Deo." Leont. p. 701 B. "Cum Verbo Dei simul adoratur caro." p. 702 C, D. "Unione Deus habetur, non natura." *ibid.* "In unione esse perseverat." *ibid.* His formula was "Unio non est homoüsion." p. 703 A]

6. Even on this more cautious ground, questions had to be met and satisfied. If the Word and His flesh were in Emmanuel as rational soul and body, the Divine Nature suffers in Him, as the soul suffers in and with the body. His party answered that it was His animal soul that suffered; but could the mere animal soul say, "Eli, Eli, lama," &c.? However, there was an alternative by which to escape the conclusion that the Divine Nature suffered; viz. to maintain that there had been no passion at all, only a manifestation of the Word.

[Apollinaris held the ἀπάθεια of the Word; vid. Theod. *Eran.* p. 256.

But Athanasius and Epiphanius accuse the party of ascribing πάθη to the Divinity. οὐσίαν τοῦ λόγου παθητὴν λέγοντες. Ath. *Apoll.* i. 3. Epiph. *Hær.* 77, 32. The Apollinarian in Incert. *Dial.* iv. 4, says, οὐκ ἔπαθεν οὖν ὁ λόγος; ὅλως ἔπαθεν. Gregory Naz. however, with a treatise of Apollinaris before him, says that he maintained our Lord τῇ ἰδίᾳ αὐτοῦ θεότητι πάθος δέξασθαι. *Ep.* 202, p. 168.]

7. A further difficulty lay in our Lord's death. As the cessation of warmth, sense, and motion are signs of death on the part of the body, so on the part of the soul is the descent into Hades; now the Word was the soul of Emmanuel; did the Word then take a place among disembodied spirits? Again, was His body any longer divine, now that the Word had left it? But why need they embarrass themselves with teaching His death, since His coming was only a manifestation? And to this conclusion they inclined.

["Non solum non succumbit morti, sed eam solvit," says Apollinaris. Leont. p. 707. Athan. *Apoll.* i. 6, 14. *Epict.* 8 *fin.* Incert. *Dial.* v. 3.]

8. Now to turn to those, as Timotheus, who adopted the extreme views to which the heresy led. They maintained our Lord's body became, on its union, consubstantial with the Divine nature; else, it was idolatry to worship Him as incarnate. Hence they were called συνουσιασταί.

[Leont. p. 703 E, p. 704, and p. 707 A. ὁμοούσιον τὸ ἐκ Μαρίας σῶμα τῇ τοῦ λόγου θεότητι. Athan. *Epict.* 2. σάρκα προαιώνιόν τινα καὶ συνουσιωμένην. Naz. *Ep.* 202. Theod. *Hær.* iv. 9. Facund. viii. 4, p. 471 and note. (Yet Malchion says θεὸν συνουσιωμένον τῷ ἀνθρώπῳ. *infr. Cyril's Formula*, 17.) That our Lord was not in His human nature consubstantial with us, was one of the two points of Eutychianism, though he wavered about it. *vid. Concil.* t. 2, p. 164, 5. Flavian *ap.* Leon. *Ep.* 26, *Ep.* 30.]

9. But, if this was so, that a change of substance took place in our Lord's body on His assuming it, so that it even was increate and everlasting, how was it a body at all? For if it could remain a body, after this change, then that into which it was changed would itself be of a material nature already. Either this, or it was no longer a body, but a phantom, as the old Docetæ had said. And thus, when they called His body increate, perhaps they meant non-create, that is, that it never had been brought into existence at all.

[μὴ ἐπίκτητον εἶναι τὴν σάρκα, ἀλλ' ἐξ ἀρχῆς ἐν τῷ υἱῷ. Naz. *Ep.* 202, p. 168. μὴ νεώτερον εἶναι τὸ σῶμα τῆς τοῦ λόγου θεότητος, ἀλλὰ συναΐδιον αὐτῷ, ἐπεὶ ἐκ τῆς οὐσίας τῆς σοφίας συνέστη. Athan. *Epict.* 2. πόθεν ὑμῖν κατηγγέλθη σάρκα ἄκτιστον λέγειν, ὥστε ἢ τὴν θεότητα τοῦ λόγου εἰς μετάπτωσιν σαρκὸς φαντάζεσθαι, ἢ τὴν οἰκονομίαν τοῦ πάθους καὶ τοῦ θανάτου καὶ τῆς ἀναστάσεως ὡς δόκησιν νομίζειν; Apoll. i. 3. *vid.* the same dilemma in Theod. *Eran.* p. 10, quoted *supr.* p. 318. σκιώδη τὴν δεῖξιν ἐποιεῖτο ὁ θεός. Athan. *Apoll.* i. 7. ὡς ἐν δοκήσει. *ibid.* ii. 5. μὴ δοκήσει. Incert. *Dial.* iv. 7. ὡς φαντασίας τινὸς ἀπατηλῆς καὶ δοκήσεως. Naz. *Ep.* 2. *Cledon.* p. 96. θέσει καὶ οὐ φύσει σῶμα πεφόρηκεν. Athan. *Epict.* 2. Unus verus, qui sine carne in carne apparuit. Leont. p. 707 A. ἐν τοῖς ποιήμασι τὸ λεγόμενον ἄκτιστον τὸ μηδέπω ὑπάρξαν λέγεται. Athan. *Apoll.* i. 5.]

10. Another question arose. They confessed that our Lord's body was originally human; did this mean that it had existed before its union with the Word? If so, they were falling into the heresy afterwards called Nestorianism.

[Athan. *Epict.* 8. Leont. *de Sectis*, vii. 1. *vid.* Petav. *Incarn.* i. 14, 5, p. 35.]

11. There are those, among whom is numbered Apollinaris himself, who made short work with this difficulty by maintaining our Lord's body was of a divine nature from the first, being taken, not from the Blessed Virgin, but from the internal essence of the Word Himself, a celestial development, for the purpose of a manifestation.

[ἐξ ἑαυτοῦ μεταποιήσας σάρκα ὁ λόγος. Athan. *Apoll.* ii. 12. οὐκ ἐκ Μαρίας, ἀλλ' ἐκ τῆς ἑαυτοῦ οὐσίας. *Epict.* 2. ἐξ ἀρχῆς ἐν τῷ υἱῷ τὴν σαρκώδη ἐκείνην φύσιν εἶναι. Naz. *Ep.* 202, p. 168. So Valentinus, the Gnostic, "Verbum ex se caro factum est." Tertull. *Carn. Ch.* 19-21. And Eutyches, "Seipsum replasmavit." Vigil. Th. *contr. Eut.* Hence ἄκτιστον καὶ ἐπουράνιον λέγοντες τὴν τοῦ Χριστοῦ σάρκα. Athan. *Apoll.* i. 2. ἐξ οὐρανοῦ τό σῶμα. *ibid.* 7. Χριστὸς οὐ χοϊκὸς, ἀλλ' ἐπουράνιος. Incert. *Dial.* v. 4. Neque caro e cœlo nec æterna, ut vos dicitis. Leont. p. 703. *vid.* Naz. *Ep.* 202. p. 168. Nyssen. *Antirrh* 13. Epiph. *Hær.* 77. 2.]

12. It is obvious how easily this last opinion might pass into Sabellianism by identifying the Word with this mere visible development, which was superficial to the Divine Essence. Accordingly, we find one large section of the Apollinarians accused of that heresy, and they favoured this imputation by teaching that our Lord was the image of the Father, not in His divine, but in His human nature.

[*Vid.* as to Apollinaris himself Basil. *Epp.* 129, 265. Theod *Hær.* iv. 8. Athan *Apoll.* i. 20, ii. 3, 5. On the other hand, Leont. *de Sect.* iv. 2. *vid.* Benedictine note on Ambros. *Incarn.* 11.]

13. On the other hand, those who scrupled to assert that the Divine Nature suffered on the Cross, yet denied with Apollinaris that Christ had a human mind, would

be tempted to consider Him not strictly God at all, and therefore of course passible. And in fact the Apollinarians are accused by some writers of considering the Son inferior to the Father, and the Spirit to the Son, which is the heresy of Arius.

[Naz. *Ep.* 1. *Cledon.* p. 92.]

14. As we know that the party of Valentinus were not Sabellians, it is probable that it was the Timotheans who favoured Sabellius, and the Valentinians who inclined towards Arianism.

[*Vid.* Tillemont, *Mém.* t. 7, p. 602, &c.]

V.

ON ST. CYRIL'S FORMULA
ΜΙΑ ΦΥΣΙΣ ΣΕΣΑΡΚΩΜΕΝΗ.

(From the Atlantis of July, 1858.)

ANALYSIS OF THE ARGUMENT.

THE inquiry—turns upon the use of terms—Phraseology of science gradually perfected—especially in the province of Revelation—Mistakes during the process—Reluctance of early Catholics to pursue it—illustrated by the *Homoüsion*—and by other terms—especially the *hypostasis*.

Yet this no proof of carelessness about dogma—Athanasius dogmatic, though without science—his varying application of *hypostasis*—One *hypostasis* taught in fourth century—and in third—Three by Alexandrians—both One and Three by Athanasius,—who innovates on the Alexandrian usage,—yet without changing the general sense of the term—which denotes the One Supreme Being—as individual, personal—and the God of natural theology—and also as being any or each of the Three divine Persons—Latitude in the sense of the term—illustration from Athanasius.

Usia has a like meaning—and is preferred by Athanasius,—as a synonyme for *hypostasis*—and *physis* also—and *eidos*.—These terms are inapplicable in their full sense to the Word's humanity—yet they are so applied—*e.g. hypostasis*—and *usia*—and *physis*—but not in their full sense.

Especially not *physis*—first on Scripture grounds—next on grounds of reason—The divine *physis* must retain the fulness of its attributes—therefore the human *physis* must have a restricted meaning—How then is there a human *physis* at all?—Hence the form and the force of Cyril's Formula.

Illustration from the Council of Antioch—which teaches the unalterableness of the divine *usia*—together with the Catholic Doctors generally—with Athanasius—and other Fathers—some of whom therefore attribute the human conception to the operation of the Word—Thus Cyril too by the "One Nature" denotes—the Word's eternity,—unity,—unalterableness.

The same Council teaches that the Word's *usia* occupies the humanity—and that the humanity is taken up into the Word's *usia*—as, analogously, the creation also is established in His *usia*—Contrast between *physis* and *usia*—The proper meaning of *physis*—shows the delicacy of applying the term to His humanity—which is in a state above nature—and therefore was not commonly called a *physis*—till Leo and the Council of Chalcedon.

This is clear from the early Fathers—who appropriate the term to the divinity—and describe the humanity as an envelopment—as an adjunct—as a first-fruit—not, as *homoüsion* with us—and omit the obvious contrast of the Two Natures—the term "man" equivalent to "nature".

Recapitulation—The Word's Nature—is One—and is Incarnate—Fortunes of the Formula.

ΜΙΑ ΦΥΣΙΣ ΤΟΥ ΘΕΟΥ ΛΟΓΟΥ ΣΕΣΑΡΚΩΜΕΝΗ

I.

THIS celebrated Formula of St. Cyril's, perhaps of St. Athanasius's, was, as is well known, one of the main supports of the Monophysites, in controversy with the Catholics of the fifth and following centuries. It has been so fully discussed by theologians from his day to our own, that it hardly allows of any explanation, which would be at once original and true; still, room is left for collateral illustration and remarks in detail; and so much shall be attempted here. *The inquiry*

First of all, and in as few words as possible, and *ex abundanti cautela* :—Every Catholic holds that the Christian dogmas were in the Church from the time of the Apostles; that they were ever in their substance what they are now; that they existed before the formulas were publicly adopted, in which, as time went on, they were defined and recorded, and that such formulas, when sanctioned by the due ecclesiastical acts, are binding on the faith of Catholics, and have a dogmatic authority. With *turns upon the use of terms.*

this profession once for all, I put the strictly theological question aside; for I am concerned in a purely historical investigation into the use and fortunes of certain scientific terms.

2.

Phraseology of science gradually perfected, Even before we take into account the effect which would naturally be produced on the first Christians by the novelty and mysteriousness of doctrines which depend for their reception simply upon Revelation, we have reason to anticipate that there would be difficulties and mistakes in expressing them, when they first came to be set forth by unauthoritative writers. Even in secular sciences, inaccuracy of thought and language is but gradually corrected; that is, in proportion as their subject-matter is thoroughly scrutinised and mastered by the co-operation of many independent intellects, successively engaged upon it. Thus, for instance, the word *Person* requires the rejection of various popular senses, and a careful definition, before it can serve for philosophical uses. We sometimes use it for an *individual* as contrasted with a class or multitude, as when we speak of having "personal objections" to another; sometimes for the *body*, in contrast to the soul, as when we speak of "beauty of person." We sometimes use it in the abstract, as when we speak of another as "insignificant in person;" sometimes in the concrete, as when we call him "an insignificant person." How divergent in meaning are the derivatives, *personable, personalities, personify, personation, personage, parsonage!* This variety arises partly from our own carelessness, partly from the necessary developments of language, partly from the exuberance of human thought, partly from the defects of our vernacular tongue.

Language then requires to be refashioned even for sciences which are based on the senses and the reason; but much more will this be the case, when we are concerned with subject-matters, of which, in our present state, we cannot possibly form any complete or consistent conception, such as the Catholic doctrines of the Trinity and Incarnation. Since they are from the nature of the case above our intellectual reach, and were unknown till the preaching of Christianity, they required on their first promulgation new words, or words used in new senses, for their due enunciation ; and, since these were not definitely supplied by Scripture or by tradition, nor for centuries by ecclesiastical authority, variety in the use, and coufusion in the apprehension of them, were unavoidable in the interval. This conclusion is necessary, admitting the premisses, antecedently to particular instances in proof·

especially in the province of revelation.

Moreover, there is a presumption equally strong, that the variety and confusion which I have anticipated, would in matter of fact issue here or there in actual heterodoxy, as often as the language of theologians was misunderstood by hearers or readers, and deductions were made from it which the teacher did not intend. Thus, for instance, the word *Person*, used in the doctrine of the Holy Trinity, would on first hearing suggest Tritheism to one who made the word synonymous with *individual;* and Unitarianism to another, who accepted it in the classical sense of a *mask* or *character.*

Mistakes during the process.

Even to this day our theological language is wanting in accuracy: thus, we sometimes speak of the controversies concerning the *Person* of Christ, when we mean to include in them those which belong to the two *natures* which are predicated of Him.

3.

Reluctance of early Catholics to pursue it

Indeed, the difficulties of forming a theological phraseology for the whole of Christendom were obviously so great, that we need not wonder at the reluctance which the first age of Catholic divines showed in attempting it, even apart from the obstacles caused by the distraction and isolation of the churches in times of persecution. Not only had the words to be adjusted and explained which were peculiar to different schools or traditional in different places, but there was the formidable necessity of creating a common measure between two, or rather three languages,—Latin, Greek, and Syriac. The intellect had to be satisfied, error had to be successfully excluded, parties the most contrary to each other, and the most obstinate, had to be convinced. The very confidence which would be felt by Christians in general that Apostolic truth would never fail,—and that they held it themselves, each in his own country, and the *orbis terrarum* with them, in spite of all verbal contrarieties,—would indispose them to define it, till definition became an imperative duty.

Illustrated by the homoüsion,

I think this plain from the nature of the case; and history confirms me in the instance of the imposition of the *homoüsion*, which, as one of the first and most necessary steps, so again was apparently one of the most discouraging, in giving a scientific expression to doctrine. This formula, as Athanasius, Hilary, and Basil affirm, had been disowned as consistent with heterodoxy by the Councils of Antioch, A.D. 264-72, yet, in spite of this disavowal on the part of bishops of the highest authority, it was imposed on all the faithful to the end of time in the Ecumenical Council of Nicæa, A.D. 325, as the best and truest safeguard, as it really is, of orthodox teaching. The misapprehensions and protests, which, after such antecedents, its adoption occasioned for many years, may be easily imagined. Though above three hundred bishops had accepted it, large numbers of them in the next generation were but imperfectly convinced of its expedience; and Athanasius himself, whose imperishable name is bound up with it, showed himself most cautious in putting it forward, though it had the sanction of an Ecumenical Council He introduces the word, I think, only once into his three celebrated Orations, and then rather in a formal statement of doctrine than in the flow of his discussion, viz. *Orat.* i. 4. Twice he gives utterance to it in the Collection of Notes which make up what is called his fourth Oration (*Orat.* iv. 9, 12). We find it indeed in his *de Decretis Nic. Conc.* and his *de Synodis;* but there it constitutes his direct subject, and he discusses it in order, when challenged, to defend it. And in his work against Apollinaris he says ὁμοούσιος ἡ τριάς, i. 9. But there are passages of his Orations in which he omits it, when it was the natural word to use; *vid.* the notes on *Orat.* i. 20, 21, and 58 *fin. Oxf. transl.* Moreover, the word does not occur in the

Catecheses of St. Cyril of Jerusalem, A.D. 347, nor in the recantation made before Pope Julius by Ursacius and Valens, A.D. 349, nor in the cross-questionings to which St. Ambrose subjected Palladius and Secundianus, A.D. 381. At Seleucia, A.D. 359, a hundred and fifty Eastern Bishops (with the exception of a few Egyptians) were found to abandon it, while at Ariminum in the same year the celebrated scene took place of four hundred bishops of the West being worried and tricked into a momentary act of the same character. They had not yet got it deeply fixed into their minds, as a sort of first principle, that to abandon the Formula was to betray the faith. We may think how strong and general the indisposition was thus to regard the matter, when even Pope Liberius consented to sign a creed in which it was omitted (*vid.* Athan. *Histor. Arian.* 41 *fin.*).

<small>and by other terms,</small> This disinclination on the part of Catholics to dogmatic definitions was not confined to the instance of the ὁμοούσιον. It was one of the successful stratagems of the Arians to urge upon Catholics the propriety of confining their statement of doctrine to the language of Scripture, and of rejecting ὑπόστασις, οὐσία, and similar terms, which when once used in a definite sense, that is, scientifically, in Christian teaching, would become the protection and record of orthodoxy.

<small>especially the *hypostasis*;</small> In the instance of the word ὑπόστασις, we find Athanasius, Eusebius of Vercelli, and other Catholic Confessors of the day, recognising and allowing the two acceptations then in use, in the Council which they held in Alexandria, A.D. 362.

4.

Such a reluctance to fix the phraseology of doctrine cannot be logically taken to imply an indisposition towards dogma itself; and in matter of fact it is historically contemporaneous with the most unequivocal dogmatic statements. Scientific terms are not the only token of science. Distinction or antithesis is as much a characteristic of it as definition can be, though not so perfect an instrument. The Epistles of Ignatius, for instance, who belongs to the Apostolical age of the Church, are in places unmistakeably dogmatic, without any use of technical terms. Such is the fragment preserved by Athanasius (*de Syn.* 47): Εἷς ἰατρός ἐστι σαρκικὸς καὶ πνευματικός, γενητὸς καὶ ἀγένητος, &c. I refer the reader to the remarks on those Epistles made in Tract ii. in this volume; also *supra*, p. 51; but the subject would admit of large illustration.

yet this no proof of carelessness about dogma.

Indeed no better illustration can be given of that intrinsic independence of a fixed terminology which belongs to the Catholic Creed, than the writings of Athanasius himself, the special Doctor from whom the subsequent treatises of Basil, the two Gregories, and Cyril are derived. This great author scarcely uses any of the scientific phrases which have since been received in the Church and have become dogmatic; or, if he introduces them, it is to give them senses which have long been superseded. A good instance of his manner is afforded by the long passage, *Orat.* iii. 30-58, which is full of

Athanasius dogmatic, though without professing science.

theology, with scarcely a dogmatic word. The case is the same with his treatment of the Incarnation. No one surely can read his works without being struck with the force and exactness with which he lays down the outlines and fills up the details of the Catholic dogma, as it has been defined since the controversies with Nestorius and Eutyches, who lived in the following century; yet the word θεοτόκος, which had come down to him, like ὁμοούσιος by tradition, is nearly the only one among those which he uses, which would now be recognised as dogmatic.

5.

His varying application of hy- postasis. Sometimes too he varies the use which he makes of such terms as really are of a scientific character. An instance of this is supplied by *hypostasis*, a word to which reference has already been made. It was usual, at least in the West and in St Athanasius's day, to speak of one *hypostasis*, as of one *usia*, of the Divine Nature. Thus the so-called Sardican Creed, A.D. 347, speaks of μία ὑπόστασις, ἣν αὐτοὶ οἱ αἱρετικοὶ οὐσίαν προσαγορεύουσι. Theod. *Hist.* ii. 8; the Roman Council under Damasus, *One hypo- stasis taught in 4th century,* A.D. 371, says that the Three Persons are τῆς αὐτῆς ὑποστά- σεως καὶ οὐσίας; and the Nicene Anathematism condemns those who say that the Son ἐγένετο ἐξ ἑτέρας ὑποστάσεως ἢ οὐσίας; for that the words are synonymes I have argued, after Petavius against Bull, in one of the Dissertations to which I have already referred, *vid. supr.* p. 78. Epiphanius too speaks of μία ὑπόστασις, *Hær.* 74, 4, *Ancor.* 6 (and though he has αἱ ὑποστάσεις *Hær.* 62, 3. 72, 1, yet he is

of the μία φύσις.   341

shy of the plural, and prefers πατὴρ ἐνυπόστατος, υἱὸς ἐνυπόστατος, &c., *ibid.* 3 and 4. *Ancor.* 6, and τρία as *Hær.* 74, 4, where he says τρία ἐνυπόστατα τῆς αὐτῆς ὑποστάσεως. *Vid.* also ἐν ὑποστάσει τελειότητος. *Hær.* 74, 12. *Ancor.* 7 *et alibi*); and Cyril of Jerusalem of the μονοειδὴς ὑπόστασις of God, *Catech.* vi. 7, *vid.* also xvi. 12 and xvii. 9 (though the word may be construed one out of three in *Cat.* xi. 3), and Gregory Nazianzen, *Orat.* xxviii. 9, where he is speaking as a natural, not as a Christian theologian.

In the preceding century Gregory Thaumaturgus had laid it down that the Father and Son were ὑποστάσει ἕν; and the Council of Antioch, between A.D. 264 and 272, calls the Son οὐσίᾳ καὶ ὑποστάσει θεὸν θεοῦ υἱόν. Routh, *Reliq.* t. 2, p. 466. Accordingly Athanasius expressly tells us, "*Hypostasis* is *usia*, and means nothing else but αὐτὸ τὸ ὄν," *ad Afros*, 4. Jerome says that "Tota sæcularium litterarum schola nihil aliud *hypostasin* nisi *usiam* novit." *Epist.* xv. 4. Basil, the Semi-Arian, that "the Fathers have called *hypostasis usia*." Epiph. *Hær.* 73, 12 *fin.* And Socrates says that at least it was frequently used for *usia*, when it had entered into the philosophical schools. *Hist.* iii. 7.   *and in 3rd century.*

On the other hand the Alexandrians, Origen (*in Joan.* ii. 6 *et alibi*), Ammonius (*ap. Caten. in Joan.* x. 30, if genuine), Dionysius (*ap.* Basil. *de Sp. S.* n. 72), and Alexander (*ap.* Theod. *Hist.* i. 4), speak of more *hypostases* than one in the Divine Nature, that is, of three; and apparently without the support of the divines of any other school, unless Eusebius, who is half an Alexandrian, be an exception. Going down beyond the middle of the   *Three by Alexandrians.*

fourth century and the Council of A.D. 362 above referred to, we find the Alexandrian Didymus committing himself to bold and strong enunciations of the three *Hypostases*, beyond what I have elsewhere found in patristical literature.

Both one and three by Athanasius,

It is remarkable that Athanasius should so far innovate on the custom of his own Church, as to use the word in each of these two applications of it. In his *In illud Omnia* he speaks of τὰς τρεῖς ὑποστάσεις τελείας. He says, μία ἡ θεότης, καὶ εἷς θεὸς ἐν τρισὶν ὑποστάσεσι, *Incarn. c. Arian.* if the work be genuine. In *contr. Apoll.* i. 12, he seems to contrast οὐσία and φύσις with ὑπόστασις, saying τὸ ὁμοούσιον ἕνωσιν καθ᾿ ὑπόστασιν οὐκ ἐπιδεχόμενόν ἐστι, ἀλλὰ κατὰ φύσιν. Parallel instances occur in *Expos. Fid.* 2, and in *Orat.* iv. 25, though the words may be otherwise explained. On the other hand, he makes *usia* and *hypostasis* synonymous in *Orat.* iii. 65, 66. *Orat.* iv. 1 and 33 *fin.* Vid. also *Quod Unus est Christus*, and the fragment in Euthym. *Panopl.* p. 1, tit. 9; the genuineness of both being more than doubtful.

who innovates on the Alexandrian usage,

There is something more remarkable still in this innovation, in which Athanasius permits himself, on the practice of his Church. Alexander, his immediate predecessor and master, published, A.D. 320-324, two formal letters against Arius, one addressed to his namesake of Constantinople, the other encyclical. It is scarcely possible to doubt that the latter was written by Athanasius; it is so unlike the former in style and diction, so like the writings of Athanasius. Now it is observable that in the former the word *hypostasis* occurs in its Alexandrian sense at least five times; in the latter, which I attribute to Athanasius, it is dropt, and *usia* is introduced, which is absent from the former. That is, Athanasius has, on this supposition, when writing in his Bishop's name a formal document, pointedly innovated on his Bishop's theological language, and that the received language of his own Church. I am not supposing he did this without Alexander's sanction. Indeed, the character of the Arian polemic would naturally lead Alexander, as well as Athanasius, to be jealous of the formula of the τρεῖς ὑποστάσεις, which Arianism was using against them; and the latter would be confirmed in this feeling by his subsequent familiarity with Latin theology, and the usage of the Holy See, which, under Pope Damasus, as we have seen, A.D. 371, spoke of one *hypostasis*, and in the previous century, A.D. 260, protested by anticipation, in the person of Pope Dionysius, against the use which might be made, in the hands of enemies, of the formula of the three *hypostases*. Still it is undeniable that Athanasius does at least once speak of three, though his practice is to dispense with the word and to use others instead of it.

Now then we have to find an explanation of this difference of usage amongst Catholic writers in their application of the word. It is difficult to believe that so accurate a thinker as Athanasius really used an important term in two distinct, nay, contrasted senses; and I cannot but question the fact, so commonly taken for granted, that the divines of the beginning of the fourth century had appropriated any word whatever definitely to express either the idea of *Person* as contrasted with that of *Essence*, or of

yet without changing the general sense of the term,

Essence as contrasted with *Person*. I altogether doubt whether we are correct in saying that they meant by *hypostasis*, in one country *Person*, in another *Essence*. I think such propositions should be carefully proved, instead of being taken for granted, as at present is the case. Meanwhile, I have an hypothesis of my own. I think they used the word in East and West with only such a slight variation in its meaning, as would admit of Athanasius speaking of one *hypostasis* or three, without any great violence to that meaning, which remained substantially one and the same. What this sense is I proceed to explain.

6.

which denotes the one Supreme Being,

The Schoolmen are known to have insisted with great earnestness on the numerical unity of the Divine Being; each of the Three Divine Persons being one and the same God, unicus, singularis, et totus Deus. In this, however, they did but follow the recorded doctrine of the Western theologians of the fifth century, as I suppose will be allowed by critics generally. So forcible is St. Austin upon the strict unity of God, that he even thinks it necessary to caution his readers against supposing that he could allow them to speak of One Person as well as of Three in the Divine Nature, *de Trin.* vii. 11. Again, in the Creed *Quicunque*, the same elementary truth is emphatically insisted on. The neuter *unum* of former divines is changed into the masculine, in enunciating the mystery. "Non tres æterni, sed unus æternus." I suppose this means, that Each Divine Person is to be received as the one God as entirely and absolutely as He would be held to be, if we had never heard of the other Two, and that He is not in any respect less than the one and only God, because They are Each that same one God also; or in other words, that, as each human individual being has one personality, the Divine Being has three.

Returning then to Athanasius, I consider that this same mystery is implied in his twofold application of the word *hypostasis*. The polytheism and pantheism of the heathen world imagined,—not the God whom natural reason can discover, conceive, and worship, one, individual, living, and personal,—but a *divinitas*, which was either a quality, whether energy or life, or an extended substance, or something else equally inadequate to the real idea which the word, God, conveys. Such a divinity could not properly be called an *hypostasis* or said to be *in hypostasi* (except indeed as brute matter in one sense may be called an *hypostasis*), and therefore it was, that that word had some fitness, especially after the Apostle's adoption of it, *Hebr.* i. 3, to denote the Christian's God. And this may account for the remark of Socrates, that it was a new word, strange to the schools of ancient philosophy, which had seldom professed pure theism, or natural theology. "The teachers of philosophy among the Greeks," he says, "have defined *usia* in many ways; but of *hypostasis* they have made no mention at all. Irenæus the grammarian affirms that the word is barbarous." *Hist.* iii. 7. The better then was it fitted to express that highest object of thought, of which the "barbarians" of Palestine had been the special witnesses. When the divine *hypostasis* was confessed, the

[margin: as individual, personal,]

word expressed or suggested the attributes of individuality, self-subsistence, self-action, and personality, such as go to form the idea of the Divine Being to the natural theologian; and, since the difference between the theist and the Catholic divine in their idea of His nature is simply this, that, in opposition to the Pantheist, who cannot understand how the Infinite can be Personal at all, the one ascribes to Him one personality and the other three, it will be easily seen how a word, thus characterised and circumstanced, would admit of being used, with but a slight modification of its sense, of the Trinity as well as of the Unity.

as the God of natural theology,

Let us take, by way of illustration, the word μονάς, which, when applied to intellectual beings, includes the idea of personality. Dionysius of Alexandria, for instance, speaks of the μονάς and the τριάς: now, would it be very harsh, if, as he has spoken of "three *hypostases* ἐν μονάδι," so he had instead spoken of "the three μονάδες," that is, in the sense of τρισυπόστατος μονάς, as if the intrinsic force of the word *monas* would preclude the possibility of his use of the plural μονάδες being mistaken to imply that he held more *monads* than one? To take an analogous case, it would be about the same improper use of plural for singular, if we said that a martyr by his one act gained three victories, instead of a triple victory, over his three spiritual foes.

and also as being any and each of the Three Divine Persons.

This then is what I conceive Athanasius to mean, by sometimes speaking of one, sometimes of three *hypostases*. The word *hypostasis* neither means *Person* nor *Essence* exclusively; but it means the one personal God of natural theology, the notion of whom the Catholic corrects and completes as often as he views Him as a Trinity; of which correction Nazianzen's language (ὃν αὐτὸς κατὰ τὴν φύσιν καὶ τὴν ὑπόστασιν, Orat. xxviii. 9), completed by his usual formula (vid. Orat. xx. 6) of the three *hypostases*, is an illustration. The specification of three *hypostases* does not substantially alter the sense of the word itself, but is a sort of *catachresis* by which this Catholic doctrine is forcibly brought out (as it would be by the phrase "three monads"), viz. that each of the Divine Persons is simply the Unus et Singularis Deus. If it be objected, that by the same mode of reasoning, Athanasius might have said *catachrestically* not only three *monads* or three *hypostases*, but three Gods, I deny it, and for this reason; because *hypostasis* is not equivalent to the simple idea of God, but is rather a definition of Him, and that in some special elementary points, as essence, personality, &c., and because such a mere improper use or varying application of the term would not tend to compromise a truth, which never must even in forms of speech be trifled with, the absolute numerical unity of the Supreme Being. Though a Catholic could not say that there are three Gods, he could say that the definition of God applies to *unus* and *tres*. Perhaps it is for this reason that Epiphanius speaks of τρία ἐνυπόστατα, συνυπόστατα, τῆς αὐτῆς ὑποστάσεως. *Hær.* lxxiv. 4 (vid. Jerome, *Ep.* xv. 3), in the spirit in which St. Thomas, I believe, interprets the "non tres æterni, sed unus æternus," to turn on the contrast of adjective and substantive.

Latitude in the sense of the term

Petavius makes a remark which is apposite to my present purpose. "Nomen Dei," he says, *de Trin.* iii. 9, § 10, "cum sit ex eorum genere quæ concreta dicuntur, formam significat, non abstractam ab individuis proprietatibus, ... sed in iis subsistentem. Est enim Deus substantia aliqua divinitatem habens. Sicut homo non humanam naturam separatam, sed in aliquo individuo subsistentem exprimit, ita tamen ut individuum ac personam, non certam ac determinatam, sed confuse infiniteque representet, hoc est, *naturam in aliquo*, ut diximus, *consistentem* . . . sic nomen Dei proprie ac directe divinitatem naturamve divinam indicat, *assignificat autem eundem, ut in quapiam persona subsistentem, nullam de tribus expresse designans, sed confuse et universe.*" Here this great author seems to say, that even the word "Deus" may stand, not barely for the Divine Being, but besides "in quapiam persona subsistentem," without denoting *which* Person; and in like manner I would understand *hypostasis* to mean the *monas* with a like undeterminate notion of personality (without which attribute the idea of God cannot be), and thus, according as one *hypostasis* is spoken of, or three, the word may be roughly translated, in one case "personal substance," or "being with personality," in the other "substantial person," or "person which is in being." In all cases it will be equivalent to the θεότης, the μονάς, the divine οὐσία, &c., though with that peculiarity of meaning which I have insisted on.

Illustrated from Athanasius, &c

These remarks might be illustrated by a number of passages from Athanasius, in which he certainly implies that the μονάς, that is, the indivisible, numerically one God, is at once Father and Son; that the Father, who is the μονάς, gives to the Son also to be the μονάς; and to have His (the Father's) *hypostasis*, *i.e.* to be that *hypostasis*, which the Father is. For instance, he says that the μονὰς θεότητος is ἀδιαίρετος, though Father and Son are two;—*Orat.* iv. 1, 2. He speaks of the ταὐτότης τῆς θεότητος, and the ἑνότης τῆς οὐσίας, *Orat.* iii. 3; of the ἑνότης τῆς ὁμοιώσεως, *de Syn.* 45; of the ταὐτότης τοῦ φωτός, *de Decr.* 24; of "the Father's *hypostasis* being ascribed to the Son," *Orat.* iv. 33; of the πατρικὴ θεότης being τὸ εἶναι τοῦ υἱοῦ, *Orat.* iii. 3; of τὸ εἶναι τοῦ υἱοῦ being τῆς τοῦ πατρὸς οὐσίας ἴδιον. *ibid.*; of the Son being the πατρικὴ ἰδιότης, *Orat.* i. 42; of the Father's θεότης being in the Son, *de Syn.* 52 (whereas the Arians made the two θεότητες different in kind); of the Son's θεότης being the Father's, *Orat.* iii. 36; of the Son's πατρικὴ θεότης, *Orat.* i. 45, 49; ii. 18, 73; iii. 26; of the Son's πατρικὴ φύσις, *Orat.* i. 40; of the Son being τὸ πατρικὸν φῶς, iii. 53; and of the Son being the πλήρωμα τῆς θεότητος, *Orat.* iii. 1. *Vid.* also Didym. *Trin.* i. 15, p. 27; 16, p. 41; 18, p. 45; 27, p. 80; iii. 17, p. 377; 23, p. 409. Nyss. *Test. c. Jud.* i. p. 292; Cyril, *c. Nest.* iii. p. 80 b.

.

7.

Since, as has been said above, *hypostasis* is a word more peculiarly Christian than *usia*, I have judged it best to speak of it first, that the meaning of it, as it is ascertained

Usia has a like meaning.

on inquiry, may serve as a key for explaining other parallel terms. *Usia* is one of these the most in use, certain in the works of Athanasius, and we have his authority, as well as St. Jerome's, for stating that it had been simply synonymous with *hypostasis*. Moreover, in *Orat.* iii. 65, he uses the two words as equivalent to each other. If this be so, what has been said above, in explanation of the sense he put on the word *hypostasis*, will apply to *usia* also.

This conclusion is corroborated by the proper meaning of the word *usia* itself, which answers to the English word "being." But, when we speak of the Divine Being, we mean to speak of Him, as what He is, ὁ ὤν, including generally His attributes and characteristics, and among them, at least obscurely, His personality. By the "Divine *Being*" we do not commonly mean a mere *anima mundi*, or first principle of life, or system of laws. *Usia* then, thus considered, agrees very nearly in sense, from its very etymology, with *hypostasis*. Further, this was the sense in which Aristotle used it, viz. for what is "individuum," and "numero unum;" and it must not be forgotten that the Neo-Platonists, who exerted so great an influence on the Alexandrian Church, professed the Aristotelic logic. Nay, to St. Cyril himself, the successor of Athanasius, whose formula these remarks are intended to illustrate, is ascribed a definition, which makes *usia* to be an individual essence: οὐσία, πρᾶγμα αὐθύπαρκτον, μὴ δεόμενον ἑτέρου πρὸς τὴν ἑαυτοῦ σύστασιν. *Vid.* Suicer. *Thes. in voc.*

and is preferred by Athanasius. Yet this is the word, and not *hypostasis*, which Athana-

of the μία φύσις.

sius commonly uses, in controversy with the Arians, to express the divinity of the Word. In one passage alone, as far as I recollect, does he use *hypostasis* : οὐ τὴν ὑπόστασιν χωρίζων τοῦ θεοῦ λόγου ἀπὸ τοῦ ἐκ Μαρίας ἀνθρώπου. *Orat.* iv. 35. His usual term is *usia*:—for instance, τὴν θείαν οὐσίαν τοῦ λόγου ἡνωμένον φύσει τῷ ἑαυτοῦ πατρί. *In Illud Omnia*, 4. Again, ἡ οὐσία αὕτη τῆς οὐσίας τῆς πατρικῆς ἐστι γέννημα. *de Syn.* 48;—two remarkable passages, which remind us of the two οὐσίαι and two φύσεις, used by the Alexandrian Pierius (Phot. *Cod.* 119), and of the words of Theognostus, another Alexandrian, ἡ τοῦ υἱοῦ οὐσία ἐκ τῆς τοῦ πατρὸς οὐσίας ἔφυ. *ap.* Athan. *de Decr. Nic.* c. 25. Other instances of the *usia* of the Word in Athanasius are such as the following, though there are many more than can be enumerated:—*Orat.* i. 10, 45, 57, 59, 62, 64 *fin.*; ii. 7, 9, 11, 12, 13, 18, 22, 47, 56.

In all these instances *usia*, I conceive, is substantially equivalent to *hypostasis*, as I have explained it, viz. expressing the divine μονάς with an obscure intimation of personality inclusively; and here I think I am able to quote the words of Father Passaglia, as agreeing (so far) in what I have said. "Quum *hypostasis*," he says, *de Trinitate*, p. 1302, "esse nequeat sine substantia, nihil vetabat quominus trium hypostasum defensores *hypostasim* interdum pro substantia sumerent, præsertim ubi *hypostasis* opponitur rei non subsistenti, ac efficientiæ." I should wish to complete his admission by adding, "Since an intellectual *usia* ordinarily implies an *hypostasis*, there was nothing to hinder *usia* being used, when

as a synonyme for hypostasis

hypostasis had to be expressed." Nor can I construe *usia* in any other way in the two passages from *In Illud Omnia*, 4, and *de Syn.* 48, quoted above, to which may be added *Orat.* ii. 47, *init.* where Athanasius speaks of the Word as τὴν οὐσίαν ἑαυτοῦ γινώσκων μονογενῆ σοφίαν καὶ γέννημα τοῦ πατρός. Again he says, *Orat.* iv. 1, that he is ἐξ οὐσίας οὐσιώδης καὶ ἐνούσιος, ἐξ ὄντος ὤν.

If we want a later instance, and from another school, of *usia* and *hypostasis* being taken as practically synonymous, when contrasted with the *economia*, we may find one in Nyssen *c. Eunom. Orat.* v. p. 169.

8.

and *physis* also,

After what I have said of *usia* and *hypostasis*, it will not surprise the reader if I consider that *physis* also, in the Alexandrian theology, was equally capable of being applied to the Divine Being viewed as one, or viewed as three, or as each of the three separately. Thus Athanasius says, μία ἡ θεία φύσις. *contr. Apoll.* ii. 13 *fin.* and *de Incarn.* V. *fin.* Alexander, on the other hand, calls the Father and Son τὰς τῇ ὑποστάσει δύο φύσεις (as Pierius, to whom I have already referred, uses the word), Theod. *Hist.* i. 4, p. 15; and so Clement, also of the Alexandrian school, ἡ υἱοῦ φύσις ἡ τῷ μόνῳ παντοκράτορι προσεχεστάτη, *Strom.* vii. 2. In the same epistle Alexander speaks of the μεσιτεύουσα φύσις μονογενής; and Athanasius speaks of the φύσις of the Son being less divisible from the Father than the radiance from the sun, *de Syn.* 52, *vid.* also *Orat.* i. 51. Cyril too, *Thesaur.* xi. p. 85, speaks of ἡ γεννήσασα φύσις and ἡ γεννηθεῖσα ἐξ αὐτῆς; and in one passage, as Petavius, *de Trin.* iv. 2, observes, implies three φύσεις in one οὐσία. Cyril moreover explains as well as instances this use of the word. The φύσις τοῦ λόγου, he says, signifies neither *hypostasis* alone, nor what is common to the *hypostases*, but τὴν κοινὴν φύσιν ἐν τῇ τοῦ λόγου ὑποστάσει ὁλικῶς θεωρουμένην. *ap.* Damasc. *F. O.* iii. 11. And thus Didymus speaks of the ἀναλλοίωτος φύσις ἐν ταὐτότητι τῶν προσώπων ἑστῶσα. *Trin.* i. 9.

Εἶδος is a word of a similar character. As it is found in John v. 37, it may be interpreted of the Divine Essence or of Person; the Vulgate translates "neque *speciem* ejus vidistis." In Athan. *Orat.* iii. 3, it is synonymous with θεότης or *usia*; as *ibid.* 6 also; and apparently *ibid.* 16, where the Son is said to have the εἶδος of the Father. And so in *de Syn.* 52. Athanasius says that there is only one εἶδος θεότητος. Yet, as taken from Gen. xxxii. 31, it is considered to denote the Son; *e.g.* Athan. *Orat.* i. 20, where it is used as synonymous with Image, εἰκών. In like manner He is called "the very εἶδος τῆς θεότητος." *Ep. Æg.* 17. But again in Athan. *Orat.* iii. 6, it is first said that the εἶδος of the Father and Son are one and the same, then that the Son is the εἶδος of the Father's θεότης, and then that the Son is the εἶδος of the Father.

and εἶδος.

9.

So much on the sense of the words οὐσία, ὑπόστασις, φύσις, and εἶδος, among the Alexandrians of the fourth and fifth centuries, as denoting fully and absolutely all that the natural theologian attaches to the notion of the Divine Being,—as denoting the God of natural theology, with

These terms inapplicable in their full sense to the Word's humanity.

only such variation of sense in particular passages as the context determines, and as takes place when we say, "God of heaven," "God of our fathers," "God of armies," "God of peace;" (all of which epithets, as much as "one" or "three," bring out respectively different aspects of one and the same idea,) and, when applied to the second Person of the Blessed Trinity, meaning simply that same Divine Being, Deus singularis et unicus, in persona Filii. Now then the question follows, which brings us at once upon the Formula, which I have proposed to illustrate; viz., since the Word is an οὐσία, ὑπόστασις, or φύσις, can the man, ἄνθρωπος,—the manhood, humanity, human nature, flesh,—which He assumed, be designated by these three terms in a parallel full sense, as meaning that He became all that "a human being" is, man with all the attributes and characteristics of man? Was the Word a man in the precise and unrestricted sense in which any one of us is a man? The Formula denies it, for it calls Him μία φύσις σεσαρκωμένη, not δύο φύσεις; and in the sense which I have been ascribing to those three terms, it rightly denies it; for in the sense in which the Divine Being is an *usia*, &c., His human nature is not an *usia*, &c.; so that in *that* sense there are not two φύσεις, but one only, and there could not be said to be two without serious prejudice to the Catholic dogma.

10.

yet they are so applied, I have said, " in the sense in which the Divine Being is an *usia;*" for doubtless this and the other terms in ques-

of the μία φύσις.

tion need not be, and are not always taken in the sense which attaches to them in the above passages.

1. *Hypostasis*, for instance, is used for substance as opposed to appearance or imagination, in Hebr. xi. 1. And in like manner Epiphanius speaks of the Word's σαρκὸς ὑπόστασιν ἀληθινήν. *Hær.* 69, 59. And Irenæus, of "substantia carnis," *Hær.* iii. 22, which doubtless in the original was *hypostasis*, as is shown by the οὐ δοκήσει, ἀλλ' ὑποστάσει ἀληθείας, *ibid.* v. 1. In a like sense Cyril of Jerusalem seems to use the word, *Cat.* vii. 3, ix. 5, 6, x. 2. And Gregory Nyssen, *Antirrh.* 25 *fin.* and apparently in the abstract for existence, *c. Jud.* p. 291. And Cyril of Alexandria, whose Formula is in question, in his controversy with Theodoret. Σύστασις is used for it by Athan. *c. Apoll.* i. 5, ii. 5, 6, &c. *Vid.* also Max. *Opp.* t. 2, p. 303, and Malchion *ap.* Routh. *Rell.* t. 2, p. 484. The two words are brought together in Hippol. *c. Noët.* 15 *fin.* (where the word *hypostasis* is virtually denied of the human nature), and in Nyss. *Test. c. Jud.* i. p. 292. Also, ἡ σὰρξ οὐκ ὑπόστασις ἰδιοσύστατος ἐγεγόνει. Damasc. *c. Jacob.* 53. For ἰδιοσύστατος, *vid.* Didym. *Trin.* iii. 23, p. 410. Ephraëm, *ap.* Phot. *Cod.* 229, p. 785 *fin.* Max. *Opp.* t. 2, pp. 281 and 282.

e.g. Hypostasis.

2. If even *hypostasis* may be found of the Word's humanity, there is more reason to anticipate such an application of the other terms which I have classed with it. Thus as regards *usia*: θεὸς ὢν ὁμοῦ τε καὶ ἄνθρωπος τέλειος ὁ αὐτός, τὰς δύο αὐτοῦ οὐσίας ἐπιστώσατο ἡμῖν, says Melito *ap.* Routh. *Rell.* t. 1, p. 115. And Chrysostom, οὐχὶ τὰς οὐσίας συγχέων, *in Psalm.* 44, p. 166; also *in*

and usia.

Joann. Hom. ii. 2. *Vid.* also Basil. in *Eunom.* i. 18. Nyssen, *Antirrh.* 30. Cyril. 2 *ad Succ.* p. 144. But the word (*i.e. substantia*) is more common in this sense in Latin writers:—*e.g.* Tertullian. *de Carn. Christ.* 13, 16, &c. *Præscr.* 51. Novat. *de Trin.* 11 and 24. Ambros. *de Fid.* ii. 77. Augustin. *Epist.* 187, 10. Vincent *Commonit.* 13. Leon. *Epist.* 28, p. 811. As to Alexandrian writers, Origen calls the Word's soul, substantia, *Princip.* ii. 6, n. 3, as Eusebius, νοερὰ οὐσία, *de Const. L.*, p. 536. Petavius quotes Athanasius as saying, τὸ σῶμα κοινὴν ἔχον τοῖς πᾶσι τὴν οὐσίαν, *de Incarn.* x. 3, § 9, t 6, p. 13, but this may be *external* to the union, as ἀπαρχὴν λαβὼν ἐκ τῆς οὐσίας τοῦ ἀνθρώπου, Athan. *de Inc. et c. Ar.* 8 *fin.*

and *physis;* 3. The word *physis* has still more authorities in its favour than *usia*; *e.g.* φύσεις δύο, θεὸς καὶ ἄνθρωπος, Greg. Naz. *Orat.* xxxvii. 11. *Epist.* 101, pp. 85, 87. *Epist.* 102, p. 97. *Carm. in Laud. Virg.* v. 149. *de Vit. sua*, v. 652. Greg. Nyssen. *c. Apoll.* t. 2, p. 696. *c. Eunom. Orat.* 5, p. 168. *Antirrh.* 27. Amphiloch. *ap.* Theod. *Eran.* i. 66. Theod. *Hær.* v. 11, p. 422. Chrysostom, *in* 1 *Tim. Hom.* 7, 2. Basil. Seleuc. *Orat.* 33, p. 175. And so *natura*, in Hilar. *Trin.* xi. 3, 14, *in Psalm.* 118, *lit.* 14, 8. *Vid.* also Ambrose, Jerome, Augustine, &c. For other instances, *vid.* Conc. Chalc. *Act.* 2, t. 2, p. 300. Leon. *Epist.* 165. Leont. *c. Nestor. ap.* Canis. t. 1, p. 548. Anastas. *Hodeg.* x. p. 154 (ed. 1606), Gelas. *de D. N.* (*in Bibl. P.* Paris. Quart. 1624), t. 4, p. 423. As for Alexandrian writers, I do not cite Origen (*e.g. in Matth.* t. 3, pp. 852, 902, t. 4, *Append.* p. 25, &c.), because we cannot be sure that the word was found in the original Greek. But we have θεὸς

of the μία φύσις.

ἦν φύσει, καὶ γέγονεν ἄνθρωπος φύσει, Petr. Alex. *ap.* Routh. *Rell.* t. 3, pp. 344-346. And Ἐν ἑκατέραις ταῖς φύσεσι υἱὸς τοῦ θεοῦ. Isid. Pelus. *Epist.* i. 405. And Athanasius himself, ἡ μορφὴ τοῦ δούλου is ἡ νοερὰ τῆς ἀνθρώπων συστάσεως φύσις σὺν τῇ ὀργανικῇ καταστάσει. *c. Apoll.* ii. 1. *Vid.* also i. 5, ii. 11. *Orat.* ii. 70, iii. 43. Nor must it be forgotten that Cyril himself accepted the two φύσεις; *vid.* some instances at the end of Theod. *Eran.* ii *Vid.* also *c. Nest.* iii. p. 70, *d. e.* and his Answers to the Orientals and Theodoret.

11.

However, though we could bring together all the instances which Antiquity would furnish on the point, still the fact would stand, first, that these terms did not belong to the Word's humanity in the full sense in which they were used of His Divine nature; secondly, that they, or at least φύσις, were not ordinarily applied to it in any sense by Catholic writers up to the time of Cyril. <small>but not in their full sense,</small>

That they did not apply to it, especially *physis*, in that full sense in which it belonged to His divinity, was plain on considering what was said of Him in Scripture. He differed from the race, out of which His manhood was taken, in many most important respects. (1) He had no human father, Matt. i. 20; Luke i. 34, 35. Gregory Nyssen, with a reference to this doctrine, says, "He was not a man wholly (δι' ὅλου), not a man like others altogether (κοινός), but He was *as* a man." *Antirrh.* 21. (2) He had no human ἡγεμονικόν, or sovereign principle <small>especially *physis*,</small> <small>first, on Scripture grounds,</small>

of action in the soul; for if there were two κύρια or ἡγεμονικά, there were two beings together in Him, which is a tenet contrary to the whole tenor of the Gospels, and when put forth by some early Gnostics, was condemned, as it would seem, by St. John, 1 *Epist.* iv. 3. (3) He was sinless; and, though sin is not part of our nature, yet St. Paul does call us by nature children of wrath, φύσει, Eph. ii. 3, which would be a reason for being cautious of applying the term to the Word's humanity; and, though it is true that St. Paul elsewhere speaks of the law of conscience being φύσει, Rom. ii. 14, 15, yet St. Jude speaks of a base knowledge also being φυσικόν, v. 10. (4) We may consider in addition how transcendent was His state of knowledge, sanctity, &c. (5) His body was different *in fact* from ours, as regards corruptibility, as would appear from Acts ii. 31, xiii. 35. (6) It had a life-giving virtue peculiar to itself, Matt. vii. 23; John ix. 6. (7) After the resurrection it had transcendent qualities;—came and vanished; entered a closed room; ascended on high, and appeared to St. Paul on his conversion, while it was in heaven.

12.

next, on grounds of reason. But besides this argument from the sacred text, there seemed a necessity from the nature of the case to lay down restrictions so great, on the sense in which the Word took our common nature, as almost to deprive it of that name. The divine and human could not be united without some infringement upon the one or the other.

There were those indeed, who, like some early teachers of the Gnostic family, whom I just now spoke of, and the Nestorians at a later date, escaped from the difficulty by denying the union; but, granting two contraries were to meet in one, how could that union be, without affecting, in its own special attributes and state, either the human or the divine? Which side of the alternative was to be followed, is plain without a word; οὐκ ἐν σώματι ὢν ἐμολύνετο, says Athanasius, ἀλλὰ μᾶλλον καὶ τὸ σῶμα ἡγίαζεν. *Incarn V. D.* 17. There is a similar passage, Nyssen, *Antirrh.* 26. τὸν γὰρ ἡμέτερον ῥύπον, &c. Here we are concerned with the alternative itself. Either the Word must be absorbed into the man, or the man taken up into the Word. The consideration of these opposite conclusions will carry us nearly to the end of our discussion; I shall pursue the separate investigation of them under the letters *a* and *b*.

(*a*) The former of these was the conclusion in which resulted the speculations of the Sabellians and Samosatenes, who explained away the " incarnate Word " into a mere divine attribute, virtue, influence, or emanation, which dwelt in the person of one particular man, receiving its perfect development in him, and therefore imperfect before the union, changed in the act of union, dependent on him after the union. Eusebius (whose language, however, is never quite unexceptionable) may be taken as the spokesman of the Catholic body on this point. " The indwelling Word," he says, " though holding familiar intercourse with mortals, did not fall under the sympathy of their affections; nor, after the manner of

marginal note: The divine *physis* must retain the fulness of its attributes:

a man's soul, was fettered down by the body, or changed for the worse, or came short of His proper divinity." *de Laud. C.* p. 536. And then he has recourse to an illustration, common with the Fathers, and expressed by Eustathius of Antioch thus :—"If the sun, which we see with our eyes, undergoes so many indignities, yet without disgrace or infliction, do we think that the immaterial Wisdom is defiled or changes His nature, though the the temple in which He dwells be nailed to the Cross, or suffers dissolution, or sustains a wound, or admits of corruption? No, the temple is affected, but the stainless *usia* remains absolutely in its unpolluted dignity," *ap.* Theod. *Eran.* iii. p. 237. *Vid.* also Vigil. Thaps. *c. Eutych.* ii. 9, p. 727. And Anast. *Hodeg.* 12, in controversy with Apollinarians, Eutychians, &c., who were involved in the same general charge.

therefore the human *physis* must have a restricted meaning.

(*b*) But, on the other hand, if the divinity remains unchanged, change must happen to the humanity; and accordingly, the Fathers are eloquent upon the subject of this change, which from the very nature of the case, and independent of the direct testimony of scripture and tradition, was necessary. To say nothing of the celebrated passages in Nyssen, who has no special connexion with the Alexandrian Church, I shall content myself with a passage from Origen : " Si massa aliqua ferri semper in igne sit posita, omnibus suis poris omnibusque venis ignem recipiens, et tota ignis effecta, si neque ignis ab ea cesset aliquando, neque ipsa ab igne separetur, nunquidnam dicimus hanc . . . posse frigus aliquando recipere ? . . . . . . Sicut . . . totam ignem effectam dicimus, quoniam

of the μία φύσις. 361

nec aliud in ea nisi ignis cernitur, sed et si quis contingere atque attrectare tentaverit, *non ferri, sed ignis vim sentiat;* hoc ergo modo, etiam illa anima, quæ, quasi ferrum in igne, sic semper in Verbo, semper in Sapientia, semper in Deo posita est, *omne quod agit, quod sentit, quod intelligit, Deus est*," &c. de *Princ.* ii. 6, n. 6; *vid. contr. Cels.* iii. 41. p. 474. Hence Isidore, another Alexandrian, says that the Word called Himself bread, because He, as it were, baked His human substance—(τὴν ζύμην τοῦ ἀνθρωπείου φυράματος; *vid.* φύραμα also Hippol. *Elench.* p. 338)— "in the fire of His own divinity." *Epist.* i. 360. Passages from Cyril; Damascene, &c., might be quoted to the same effect, *e.g.* Cyr. *Quod unus*, p. 776. Damasc. *c. Jacob.* p. 409. Hence it was usual with Athanasius and other Fathers to call the incarnation a θέωσις or θεοποίησις of the ἀνθρώπινον (*vid.* Concil. Antioch. *infr.* p. 374. Athan. *de Decr.* 14 *fin. de Syn.* 51. *Orat.* i. 42, &c. &c.), from the great change which took place in its state, or rather difference in its state from human nature generally.

13.

But, if the humanity assumed was thus *extricated from* the common *usia* or *physis*, to which, under other circumstances, it would have belonged, and, being grafted upon the Word, existed from the very first in a *super*-natural state, how could it be properly called *nature?* In the words of Damascene, ἡ μὲν φύσις τῆς σαρκὸς θεοῦται, οὐ σαρκοῖ δὲ τὴν φύσιν τοῦ λόγου. θεοῖ μὲν τὸ πρόσλημμα, οὐ σαρκοῦται δέ. *c. Jacob.* 52, p. 409. It is but in accord-

How then is there a human physis at all?

24

ance with this train of thought to lay down, that there is only *one* nature in Christ. Here, then, we see the meaning of Cyril's Formula.

Hence the force of Cyril's Formula.
It means (*a*), first, that when the Divine Word became man, He remained one and the same in essence, attributes, and personality; in all respects the same as before, and therefore μία φύσις.

It means (*b*), secondly, that the manhood, on the contrary, which He assumed, was not in all respects the same nature as that *massa, usia, physis*, &c., out of which it was taken, 1, from the very circumstance that it was only an addition or supplement to what He was already, not a being complete in itself; and 2, because in the act of assuming it, He changed it in its qualities.

This added nature, then, was best expressed, not by a second substantive, as if collateral in its position, but by an adjective or participle, as σεσαρκωμένη. The three words answered to St. John's ὁ λόγος σὰρξ ἐγένετο, *i.e.* σεσαρκωμένος ἦν.

14.

Illustration from Council of Antioch,
We have an apposite illustration of this account of the Formula in an early passage of history, as contained in the fragmentary documents which remain to us of the Great Council of Antioch, A.D. 264-272 (to which I have already referred), in which Paul of Samosata was condemned, Malchion being the principal disputant against him. Paul denied that the Divine Being was in Christ in essence or personality; I say "in essence or person-

ality," for, as I have explained above, since the Divine Essence cannot be without personality, to deny the one was to deny the other, and the further question, whether that personality was single or trine, did not directly come into controversy. By such a doctrine, both points of Cyril's subsequent formula were sacrificed :—(*a*) the divine *physis* in Emmanuel was explained away, and (*b*) the flesh, being denied its hypostatic union, was no longer ὑπερφυής, but remained in its strictly natural *usia*, as any other individual of our race who was in the divine favour. The Synodal Epistle strikes at (*a*) the former of these errors; and the fragments of Malchion's disputation (*b*) at the latter.

15.

(*a*) Paul said that the Word was not incarnate as an *usia*, but only as a quality; the Fathers of the Council therefore declare that, on the contrary, He really was an *usia* and *hypostasis* (for they use the terms as equivalent) Routh. *Rell*. t. 2, p. 466; a ζῶσα ἐνέργεια ἐνυπόστατος, p. 469; the Creator of the universe, p. 468; and Son and God before the creation, p. 466; and that He became incarnate ἀτρέπτως. Still further to destroy the notion of a separation into two beings, they call this pre-existing Word Christ, p. 474, and they assert that He is ἓν καὶ τὸ αὐτὸ τῇ οὐσίᾳ, from first to last, on earth and in heaven. In thus speaking, they are evidently entering a protest against another contemporaneous aspect of the same doctrine, into which even Catholics had, as far as language

which teaches the unalterableness of the one divine usia,

goes, been betrayed. The opinion I have in mind is that of the προφορικὸς λόγος, or that the Word or Son, at first nascent or inchoate, had been perfected by the Incarnation. Not only had Tertullian said, speaking of the "Fiat Lux" at creation, "Hæc est nativitas *perfecta* sermonis," *c. Prax.* 7, but Hippolytus even, that the "Word, before His incarnation and καθ᾽ ἑαυτόν, was not τέλειος υἱός, though τέλειος λόγος ὢν μονογενής." *c. Noët.* 15. *Vid. supr.* pp. 272, 280.

<small>together with Catholic doctors generally,</small> Now, all these points, the oneness and identity of the Word considered in *usia*, His unalterableness in His incarnation, His perfection from eternity, His one sonship, and the impiety of dividing Word and Son, or holding two sons, were traditional matters for Catholic teaching and preaching (against those who imagined some change or other in His nature or state), from the date of this Council, two hundred years before Cyril, down to that of the Council of Chalcedon, after his death, to say nothing of other periods of history. Cyril comes in merely as one instance of the inculcation of this doctrine out of a hundred like his. His peculiarity is his using the term *physis* of the Word (which, as I have instanced *supr.* p. 352, was a specially Alexandrian word for *usia* or *hypostasis*), and yet not using it for our Lord's humanity.

<small>with Athanasius</small> All this may be illustrated from Athanasius, who, in controversy not only with Apollinarians, but with teachers of the Samosatene school, had to protest against any *degradation* of the Word's nature, and therefore to maintain His *unity*, His *unchangeableness*, and His *perfection*. "They fall into the same folly as the Arians," he says,

of the μία φύσις. 365

"for the Arians say that He was created that He might create; as if God waited till creation, for His *probole* (ἵνα προβάληται), as these say" (*vid. e.g.* Tertullian *supr.*) "or His creation, as those" (the Arians). He goes on to condemn the notion that ὁ λόγος, ἐν τῷ θεῷ ἀτελὴς γεννηθείς, is τέλειος (*vid.* Hippolytus *supr.*); "He was not anything, that He is not now, nor is He what He was not" (here is the "one and the same" of the Council *supr.*), "otherwise He will have to be *imperfect* and *alterable*.' *Orat.* iv. 11, 12. Again: "The world was made by Him; if the world is one and the creation one, it follows that Son and Word are one and the same before all creation, for by Him it came into being." 19. "As the Father is one," he says, "so also the μονογενής is one." 20. Ταὐτὸν ὁ υἱὸς καὶ λόγος. 29. "Those men degrade the Divine incarnation and think as heathens do, who conceive that it involves an *alteration*, τροπή, of the Word; ... but let a man understand the divine mystery, to be *one* and *simple*," 32. Again: "God's Word is *one and the same*; as God is one, His Image is one, His Word one, and one His Wisdom." *Orat.* ii. 36. Elsewhere he says, "God's Word is not merely προφορικός, nor by His Son is meant His command," *e.g.* Fiat lux, "but He is τέλειος ἐκ τελείου," *ibid.* ii. 35. *Vid.* also iii. 52, *Epiph. Hær.* 76. p. 945, Hilar. *Trin.* ii. 8. Also Didym. *Trin.* i. 10, *fin.* 20, p. 63, 32, p. 99, iii. 6, p. 357. Nyssen, *Antirrh* 21 and 56.

So again, αὐτὸς ἄτρεπτος μένων καὶ μὴ ἀλλοιούμενος ἐν τῇ ἀνθρωπίνῃ οἰκονομίᾳ καὶ τῇ ἐνσάρκῳ παρουσίᾳ, Athan. *Orat.* ii. 6. And so again *contr. Apoll.* ii. 3, 7. And so Pseudo-Athanasius, *ap.* Phot.: "The Word took flesh

and other Fathers.

to fulfil the economy, and not εἰς αὔξησιν οὐσίας." And so, Οὐσία μένουσα ὅπερ ἐστί, Chryst. *in Joan. Hom.* xi. 1, Naz. *Orat.* 29, 19, Procl. *ad Arm.* p. 615, Maxim. *Opp.* t. 2, p. 286. And so, "Manens id quod erat, factus quod non erat," August. *Cons. Ev.* i. 53. *Vid.* also Hilar. *Trin.* iii. 16; Vigil. *c. Eut.* i. 3, p. 723. And in like manner Leo, "*Simplex* et *incommutabilis natura* Deitatis [in Verbo] tota in sua sit semper essentia (*usia*), nec damnum sui recipiens aut augmentum, assumptam naturam beatificans." *Epist.* 35, 2. And again, "In se incommutabilis perseverans; *deitas* enim, quæ illi cum Patre communis est (*i.e.* ἡ φύσις τοῦ θεοῦ λόγου) nullum detrimentum omnipotentiæ subiit (*i.e.* μία ἐστίν); . . . quia summa et sempiterna *essentia* (*i.e.* οὐσία μία)," &c. &c. Leon. *Serm.* 27, 1.

who therefore attribute the human conception to the operation of the Word.

Moreover, I do not think it a refinement to suggest that this was one reason why so many of the Fathers interpret Luke i. 35 of the Word, not of the Spirit. It was their wish to enforce His personal being and omnipotent life before and in the first beginnings of the economy; as is done by Athanasius by saying λόγος ἐν τῷ πνεύματι ἔπλαττε τὸ σῶμα. *Serap.* 1, 31, and elsewhere by referring to *Prov.* ix. 1; *e.g. Orat.* ii. 44, and so Leo, *Epist.* 31, 2. Thus Irenæus (after insisting on the real existence of both natures, and saying, "if what had existed in truth, οὐκ ἔμεινε πνεῦμα after the incarnation, truth was not in Him") proceeds to say that the "*Verbum* Patris et Spiritus Dei viventem et perfectum effecit hominem." *Hær.* v. 1. Hilary too, after laying down "Forma Dei *manebat*," *Trin.* ix. 14, adds, "ut *manens* Spiritus Christus, *idem* Christus homo esset," with a reference to the passage in St. Luke. Clement, too, says, contrasting the personality of the Christian λόγος with the Platonic, ὁ λόγος ἑαυτὸν γεννᾷ, *Strom.* v. 3. This doctrine of one υἱότης with a double γέννησις, must not be confounded with the Sabellian tenet of the υἱοπατώρ, which related to the Trinity, not the Incarnation. It is with the same purport that the creed in Epiphanius speaks of the Son as "not *in* man, but εἰς ἑαυτὸν σάρκα ἀναπλάσαντα, εἰς μίαν ἁγίαν ἑνότητα." *Ancor. fin.*

16.

So much on the light thrown upon the μία φύσις (viz. τοῦ θεοῦ λόγου), by the language of other Fathers. Cyril, too, in like manner, does but teach that the φύσις of the Word is μία, one and the same. His "One nature of God" implies, with the Council of Antioch, a protest against that alterableness and imperfection, which the anti-Catholic schools affixed to their notion of the Word. The Council says "one and the same in *usia*:" it is not speaking of a human *usia* in Christ, but of the divine. The case is the same in Cyril's Formula; he speaks of a μία θεία φύσις in the Word. He has, in like manner, written a treatise entitled "Quod unus sit Christus;" and in one of his Paschal Epistles he enlarges on the text, "Jesus Christ yesterday and to-day the same and for ever." His great theme in these works is, not the coalescing of the two natures into one, but the error of making two sons, one before and one upon the Incarnation, one divine, one human, or again of degrading the

Thus Cyril, too, by the One nature denotes

divine *usia* by making it subject to the humanity. *Vid.* also his Answers *adv. Oriental. et Theod. passim.*

<small>the Word's eternity,</small> Thus, for instance, he says to Nestorius: "It is at once ignorant and impious even to imagine that the Word of the Father should be called to a *second beginning of being*, or to have taken flesh of the Holy Virgin, as some kind of *root of his own existence*," *c. Nest.* i. p. 7. *Vid.* also *ibid.* p. 5, *c.*

<small>unity,</small> So to Successus, "There is *one* Son, *one* Lord, before the incarnation and after; the Word was not one Son, and the child of the Virgin another; but αὐτὸς ἐκεῖνος ὁ προαιώνιος, man, not by *change of nature*, but by economical good pleasure." *Ep.* 1, pp. 136-7. *Vid. c. Nest.* iv. *fin.* Χριστὸν ἕνα καὶ υἱὸν καὶ κύριον ἀποτετέλεκε τὸν αὐτὸν ὄντα θεὸν καὶ ἄνθρωπον, *ibid.* ii. 58. "The *nature* of the Word *remained* what it was," *ibid.* i. p. 15. Μεμένηκε ἐν ἀνθρωπότητι θεός, *ibid.* iii. p. 73. "He is one, καὶ οὐ δίχα σαρκός, who *in His own nature* is ἔξω σαρκός, *ibid.* p. 45. Εἷς νοεῖται μετὰ σαρκός," *ibid.* 55. *Vid.* also ii. p. 60 A, and *ad Succ. Ep.* 2, p. 145.

And when he is formally called on to explain his Formula, his language is still more explicit in the same sense. <small>unalterableness.</small> "He *remained* what He was, φύσει θεός; and He remained *one* Son; but *not without flesh*," *ad Succ. Ep.* 2, p. 142. "The φύσις of the Word has not *changed* into τὴν τῆς σαρκὸς φύσιν, nor the reverse; but each *remaining* and being recognised ἐν ἰδιότητι τῇ κατὰ φύσιν by an ineffable union, He shows to us μίαν υἱοῦ φύσιν, but that φύσιν σεσαρκωμένην," *ibid.* "Had we," he continues, "stopped without adding σεσαρκωμένη, they might have had some pretence for speaking, but ἡ ἐν ἀνθρωπότητι τελειότης and ἡ καθ' ἡμᾶς οὐσία is conveyed in the word σεσαρκωμένη," ibid. p. 144, &c.

17.

(b) Now we come in the next place to σεσαρκωμένη, and must return to the Council of Antioch and Paul of Samosata, and to Malchion, who was appointed by the Council to dispute with him.

The same Council teaches that the Word's usia occupies the humanity.

Malchion views Paul's doctrine in its consequences to the humanity assumed. He accuses him of denying οὐσιῶσθαι ἐν τῷ ὅλῳ σωτῆρι τὸν υἱὸν τὸν μονογενῆ, Routh. Rell. t. 2, p. 476; τὴν σοφίαν συγγεγενῆσθαι τῷ ἀνθρωπίνῳ οὐσιωδῶς, p. 484; δι' ἑαυτῆς ἐπιδεδημηκέναι οὐσιωδῶς ἐν τῷ σώματι, p. 485; οὐσίαν εἶναι οὐσιωμένην ἐν σώματι, p. 485; θεὸν συνουσιωμένον τῷ ἀνθρώπῳ, p. 486; that is, of denying that the divine *usia* in its fulness had simply taken possession of, occupied, and permeated an individual of our race, and that all that was in His human nature, totum quantumcumque, was lived in by, and assumed into, the *usia* of the Word. What had been from eternity an *usia* only in itself, now manifested itself as ἐν τῇ κτίσει or ἐν τοῖς γενητοῖς; whereas Paul held nothing more than that a human *usia* had received the Divine Wisdom κατὰ ποιότητα, p. 484. In a fragment of Africanus (A.D. 220), we find a statement parallel to Malchion's, the same prominence being given to the Divine Nature in contrast with the economy. Ἐν τῇ οἰκονομίᾳ, ὡς κατὰ τὴν οὐσίαν ὅλην οὐσιωθείς, ἄνθρωπος λέγεται, ibid. p. 125; that is, His absolute and whole divinity, not an emanation, or virtue, or attribute, simply filled, energetically appropriated, and sovereignly ruled a human nature as an adjunct; and he refers to Col. ii. 9, in which it is said that in Him, that is, in the human nature, dwells the whole fulness of the Divinity σωματικῶς, substantially. *Vid.* the striking passage in Cyril, *c. Nest.* i. p. 28, *a. b.* and παχύνεται, Damasc. *c. Jacob.* p. 409. In these statements, the *usia* of the Word is put so prominently forward as to imply *prima facie* that in His economy there is no *usia* besides it. Compare with them Athanasius's words, in his *de Decretis*:—"As we, by receiving the Spirit, do not lose our proper *usia*, so the Lord, when made man for us, and bearing a body, was no less God: for He was not lessened by the envelopment of the body, but rather deified it and rendered it immortal;" 14. If we were to bring out in a formal statement the impression which such a parallel creates, it would be this—that the Word had one *usia*, divine; and we one *usia*, human; and that as our proper *usia* remains one and the same, μία φύσις, though it received grace, so the divine *usia* remained one and the same, though it took upon it humanity, as an adjunct or possession. And, in like manner, Didymus, on Acts ii. 36, after contrasting the *usia* of the Word with the Word as "conformed to our *humiliation*," says, "To describe a thing as being *in this way or that*, is not to declare its *usia*;" *Trin.* iii. 6.

and that the humanity is taken up into the Word's usia.   Now there is another way of expressing the same doctrine, viz., to say, not that the Word came as an *usia* into a created nature, but became an *usia* to, or the *usia* of, a created nature. In this mode of statement it is not said that the Word οὐσιώθη ἐν τῇ κτίσει, but ἡ κτίσις οὐσιώθη in the Word; but the meaning is the same, for in both cases only one *Usia* is spoken of, who, besides being what He is in and for Himself, καθ' ἑαυτὸν, ἐφ' ἑαυτοῦ, &c., also makes Himself, and serves as, an *usia* to the created nature which He assumes. Thus (for illustration, but illustration only), fire οὐσιώθη in iron, or is *in* iron, because its real and substantial presence is in every part of the mass, which is simply mastered by it; and iron οὐσιώθη in fire, or is *in* fire, in the sense that it is transformed into a new nature, which depends for what it is solely on the presence of the fire. Accordingly Nazianzen, after saying θεοῦ δ' ὅλου μετέσχεν ἀνθρώπου φύσις, that is θεὸς οὐσιώθη ἐν φύσει ἀνθρώπου, goes on to speak of human nature as οὐσιωθεῖσ' (*i.e.* ἐν θεῷ) ὥσπερ αὐγαῖς ἥλιος, *de Vit. sua*, v. 642, the material body of the sun being flooded with light. Here then, as little as in the former form of speech, are two *usias* spoken of.

This latter mode of speaking will be illustrated by the parallel use of it by Athanasius in relation to the creation generally, not to the hypostatic union. He says (analogously) that the whole universe depends for its stability upon the Word; that the φύσις τῶν γενητῶν, as having its *hypostasis* ἐξ οὐκ ὄντων (*i.e.* from what has no οὐσία), is evanescent, and must be protected against itself. Accordingly, the Creator, οὐσιώσας τὴν κτίσιν *in* His Word, does not abandon it τῇ ἑαυτῆς φύσει φέρεσθαι, &c., *c. Gent.* 41, *vid.* Didym. *Trin.* iii. 4, p. 351.

as analogously the creation also is established in His *usia*.

And this illustration enables us to advance a step Contrast between *physis* and *usia*.

further. Even in Nazianzen's verses *supr. usia* is contrasted with *physis* as with something inferior to itself; the contrast is brought out more pointedly in the last statement of Athanasius, and it will appear that, if there were reasons for backwardness in calling the Word's humanity an *usia*, lest it should introduce the notion of a second and independent being, so there were even stronger reasons against calling it a *physis*.

18.

The proper meaning of physis

Physis is a word of far wider extent of meaning than *usia*, and may be said to be a predicate of which *usia* may be made the subject. When applied to the Supreme Being, it means His attributes; as, ἴδιον γνώρισμα τῆς θείας φύσεως ἡ φιλανθρωπία, Nyssen. *Orat. Catech.* 15. When applied to the universe, it means *phænomena*; hence, those who investigate them, as distinct from ontologists, whose subject is *usia*, are called physicists. When applied to man, it means his moral disposition, &c., as the poet's "*Naturam expellas furca*," &c., and as we speak of good and ill nature. When applied to the moral (as well as to the material) world, it means the *constitution* or *laws* which characterise it; Butler saying, that "the only distinct meaning of the word is *stated, fixed, settled*," *Anal.*, part i. ch. i. Hence, though in the Catholic doctrine of the Holy Eucharist, the *substance* of the bread ceases to be, the *natura*, as being what schoolmen have called the accidents, may be said to remain, as in the Epistle to Cæsarius ascribed to Chrysostom, in which we read, "divina sanctificante gratia, mediante Sacerdote, dignus habitus est, [panis] dominici corporis appellatione etiamsi *natura* panis in ipso permansit."

But if *physis* or *natura* is thus to be taken for the attributes and properties of humanity generally, as contrasted with *usia* or essence, it became a grave question whether, in applying it to the Word's humanity, there was not the risk of that very degradation of the divine *usia*, against which the Catholic writers, as we have seen, so strongly protested. If an human *usia* involved the risk of two beings or personalities, a human *physis* implied a contamination with human passions and excesses. St. Hilary, while he adopts the word, illustrates the abuse which might be made of it. " Si assumpta caro," he says, " id est, totus homo, *passionum* est permissa *naturis*," &c. *Trin.* x. 24. Tertullian, on the other hand, taking the word in the same general sense, repudiates it, and adopts *substantia* (*usia*) instead, making *natura* equivalent to *culpa*. He says that the Word, in taking flesh, abolished, "non carnem peccati sed peccatum carnis, non materiam sed *naturam*, non substantiam sed *culpam*." *de Carn. Christ*. 16. Leo corrects this language pointedly, saying, " Assumpta est natura non culpa." *Serm*. 22, 3. Athanasius, too, as the Greek Fathers and Catholics generally, reserves the word *physis* for our moral constitution as it came from the Creator, and refers sin to the will of the individual. He says that it is " the impiety of the Manichees to say that the φύσις of the σάρξ, and not merely the πρᾶξις, is sin." *c. Apoll*. i. 12-19 ; *vid*. also ii. 6-9, and *Vit. Ant*. 20..

[shows the delicacy of applying the term to His humanity.]

<small>which is in a state above nature,</small>

But, on the other hand, in matter of fact, the humanity of the Word was *not* left in its natural state, but as the Council of Antioch had said, τεθεοποίηται; since then it was beyond all doubt in a state *above* nature or *super*natural, why (as I have said above) should it be any longer called a nature? It was that which *would have been* a nature, had it not been destined to be united from the first to the Word; but *in fact* it had been taken out of the massa, the φύραμα, τῶν γενητῶν, and been refashioned, as Isidor said, *supr.*, "by fire of the divinity." "The body itself," says Athanasius, "which had a mortal φόσιν, rose again ὑπὲρ φύσιν, on account of the Word which was in it, and lost the corruption which is κατὰ φύσιν, and became incorruptible, being clad in the Word, which is ὑπὲρ ἄνθρωπον." ad *Epict.* 10. That which had a special fulfilment after the resurrection, was analogously true in the incarnation itself.

When then Cyril said σεσαρκωμένη, he meant to express that our Lord's humanity had neither the ἡγεμονικόν of an *usia*, nor the imperfections and faults of a *physis*.

19.

<small>and therefore not commonly called *physis*,</small>

No wonder then, these things being considered, that, after we have done our utmost, we shall be unable to discover more than a few instances in the early Fathers, compared with the multitude of opportunities which the subject-matter of their works admits, of dogmatic statements verbally contrary to Cyril's Formula, while, on the other hand, that Formula admits, or even requires by its very wording, an explanation absolutely consistent with the Catholic dogma, as expressed, at least in Alexandria, up to his time. No wonder that, while the whole body of theologians admitted the ἐκ δύο φύσεων, it remained for a Pope, who saw with a Pope's instinctive sagacity the need of the times, to explain the old truth, in which all parts of Christendom agreed, under the comparatively new formula of the ἐν δυσὶ φύσεσι. To prove a negative, difficult at all times, cannot be expected here; but as I have given specimens of the Catholic use of *physis* or *natura*, in application to the humanity of the Word, which, though not near all which could be found, are sufficient to justify the Council of Chalcedon in adopting it into their formal definition of faith; so now, in conclusion, I will, in addition to the general considerations which I have enlarged on in explanation of Cyril's Formula, set down some instances of the absence of the word *physis* in great theological authorities and others during the first four centuries, in denoting the Word's humanity, where it might naturally have been expected. *[till Leo and the Council of Chalcedon,] [as proved from the early Fathers]*

20.

1. Thus Athanasius, in a remarkable passage, in which his eagerness to avoid ascribing human imperfection to the Word's humanity makes him speak as if he would deny to it a will (which is contrary to his categorical statement elsewhere, *de Incarn. et c. Ar.* 21), uses *physis* simply for His divine nature. "He set up anew," he says, "the form of man in Himself, in the spectacle of a flesh which *[who appropriate the term to the divinity,]*

had no fleshly wills or human thoughts, in an image of renovation. For the will is of the θεότης alone; since the whole φύσις of the Word was there." *c. Apoll.* ii. 10. And he argues, against the Arian objection from "The Lord created me," &c., in *Prov.* viii. 22, not simply that it refers to the Word's *human usia*, but that it does *not* refer to His *usia* (as if He had no *usia* but one), that it refers to something happening περὶ ἐκεῖνον, something adventitious, an adjunct or circumstance, which is not such as at all to warrant the inference that "what is said to be created is at once *in nature and usia* a creature." *Orat.* ii. 45.

and describe the humanity as an envelopment,

2. The force of this last expression περὶ ἐκεῖνον will be seen in the *de Decr.* 22, where he not only denies that the divine *usia* admits of accidents, but that it has anything "about it" necessary for its perfection; ἔξωθέν τινα περιβολὴν ἔχειν, καὶ καλύπτεσθαι, ἢ εἶναί τινα περὶ αὐτόν. Such a περιβολή then, or κάλυμμα, he considers the humanity. Hence, in spite of the Apollinarian perversion of the idea, we find it called a περιβολή, Theod. *Eran.* i. p. 23; κάλυμμα, Athan. *Sabell. Greg.* 4; προκάλυμμα, Theod. *ibid.* also *Gent.* vi. p. 877; καταπέτασμα, Athan. *ad Adelph.* 5, Cyril. *Cat.* xii. 26. xiii. 22. Cyril. Alex. *Quod unus*, p. 761. προπέτασμα, Athan. *Sabell. Greg.* 4. παραπέτασμα, Theod. *ibid.* p. 22. στολή, *ibid.* p. 23. Velamen, Leon. *Epist.* 59, p. 979. *Serm.* 22, p. 70. 25, p. 84. *Vid.* also the striking illustration, Athan. *Orat.* ii. 7, 8.

as an adjunct,

3. A safer term, which became a term of science, was πρόσλημμα and the parts of its verb; ὁ πρὸς αὐτὸν ληφθείς, Athan. *Orat.* iv. 3. ὁ προσληφθεὶς ἄνθρωπος, Nyssen. *Antirrh.*

of the μία φύσις. 377

35. τὸ ληφθέν, Cyril. *c. Nest.* iii. p. 69. τὸ προσλαβὸν καὶ τὸ προσληφθέν, Naz. *Orat.* xxxvii. 11. προσλαβών, Isid. *Ep.* i. 323. κατὰ πρόσληψιν, Cyril. *ad Succ. Ep.* 2, p. 1422. πρόσλημμα Naz. *de Vit. sua*, v. 648. Damasc. *F. O.* iii. 1.

4. These words denote the humanity in relation to the divine *usia*; another word, "first-fruits," which is taken from St. Paul, considers it in relation to that universal human *physis*, from which it was taken; but marks still the same reluctance in theologians to call it distinctly by the latter name. Ἀπαρχὴ ἐκ τῆς οὐσίας τῶν ἀνθρώπων, says Athanasius, *de Incarn. et c. Ar.* 8. And so *Orat.* iv. 33. Didym. *Trin.* iii. 9 *fin.* Cyril. *c. Nest.* i. p. 5. Nyssen. *Antirrh.* 15 *fin.* <small>as first-fruits</small>

5. The same reluctance is evidenced by the omission of the phrase ὁμοούσιος ἡμῖν, in relation to the humanity. This phrase is found in Eustathius and Theophilus *ap.* Theod. *Eran.* i. p. 56, ii. p. 154, and in Amphilochius *ap.* Phot. *Cod.* 229, p. 789; as is ὁμόφυλος in Procl. *ad Arm.* pp. 613, 618, and ὁμογενής Athan. *S. D.* 10. But the word ὁμοούσιος itself Athanasius singularly avoids in this last passage, though he has just used it in expounding John xv. 1, &c. And he still more remarkably avoids it in his *ad Epict.* and *contr. Apoll.*, where it was the natural amendment upon ὁμοούσιος τῇ θεότητι, which he is combating; yet he does not use it once, nay, he scarcely once, if ever, uses even ἐξ οὐσίας Μαρίας, substituting for it simply ἐκ Μαρίας. <small>not as homoousion with us,</small>

6. In like manner, in the antithesis between the divine and human natures, which is of constant occurrence in the Fathers, the word *physis* for the latter is scarcely <small>and omit the obvious contrast of the Two Natures.</small>

found, but ἀνθρωπότης, σάρξ, οἰκονομία, &c. For instance, Athanasius says, "The Word was by *nature* Son of God, but by *economy* son of Adam." *de Inc. et c. Ar.* 8. "He was by *nature and usia* the Word of God, and, *according to the flesh,* man." *ad Epict.* 12. Or, as Basil of Seleucia says, speaking of texts which refer to His mission, "These refer to His economy, *not* to His *usia*." *Orat.* 32, p. 171.

I set down some instances of this contrast:—

1. θεὸς ἐν ἀνθρωπότητι. Cyril. *c. Nest.* iii. p. 84.
2. θεὸς ἐν σαρκί. Athan. *Orat.* ii. 71. *ad Epict.* 10.
3. θεὸς ἐν σώματι. *Orat.* ii. 12. *ad Epict.* 10. Nyssen. *Antirrh.* 55.
4. δημιουργὸς ἐν σώματι. Athan. *ad Epict.* 10.
5. υἱὸς ἐν σώματι. *Orat.* i. 44.
6. λόγος ἐν σώματι. *Sent. D.* 8.
7. κύριος ἐν σώματι. *Orat.* i. 43.
8. λόγος ἐν σαρκί. *ibid.* iii. 54.
9. κύριος and his σάρξ. Nyssen. *Antirrh.* 44.
10. λόγος and his σάρξ. Athan. *Orat.* I. 47. iii. 38.
11. λόγος and his ἄνθρωπος. *ibid.* iv. 7.
12. λόγος and his ἐνανθρώπησις. Cyril. *c. Nest.* iv. p. 109.
13. λόγος and his οἰκονομία. Didym. *Trin.* iii. 21. Cyril. *c. Nest.* iii. p. 58.
14. υἱός and his οἰκονομία. Athan. *Orat.* ii. 76.
15. his οὐσία and his οἰκονομία. *ibid.* ii. 45. iii. 51.
16. his οὐσία and his διακονία. *ibid.* i. 12.
17. his οὐσία and his ἐπιδημία. Origen. *Caten. in Joan.* i. p. 45.
18. his οὐσία and his ἐπιφάνεια. Origen. *c. Cels.* viii.

19. his οὐσία and his ταπεινότης. Didym. *Trin.* iii. 6.

20. his οὐσία and his δουλικὴ μορφή. Nyssen. *Antirrhet.* 25.

21. his οὐσία and his ἀνθρώπινον. Athan. *Orat.* iii. 51.

22. his οὐσία and his ἄνθρωπος. Origen. *c. Cels.* vii. 16.

23. his ὑπόστασις and his ἄνθρωπος. Athan. *Orat.* iv. 35.

24. his φύσις and his ἄνθρωπος. Origen. *in Joan.* tom. i. 30.

25. his φύσις and his ἀνθρωπότης. Cyril. *Schol.* 25.

26. his φύσις and his σῶμα. Athan. *Orat.* ii. p. 57.

27. his φύσις and his σάρξ. Athan. *Orat.* iii. 34. Cyril. *c. Nest.* v. p. 132.

28. his θεότης and his σάρξ. Didym. *Trin.* iii. 8.

29. his ἔνσαρκος ἐπιδημία. Athan. *Orat.* i. 59.

30. his ἔνσαρκος παρουσία. *ibid.* i. 8, 49, &c. &c. *Incarn.* 20. *Sent. D.* 9. *Ep. Æg.* 4. *Serap.* i. 3, 9. Cyril. *Cat.* iii. 11 *et alibi.* Epiph. *Hær.* 77, 67, &c. &c.

31. his σωματικὴ παρουσία. Athan. *Orat.* ii. 10.

It may seem to some readers that the word ἄνθρωπος, which occurs among these instances, expresses the doctrine of a human nature even more strongly than φύσις could do, and even with some sort of countenance of the Nestorian doctrine of a double personality. But the word is in too frequent use with the Alexandrian and other divines to admit of the suspicion. I will set down one or two specimens of the parallel use of *homo* among the Latins. "Deus cum homine miscetur; hominem induit." Cyprian. *Idol. Van.* p. 538. "Assumptus a Dei Filio

The term "man" equivalent to "nature."

homo." Hilar. *in Ps.* 64. 6, "Assumptus homo in Filium Dei." Leon. *Serm.* 28, p. 101. "*Suus,*" the Word's, "homo." *ibid.* 22, p. 70. "*Hic* homo." Leon. *Ep.* 31, p. 855. "*Ille* homo, quem Deus suscepit." Augustin. *Ep.* 24, 3.

<small>Parallel of Hilary's phraseology.</small>   The word "assumptus" in some of these passages is the Latin of the προσληφθείς spoken of above, and reminds us of Hilary's division of the Word's attributes into *naturalia* and *assumpta,* from which we might draw an additional illustration, did we choose to pursue it, of the early theological language, and that the more striking, because, as we have seen, that Father has no difficulty of using the word *natura,* when the occasion calls for it, of the Word's humanity. *Vid.* the Benedictine Preface in *Hilar. Opera.*

21.

<small>Recapitulation.</small>   To recapitulate the conclusions to which we have arrived, concerning the sense of the Formula, μία φύσις σεσαρκωμένη.

<small>The Word's nature</small>   1. φύσις is the Divine Essence, substantial and personal, in the fulness of its attributes—the One God. And, τοῦ λόγου being added, it is that One God, considered in the Person of the Son.

<small>is one</small>   2. It is called μία (1) because, even after the Incarnation, it and no other nature is, strictly speaking, ἴδια, His own, the flesh being "assumpta;" (2) because it, and no other, has been His from the first; and (3) because it has ever been one and the same, in nowise affected as to its perfection by the incarnation.

<small>and incarnate.</small>   3. It is called σεσαρκωμένη, in order to express the de-

pendence, subordination, and restriction of His humanity, which (1) has neither ἡγεμονικόν nor personality; (2) has no distinct υἱότης, though it involved a new γέννησις; (3) is not possessed of the fulness of characteristics which attaches to any other specimen of our race. On which account, while it is recognised as a perfect nature, it may be spoken of as existing after the manner of an attribute rather than of a substantive being, which it really is, as in a parallel way Catholics speak of its presence in the Eucharist, though corporeal, being after the manner of a spirit.

22.

It only remains to add concerning the Formula, that, in spite of the misapprehensions to which it has given rise, and the suspicion with which it has been viewed, it is of recognised authority in the Catholic Church. Whether Athanasius himself used it, is a contested point. Flavian admitted it at the Latrocinium, A.D. 449, in the presence of its partisans, the Eutychians, who condemned and murdered him there. It was indirectly recognised at the fourth General Council at Chalcedon, A.D. 452, in the Council's reception of Flavian's confession, which contained it. It was also received in the fifth General, and in the Lateran of A.D. 649. But, for this point of history, I refer the reader to Petavius *de Incarn.* iv. 6, who brings together all that has to be said upon it in the course of a few pages.

Fortunes of the Formula.

It is perhaps scarcely necessary to observe, that my

reason for not referring in the above inquiry to the works of the Areopagite, to the disputation between Dionysius and Paul of Samosata, to Hippolytus *contr. Beron. et Helic.* and some other works and fragments, has been a disbelief of their genuineness.

VI.
THE ORDO DE TEMPORE IN THE ROMAN BREVIARY.

(From the "Atlantis" of February, 1870.)

THE ORDO DE TEMPORE.

I DO not know where to find, what doubtless is to be found somewhere, a perfect analysis of the *Ordo de Tempore*, (that is, the succession of ecclesiastical seasons,) as it stands in the Catholic Calendar. The *Ordo* has to deal with some considerable difficulties, and its disposal of them is very beautiful. I sometimes fancy I could interest a reader in it, and I will try; and though I must do so in my own way for want of a better, and though in consequence I am obliged to speak under correction of any authoritative exposition of it, if such exists, still I do not think I can be much out in my analysis, even though it be incomplete.

The *Ordo de Sanctis* is invariable through the year. Each saint has his day, which is never changed year after year, except by an accidental transference or postponement. Here, the only call for arrangement and adjustment in it rises out of the necessity of reconciling this *Ordo* with the *Ordo de Tempore*. For the *Ordo de Tempore* is far from invariable year after year; on the contrary, as I have intimated, it even disturbs the tranquil course of the *Ordo de Sanctis*. It is on this account especially that the yearly Directory called the "Ordo

Recitandi" is necessary; for the *Ordo de Tempore* is not only variable itself, but it interferes with the harmonious succession of Saints' Days in the *Ordo de Sanctis*. If we look at the table of Transferred Saints' Days in the yearly "Ordo Recitandi," we shall find that they are all occasioned by the collision between the two *Ordines*, *de Sanctis* and *de Tempore*. For instance, in the present year (1869), St. Thomas was thrown out of his day, March 7, because it was the Fourth Sunday in Lent; and the Seven Dolours lost its Friday because it was the Feast of St. Joseph.

Left to itself, the *Ordo de Sanctis* is invariable, but the *Ordo de Tempore* is never the same two years running. Its chief features indeed, viewed relatively to each other, are always the same—Advent, Christmas, Epiphany, Lent, Easter, and Pentecost come in succession; but these seasons are not fixed to determinate days in the civil year, as the Festivals of the Saints are. Easter Day is in one year upon one day in March or April, in another year on another. The coincidence then of days in the civil year and in the ecclesiastical year has to be reduced to rule; and this is done, I consider, very beautifully by the provisions of the Calendar, as I propose to show in these pages.

I.

The first and chief difficulty in the *Ordo de Tempore* is obviously this—that Easter Day depends upon, is later than, the full moon in March or in April, and the full moon is not fixed to any certain day in either month. The lunar month is about 29 days, the civil varies from

28 to 31. As the full moon is not constant to one day of either month, neither is the Easter Day. Next, there is this additional disturbance, that Easter Day is always kept on a Sunday, the Sunday after the full moon (mean time) which follows upon March 21. Thus, even were the day of the full moon fixed to a given day of a given month in the civil calendar, say March 22, Easter Day would not on that account be a fixed day, for it must be a Sunday, and the Sunday after that March 22 may be any one of the seven following days. Easter Day then is variable, first, because the full moon may fall on any one day out of 29 civil days, and next because Sunday may fall on any day out of the seven, which follow the full moon.

Nor is this the whole of the difficulty. Easter Day is one great centre of feasts and seasons in the ecclesiastical year; but there is another such centre, and that is Christmas Day. And though Christmas Day is fixed in the civil year, Advent Sunday, which precedes and depends upon it, is not. It is the fourth Sunday before Christmas Day; and since Christmas Day, as being fixed in the month, may be any one of the seven days of the week, it follows that Advent Sunday may be one or other of seven days of the month. When, for instance, Christmas Day is Monday, the fourth Sunday in Advent is the day before, that is, December 24, and the first Sunday in Advent, or Advent Sunday, will be December 3. When Christmas Day is Tuesday, then Advent Sunday will be December 2, and so on through the seven days. The range of Advent Sundays, then, is from November 27 to December 3 inclusive.

Christmas with Advent, then, and Easter, are the two centres of the sacred year, with an assemblage or body of seasons and feasts about each of them, and all inserted and having a place, a shifting place, in the civil year; and the problem to be solved in the *Ordo de Tempore* is how to overcome the disarrangement caused by the varying distance from each other of these two oscillating bodies, standing in relation, as they do, to the course of weeks and months. When are we to cease, for example, to date with a reference to Christmas? When with a reference to Easter? Were both Christmas with Advent, and Easter, fixed, there would be nothing more to settle; but the interval between Advent Sunday and the following Easter Sunday varies year by year, and also the interval between Easter and Advent; and it has to be determined when the one period is to end and the other to begin. And there is this additional difficulty, that the Easter before a given Advent being always a different day in the year from the Easter after Advent, there are three dates to be taken into account, and reduced to system, one Advent and two Easters.

Now let us see how these variations are actually adjusted; that is, what is the abstract scientific arrangement, which, year by year as it comes, is to be appealed to and applied. I speak of the scientific theory of arrangement for obvious reasons; for instance, leap-year introduces a disturbance, which must be neglected in the theory—that is the sun's doing. The moon is the cause of a disturbance of a different sort, viz., though many consecutive days are, on this year or that, possible Easter days, still Easter days do not actually proceed in course year by year in regular succession. I mean the 6th of April is not Easter Day in one year, the 7th in year two, the 8th in year three, and so on; but for the scientific theory I shall place them in sequence, that is, following, not the chronological order, as it is sometimes called, or order in fact, but the logical, or order in system. Nor am I concerned with the condition of mean time.

2.

I observe first, as a matter of fact, to be taken as a *datum* and not to be proved here, that Easter Day may fall on any one of thirty-five successive days, that is, on any day of five successive weeks, from March 22 to April 25, both inclusive. Let us suppose, then, a column made of these thirty-five days, one after another, March 22, 23, 24, &c, and so on to April 22, 23, 24, 25. This is the Easter Day range.

Next, I shall place two other columns of dates, one on each side of this central column, and each of them dependent upon it.

The one on the left of the Easter column shall be the Septuagesima column. Septuagesima Sunday is always nine weeks or sixty-three days before Easter Sunday. As then there are thirty-five days on which Easter Sunday may fall, so there are thirty-five days on which Septuagesima Sunday may fall. The first of these, counting back nine weeks from Easter Day, March 22 (and taking no account of leap-year), is January 18; and the last, counting back from Easter Day, April 25, is February 21.

This is the Septuagesima range of days, on the left of the Easter column.

The column on the right of the Easter column will consist of the Post-Pentecostal range ; and the Sundays, which are marked down it, must be the days on which may fall the 23rd Sunday after Pentecost. This is the last proper Pentecost Sunday ; there is no proper 24th, &c., and the "ultima" is shifting. Up to the 23rd Sunday, the order of Sundays after Easter Day is as regular and invariable as the nine Sundays back to Septuagesima before Easter Day. How many Sundays is it from Easter Day to the 23rd after Pentecost ? Seven to the day of Pentecost, or Whit-Sunday, and twenty-three more to the 23rd after it ; that is, altogether thirty Sundays or weeks —invariable, I say, following one the other in fixed order. This is the column to the right of the Easter column.

Here then we have the whole Paschal period, from Septuagesima Sunday to the 23rd Sunday after Pentecost ; nine weeks before Easter Day, and thirty weeks after, altogether thirty-nine weeks, or precisely nine calendar months, or three-quarters of a year. Though the Paschal period, as I have called it, varies year by year in its place in the civil year, because Easter Day varies, the Paschal period does not vary in its length, it is always nine calendar months precisely. There is a fixed succession of thirty-nine weeks from Septuagesima Sunday to the 23rd Sunday after Pentecost.

One other result is this : that as Septuagesima falls in January or February, and Easter Day falls in March or April, so does Pentecost 23rd fall always in October

The Ordo de Tempore.

or November. Nay, further than this, since it is exactly nine calendar months from Septuagesima to Pentecost 23rd, it follows that, whatever be the day of the month in January or February on which Septuagesima falls, on the same day of the month in October or November respectively does Pentecost 23rd fall. Thus, if Septuagesima is January 18, then Pentecost 23rd is October 18; if the former falls on February 1, the latter falls on November 1; if the former on February 21, then the latter on November 21. And all along the two series of possible Septuagesima and possible 23rd Pentecost Days, the number of the day of the month on which Septuagesima Sunday falls is the same as the number of the day of the month on which, in the same year, the 23rd Sunday after Pentecost falls.

Now, then, we can fill up the dates in the third column or 23rd Pentecost, which is on the right of the Easter column. We shall have to go through thirty-five days from October 18 to November 21; putting October 18 against January 18, and so on till we end with November 21 against February 21. Thus:—

Septuagesima Sunday.	Easter Day.	23rd Sunday after Pentecost.
January 18	March 22	October 18
,, 19	,, 23	,, 19
,, 20	,, 24	,, 20
,, 21	,, 25	,, 21
&c., &c.	&c., &c.	&c., &c.
to	to	to
February 19	April 23	November 19
,, 20	,, 24	,, 20
,, 21	,, 25	,, 21

Now, in order to apply a test to what I have said, let us have recourse to the "Ordo Recitandi," as in use with us, for the six years from 1849 to 1851 and from 1853 to 1855. It will be found to bear out the conclusions, at which I have arrived theoretically.

	Septuagesima.	Easter.	Pentecost 23rd.
1849	February 4	April 8	November 4
1850	January 27	March 31	October 27
1851	February 16	April 20	November 16
1853	January 23	March 27	October 23
1854	February 12	April 16	November 12
1855	February 4	April 8	November 4

The years 1852 and 1856 were leap-years, which ought to throw out the exact correspondence of Sundays by one day; and hence, in accordance with the above rule, we find from the "Ordo Recitandi" in fact, that Septuagesima was February 8, but Pentecost 23rd was November 7 in 1852, and Septuagesima January 20, and Pentecost 23rd October 19, in 1856.

3.

So much on the connexion of Easter Day with Septuagesima and Pentecost 23rd; but can nothing be done to make the actual succession of Easter Days less variable than it seems to be at first sight? Yes, something, as I proceed to show.

Let it be observed, that as Christmas Day is a fixed day of the month, it may be on any day of the week; it runs through seven days, and, as the days in the year exceed fifty-two weeks by one day, a fixed day in any month travels forward along the days of the week in a succession of years. Thus (neglecting leap-years), if the 25th of December, Christmas Day, be on Monday in this year, it will be on Tuesday next year, and on Wednesday the year after, and so on to Sunday inclusive; and, after completing the week, it will next year be on Monday again, and so on for ever. In consequence, the Fourth Sunday in Advent, being the Sunday immediately before Christmas Day, will travel backwards, in those same successive years, along the days of the month; when Christmas Day is on Monday, the 4th Advent Sunday will be on the 24th; when Christmas Day is on Tuesday, it will be on the 23rd; and so on successively the 22nd, 21st, 20th, 19th, and 18th, and so on, over and over again, for ever. And again, Advent Sunday, which is three weeks before that fourth Sunday, will be successively, as I have said already, on December 3, 2, 1, November 30, 29, 28, 27, in never-ending routine. To these seven days Advent Sunday is tethered. The feast of St. Andrew is just in the middle of them, November 30, with three possible Advent Sundays before it, and three after.

Now let us observe what we have hereby gained. Advent begins with a Sunday, and must be one of a certain seven days; but Pentecost 23rd, which ends what I have called the Paschal period, is also a Sunday; therefore there must be also a whole number of weeks without any days over, between the last Sunday of the Paschal period and Advent Sunday, which is the commencement of the

Christmas period. If, for instance, Advent Sunday falls on November 27, Pentecost 23rd cannot fall on any whatever of the thirty-five possible days from October 18 to November 21, which constitute the range of the latter Sunday, but it must fall on such a day out of the thirty-five as will secure a round number of weeks between it, and November 27.

How many such days are there in its whole range? Of course, one in seven. Therefore out of the thirty-five possible days for Pentecost 23rd, only five are actually possible in this particular case of Advent Sunday falling on November 27. The possible days, counting backwards, are November 20, 13, 6, October 30, and 23. And in like manner when Advent Sunday is November 28, there are only five possible days on which the previous Pentecost 23rd can fall; and so on in the case of all the Advent Sunday month-days, November 29, 30, December 1, 2, and 3.

And, since Easter Sunday and Septuagesima Sunday vary, as regards the day of the month, with Pentecost 23rd, it follows that out of the whole thirty-five possible days on which Easter may fall there are only five days possible, when Advent Sunday is November 27; and the same is true for all the other days of the month which are possible for Advent Sunday. It seems then that in every year Easter Day is one out of five days, and which the five days are is determined (practically) by the day on which the following Advent Sunday falls. And this is true of Septuagesima Sunday also.

Moreover, as the day of the month on which Advent Sunday falls, depends on the day of the week on which

Christmas Day falls, on Christmas Day also depend the five days which in every year are possible for all three, Septuagesima, Easter Day, and Pentecost 23rd.

Once more; it is awkward to make a day at the end of the year, December 25, the index or pivot of days and seasons which have gone before it. I observe then that (neglecting leap-year) as December 25 falls on this or that day of the week, the preceding January 1 falls on a day in correspondence with it, so that, according to the day of the week on which the first day of any year falls are the five possible days determined for Septuagesima, Easter, and Pentecost 23rd in that year. When December 25 is on a Monday, then New Year's Day preceding was on Sunday; when on Tuesday, New Year's Day was on Monday, &c. I shall call the seven years which successively begin with Sunday, Saturday, Friday, &c., years A, B, C, D, E, F, G, and then we have the following table:—

Year.	Jan. 1.	Septuagesima.		Easter Day.		Pentecost 23rd.		Advent Sunday.		Christmas Day
		Jan.	Feb.	Mar.	April.	Oct.	Nov.			
D	Th.	18, 25.	1, 8, 15	22, 29.	5, 12, 19	18, 25.	1, 8, 15	Nov. 29		Fr.
E	We.	19, 26.	2, 9, 16	23, 30.	6, 13, 20	19, 26.	2, 9, 16	„	30	Th.
F	Tu.	20, 27.	3, 10, 17	24, 31.	7, 14, 21	20, 27.	3, 10, 17	Dec.	1	We.
G	Mo.	21, 28.	4, 11, 18	25.	1, 8, 15, 22	21, 28.	4, 11, 18	„	2	Tu.
A	Su.	22, 29.	5, 12, 19	26.	2, 9, 16, 23	22, 29.	5, 12, 19	„	3	Mo.
B	Sa.	23, 30.	6, 13. 20	27.	3, 10, 17, 24	23, 30.	6, 13, 20	Nov. 27		Su.
C	Fr.	24, 31.	7, 14, 21	28.	4, 11, 18, 25	24, 31.	7, 14, 21	„	28	Sa.

This table, which has been formed from the preceding analysis, will be found to agree with the Tabula Paschalis of the Missal and Breviary, the letter of the alphabet by which I have denoted the year, being the Litera Dominicalis of the Tabula. However, that Tabula has no occasion to mention, nor does mention, Pentecost 23rd, or its connexion with Septuagesima, of which I have made such use above, and shall also avail myself in what follows.

4.

Hitherto I have been speaking of the Christmas period only in its bearings upon the Paschal period: now let me speak of it for its own sake.

The Paschal period varies in its dates in the civil year, but never in its length; it is always thirty-nine weeks, or nine calendar months. But, unlike Easter Day, Christmas Day is fixed; is its period fixed also, or does it vary in its length? I cannot answer this question till I know what is meant by the Christmas period; do we mean by it (1) that season which the Paschal nine months interrupt, that divided season, lying at the extremities, the beginning and the end of one and the same year, and which, because divided, has no proper title to be called a period at all? or do we mean (2) that continuous lapse of weeks lying partly at the end of one year and partly at the beginning of the next? Let us take these two cases separately, and the second case first.

The actual continuous Christmas period lying partly in one year, partly in the next, between Pentecost 23rd of one year and Septuagesima of the next, is not only variable in length, but too variable to admit of being reduced to rule.

At first sight it admits of as many as twenty-five different lengths; for every year, as I have shown, allows of five possible dates for Septuagesima and Pentecost 23rd; now the continuous Christmas period is from the Pentecost 23rd of this year to the Septuagesima of the next; since then the Pentecost 23rd may be any one out of five dates, and the next Septuagesima also any one of five, there result twenty-five possible lengths of the continuous Christmas period. Nor is there any easy rule for determining the succession of their variations in consecutive years. I do not propose any formula then for determining the length of the continuous Christmas period; for it depends on two conditions, practically independent of each other, the dates of the previous and of the succeeding Easter.

Some idea of these variations will be gained by the inspection of them as they occurred between 1848 and 1857 :—

	1848-9.		1849-50.		1850-1.		1851-2.	
	Weeks.		Weeks.		Weeks.		Weeks.	
1. Before Advent.	2	Nov. 19 Nov. 26	4	Nov. 4 11 18 25	5	Oct. 27 Nov. 3 10 17 24	2	Nov. 16 23
2. Advent to Epiphany.	5	Dec. 3 10 17 24 31	6	Dec. 2 9 16 23 30 Jan. 6	6	Dec. 1 8 15 22 29 Jan. 5	6	30 Dec. 7 14 21 28 Jan. 4
3. After Epiphany.	4	Jan. 7 14 21 28	2	13 20	5	12 19 26 Feb. 2 9	4	11 18 25 Feb. 1
Sum Total	11		12		16		12	

	1852-3.		1853-4.		1854-5.	1855-6.	1856-7.
	Weeks.		Weeks.		Weeks.	Weeks.	Weeks.
1. Before Advent.	3	Nov. 7 14 21	5	Oct. 23 30 Nov. 6 13 20	3	4	6
2. Advent to Epiphany.	6	28 Dec. 5 12 19 26 Jan. 2	6	27 Dec. 4 11 18 25 Jan. 1	5	6	6
3. After Epiphany.	2	9 16	5	8 15 22 29 Feb. 5	4	1	4
Sum Total	11		16		12	11	16

However, in spite of this irregularity in the continuous Christmas period, it has some kind of intelligible shape, thus :—

In the first place, since we know the earliest and latest possible dates of Pentecost 23rd and Septuagesima, we can ascertain the longest and shortest measure of the Christmas period. Pentecost 23rd may be as early as October 18; Septuagesima as late as February 21; this whole interval from October 18 in one year to February 21 in the next, is one hundred and twenty-five days, or eighteen weeks. Again, Pentecost 23rd may fall on November 21, and the following Septuagesima as early as January 18, that is, at an interval from it of fifty-seven days, or eight weeks. Thus eighteen weeks is the longest, and eight weeks the shortest continuous Christmas period.

Next, this period, whatever its length, is made up of three parts: 1. The central portion, which I might call the Tempus Natale, from Advent Sunday to the first Sunday after Epiphany. 2. The Ante-natal portion been Pentecost 23rd and Advent Sunday. 3. The Epiphany or Post-natal, between the first Sunday after Epiphany and Septuagesima.

Now the possible length of each of these three is easy to ascertain. 1. The Natal Time is ordinarily six weeks (*i.e.* except when Advent Sunday falls on December 3, for then, the Epiphany falling on Saturday, the Natal portion loses a week). 2. The Ante-natal portion varies from one week (viz. when Pentecost 23rd falls on November 20 or 21, and is the "ultima" Sunday) to six weeks (viz. when Pentecost 23rd falls between October 18 and 22 inclusive, and there are twenty-eight Sundays after Pentecost). 3. The Post-natal portion also varies from one week to six; for, if the Sunday after Epiphany be January 11, 12, or 13, and the following Septuagesima be January 18, 19, or 20, it is one week; and if the former of these Sundays be January 7-9, and the latter February 18-21, then there will be all the six Sundays, as they stand in the *Ordo de Tempore*.

It appears then that the longest Christmas period consists of six, six, and six weeks; that is, eighteen weeks, which agrees with my former calculation; and the shortest is one, six, and one, that is, eight weeks, which also agrees with what I have determined above.

5.

Now, secondly, let us consider the Christmas weeks, as contained in one and the same year, that is, as partly at the beginning of it, and partly at the end: can we determine the length of these two portions taken together? Certainly we can, and, as it would seem at first sight, without any difficulty; for, as the Paschal period takes up exactly nine calendar months or thirty-nine weeks, there are three months or thirteen weeks left for the Christmas. And, as to the separate portions, they are always the same, though not in the same place in the civil year; for, in order to allow for the variation of the date of Easter Day (which ranges through thirty-five days or five weeks), of the six Sundays after Epiphany, those are omitted year by year, which would interfere with an early Septuagesima, and are introduced instead between Pentecost 23rd and Advent. This is so simple an arrangement, that it would seem as

The Ordo de Tempore.

if it could have no difficulty, and there would be nothing to observe upon it; for as many weeks as are taken out of the Christmas three months by an early Septuagesima of any year, just so many are paid back to it by the corresponding early Pentecost 23rd of that year; however, the arrangement does not run quite smoothly, as the following table shows:—

Variations.	Epiphany Sundays before Septuagesima.	Septuagesima to Pentecost 23 39 Weeks or 9 Calendar Months.		Epiphany Sundays intercalated after Pentecost 23 and before Pent. ult.	Sundays after Pentecost.	Advent Sunday.	
1	1. [2 dropped]	Jan. 18	Oct. 18	3. 4. 5. 6.	28	Nov.	29
2	1. [2 dropped]	,, 19	,, 19	3. 4. 5. 6.	28	,,	30
3	1. [2 dropped]	,, 20	,, 20	3. 4. 5. 6.	28	Dec.	1
4	1. 2.	,, 21	,, 21	3. 4. 5. 6.	28	,,	2
5	1. 2.	,, 22	,, 22	3. 4. 5. 6.	28	,,	3
6	1. 2. [3 dr.]	,, 23	,, 23	4. 5. 6.	28	Nov.	27
7	1. 2. [3 dr.]	,, 24	,, 24	4. 5. 6.	27	,,	28
8	1. 2. [3 dr.]	,, 25	,, 25	4. 5. 6.	27	,,	29
9	1. 2. [3 dr.]	,, 26	,, 26	4. 5. 6.	27	,,	30
10	1. 2. [3 dr.]	,, 27	,, 27	4. 5. 6.	27	Dec.	1
11	1. 2. 3.	,, 28	,, 28	4. 5. 6.	27	,,	2
12	1. 2. 3.	,, 29	,, 29	4. 5. 6.	27	,,	3
13	1. 2. 3. [4]	,, 30	,, 30	5. 6.	27	Nov.	27
14	1. 2. 3. [4]	,, 31	,, 31	5. 6.	26	,,	28
15	1. 2. 3. [4]	Feb. 1	Nov. 1	5. 6.	26	,,	29
16	1. 2. 3. [4]	,, 2	,, 2	5. 6.	26	,,	30
17	1. 2. 3. [4]	,, 3	,, 3	5. 6.	26	Dec.	1
18	1. 2. 3. 4.	,, 4	,, 4	5. 6.	26	,,	2
19	1. 2. 3. 4.	,, 5	,, 5	5. 6.	26	,,	3
20	1. 2. 3. 4. [5]	,, 6	,, 6	6.	26	Nov.	27
21	1. 2. 3. 4. [5]	,, 7	,, 7	6.	25	,,	28
22	1. 2. 3. 4. [5]	,, 8	,, 8	6.	25	,,	29
23	1. 2. 3. 4. [5]	,, 9	,, 9	6.	25	,,	30
24	1. 2. 3. 4. [5]	,, 10	,, 10	6.	25	Dec.	1
25	1. 2. 3. 4. 5.	,, 11	,, 11	6.	25	,,	2
26	1. 2. 3. 4. 5.	,, 12	,, 12	6.	25	,,	3
27	1. 2. 3. 4. 5. [6]	,, 13	,, 13	0.	25	Nov.	27
28	1. 2. 3. 4. 5. [6]	,, 14	,, 14	0.	24	,,	28
29	1. 2. 3. 4. 5. [6]	,, 15	,, 15	0.	24	,,	29
30	1. 2. 3. 4. 5. [6]	,, 16	,, 16	0.	24	,,	30
31	1. 2. 3. 4. 5. [6]	,, 17	,, 17	0.	24	Dec.	1
32	1. 2. 3. 4. 5. 6.	,, 18	,, 18	0.	24	,,	2
33	1. 2. 3. 4. 5. 6.	,, 19	,, 19	0.*	24	,,	3
34	1. 2. 3. 4. 5. 6.	,, 20	,, 20	—1.	23	Nov.	27
35	1. 2. 3. 4. 5. 6.	,, 21	,, 21	—1.	23	,,	28

* The expression "—1" means that the Pent. 23 is merged in or becomes the "ultima" before Advent, and a week suppressed.

It will be observed in this table, that of the six Epiphany Sundays (whether in their place or intercalated before Advent), in five years out of seven, one is dropped, that is, there is no place for it. The reason is this: the Calendar contemplates only one Sunday after Christmas; it does not contemplate a second, as if the Epiphany certainly fell in the week of that first Sunday after Christmas, and the first Sunday after Epiphany were the next Sunday immediately upon that first Christmas Sunday. But, in matter of fact, in five years out of seven, there are two Sundays between Christmas day and the first Sunday after the Epiphany. For this second Sunday the Calendar makes no provision or room; it is as if it had reckoned it as one of the six Epiphany Sundays, and it (the Sunday) had, in those five years, got (as it were) by accident on the wrong side of the Epiphany. The consequence is, that in those years in which there is a Sunday too much before the Epiphany, there is no room for the whole number of Sundays after Epiphany, and one Epiphany Sunday has to be suppressed.

VII.

THE HISTORY OF THE TEXT OF THE RHEIMS AND DOUAY VERSION OF HOLY SCRIPTURE.

(From the "Rambler" of July, 1859.)

THE RHEIMS AND DOUAY VERSION OF HOLY SCRIPTURE.

IN attempting to trace the history, and to ascertain the present state, of the text of the Rheims and Douay version of Holy Scripture, we cannot avoid availing ourselves of the elaborate work on the subject, recently published by a dignitary of the Irish Establishment. We mean Archdeacon Cotton's *Attempt to show what has been done by Roman Catholics for the Diffusion of the Holy Scriptures in English*, published at the Oxford University Press in 1855.

Not that it needs any apology for using the investigations of a learned Protestant, or for feeling grateful to him, so far as he has anticipated the necessity of researches of our own, by such minute, exact, and persevering diligence as he has taken in a subject-matter which could not be of any the slightest personal interest to himself. But, painful as it is to say it, in spite of his stating in his preface, that "the design of his book is not controversial but literary," he has made it the vehicle of so much incidental insinuation, sometimes unfair, sometimes ignorant, always ill-natured, to the disadvantage of Catholic ecclesiastics, that we are unable to regard him with that unmixed respect, and to use him with that ready and unfaltering confidence, which would be natural in those who, like ourselves, have long known his claims, both as a gentleman and a scholar, on public estimation. Perhaps, however, it is well that he should have allowed his *animus* against the Catholic Church to appear so distinctly; otherwise, from admiration of the long and patient pains with which he has prosecuted an irksome labour, we might have been led to such full reliance on his statements as it is never right to place on any writer whatever, much less on one who, whatever his personal worth, is naturally open to the prejudices of his creed and party. As things stand, while we shall use him in the following pages, we are warned at the same time to verify his various statements, as far as may be, and where this cannot be done, not to adopt them without distinct reference to him as our authority. At the same time, in so difficult and intricate an inquiry, we have no right to anticipate that, whatever be our care, we shall succeed, whether we use him or not, in guarding against inaccuracies and errors of our own in matters of detail.

§ I. RHEIMS AND DOUAY BIBLE.

The circumstances under which the existing Catholic translation of Holy Scripture was made are rendered familiar to us by Mr. Tierney's edition of Dod's *History*, not to refer to other authorities. The College or Seminary of Douay had been founded in 1568 by the exertions of Cardinal Allen, some time fellow of Oriel College, Oxford. A few years afterwards, its members were obliged, by the political troubles of Flanders, to migrate for a time to France, and to establish themselves at Rheims. One of their first works in the service of their countrymen was an English version of Holy Scripture. The divines chiefly concerned in the translation of the New Testament were the aforesaid Dr. William Allen, afterwards Cardinal; Dr. Gregory Martin, of St. John's College, Oxford; Dr. Richard Bristow, of Christ Church and Exeter; and John Reynolds, of New College. Martin translated the text, and the rest revised; the Annotations were written by Bristow and Allen. Martin was also the translator of the Old Testament, the notes to which were written by Dr. Worthington, who, according to Dr. Cotton, eventually joined the Oratory. This, however, was not the case; for we find his name in Alegambe's *Script. Soc. Jes.* p. 438. He joined the Society, "ætate jam grandævus," dying in 1626. Martin died of an illness, the consequence of his labours, in the very year in which his New Testament made its appearance.

The reasons which actuated them in their work are detailed in the Prefaces with which both Old and New Testaments are introduced to the reader. " Now since Luther's revolt also," says the preface to the New Testament, " diverse learned Catholics, for the more speedy abolishing of a number of false and impious translations put forth by sundry sects, and for the better preservation or reclaim of many good souls endangered thereby, have published the Bible in the several languages of almost all the principal provinces of the Latin Church, no other books in the world being so pernicious as heretical translations of the Scriptures, poisoning the people under colour of divine authority, and not many other remedies being more sovereign against the same (if it be used in order, discretion, and humility) than the true, faithful, and sincere interpretation opposed thereunto. . . . We, therefore, having compassion to see our beloved countrymen, with extreme danger of their souls, to use only such profane translations and erroneous men's mere fantasies, for the pure and blessed word of truth, much also moved thereunto by the desires of many devout persons, have set forth for you, benign readers, the New Testament to begin withal, trusting that it may give occasion to you, after diligent perusal thereof, to lay away at least such their impure versions as hitherto you have been forced to occupy."

The preface to the whole Bible speaks to the same effect: " Now since Luther and his followers have pretended that the Catholic Roman faith and doctrine should be contrary to God's written word, and that the Scriptures were not suffered in vulgar languages, lest the people should see the truth, and withal these new masters corruptly turning the Scriptures into diverse tongues, as might best serve their own opinions, against this false suggestion and practice, Catholic pastors have, for one especial remedy, set forth true and sincere translations in most languages of the Latin Church."

The translation was made, as we have noticed, soon after the establishment of the college; but, owing to a "lack of means," as the preface says, in their "poor estate in banishment," "to publish the whole in such sort as a work of so great charge and importance" required, it "lay by them," the New Testament till 1582, the Old till 1609-10. At these dates the versions of the New and Old Testaments were respectively published in quarto; that of the New at Rheims, that of the Old at Douay, whither they returned in the course of the year. The Old Testament came to a second edition (quarto) in 1635, without alterations or corrections. The New Testament came to a second edition (quarto) in 1600, with some few alterations and corrections; to a third (16mo) in 1621; and to a fourth (quarto) in 1633. After these there was no new edition of either Old or New Testament for above a hundred years, when at length, in 1738, the fifth was published (folio) of the New Testament. In this reprint the spelling is modernised, and the text and annotations have a few verbal alterations, but in substance it is the edition of 1600 and 1633. A sixth edition of the New Testament (folio) was published fifty years afterwards (1788) at Liverpool, with the original preface and annotations, after the edition of 1738.

In 1816-1818 an edition, or editions, of the whole Bible were published in Ireland, in which, as regards the New Testament, the Rhemish text and annotations were mainly adopted. This edition was printed in different places, with duplicate sheets, and various cancels; and the Old Testament follows mainly, both in text and notes, Dr. Challoner's revision, which will be described lower down. This may be considered the seventh edition of the original Rhemish version of the New Testament.

An eighth edition, both text and notes, was published

in New York, in octavo, in 1834, by a Protestant party, which hoped to make use of it as a weapon in controversy against Catholics. It professes to be "exactly printed from the original volume."

Such is the history of the Rheims and Douay Bible, of which there have been two editions of the Old Testament, 1609-10 and 1635, and eight (including the New York Protestant reprint) of the New, 1582, 1600, 1621, 1633, 1738, 1788, 1816-1818, and 1834. This version comes to us on the authority of certain divines of the Cathedral and College of Rheims and of the University of Douay, confirmed by the subsequent indirect recognition of English, Scotch, and Irish bishops, and by its general reception by the faithful. It never has had any episcopal *imprimatur*, much less has it received any formal Approbation from the Holy See.

§ 2. DR. CHALLONER'S BIBLE.

We now come to review the labours of Dr. Challoner, Vicar-Apostolic of the London district, in the middle of last century.

Before that time the need of a revision of the Rheims and Douay version had been felt and acknowledged. During the greater part of the seventeenth century, indeed, from 1635 till the first years of the eighteenth, the inconvenience was borne of necessity; for no reprint was, during that long time, called for; but when, at length, the old edition was exhausted and a new one required, then the latent dissatisfaction of Catholics with the existing version showed itself, for two translations of the New Testament successively appeared in rivalry of the Rheims, and as substitutes for it. The former of these new translations was that of Dr. Cornelius Nary, in the year 1718; the latter, that of Dr. Witham of Douay. Of these two translators, Dr. Nary was parish-priest of St. Michan's, Dublin; and the version which he published had the approbation of four Irish divines, of Paris and of Dublin. The translator observes of "the Douay Bible and the Rheims Testament," that the "language is so old, the words so obsolete, the orthography so bad, and the translation so literal, that in a number of places it is unintelligible, and all over so grating to the ears of such as are accustomed to speak, in a manner, another language, that most people will not be at the pains of reading them."

An additional reason which Dr. Nary assigns for a new translation is the inconvenience of the folio or quarto size, in which the hitherto editions (excepting the third of the New Testament) had been published. "They are so bulky," he says, "that they cannot conveniently be carried about for public devotion; and so scarce and dear, that the generality of people neither have, nor can procure them for their private use."

Dr. Witham, the latter of these two translators, was president of Douay College in 1730. He too complains of the obscurity arising out of the literal renderings of the Douay translators. "They followed," he says, "with a nice exactness the Latin text, which they undertook to translate, at the same time always consulting and comparing it with the Greek, as every accurate translator must do, not to mistake the true sense of the Latin text. They perhaps followed too scrupulously the Latin, even as to the placing of the words; but what makes that edition seem so obscure at present, and scarce intelligible, is the difference of the English tongue, as it was spoken at that time, and as it is now changed and refined ; so that many words and expressions, both in the translation and annotations, by length of time are become obsolete, and no longer in use."

These two translations appeared in 1718 and 1730; and in 1738, as I have said above, in spite of them, a new edition of the Rheims was published, probably, says Dr. Cotton, in London. However, though they were superseded, the force of the considerations which led to their publication seems to have been felt, and resulted in the revision of the Rheims and Douay text by Dr. Challoner in 1749 and following years. That this pious prelate, to whom the English Church is so much indebted, concurred in the dissatisfaction which Nary and Witham felt with the text itself, is proved from the very fact of his altering it. That he recognised the justice of the complaint which they urged against the size which had been selected for the Rheims and Douay, may be argued from the circumstance, that he prints his own edition, not in folio or quarto, but in 12mo.

The first edition of Dr. Challoner's revision was published in 1749. It consisted of the New Testament only, and professed in the title-page to be " newly revised and corrected according to the Clementine edition of the Scriptures" (the standard Vulgate). The approbation of two English divines is prefixed to the volume, but of no Bishop, which perhaps was unnecessary, considering he was a co-adjutor Bishop himself. In the next year, 1750, he published an edition of the whole Bible, including, therefore, a second edition of the New Testament. In 1752 he published a third edition of the New Testament; in 1763-4, a second edition of both Testaments, which included a fourth edition of the New. In 1752 he published a fifth edition of it; which was followed in 1777 by a sixth, according to Mr. C. Butler, and the last in the editor's lifetime; for he died of the shock caused him by Lord George Gordon's riots, and the trouble in which he was involved in consequence. This was in the beginning of 1781, when he was in his ninetieth year.

As to the alterations of text which he introduced, he has given us no preface or other notice which would serve as our informant of the principle, the source, or the extent of them. On an inspection of the text itself, we find them to be very considerable. We say so on a comparison, as regards the Old Testament, of the edition of 1750 with the Douay of 1635, in seven passages taken at random, viz. Gen. i. 1-10; Exod. xv. 1-10; Judges xiii. 1-10; 3 Kings xviii. 18-27; Job xxxviii. 30-39; Psalm cvi. 21-30; and Ezek. xxxiii. 1-10. In these passages, reckoning roughly, there are altogether 170 variations in 70 verses: 11 in the first passage, 20 in the second, 32 in the third, 35 in the fourth, 21 in the fifth, 25 in the sixth, and 26 in the seventh. The variation in the number of alterations in the several passages, compared one with another, may partly be accounted for by the varying length of the verses of which they are composed, and partly from the greater or less difficulty of translating. The principle of the alterations seems to be, that of making the text more intelligible to the reader; and, with this object, old words and old collocations are superseded by modern, and less usual ones are exchanged for those which are more in use and even familiar.

Thus, for "God also said," Challoner corrects "And God said;" for "Be a firmament," "Let there be." "It was so," for "it was so done;" "Then Moses sung," for "Then sang Moses." For "song," "canticle;" for "to whom," "to her;" for "sicer," "strong drink." "I have not troubled," for "not I have troubled;" "call ye," for "invocate ye;" "fasten," for "compact;" "wilt," for "shalt," in the sense of simple futurity; "food," for "meat;" "give glory to," for "confess to;" "affliction," for "tribulation;" "indeed," for "certes;" "I will require his blood," for "his blood I will require;" "The word of the Lord came," for "was made;" "be converted," for "convert." There seems no desire to substitute Saxon words for Latin, for "set forth" is altered into "declare;" nor, perhaps, to approach the Protestant version, though there often is an approach, in fact, from the editor's desire to improve the English of his own text. Thus, for "between waters and waters," he writes "the waters from the waters;" for "named Manue," he has adopted "whose name was,"

&c.; for "having a wife barren," "and his wife was barren;" for "the waters were quiet," "the waves were still;" for "were moved," "reeled;" for "if thou speak not that the impious may keep himself from sin," "if thou dost not speak to warn the wicked from his way." On the other hand, there are instances in which he leaves both the Douay and Protestant versions, which agree together, for a rendering of his own. Thus for "terrible" he puts "awful;" for "fill the appetite," "satisfy the appetite;" for the inverted sentence "his blood will I require," "I will require his blood."

At the same time, it can scarcely be denied that, in these specimens of Dr. Challoner's edition, there do seem to be cases in which he adopts the Protestant version by preference. Thus, for "the gathering of waters together," he writes "the gathering together of the waters;" for "hastened," "made haste;" for "the house of thy father," "thy father's house;" for "if Baal, follow him," "if Baal, *then* follow him;" for "till midday," "even till [until, Pr.] noon;" for "the depths have overwhelmed," "the depths have covered." And undoubtedly he has sacrificed force and vividness in some of his changes; as, for instance, in his dispensing with all inversions of words, as, "his blood will I require," as already quoted; in altering "the haven of their will" of the Douay into "the haven which they wished for;" "fill," into "satisfy;" "marvellous" into "wonderful;" "making traffic" into "doing business;" "the blast of the storm stood," in a poetical passage, into "there arose a storm of wind." It is observable that for "*our* Lord" (as in "the commandments of *our* Lord," "if our Lord be God," "the word of our Lord came," &c.) he uses "*the* Lord" *passim*.

So much of particular passages :—Looking at Dr. Challoner's labours on the Old Testament as a whole, we may pronounce that they issue in little short of a new translation. They can as little be said to be made on the basis of the Douay as on the basis of the Protestant version. Of course there must be a certain resemblance between any two Catholic versions whatever, because they are both translations of the same Vulgate; but, this connexion between the Douay and Challoner being allowed for, Challoner's version is even nearer to the Protestant than it is to the Douay; nearer, that is, not in grammatical structure, but in phraseology and diction. We will take Psalm lii. as an example, selected at hazard; and we will go through it in the three versions, member by member, denoting the three by the initials of Douay, Protestant, and Challoner respectively.

1. The fool hath said in his heart, There is no God. D. P. The fool said in his heart, there is no God. C.

2. They are corrupt. D. Corrupt are they. P. They are corrupted. C.

and become abominable in iniquities. D. C. and have done abominable iniquity. P.

There is not that doth good. D. There is none that doeth [doth C.] good. P. C.

3. God hath looked forth from heaven. D. God looked down from heaven. P. C.

upon the children of men. D. P. on the children of men. C.

to see if there be that understandeth. D. to see if there were any that did understand. P. C.

or D. C. that. P.

seeketh after God. D. did seek God. P. C.

4. All. D. C. Every one. P.

of them, *omitted by* D. of them. P. C.

have declined. D. is gone back. P. have gone aside. C.

they are become unprofitable together. D. C. they are altogether become filthy. P.

there is not that doth good, no there is not one. D. there is none that doeth [doth. C.] good, no, not one. P. C.

5. Shall they not all . . . know. D. C. Have . . . no knowledge. P.

that work iniquity. D. the workers of iniquity. P. C.

that devour my people as food of bread. D. who eat up my people as they eat bread. P. C.

6. God they have not invocated. D. they have not called upon God. P. C.

there have they trembled for fear. D. C. there were they in great fear. P.

where no fear was. D. P. where there was no fear. C.

because God had dissipated the bones. D. for God hath scattered the bones. P. C.

of them that please men. D. C. of him that encampeth against thee. P.

they are [have been. C.] confounded. D. C. thou hast put them to shame. P.

because God hath despised them. D. P. C.

7. Who will give out of Sion the salvation of Israel. D. C. O that the salvation of Israel were come out of Zion. P.

when God shall convert the captivity of his people. D. when God bringeth [shall bring. C.] back the captivity of his people. P. C.

Jacob shall rejoice, and Israel shall be glad. D. P. C.

Now, on this collation we observe : 1. That there is (with one exception) no instance of difference between the Douay and Protestant in which Challoner leaves the Douay but he leaves it for the Protestant. The exception is in v. 4, where, for the Douay " declined," he does not substitute the Protestant "gone back," but "gone aside."

2. Next, we observe that, of the nine instances in which Challoner sides with the Douay against the Protestant, eight are cases of mere construction of the Latin Vulgate, not of diction, viz. " become abominable in," v. 2, "or," v. 3, "all," v. 4, " unprofitable," *ibid.*, "shall not . . . know," v. 5, " trembled," v. 6, " please men," *ibid.*, and " who will give," v. 7. Such fidelity to the Douay was a simple matter of duty.

3. Subtracting these from the nine cases in which Challoner sides with the Douay against the Protestant, we have only one remaining in which he does so freely and by his own choice, viz. " confounded " for " put to shame," v. 6.

4. It is true there are other cases in which Challoner abstains from the Protestant, but in these the Protestant agrees with the Douay. There are three of these, that is to say, three instances of the Douay siding with the Protestant against Challoner; and thus there are more instances of the Douay siding with the Protestant than of Challoner siding with the Douay.

5. On the other hand, there are eleven instances in which Challoner leaves the Douay for the Protestant.

We really cannot say whether this Psalm supplies a fair instance of the general character of Challoner's Old Testament, though we have taken it at random; but, after all allowances for the accident of the selection, it is difficult to avoid the conclusion, that at this day the

Douay Old Testament no longer exists as a received version of the authorised Vulgate.

So much as to the Old Testament; as to the New, we are not in possession of Dr. Challoner's first edition (1749), but we have compared with the Rheims of 1738 (which is the edition of the New Testament immediately before his own) his third edition of 1752, correcting it back into the text of his first, by means of the collations between the editions of 1749 and 1752, which Dr. Cotton has made. We have made the comparison in three places, taken at random—Luke viii. 1-10; John xiii. 6-15; and Heb. iv. 1-10.

In the first of these three passages there are about twenty-two corrections of the Rheims; of these fifteen are adoptions of the Protestant version, and seven alter the Rheims, yet differ from the Protestant.

In the second passage, John xiii. 6-15, there are but seven corrections of text; of these, at least six are made in accordance with the Protestant version, and one of these is even an insertion of a word, not in the Vulgate, which the Protestant inserts. As these changes are remarkable, we cite them. They are, "what I do," for "that which I do;" "but thou shalt know hereafter," for "hereafter thou shalt know;" "Thou shalt never wash my feet," for "Thou shalt not wash my feet for ever;" "for so I am," instead of "for I am so;" "*your* Lord and Master," for "Lord and Master;" "you also ought," for "you ought."

As regards the third passage, instead of a collation throughout, we will set down a few verses as a specimen:

Verse 1.

Rheims, 1738. Let us fear therefore, lest perhaps *forsaking the promise* of entering into his rest, *some* of you be thought to be wanting.

Protestant. Let us therefore fear, lest, a *promise being left* us of entering into his rest, *any* of you should seem to come short of it.

Challoner, 1749. Let us fear therefore, lest, *the promise being left* of entering into his rest, *any*, of you should be thought to be wanting.

Verse 3.

Rheims. For we, that have believed, shall enter *into the rest*, as he said, As I *sware* in my wrath, if they shall enter into my rest; and truly the works from the foundation of the world *being perfected*.

Protestant. For we which have believed do enter *into rest*, as he said, As I *have sworn* in my wrath, if they shall enter into my rest: although the works *were finished* from the foundation of the world.

Challoner. For we who believed shall enter *into rest;* as he said, As I *have sworn* in my wrath, If they shall enter into my rest; and this, when the works from the foundation of the world *were finished.*

Verse 6.

Rheims. Because then it remaineth that *certain* enter into it, and they, to whom *first it was* preached, did not enter because of *incredulity.*

Protestant. Seeing therefore it remaineth that *some* must enter therein, and they to whom it *was first* preached entered not in because of *unbelief.*

Challoner. Seeing then it remaineth that *some* are to enter into it, and they, to whom it *was first* preached, did not enter in because of *unbelief.*

A comparison of these verses again suggests to us some of the rules which Dr. Challoner kept in view in approximating, or not approximating, to the Protestant version. As we have said, he could not be unfaithful to the Vulgate: he never would leave its literal sense for the Protestant text, which, on the other hand, is translated from the Greek. Hence, in the contrast of the Greek δοκῇ τις and the Latin *existimetur aliquis*, he keeps to the Rheims; and in like manner, in ὑστερηκέναι as contrasted with *deesse*, and in καίτοι γενηθέντων with *et quidem operibus perfectis*. It is remarkable, however, that in one case, where the Rheims is with the Greek, he leaves it for the Protestant, which is not faithful to the Greek, viz. εἰς τὴν κατάπαυσιν, *in requiem*. In one case he modifies the interpretation which the Rheims gives of the Vulgate by the Protestant, *relictâ pollicitatione*. Again, one object with him was to popularise the style; hence he puts *unbelief* for *incredulity*. Hence he alters the *we that have* of the Rheims, not to the *we which have* of the Protestant, but into *we who have*. Hence, too, he retains the *enter into it* of the Rheims, where the Protestant has *enter therein;* and the *did not enter* of the Rheims, where the Protestant translates *entered not*. Yet he is not always consistent: *herein* or *therein* occurs elsewhere in his revision; and *unto* for *to* very frequently. Vide also Cotton, note t, p. 49. In John vi. 53 he has altered the "Unless ye eat" of the Rheims into the less accurate or obsolete Protestant rendering, "Except ye eat." Vide also John iii. 3.

We have already implied that Dr. Challoner made corrections of his own editions of the New Testament as they successively issued from the press. The second edition (1750) differs from the first, according to the collations which Dr. Cotton has printed, in about 124 passages; the third (1752) in more than 2000. These alterations, Dr. Cotton tell us, are all in the direction of the Protestant version; how far this is the case, and in what sense, the above examination of particular texts may serve to explain.

Challoner's text was the first which was published with an episcopal sanction; for it must be borne in mind that he was a Bishop, and the coadjutor of the Vicar-Apostolic of London, at the time of his first edition.

§ 3. DR. TROY'S BIBLE.

Dr. Challoner died in 1781; while he lived, no editions were published but such as followed his Revision. A few years, however, after his death, as we have noticed above, there was a return to the original Rheims of the New Testament, which was published in a sixth edition at Liverpool in 1788. But this had been preceded by an edition at Dublin which, as being the first of a series of editions of the New Testament upon a new revision of the Rheims version, requires some distinct notice. It was made on the basis of Dr. Challoner's, but still with considerable changes of text. The revisor was the Rev. Bernard Macmahon, a Dublin priest, who published his first edition in 1783, in 12mo, with the formal approbation of his Archbishop, Dr. Carpenter. There is reason for supposing that it professed to be a continuation of Dr. Challoner's labours; for, as that venerable prelate published successively three corrected editions of the New

Testament, in 1749, 1750, and 1752 (for the subsequent editions are not new corrections, but almost *fac-similes* of the preceding: vide Cotton, p. 20, &c.), so this new Dublin edition is called, in the Archbishop's approbation prefixed to it, "the *fourth* edition revised and corrected anew." This is Dr. Cotton's conjecture also, though he accompanies it, as is not unusual with him, with a gratuitous piece of ill-nature. If the "fourth" does not mean this, it is difficult to say to what previous edition it refers; for, at the time that it was published, there had been already five editions of the Rheims. Leaving this point, we are told by Dr. Cotton that the variations from Challoner's text, in the Gospels, are about 50; in the Acts and subsequent books, above 500. Eight years afterwards, in 1791, the same clergyman was selected by Dr. Troy, his then Archbishop, to superintend an edition of the whole Bible in quarto; and on this occasion, according to the same authority, he introduced into the New Testament above 200 changes more, calling it the "fifth edition." In 1794 it was reprinted in folio, forming "the sixth;" a "seventh edition" of the New Testament was published in 12mo in 1803, with above 100 variations from the text of 1791, in favour of that of 1783; and an "eighth" in 1810, in 12mo also, after the text of the seventh.

Thus we have five editions of the revision of Mr. Macmahon, with the titles of fourth, fifth, sixth, seventh, and eighth. Of these the editions of 1783, 1803, and 1810 are of the New Testament only; those of 1791 and 1794 of the whole Bible. The text has also been adopted in the Philadelphian edition of the Bible in 1805, which styles itself "the first American from the fifth Dublin edition."

If we are to follow Dr. Cotton, we ought to notice it as a peculiarity of this revision, that, whereas Dr. Challoner's alterations were in the direction of the Protestant version, those of Mr. Macmahon (or of his successors in the editorship) were in the opposite direction. We should not have been surprised at this being the case, without imputing to the English Bishop any wish to favour that version, or to the Irish priest a wish to protest against it. From the respective circumstances of the two countries, it has come about, as we are informed by those who ought to know, that the English language in Ireland has, in its diction and construction, more of a French or Latin character than in England. If this be so, the idioms and words, which each revisor would consider to be an improvement on the Rheims, might in one case approximate to the Protestant text, in the other recede from it. However, we are not sure of the accuracy of Dr. Cotton's alleged fact, nor of the actual operation, in this instance, of the principle to which we have referred it. We doubt whether Macmahon's alterations *have* a foreign cast, and we doubt whether he *is* further from the Protestant version than Dr. Challoner.

As to the character of his alterations, as regards the New Testament, they are sometimes more colloquial than Challoner's, and sometimes not so English, without being foreign. Thus, the Rheims and Challoner speak of "the multitude," and the Protestant of "the people," being "put forth," when Mr. Macmahon speaks of "the crowd" being "turned out" (Matt. ix. 25). Where the Rheims translates "it shall break him to powder," and the Protestant and Challoner, "it will grind him to powder," Mr. Macmahon writes, "it will dash him to pieces" (Luke xx. 18). Where the Rheims has "they were in doubt of them, what would befall," Challoner, "they were in doubt concerning them, what would come to pass," and the Protestant, "they doubted of them, whereunto this would grow," Mr. Macmahon has adopted, "they were in doubt what was become of them" (Acts v. 24). The "Barnabas would have taken with them John" of the Rheims, "Barnabas would have taken with him John" of Challoner, "Barnabas determined to take with them John" of the Protestant, is rendered by Mr. Macmahon, "Barnabas had a mind to take along with him John" (Acts xv. 37). And for "that which is the foolish of God" according to the Rheims, and "the foolishness of God" of the Protestant and Challoner, Mr. Macmahon substitutes "that which appeareth foolish of God."

We could not, then, account for the fact, supposing it to hold, that Mr. Macmahon receded from the Protestant approximations of Challoner's text, by his supposed preference of an English style less vernacular than what is in use among ourselves. However, we are not sure that the fact is as Dr. Cotton represents it. He says, "Of the passages rendered differently from Challoner, many recede much further from the authorised version than he (Dr. Challoner) did" (p. 55). We do not set our own diligence or accuracy in competition with Dr. Cotton's, still we do but state a fact when we say that our own experiments at collating the two revisions do not bear out the impression which his words convey. The edition, indeed, of the New Testament of 1783 hardly exists, and is unknown to us; but Dr. Troy's edition of 1794, which we have used, "follows," says Dr. Cotton (p. 77), "the quarto Bible of 1791 exactly," the text of which "is the text of Mr. Macmahon's Testament of 1783, with upwards of two hundred additional departures from Challoner" (p. 58). With this New Testament, then, of 1794 we have compared Dr. Challoner's of 1752, and the Rheims of 1621, with the following result.

In twenty specimens, taken at random, we found that, while in ten of them Dr. Challoner had left the Rheims for the Protestant, and in six Mr. Macmahon (or his editorial successor) had returned from Dr. Challoner's to the Rheims; on the other hand, in four, in which Dr. C. had retained the Rheims, Mr. Macmahon had adopted the Protestant; that is, on the whole, that out of *twenty* instances of variation, Dr. Challoner and Mr. Macmahon had left the Rheims for the Protestant in the same *four;* that Dr. Challoner had adopted altogether *ten* Protestant renderings, and Mr. Macmahon *eight;* that Dr. C. had kept the Rheims where Mr. M. had adopted the Protestant in *four*, and that Mr. M. had kept the Rheims where Dr. C. had adopted the Protestant in *six*.

Again, taking Hebrews xiii. and collating the three

texts of 1621, 1752, and 1794 with the Protestant version, we find Challoner and Macmahon have *eleven* differences from each other; in *two* Challoner leaves the Rheims for the Protestant, where Macmahon retains it, viz. in the position, &c. of words in vv. 7 and 11; in *four* Macmahon leaves the Rheims for the Protestant, where Challoner retains it, viz. " carried," 9; " now the God," &c. 20, 21; " working," 21; and " few," 22. In *three* C. retains and M. leaves both Rheims and Protestant, where the latter two agree together; and in *two* M. retains the Rheims and C. leaves it, though not for the Protestant.

Again, in James i. there are *nine* differences between Challoner and Macmahon; in which C. retains *three* of the Rheims, which M. changes, and C. changes into the Protestant *five* of the Rheims, which M. retains. In the *ninth* all four renderings are different from each other.

Again, in St. Jude's Epistle, 1-10, out of Macmahon's *twenty-six* alterations of the Rheims, *twenty-four* are from Challoner; but in the other *two* Challoner retains the Rheims, which Macmahon leaves for the Protestant.

And in 2 Ep. St. John, out of Macmahon's *eighteen* alterations from the Rheims, *fifteen* are from Challoner, and *three* are made where C. follows the Rheims.

On the whole, then, we are not able to corroborate Dr. Cotton's remark as to Mr. Macmahon's dissatisfaction, greater or less, with the Protestant leaning of Dr. Challoner's revision of the Rheims, though it is a real perplexity to us that we should find ourselves differing from him. So much as regards the New Testament. As regards the Douay translation of the Old, there seems to be very little difference between the texts of Dr. Challoner and Mr. Macmahon. We have collated seven chapters taken at random: Numb. xxiv., Deuter. i., Esther v., Psalm lxxviii., Ecclus. v., Isai. xv. and Abdias. In four of these there is not a single difference between Dr. C. and Mr. M. In Deut. i. the only difference is C.'s " unto " for M.'s " to," in verse 3. In Psalm lxxviii., the last words " unto all generations," which C. adopts after the Protestant, instead of the " unto generation and generation" of the Douay, which M. retains. In Abdias the only difference is C.'s "speak proudly" after the Protestant, where M. retains the " magnify thy mouth " of the Douay. That is, in one hundred and forty-six verses there are only three, or rather two, differences; in these Macmahon returns to the Douay, which Challoner had left for the Protestant. These collations bear out, as far as they go, Dr. Cotton's remark, that "the text of this edition (the Dublin), so far as concerns the Old Testament, does not differ materially from that of Dr. Challoner's " (p. 58).

This series of editions, commenced by Mr. Macmahon's New Testament, and extending from 1783 to 1810, may be fitly called Dr. Troy's Bible, from the Approbation which he gave to it in 1791. As that Approbation sums up the history of the version hitherto, and connects his own revision with that of Dr. Challoner, a portion of it shall be given here. " By our authority," the Archbishop says in Latin, "we approve this new English edition of the Holy Bible, ... which has by our order been carefully collated by the Rev. Bernard Macmahon with the Clementine Vulgate, also with the Douay Old Testament of 1609, and the Rheims New Testament of 1582, and with the London Old and New Testament of 1752, approved English versions."

§ 4. EDITIONS SINCE DR. TROY'S BIBLE.

Challoner's revision is the first and the last to which the Douay version of the Old Testament has been subjected; the text remains almost *verbatim* as he left it. What qualifications must be made of this statement, on the score of certain passages in Dr. Troy's Bible, shall be considered when we speak of the now current editions. The same, however, cannot be said of Challoner's New Testament, and for this reason, if for no other, that the texts of his own editions vary from each other; and, moreover, as he was not the author of all the changes introduced into the later editions (for Mr. C. Butler tells us, " alterations were made in every" edition, "*to his dissatisfaction,*" Cotton, p. 50), it is not wonderful that the tendency to fresh changes, which was powerful enough even in his lifetime to introduce itself, in spite of his wishes, into his own work, should have had actual results after his death. Dr. Troy's (*i.e.* Mr. Macmahon's) emendations have already been spoken of. Subsequent editors have had to choose between this or that of Challoner's three texts of the New Testament, and Dr. Troy's text; and, as might have been expected, they have chosen variously. The principal of these editions shall now be enumerated.

1. Dr. Hay's Bible.

1. In 1761 an edition of the whole Bible was printed in Edinburgh, 5 volumes, 12mo, under the inspection of Dr. Hay, one of the Vicars-Apostolic in Scotland, so well known by his publications. We introduce Dr. Hay's name on Dr. Cotton's authority, as we do not find it in our own copy, which is of the second edition.[2]

2. In 1804-5 " the same printer (Mr. John Moir) issued a re-impression." About 3000 and 2000 copies were struck off in these two editions.

3. In 1811 a great number of unsold copies were published in Dublin with new title-pages, some engravings, and a long list of subscribers, with the imprint, "Dublin, 1811." This may be called the third edition.

4. In the same year an actual reprint of the New Testament was published by the same Dublin publisher. It also has a list of subscribers ; among whom are Dr. Troy, Dr. Murray, &c.

5. In 1814 this New Testament came to a fifth edition at Dublin, in 12mo.

6. And in 1817, it probably supplied the text to the 12mo edition printed at Belfast.

Of the text of Dr. Hay's New Testament (for, as we

---

[2] It appears from a private letter of the date of 1792, which has been shown me by the kindness of Canon Toole, that the actual revisor of this edition was the Rev. James Robertson, of the order of St. Benedict.

have said, the text of the Old Testament has not substantially varied since Challoner's time), Dr. Cotton says: "It in general follows Challoner's edition of 1763-4; but occasionally it deserts that edition for the first, of 1749, as in Matt. i. 25, iii. 13, iv. 9, v. 37, vi. 16, viii. 17, x. 22, xxi. 40; Acts v. 38; Eph. i. 21, and some other places. In a few passages, it agrees with Dr. Troy's Bible of 1791, as at Matt. ii. 23, iv. 9; Gal. vi. 9, &c." (p. 77).

2. *Dr. Gibson's Bible.*

1. In 1816-17, an edition of the Bible was published at Liverpool, in folio. It bore "on the title-page that it was published with his (Dr. Gibson's) sanction" (p. 110).

2. In 1822-23, a reprint of this Bible, in folio, was published in London.

3. In 1829, a third was published in London also, and in folio, and "very handsomely executed." It was put forth under the sanction of Dr. Bramston, then Vicar-Apostolic, and calls itself "the third edition" (*ibid.*).

It is not certain that these three editions belong to each other, though the printers and publishers of all three, and the approving Bishop of the first two, are the same, and though the last two distinctly call themselves "the second and third" respectively, if we understand Dr. Cotton (pp. 110, 127). Our reason for this remark is, that the second edition is said to be "*revised and corrected*" by two Liverpool clergymen, and that the third edition has not the same episcopal sanction as the first two.

As to the text of the New Testament, Dr. Cotton tells

us that, in the edition of 1816-17, it is "taken almost without exception from Challoner's later edition;" in the third it "appears to agree with that of Dr. Challoner in 1763-4." These statements coincide.

3. Dr. Poynter's New Testament.

1. 1815;—A New Testament was published in two sizes, "12mo and a handsome 8vo" (p. 99). It professes in the title-page to be "stereotyped from the edition published by authority in 1749," that is, from Challoner's first. It has a preliminary "Address," anonymous, but according to Mr. C. Butler, written by Dr. Poynter. "The superintendence of this edition," says Dr. Cotton, "was confided to the care of the Rev. Dr. Rigby, afterwards Vicar-Apostolic of the London District. . . . The text," he continues, "as was above stated, agrees with that of the edition of 1749. I have only detected a single slight variation, viz. at Phil. ii. 7." The reading of Dr. Poynter's edition, in this place, is "debased himself," taken from Challoner's text of 1752; for the reading in those of 1749 and 1750 is "emptied himself."

2. In 1818, a new edition of this New Testament was prepared by the Rev. Mr. Horrabin, under the sanction of Dr. Poynter. It was in 12mo, and was sold at a low price for the use of the poorer class.

3. In 1823, the stereotype plates of the edition of 1815 were used for an edition published by Mr. Bagster, which is still in circulation.

4. 1825. A fresh edition of Dr. Poynter's New Testament, in 8vo. Dr. Cotton tells us that it follows the edition of 1815 "both in text and notes, *with exception* of reading 'debased' *instead* of "emptied' at Phil. ii. 7." This perplexes us; for Dr. Poynter's edition of 1815, and Bagster's from the same plates, in 1823, both of which lie before us, both read "debased" already. We have not the means of comparing the edition of 1825 with them.

5. 1826. A new stereotyped edition of Dr. Poynter's New Testament, in 12mo. It was published at Dublin, at the expense of the Commissioners of Irish Education, with the *imprimatur* of the four Archbishops of Ireland.

6. 1834, 35, 37, 40. The edition of 1826 with new title-pages (Cotton, p. 242).

7. 1842. The edition of 1825 was "reissued with a new title-page and a new printer's name" (p. 123).

4 *Dr. Troy's Testament without notes.*

1. 1820. This edition is quite distinct from the series of editions on which we have enlarged as Mr. Macmahon's revision. It is quite distinct, too, from Dr. Troy's Bible of 1816-18, which, as regards its New Testament, we have mentioned above (p. 409), as being a reprint, Text and Notes, of the Rhemish. It is remarkable for having no notes at all appended to the verses or chapters. The whole sacred text stands absolutely by itself, a supplement being added with the usual notes, which might or might not, according to the purchaser's pleasure, be bound up with it. Of this edition 20,000 copies were struck off. Dr. Troy,

in his Approbation, speaks of it as "conformable particularly to the text of the Douay English version sanctioned by him, and published in 1791;" however, Dr. Cotton tells us that "the text is taken literally from that of Dr. Challoner's second edition, 1750, and is," as he believes, "the first, if not the only, modern representation of that particular text" (p. 120).

2. 1825. Copies of the above were reissued in London with a new title-page.

5. Dr. Murray's Bible.

1. 1825. This edition is in 8vo, stereotyped, and its plates are still in use. There have been fresh impressions of it from time to time, in 1829, 33, 40, 44, 47, &c.

As to the text of the New Testament, "it rather follows Dr. Challoner's early editions of 1749 and 1750" (Cotton, p. 124). He adds, "The Bible appears to have given great satisfaction to the Roman Catholic public, and to have been made a sort of standard or exemplar for some editions since issued both in Great Britain and Ireland."

2. 1833-36. The Glasgow Bible, 8vo, published with the Approbation of the Vicars-Apostolic of England and Scotland.

3. 1838. Dr. Blake's New Testament, 8vo, Newry, appears to adopt "the text of Dr. Murray, agreeing with the early editions of Challoner" (p. 140.) It was reprinted at Belfast, 1846-7.

4. 1838. Dr. Denvir's series of reprints at Belfast of

the New Testament begin apparently in 1836; Dr. Cotton sets down one under the date of 1837. Subsequent reprints, or fresh issues, are dated 1839, 41, 43, 45, and nearly every successive year; and the whole Bible in 1839, 47, &c. In another issue of Bibles his name appears in conjunction with Dr. Crolly's, in 1846, and 52.

The text of the New Testament in these editions, at least in that of 1839, "appears to agree with Dr. Murray's edition of 1825"(p. 146). We have collated Dr. Murray's text of 1825 with Dr. Denvir's of 1853, in Rom. xiii. There is a variation in verse 11, viz. "time" in edition 1853 for "season" in edition 1825. "Time" stands in Troy's edition, 1794; but the text is certainly not Troy's, from whose text in the same chapter it has the following variations: "princes" for "rulers," v. 3; "God's minister" for "minister of God," twice in v. 4; "to love" for "that you love," v. 8; and "our neighbour" for "the neighbour," v. 10.

5. 1840. At Philadelphia, U.S., a New Testament, apparently a reprint of Dr. Murray's text of 1825, with the approbation of Archbishops Kenrick and Hughes.

6. 1846. Dr. MacHale's New Testament. "Both the text and notes seem to agree with Dr. Murray's Bible published in 1825" (Cotton, p. 148).

6. *Cardinal Wiseman's Bible.*

1847. This edition is printed in 8vo by Messrs. Richardson, London and Derby. It has the approbation of Dr. Walsh, Vicar-Apostolic, and Dr. Wiseman, his coadjutor.

The text seems to follow Dr. Troy's of 1791, or of 1803, which inclines to Mr. Macmahon's original edition of 1783. This seems to be Dr. Cotton's account, *vide* pp. 78, 149. Out of twenty-seven instances of variation of text taken at random, we find none to side with Challoner against Troy, twenty-six side with Troy against Challoner, and in one the reading is without precedent, viz. in 1 John iv. 2: "Every spirit that confesseth Jesus Christ *to come* in the flesh is of God."

We must not conclude this enumeration of revisions and reprints of the Rheims and Douay, without giving some account of two rival folio editions, which were published (or rather sold to subscribers in parts) without direct episcopal sanction, though one of them has since risen into great reputation, and has received, first the approbation of the Vicars-Apostolic of Scotland, and of various Archbishops and Bishops of Ireland, and lately that of the Archbishop of New York, where it has been republished, together with the recommendation of a great number of North American Bishops, in letters prefixed to the edition, as well as that of our own Cardinal Archbishop and of the late Archbishop of Milan. This is Haydock's Bible, originally published at Manchester and Dublin in 1811-12 and 1814; its rival being that of Oswald Syers, published at Manchester in 1811-13. Mr. Haydock and Mr. Syers, the respective publishers, were printers; but the editor and annotator employed by the former was his own brother, who was a priest, the Rev. George Haydock, to whom the edition owes its celebrity

7. *Syers' Bible.*

1811-13. The Bible "bears no approbation of any living ecclesiastical authority; nor any preface or other introductory matter to explain the principle adopted in this edition, or the sources from which the annotations are derived" (Cotton, p. 91). With the annotations we are not here concerned; "the text," he continues, "appears rather to agree with that of Dr. Challoner, and in the New Testament it rather follows his early editions, 1749 and 1750, than his later ones, 1752, &c." We do not think it very necessary to go to any great pains in verifying what Dr. Cotton has so diligently examined. In Phil. ii. 7, this edition follows Challoner's later edition of 1752; otherwise our collations, as far as they have gone, lead us to agree with Dr. Cotton.

8. *Haydock's Bible.*

1. 1811-12 and 1814, fol. The characteristic of this edition is its series of new and copious Annotations. As to the text, the editor professes in his advertisement his intention to "adhere to the text of the Venerable and Right Rev. Dr. Richard Challoner;" on which Dr. Cotton remarks, "it is not exactly true that Dr. Challoner's text is followed universally" (p. 87). As regards the New Testament, the justice of Dr. Cotton's remark will be plain on a very superficial examination, however the

fact is to be accounted for. Out of twenty instances taken at hazard, we found Haydock's text to agree with Dr. Troy's of 1794, as against any of Challoner's texts, in eighteen; to agree with Challoner against Troy in one; and in one to differ from both.

2. 1822-24. In 1822 "an 8vo edition of Haydock's Bible with short notes was issued in Dublin; and two years later, a new title-page was prefixed to it with the date 1824, calling itself 'the second edition.' The book is very carelessly printed, and full of errors. The text of the New Testament seems to have been taken from Dr. Troy's Bible of 1791 and 1794" (Cotton, p. 123).

3. 1845-48. "A republication of Haydock's Bible at Edinburgh and London, with all its notes, in a handsome quarto form" (*ibid.* p. 149), with the approbation of the Vicars-Apostolic of Scotland, with their coadjutors, of the Archbishops of Armagh and Dublin, and of the Bishops of Belfast, Waterford, and Limerick. This edition was printed from Haydock's earliest impressions of his Bible in 1811, as Dr. Cotton tells us, *verbum verbo*, in consequence of the wish expressed by Dr. Scott, one of the Scotch Vicars-Apostolic.

4. 1852-56. This splendid edition, which is published by Messrs. Dunigan of New York, in quarto, is introduced to the public by those many high approbations and recommendations to which we have already referred. Dr. Cotton says that "it appears to have been copied from Haydock's first impression of 1811." We do not know how to follow him in this conclusion; but we have not been able to find any information on the subject in the edition itself. Our

reason for questioning Dr. Cotton's belief is, that, on taking twenty instances of text at hazard in the editions of 1811-14 and of 1852-56 we found the latter to differ from the former in seven, of which four are altered back to Challoner's editions, one agrees with Cardinal Wiseman's, and two with no edition with which we are acquainted.

5. 1853. This edition in quarto, with Haydock's notes abridged, is due to the Very Rev. Dr. Husenbeth, who undertook it, as he informs us, "with the approbation and sanction of his ecclesiastical superior, the Right Rev. Dr. Wareing, and with the concurrent approbation and sanction of all the Right Rev. Vicars-Apostolic of Great Britain." Approbations from the Vicars-Apostolic of England and Scotland follow.

§ 5. CURRENT EDITIONS.

We may fitly sum up this account of public and authorised editions of the Catholic English Bible with a notice of its existing texts and their relation to the text of the original Rheims and Douay. We conceive these texts may be represented by the editions of Cardinal Wiseman in England, and of Dr. Murray and Dr. Denvir in Ireland, to which may be added Mr. Haydock's in the United States, till the learned Archbishop of Baltimore completes the laborious work to which he has so long devoted himself.

1. *The Old Testament.*

As to the Old Testament, as we have already said, there

have been no material alterations in its text since the revision or retranslation executed by Dr. Challoner. (1) Dr. Hay's text exactly follows Dr. Challoner's edition of 1763-4. So says Dr. Cotton, p. 77; and we can corroborate him as far as this, that, on comparing Challoner's 1750 with Hay's, we find that, all through the four volumes of the Old Testament, page answers faithfully to page: *e.g.* there are 507 pages in each first volume, ending with Ruth; 487 in the second, ending with Esther; and so on. So again, p. 300, vol. iii., ends with Eccles. iv. 9, in both; p. 400 in vol. iv. ends with Mal. iii. 9, in both, &c. (2) Again, Dr. Gibson's text "is taken from Bishop Challoner" (*ibid.* p. 110). (3) Of Syers's, the same authority says that "the text appears to agree with that of Dr. Challoner." We have collated it with Dr. Challoner's of 1750, in Eccles. x. and Isai. i., and find, as he would lead us to expect, not a single difference of reading between them. (4) Lastly, as to Dr. Troy's Bibles of 1791 and 1816. Speaking of the former of these, Dr. Cotton says: "I have observed a few variations [from Dr. Challoner] in several of the books, as in Dan. ii.," &c., p. 58. In these instances the text of 1791 is followed by that of 1816, which "generally follows Dr. Challoner, but occasionally differs, as in Neh. [2 Esdr.] ix. 17, Job xxvi. 13, Isai. viii. 19, Ezech. xix. 5," p. 115. Considering, then, Dr. Troy is followed by the editions of Haydock, Dr. Murray, Dr. Denvir, and Cardinal Wiseman, pp. 124, 146, 149, which we have taken to represent the current text or texts of the day, we are safe in saying, first, that Challoner's revision has been hitherto a final one; next that there is at present, as regards the Old Testament, one, and only one, received text, or very nearly so.

In verification of Dr. Cotton's statements, we have compared together the text of five passages in the Old Testament, taken at random in five editions: viz. in Dr. Challoner's of 1750, and in the current editions of 1847, Richardsons, London (Cardinal Wiseman's); of 1853, Dolman, London (Dr. Denvir's); of 1854, Duffy, Dublin (Dr. Murray's); and of 1856, Dunigan, New York (Haydock's); with the following results:—

1. 4 Kings xx. 1-11. They all agree *verbatim*, except that in v. 8, Haydock, instead of " What shall be the sign that I *shall* go up to the temple," reads " What is the sign that I *will* go up." This is correctly printed after Haydock's text of 1811. Again, in v. 11, where the other four read " *in* the dial," Haydock, 1856 (after the edition of 1811), reads " *on* the dial."

2. Job xiii. 1-10. Where Challoner has changed the Douay " or shall *it* please him," v. 9, into " shall *this*," the four current editions have gone back to " it."

3. Psalm x. For " *the* Psalm *of* David " of the Douay 1635, Challoner reads " *a* Psalm *for* David." He is followed by Cardinal Wiseman, Dr. Murray, and Dr. Denvir; but Haydock (after ed. 1811) substitutes " *a* Psalm *to* David."

4. Psalm lxvii. 12-21. For Challoner's " amongst," v. 14, the four current editions read " among." For the " Sina," v. 18, of Douay, Challoner, Cardinal Wiseman,

Dr. Murray, and Dr. Denvir, Haydock (after ed. 1811) reads "Sinai."

5. Isai. xxviii. 20-29. For "the mountain of divisions," v. 21, of Challoner, Murray, Dr. Denvir, and Haydock, Cardinal Wiseman reads "division." In v. 21 Murray, apparently by an error of press, leaves out "that he may do his work, his strange work." The same edition and Dr. Denvir's read "thrash," where the others read "thresh."

These are all the variations which we have discovered between Dr. Challoner and the four modern editions, in the passages in question. On the other hand, if we would see the concordant divergence of all five from the old Douay of 1635, we may take the following instances out of the same passages:—

1. Where the four editions all read, "In the Lord I put my trust, how then do you say to my soul, Get thee away from hence to the mountain like a sparrow?" in the Douay we find, "I trust in the Lord, How say ye to my soul, Pass over unto the mountain as a sparrow?"

2. Where the four editions read, "For they have destroyed the things which thou hast made; but what has the just man done?" the Douay has, "For they have destroyed the things which thou didst perfect; but the just, what hath he done?"

3. Where the four editions read, "The Lord shall give the word to them that preach good tidings with great power; the king of powers is of the beloved, of the beloved, and the beauty of the house shall divide spoils;" the Douay runs, "Our Lord shall give the word to them that

evangelise with great power; the king of hosts, the beloved of the beloved, and to the beauty of the house to divide the spoils."

4. And where the four editions read, "And now do not mock, lest your bonds be tied strait, for I have heard of the Lord, the God of hosts, a consumption and a cutting short upon all the earth. Give ear and hear my voice, hearken and hear my speech;" the Douay reads, "And now mock not, lest perhaps your bonds be tied strait; for I have heard of our Lord, the God of hosts, consummation and abridgment upon all the earth. Hearken with your ears, and hear my voice; attend, and hear my speech."

2. *The New Testament.*

Now, lastly, we come to the current editions of the New Testament. Of the four current editions which we have been using, Dr. Cotton has given us, as we have said above, the following account: that Dr. Murray's text rather follows Dr. Challoner's early editions of 1749-50; that Dr. Denvir's agrees with Dr. Murray's; that Cardinal Wiseman's seems to follow Dr. Troy's of 1791 or 1803 and Haydock's; and that Haydock, professing to follow Challoner, does not always do so.

We have thought it sufficient, in corroboration, to take at hazard two passages, 1 Thess. iii. 1-5 and Apoc. xvi. 1-6. On collating together the text of these in the four current editions of 1847, 1853, 1854, 1856, we find altogether twelve variations between them; one in the passage of the Thessalonians, eleven in that of the Apocalypse. And we are able to trace them all to one or other of Challoner's editions of 1749, 1750, 1752, and of Troy's of 1791, 1794, except three of 1856 (Haydock's, New York). We shall show this best by throwing the variations into a tabular form.

Var.	Murray, 1854, follows.	Denvir, 1853, follows.	Wiseman, 1847, follows.	Haydock, 1856. follows.
1	Challoner.	Troy, 1794.	T. 1794.	T. 1794.
2	C. 1749.	C. 1749.	C. 1752.	C. 1752.
3	C. 1749.	C. 1749.	C. 1752.	C. 1752.
4	C.	C.	T.	T.
5	C.	C.	T.	T.
6	C.	C.	T.	T.
7	C.	C.	T. 1794.	T. 1794.
8	C.	C.	T. 1794.	?
9	C.	C.	T. 1791.	?
10	C. 1749.	C. 1749.	C. 1752.	C. 1752.
11	C.	C.	T.	T.
12	C.	C.	T. 1794.	?

It appears from this analysis, as far as it is a fair specimen of the respective texts, that Dr. Murray and Dr. Denvir follow Challoner's early editions, and that Cardinal Wiseman and Mr. Haydock follow his later editions and Dr. Troy's; and this is pretty much what Dr. Cotton has said. As to the three readings, which are referable to no former edition, of which we are possessed, these all occur in no other of the four current editions besides the New York Haydock, and, what is remarkable, they do not occur in the Haydock of 1811-14, which follows in all three passages Dr. Troy's edition of 1794. The probability is, that the New York editor has fairly used the same liberty of alteration which has been exercised by other editors before him.

We here close our sketch of the history of the received version, from the date of the Rheims and Douay translators to the present day. The versions of the New Testament, or portions of the Old or New, which have at various times been given to the world by divines and scholars,—such as Mr. Nary, Dr. Witham, and of late years by Dr. Lingard and the Archbishop of Baltimore,—also the Annotations which have accompanied the various editions, demand a separate consideration.

THE END.

www.ingramcontent.com/pod-product-compliance
Lightning Source LLC
Chambersburg PA
CBHW032010300426
44117CB00008B/966